David Davis,
Abraham Lincoln's
Favorite Judge

David Davis, Abraham Lincoln's Favorite Judge

RAYMOND J. McKOSKI

UNIVERSITY OF
ILLINOIS PRESS
Urbana, Chicago, and Springfield

© 2025 by the Board of Trustees
of the University of Illinois
All rights reserved
Manufactured in the United States of America
C 5 4 3 2 1
∞ This book is printed on acid-free paper.

Library of Congress Cataloging-in-Publication Data
Names: McKoski, Raymond J., author.
Title: David Davis, Abraham Lincoln's favorite judge /
    Raymond J. McKoski.
Description: Urbana : University of Illinois Press, 2025. |
    Includes bibliographical references and index.
Identifiers: LCCN 2024060682 (print) | LCCN 2024060683
    (ebook) | ISBN 9780252046636 (cloth) | ISBN
    9780252047947 (ebook)
Subjects: LCSH: Davis, David, 1815–1886. | Judges—
    United States—Biography. | United States—Politics
    and government—1829–1837. | Republican Party
    (U.S.)—History—19th century.
Classification: LCC KF373.D38 M35 2025 (print) | LCC
    KF373.D38 (ebook) | DDC 347.73/2634 [B]—dc23/
    eng/20250107
LC record available at https://lccn.loc.gov/2024060682
LC ebook record available at https://lccn.loc.gov/
    2024060683

To Nora Rae Partin

Contents

Photographs follow page 155

Acknowledgments

First and foremost, thanks to my wife, Janis, for introducing me to Judge Davis by suggesting that we stop at the David Davis Mansion in Bloomington, Illinois, on our trip home from the Abraham Lincoln Presidential Library and Museum in Springfield, Illinois. The knowledge and enthusiasm of the mansion's docent quickly hooked me on the unique and important life of Lincoln's favorite judge. The staff and volunteers of the David Davis Mansion Foundation have been instrumental in educating the public about the judge and carrying on his legacy. One of the volunteers, foundation researcher Patricia Kasbohm Schley, has transcribed more than a thousand letters to and from the Davis family. As I wrote to Pat in September 2013, after making a presentation in Bloomington on Davis's impartiality as a judge, "You are providing an unbelievably valuable service for historical research and future generations." Little did I know that ten years later I would rely on her work in documenting the thoughts and activities of the judge, his family, Abraham Lincoln, and their contemporaries.

Electronically available primary source material indispensably aids someone like me in writing a book. The Papers of Abraham Lincoln, the Law Practice of Abraham Lincoln, the Collected Works of Abraham Lincoln, David & Sarah Davis Family Correspondence (Illinois Wesleyan University), Chronicling America and other newspaper archives, to mention a few, permit authors to do much research from home. Several institutions welcomed me to use their facilities and collections, including the Abraham Lincoln Presidential Library and Museum, the Chicago History Museum, the University of St. Mary of the Lake, the University Center of Lake County, Illinois, the University of Wisconsin–Parkside, and the Lake Villa Township Library. Special recognition goes to Meghan Harmon, Megan Klintworth, Michelle Miller, Christopher Schnell, and Matthew Deihl of the Abraham Lincoln Presidential Library and Museum for their valuable assistance in tracking down and obtaining copies of documents from the library's collections. Similarly, Autumn Haag of the University of Rochester was very helpful in securing documents from the Thurlow Weed Papers and the William H. Seward Papers. Further thanks to the curators of the US Supreme Court and US Senate and to the University of Illinois Library Special Collections staff.

Willard King must be credited for his fine biography of David Davis and for sharing his research notes. Thanks to William W. Freehling, who, in *Becoming Lincoln*, first described Davis as "Lincoln's favorite Illinois judge." But Lincoln's partiality toward the judge saw no geographical boundaries.

Alison Syring, University of Illinois Press acquisitions editor, wholeheartedly supported this endeavor, provided valuable suggestions to improve the manuscript, and guided me through the publishing process. The insightful comments and recommendations of the two anonymous reviewers immensely benefited the final product. The entire University of Illinois Press staff has earned my respect and gratitude.

Let me end my thanks where it began, with my wife, who not only took me to Judge Davis's home but also patiently tolerated my many hours at the computer and my continuous barrage of tales about Davis and Lincoln.

Introduction

The crucial contributions of Judge David Davis to both the executive and judicial branches of government have long been understudied and undervalued. Historians acknowledge that in May 1860 Judge Davis changed the course of history when he masterminded the Republican National Convention floor fight to hand the presidential nomination to Abraham Lincoln. But the full story behind this triumph can only be understood through the eyes of Judge Davis. How did this trial court judge from central Illinois who had never attended a national political convention outstrategize, outwork, outorganize, and outmaneuver the unchallenged top campaign manager in the nation, "The Dictator," Thurlow Weed? Weed backed the odds-on favorite for the nomination, New York senator William H. Seward. As usual, Weed had "oceans of money" to dole out as he saw fit and an army of seasoned campaign operatives at his side. Davis had no funds and directed a montage of country lawyers who traveled central Illinois's Eighth Judicial Circuit with the judge and Lincoln. Seward entered the convention with a commanding lead in delegates. Davis, on the other hand, was worried that some of the Illinois delegates who really preferred Seward or Edward Bates of Missouri would bolt to their favorites after fulfilling a commitment to vote for Lincoln on the first ballot. Lincoln's floor manager overcame all obstacles and patched together enough votes to nominate dark horse Lincoln on the convention's third ballot. And the narrative continues with Davis's essential contribution in the general election as fundraiser, strategist, organizer, and troubleshooter (see chapters 3 and 4).

Certainly, a big part of the David Davis story is his unwavering commitment to advance Lincoln's political career. Davis's loyalty to his friend solidified over years of traveling together on the Eighth Judicial Circuit. Their shared Whig origins, the judge's enormous number of political and personal contacts, his organizational and leadership abilities, and, as Lincoln put it, his knack "of making a man do a thing whether he wants to or not" all combined to make Davis Lincoln's strongest and most effective political supporter.[1] Their political partnership started in earnest with Lincoln's unsuccessful efforts to gain a US Senate seat in 1855 and 1859 and culminated in the judge's pivotal role in Lincoln's presidential nomination and election. Any study of Davis must in large part focus on his role in the political rise of America's greatest president. And that political relationship cannot be understood without a long-overdue examination of the personal relationship between the two friends.

But Davis deserves approbation for more than his friendship with Lincoln and the campaign skills that he employed to Lincoln's advantage. His thirteen years as an Illinois trial court judge and his fourteen years as an associate justice of the US Supreme Court demonstrate Davis's fundamental contribution to the fabric of the judicial system: the ability to render impartial decisions free from personal, political, and social views; personal relationships; public pressure; and partisan loyalties. Independence and impartiality in court was the judge's hallmark. Davis's impartiality extended to cases involving his favorite lawyer, Abraham Lincoln, to whom he showed unmitigated partiality and loyalty in his personal and political endeavors. In the courtroom it was a different story. Lincoln actually lost more cases than he won in trials decided by Davis without a jury.

The judge's independence was on full display after Lincoln promoted him to the Supreme Court. In his most important opinion, *Ex parte Milligan*, Justice Davis was the only Republican to side with four Democrats in finding that neither the president nor Congress could employ military commissions to try civilians in nonseceding states in which the courts were open (see chapter 6).[2] In *Milligan* Davis ruled against the commissions created by the president who put him on the high court. He ruled for Lambdin P. Milligan while harboring a deep disdain for Copperheads like Milligan. It was no secret that the decision and its author would receive a severe beating at the hands of the Republican Congress and Republican press. Davis also knew that he would suffer the consequences of being the only Republican member of the Supreme Court to deny Congress the power to extend the jurisdiction of military commissions to include civilians. But regardless of his personal views and relationships, Davis never deviated from his commitment to judicial impartiality and independence during his years on the bench.

In what should be considered his second most important Supreme Court opinion, Davis rejected the Washington, Alexandria and Georgetown Railroad Company's argument that it could segregate passenger cars by race as long as the accommodations were "equal."[3] The judge's decision rested on his interpretation of the railroad's congressional charter and the "temper" of Congress at the time the charter was renewed in 1863 and 1866. Davis doubted the wisdom and practicality of social and political equality of the races, but he kept his personal opinion out of his judicial decision-making process. Unfortunately for future generations, Davis and the court's rejection of the "separate but equal" policy in 1873 was all but ignored by the Supreme Court twenty-three years later when it approved the unconstitutional and blatantly discriminatory doctrine.[4]

The aim of this book is modest. It does not attempt to tell the complete story of Davis's important and interesting life, which is briefly chronicled in the section titled "A Biographical Sketch of David Davis." Instead, the book reveals an unheralded country judge's impact on the presidency and the judiciary. Parts I and II explore the role that Davis played in the political rise of Abraham Lincoln. Part I describes Lincoln's two unsuccessful races for the US Senate. Part II continues with the story of Lincoln's nomination and election as president in 1860. This examination includes a close look at the personal, professional, and political relationships between Davis and Lincoln. Part III analyzes Davis's appointment to the US Supreme Court and his involvement in issues created by the president's wartime edicts, including the use of military tribunals to try civilians and the suppression of opposition newspapers. This analysis is not limited to Davis's judicial decisions. Rather, it includes his equally important unofficial communications with the president, which were designed to avert the necessity of embarrassing court rulings overturning some of the president's wartime actions. Part IV establishes the judge's unyielding commitment to judicial impartiality, which was fully recognized and appreciated by Lincoln. Impartiality was Davis's signature trait and vital contribution to the judicial branch of government. He consistently displayed actual impartiality on the bench even though off the bench he openly demonstrated partisan loyalties, fixed social and political beliefs, and strong opinions concerning the lawyers who appeared before him. His personal, political, and social activities simply did not interfere with his judicial fairness or his reputation for impartiality. That is no small accomplishment, considering that in Davis's time, just as today, Supreme Court decisions were often explained in strictly partisan terms rather than by the validity of their legal reasoning. Now, as in the nineteenth century, politicians and much of the media believe that high court justices decide cases to promote their own partisan or ideological agendas and that the only important aspect of a court decision is whether it hurts or helps "our side." The book concludes with some observations on the Lincoln-Davis friendship and explains how today's ethical rules governing judges, if in effect in the mid-nineteenth century, would have prohibited Judge Davis from any public participation in Lincoln's political campaigns.

This book presents important aspects of David Davis's life, character, loyalty to Lincoln, and dedication to the fundamental value of any legitimate legal system:

impartiality in the exercise of judicial duties. It does not offer a comprehensive examination of the man or his values. For instance, Davis's views on slavery, race, and reconstruction are discussed in the context that he set aside his personal views when rendering court decisions. But Davis's personal beliefs on these and other critical issues of the time deserve further investigation and analysis.

A Biographical Sketch of David Davis

The story of David Davis presents a complex and fascinating blend of personal, professional, and political experiences and associations. A brief chronological capsule of Davis's life will provide context for the detailed examination of the major themes of the book: Davis's role in Lincoln's political rise and the judge's unwavering commitment to judicial impartiality.

Ann Mercer Davis gave birth to David Davis on March 9, 1815, at her father's plantation house on the Eastern Shore of Maryland. The boy's father, Dr. David Davis, was a practicing physician. One could easily assume that little David's childhood would be secure in terms of financial and emotional support. Unfortunately, Dr. Davis's death eight months before the birth of his son foreclosed that possibility. For the first five years of his life, David lived comfortably with his widowed mother at the plantation with enslaved children as playmates. But when Ann Davis remarried in 1820 things changed. Her new husband, bookseller Franklin Betts, became the boy's guardian and unceremoniously deposited David with a family friend until arrangements could be made for him to live in Annapolis with his uncle, the Reverend Henry Lyon Davis. Reverend Henry Davis had a son, Henry Winter Davis, who was two and a half years younger than his cousin David. David and Winter became close and would remain so during their lifetimes. In adulthood they were political confidants and strategists, Winter serving in Congress and as a leader of the anti-immigrant American Party in Maryland. Both Winter and David were heavily influenced by the Reverend Davis's admiration for Henry Clay. Equally influential on the development of the cousins was Winter's mother, Jane Brown Winter Davis, described as a "cultured woman" of "elegant accomplishments." Jane's sister, Elizabeth Brown Winter, "entertained the most rigid and exacting opinions in regard to the training of children." She was in charge of educating the boys.[1]

After David spent a year with Reverend Henry Davis, Franklin Betts returned his stepson to the Betts home in Baltimore and began deducting room and board from David's $5,000 inheritance. Betts then sent David to a famous boarding school, Rock Hill Academy, operated by Isaac Sams, "a man of fine personal appearance" and "an ardent admirer of classical studies." Betts, however, was not anxious to pay the tuition of $128 per year. So after eighteen months he sent David back to live with his uncle, Reverend Henry Davis, at $100 per year, which included the child's living expenses.[2]

David lived with Reverend Davis for the next three years. After his uncle's failed attempt to remove Betts as David's guardian for mismanaging estate assets, the boy returned to live with his mother and stepfather in New Ark, Delaware. Betts enrolled David in the New Ark Academy, where he studied for two years before leaving to attend Kenyon College at the age of thirteen. In November 1828 David arrived at the college in the village of Gambier in the middle of nowhere in the middle of Ohio. Gambier, as well as Kenyon College, was founded by Bishop Philander Chase. Philander was the uncle of Salmon P. Chase, who would serve on the United States Supreme Court with David Davis. The college was still under construction, with only the foundation and basement of the permanent building completed. A log cabin was used for class and administration space, and a residence was designated for "his supreme highness," Professor William Sparrow. Bishop Chase built four temporary buildings in Gambier, each thirty-six feet by twenty-two feet and two stories high, to house students three to a bunk stacked three bunks high.[3]

The boy earned his keep by helping construct campus buildings and working on the college farm. David had to earn his own way, as he was given forty-five dollars when he departed for college and no money after that. His mother provided only three pairs of socks and a winter coat that was too small. She failed to send required texts, so the young college student purchased the books at inflated prices from his earnings for work at the college. To add insult to injury, Davis had to ask his mother not to send letters "postage due."[4]

A letter from David to his mother about eight months after he arrived at Kenyon shows that he adjusted well to his new life and liked "the institution well enough" except for the cold lodgings and poor food. Poor accommodations and poor food was a refrain Davis would often repeat while riding the court circuit as a lawyer and later as a judge in central Illinois.[5] The letter also disclosed that the absence of regular contact with his mother distressed him. David wrote to his mother: "I received your letter about three months ago and answered it and have not received one since. . . . I thought you was sick and sometimes I thought perhaps you did not receive my letter, but I hope you will answer this as soon as you receive [it] for I will be very uneasy till you do." David closed his letter with a plea for news from home and a letter from his mother.

Let me know who has moved out and in New Ark since I left there and give my respects to all of my old acquaintances and let me know if Lambert Biddle is studying Medicine in Elkton or not and let me know what the Miss Davis' are doing you did not write me whether they went to Baltimore after Sarah did or not and let me know if Frank moved out or not and if he did who he was succeeded by. Give my respects to all the family and give the children something for me.

D Davis
(write me soon)[6]

After graduating from Kenyon College in 1832, David went to Lenox, Massachusetts, to study law in the office of Henry W. Bishop. The probate judge for the county was William Perrin Walker, the father of David's future wife, Sarah Walker. On October 1, 1834, Davis left Lenox to begin studies at the New Haven Law School in Connecticut. The nondegree program, loosely affiliated with Yale College, lasted two years, but Davis left after six months.[7] By May 1, 1835, he was back in Lenox asking for Mr. and Mrs. Walker's permission to marry their daughter. The couple planned to wed in three or four years. By that time Davis felt he would be established in the legal profession. Judge Walker declined to consent to any engagement so far in advance of the marriage. However, he did say that he and Mrs. Walker would approve of the marriage in three or four years if Davis succeeded in business as he expected, if he and Sarah had the same attachment for each other, and if Judge Walker and his wife continued to harbor the same favorable opinion of Davis at the time of the marriage.[8]

Family, Profession, and Politicking in Illinois

With the Walkers' less than resounding endorsement of his marriage plans, the prospective groom headed west, intending to establish a law practice in St. Louis. Davis's relative Levi Davis, a lawyer in the Illinois state capital of Vandalia, suggested that he take up residence in central Illinois, where competition for clients would be less intense.[9] Davis took the advice and in late 1835 opened an office in Pekin, Illinois, about seventy miles north of Springfield. He quickly gained the confidence of the town's residents. Shortly after his arrival he was made part of a delegation to lobby the state legislature to bring a railroad to Pekin. In Vandalia David met three people who would dictate much of his future: Jesse W. Fell of Bloomington; Springfield lawyer John Todd Stuart, the leader of the Whigs in the legislature; and Abraham Lincoln, a state representative from Springfield. Davis's practice in Pekin, while stable, did not flourish, and he supplemented his income by teaching school.[10] After recovering from a bout with malaria, he accepted an offer to purchase Jesse Fell's law practice and moved to Bloomington in 1836. Along with the practice, Fell sold Davis several hundred acres of land. Thus began Davis's accumulation of vast holdings of what would

eventually become extremely valuable real estate.[11] In May 1838 Davis entered
a law partnership with Wells Colton, whom he had known in Massachusetts.
Neither partner excelled as a trial lawyer, so they concentrated their practice
in transactional matters such as wills and contracts.

On June 20, 1838, three years after his first attempt to acquire permission from
Judge Walker and his wife to marry their daughter Sarah, Davis sent a letter
renewing the request. The letter fastidiously set out Davis's financial condition
with ledger-like precision, listing assets, liabilities, and accounts receivable. He
did not hide or sugarcoat anything, including the fact that he "made nothing"
from the time he started his practice in Pekin until January 1837. Judge Walker
answered the letter nineteen days later after consulting his wife and Sarah;
Walker stated that he and his wife "[did] not know of any objection which we
think ought to prevent giving our consent."[12]

David and Sarah were wed in Lenox, Massachusetts, on October 30, 1838, and
arrived in Bloomington in December. Sarah brought four boxes of necessities,
including towels, sheets, comforters, nightgowns, quilts, shawls, napkins, skirts,
a teapot, a creamer, a sugar bowl, shoes, "Bible & Books," bedspreads, and bed
lace. David was not left out, as the boxes also contained multiple volumes of
the Massachusetts Supreme Court reports.[13]

The new groom was "about 5 feet 11 inches in height, with a large commanding
form, a broad expansive forehead, blue, penetrating eyes, and rather prominent
nose." At the time of the wedding, he weighed slightly over 200 pounds but soon
put on another 100 pounds.[14] After Davis came into the national limelight as a
Supreme Court justice and later as a US senator, many newspapers, especially
the Democratic papers, relentlessly made fun of his weight. The *Evening Critic*
of Washington, DC, put his weight at 375 pounds, which, according to the
paper, made him the "heaviest individual in public life" since the death of P.
T. Barnum's fat woman. That was kinder than a Wisconsin newspaper that put
the weight of "the fat man who presides over the senate of the United States"
at 500 pounds. In a manner of speaking, the *Austin Weekly Statesman* came to
Davis's "defense," stating that Davis had a right to be fat if he wanted and that
"he shouldn't be tormented about it."[15]

In 1840 Davis unsuccessfully ran for the Illinois Senate as a Whig. He was
defeated by one hundred votes in a district comprised of McLean, DeWitt, Macon, and Livingston Counties. Three months before the election, the Davises lost
their first child during childbirth. Because Sarah suffered greatly both physically
and emotionally, her mother came to stay with the Davises in Bloomington. Still
ailing in August, Sarah accompanied her mother back to Lenox, Massachusetts.
Sarah returned to Bloomington at the end of April the next year. During this
time, Davis concentrated on his law practice, traveling in the counties of the
Eighth Judicial Circuit. It was a difficult time for Davis, who was questioning

his decision to move to Illinois and doubting his ability to achieve financial and professional success.[16]

In February 1841 Davis complained to his brother-in-law, Julius Rockwell, that he was "tired of Illinois," tired of its financial condition, tired of the dominance of the Democrats, and tired of chasing his legal fees. He thought that he might win a seat in the legislature and maybe "ultimately obtain a seat in Congress." But the cost of running for Congress would be too great. John Todd Stuart spent the outlandish sum of $1,000 to be elected a congressman. Davis's fallback position was to become a judge in Iowa or "Wiskonsan," and so he asked his brother-in-law to consider using his political connections to help achieve that more attainable goal. Three months later, Davis again wrote Rockwell, this time directly asking him to make an application on Davis's behalf for a judgeship, preferably in Iowa, and if not, then in Wisconsin, adding "the Sooner—the bet-ter." Davis's dissatisfaction with Illinois did not prevent him from accepting an appointment as a McLean County representative to the Whig State Convention in December 1841.[17]

On June 3, 1842, Sarah gave birth to a son, George, without complications, and things began to look better. The proud father described his son in loving yet objective terms: "His hair is black, eyes deep blue, nose so so—mouth pretty big = & chin & neck quite handsome." Things also improved on the financial side. Davis and Colton became a leading law firm, transacting "a large amount of very important business." At the same time, the real estate holdings of the partners increased in number and in value.[18]

In August 1844 Davis was elected a state representative from McLean County. Writing to his father-in-law on New Year's Eve, he reported that other than a lot of "steam talking," the state legislature accomplished little. The newly elected legislator also said that he was "tired & sick" of the legislature since his Whig idol, Henry Clay, lost the presidency to James K. Polk and "resolved to avoid politics & to devote [himself] to making money." But in February the legislature did something that would profoundly affect Davis's future: it agreed to call a state constitutional convention.[19]

In April 1847 Davis won an uncontested seat as a delegate to the constitu-tional convention. The gathering convened in Springfield on June 7, 1847, and adjourned on August 31. On March 8, 1848, the voters ratified the new consti-tution by a margin of more than three to one. Davis took an active role in the shaping of the document. He opposed Article XIV, which directed the state legislature to "pass such laws as will effectually prohibit free persons of color from immigrating to and settling in this state." The article further provided that the legislature shall enact laws to "prevent the owners of slaves from bringing them into this state for the purpose of setting them free." But a majority of the delegates voted for Article XIV and placed it as its own separate proposition on the ratification ballot. Article XIV was passed by Illinois voters and included in the new constitution.[20]

Davis was a force behind the convention's decision to change the manner of selecting judges from appointment by the legislature to election by the people. He vehemently argued for the popular election of state judges to protect judicial independence and to prevent what he saw as the corrupting influence of the legislative appointment process. Davis might have viewed things differently if his own Whig Party, rather than the Democrats, had controlled the Illinois legislature and thereby the judicial appointments. Delegate Davis also believed that popular elections would improve the federal bench, because, unlike the president, the people "would have chosen judges, instead of broken down politicians."[21]

On September 4, 1848, the voters of the Eighth Judicial Circuit elected Davis to a judgeship created by the state constitution that he helped write. Although the Eighth Judicial Circuit would shrink over time, it then included the fourteen central Illinois counties of Sangamon, Tazewell, Woodford, McLean, Logan, DeWitt, Piatt, Champaign, Vermilion, Edgar, Shelby, Moultrie, Macon, and Christian. It was during Davis's years as a circuit judge that he solidified relationships with Lincoln and other lawyers of the Eighth Judicial Circuit who would later assist him in securing Lincoln's nomination for president (see chapter 1).

Lincoln ran for the US Senate in 1855 and again in 1859. At the time, US senators were elected by the state legislature rather than by popular vote. In both unsuccessful efforts, the judge was Lincoln's most active and committed campaign supporter. Then in May 1860 Davis temporarily absented himself from the bench to mastermind Lincoln's presidential nomination at the Republican National Convention in Chicago. In the general election the judge served as Lincoln's in-state and out-of-state troubleshooter, fundraiser, campaign strategist, event coordinator, liaison, and most trusted campaign advisor (see chapters 1–4). Davis's public, hands-on campaign activities, which were somewhat common among judges in the nineteenth century, would today be absolutely barred by ethics codes governing judges. Current judicial ethics rules would have put Judge Davis on the sidelines in each of Lincoln's campaigns.[22]

Davis Goes to Washington

When Lincoln assumed the presidency three open seats existed on the United States Supreme Court. Lincoln filled the first two openings without much thought of nominating Davis for either spot. Ignoring Davis did not sit well with Eighth Circuit lawyer Leonard Swett. Swett, who was Davis's right-hand man in all of Lincoln's campaigns, would not accept Lincoln's snub of the judge. With the help of Mary Lincoln and the lawyers of the Eighth Circuit, Swett eventually convinced the president to appoint Davis to the third court vacancy. Justice Davis took a seat on the high court on December 10, 1862.[23]

The close personal and political association between the judge and Lincoln continued after Davis joined the Supreme Court. He provided advice to the president on numerous and varied governmental matters. As Doris Kearns Goodwin noted, Abraham Lincoln "listened carefully" to David Davis when he was on the Supreme Court.[24]

As the 1864 election approached, the judge resumed his role as campaign manager. He held strategy meetings with the president and others and was asked by Lincoln to attend the national convention of the Union Party (a coalition of Republicans and War Democrats), scheduled for June in Maryland. The newest high court justice kept close tabs on delegate counts, and when the New York and Ohio delegates received instructions to vote for the president, Davis knew that Lincoln would be renominated and decided not to travel to Baltimore. If a "speck of opposition" arose, Justice Davis would have again personally directed convention efforts.[25]

During his fourteen years on the Supreme Court, Davis was involved officially and sometimes unofficially in cases that challenged Lincoln's use of the war powers. Davis's most famous and important court opinion was *Ex parte Milligan*. Writing for a bare majority of five justices and to the shock of the Republicans in Congress, he held that the military commissions created by Lincoln during the Civil War had no jurisdiction over civilians in nonseceding states in which courts were open and operating. Republicans and the Republican press bitterly condemned the decision (see chapter 6).

Davis became restless in his confining position as an associate justice of the Supreme Court. As the years went on, the tediousness of his duties weighed more and more on him. Even worse, the job required him to refrain from public comment on important issues of the day, such as the impeachment of President Andrew Johnson and Reconstruction policy.[26] By early 1868 the job and the separation from his family caused Davis to remark to Sarah, "I feel that I am on the downhill road of life."[27] So when an anti–President Grant wing of the Republican Party, known as Liberal Republicans, decided to nominate a candidate to challenge Grant's reelection bid, Davis put himself in the running. The judge hoped that his unexpected nomination by the new Labor Reform Party in February 1872 would enhance his chances for nomination at the Liberal Republican National Convention in Cincinnati that April. Leonard Swett and Jesse Fell led the floor fight at the Cincinnati convention. Swett employed the same technique that he and Davis used at the 1860 Republican National Convention: packing the house for their favorite. Davis paid the bill for many of the one thousand Illinoisans who traveled to the convention. Illinois by far had the largest contingent of any candidate. But the judge's rising momentum was quickly squelched when, on the eve of the convention, the publishers of four newspapers, the *Springfield Republican*, the *Chicago Tribune*, the *Cincinnati Commercial*, and the *Louisville Courier-Journal*, made a coordinated attack on Davis. The attack effectively ended his candidacy. Horace Greeley, editor of the *New-York Tribune*, was nominated by the Liberal Republican Party. After Greeley's nomination, Davis declined the Labor Party's nomination. The Democrats fielded no presidential candidate, swallowed their pride, and supported Greeley, who had relentlessly denounced the Democrats throughout his career. Greeley lost badly to President Ulysses Grant.[28]

Life after Lincoln's Death

The day that President Lincoln died, Robert Lincoln telegraphed Davis, asking him to immediately come to Washington to take charge of his father's affairs. At the time, the judge was sick in Bloomington but promptly left for Washington to console Mary Lincoln, help Robert and Mary make decisions about funeral and burial arrangements, and take charge of the president's estate. Through wise investments and the collection of debts, Davis increased the value of the estate's assets from $83,343.70 at the time of Lincoln's death to $110,974.62 when the estate was distributed to Mary, Robert, and fifteen-year-old Tad. While the estate was pending, Robert sent twenty-eight letters and two telegrams to Davis seeking advice and assistance concerning his own finances and law partnership, his mother's condition, his father's papers, and Tad's best interests. The judge refused any compensation and paid his own expenses. At Robert's insistence, Davis was appointed Tad's guardian in 1867.[29]

In 1877 the Illinois state legislature elected Justice Davis to replace Republican John A. Logan as US senator. The selection process ended on the fortieth ballot when the Democrats abandoned their candidate and united with independents to choose the judge.[30] Davis's appointment was mired in the intrigue surrounding the contested 1876 presidential election, which pitted Republican Rutherford B. Hayes against Democrat Samuel J. Tilden. Tilden won the popular vote and was only one electoral vote away from becoming the nineteenth US president. To determine who won the contested twenty combined electoral votes of Florida, Louisiana, Oregon, and South Carolina, Congress established a fifteen-member commission. The commission was to consist in part of four Supreme Court justices, two from each party. Those four members of the court would select a fifth justice to serve on the commission. Five senators and five members of the House of Representatives would round out the commission. Everyone knew that fourteen of the members would vote their partisan party loyalties, leaving the fifteenth member to pick the next president. Democrats and Republicans assumed that the deciding member would be "a genuine Independent," David Davis. But after he was chosen for the Senate seat, Davis refused the appointment to the electoral commission and was replaced by Supreme Court Justice Joseph P. Bradley. An appointee of President Grant, Justice Bradley voted to give Rutherford B. Hayes all twenty contested electoral votes, making him president.[31]

Davis did not seek the senatorial office, nor did the Democrats directly ask permission to place his name before the legislature. But longtime Bloomington friend Jesse Fell advised the Democrats that the judge planned to retire from the court at the end of President Grant's term in March 1877 and would then accept an appointment to the Senate.[32] As Fell predicted, Davis resigned from the court and served as a US senator from 1877 until 1883. Although not a single Illinois Republican state legislator voted for Davis, he took a seat on the Republican side of the Senate and refused to attend either party's caucus. As one Republican told the *Chicago Daily Tribune*, the new senator was less political than any of the other candidates in the Illinois senatorial race and was "about as much Republican as Democratic." A true independent, Davis voted his mind on the basis of issues rather than party affiliation.[33]

In October 1881, on a motion of the Republicans, Davis became president pro tempore of the Senate, filling the vacancy created when Vice President Chester Arthur succeeded slain President James Garfield.[34] Accepting the office, the new president pro tem emphasized two goals. First, he desired to facilitate the reunification of the country so that it could attain the "grandeur and glory" for which it was destined: "My only ambition while here is to be instrumental in bringing about perfect peace between the North and the South as the best means of promoting the permanent prosperity of the whole Union. When the rude voice of faction, which for fifteen years past in time of peace has disturbed the national fellowship that should have been restored at the close of the civil war, shall be silenced, this country will bound forward in a career of grandeur and of glory that will astound mankind."[35]

Davis achieved greater success in his second ambition: to administer the office of president pro tem "with impartiality and with entire fairness."[36] According to *Harper's Weekly*, the president pro tem maintained his independent status by winning and retaining the respect of Republicans and Democrats. As presiding officer of the Senate, Davis stood next in the line of succession for the presidency and was addressed by President Arthur and the *New York Times* as "Mr. Vice President."[37]

While Davis was a member of the Senate, "no important law bore his name; he defeated no notable measures."[38] Senator Davis did steer a bill through the upper chamber that would have created an intermediate federal court of appeals with full-time judges to hear appeals from the federal district courts. The reform would have lightened the increasing load of the members of the Supreme Court and reformed the antiquated and inefficient system in which a district court judge and a Supreme Court justice sat as a "circuit court" reviewing the district court judge's decisions. Although it passed the Senate, Davis's bill failed in the House. Not until 1891 would Congress finally create the Federal Circuit Courts of Appeals.[39]

Sarah Davis's Illness and Death

In the summer of 1879 Sarah Davis traveled to Rhode Island, confident that the eastern fresh air would remedy her constant cough. But her health deteriorated, causing her to move in with her sister in Stockbridge, Massachusetts. Sarah died there of a heart condition on November 9, 1879, at the age of sixty-five with her husband and children in attendance. Funerals were held in Stockbridge and in Bloomington, where she was interred at Evergreen Memorial Cemetery, about a mile and a half from the Davis home. The judge had lost the love of his life.[40] The letters of five decades between husband and wife demonstrate their close and loving relationship. Davis's letters are replete with declarations of his love and affection for Sarah and his inability to enjoy life without her. A paragraph in a letter to Sarah in 1864 is representative: "You are never out of my mind. Your pleasant loving face is daguerreotyped on my heart & there it will remain forever. I think of you by day & dream of you by night. I see you on Law records & on paper when writing an opinion."[41] Sarah's letters to her husband reveal the same loving relationship. In 1852 she wrote:

> Dearest Davie,
>   You are to me the dearest earthly object and life would be dreary without your love. It keeps me up when I feel sad and weary—when you are away I look for your return—and your constant kindness is ever present. Dearest love to write to you is pleasure to me—and to hear good news from you refreshes me.
>
>   Sarah
>   I hope you dried your clothes *thoroughly* before wearing them.[42]

On their thirty-second wedding anniversary Sarah wrote:

> Dear Davie
>   Mrs. Maclean . . . wished me many returns of the day—thus reminding me that this is our Wedding Anniversary—32 years to day we were made one—and a kind loving husband you have been to me—and I love you ten times more than when I stood by your side at that time—I can hardly think of any time when I did not love you—so long has your image filled my heart.[43]

During the summers, Davis brought flowers to Sarah's final resting place three times a week.[44]

After Leaving the Senate

On March 14, 1883, ten days after he left the Senate, Judge Davis married Miss Adeline Burr. Addie and the judge had been secretly engaged for some time, but Addie refused to get married until her fiancé retired from the Senate. The private wedding was held at Congressman Wharton Jackson Green's mansion, Tokay, overlooking the Cape Fear River near Fayetteville, North Carolina. Although some "irresponsible newspapers" published her age as thirty years, Addie was in fact forty years old and according to the *Bloomington Daily Pantagraph* was "certainly one of the best preserved and most elegant maidens of four decades that have ever approached the marriage altar." Davis's gifts to the bride included a diamond solitaire engagement ring and a pair of diamond solitaire earrings with "stones of great size and brilliancy." The newlyweds took a special steamer to Wilmington, Delaware, then visited Charleston, Savannah, and New Orleans before continuing to California on their honeymoon. The trip was quite different from his journey to Illinois after his first marriage when he and Sarah slept on the floor of an inn after their carriage broke down.[45]

Davis served as the seventh president of the Illinois State Bar Association in 1884. Failing health did not prevent him from making a forceful inaugural address to the bar. Davis underscored the role of the jury in protecting the rights of Americans and, quoting Alexis de Tocqueville, in educating the public and allowing ordinary citizens to be the decision-makers in the judicial branch of government. He emphasized the importance of unanimous jury verdicts and of increasing the salaries of prosecutors. He criticized the lawyers who failed to join the state bar association, noting that the association had only 279 members out of the 5,000 lawyers in the state. He particularly called out the cities of Chicago, Peoria, Quincy, and his own Bloomington for failing to enroll more members. Davis said that his "delinquent brethren" were ignoring their duty to improve the profession and thereby advance the interests of society.[46] Until his health worsened, the judge remained active in community and ceremonial events. For instance, in 1884 he presided over a reunion of delegates to the 1847 Illinois Constitutional Convention.[47]

On May 10, 1886, Leonard Swett, the judge's best and most loyal friend, now practicing law in Chicago, visited Davis in Bloomington. The judge loved Swett like a brother and admired his unselfish and self-sacrificing nature.[48] The visit was a final farewell, because according to Swett, both knew that Davis's days were numbered.[49] A week after the visit, Addie responded to reports of her husband's worsening condition by saying that David was "not as sick as the reports have represented and there is no reason for believing that he will not be fully restored to health in a week or ten days."[50] But Davis rapidly deteriorated from a malignant carbuncle on his shoulder, complicated by his diabetes and weight.

On the morning of June 21 Lawrence Weldon, a circuit-riding lawyer who backed Davis for the Supreme Court, visited the judge and found him to be "emaciated with disease" and "in [the] lowest condition of life . . . [r]ational when aroused but almost unconscious of his surroundings except when aroused."[51] The judge died at 6:00 a.m. on June 26, 1886. Honorary and active pallbearers included Robert Lincoln; Adlai Stevenson I; Leonard Swett; Jesse Fell; Governor Richard Oglesby; Judges John Caton, Henry Blodgett, Lawrence Weldon, John Scott, and Thomas Drummond; Clifton Moore; Robert B. Latham; Senator John Logan; James S. Ewing; Luman Burr; Frank D. Orme; Duncan M. Funk; Honorable D. T. Littler; Henry W. Bishop Jr.; and Lucius G. Fisher Jr.[52] Davis's real estate investments had made him a multimillionaire at the time of his death.[53] He was buried next to Sarah and his deceased children in the Davis family plot at Evergreen Memorial Cemetery. Addie Davis would subsequently marry Wharton Jackson Green, who served as a Confederate officer during the Civil War and who later served two terms as a congressman from North Carolina.[54]

I

Davis, Lincoln, and the US Senate

1 Lincoln's First US Senate Campaign

Building the Relationship

When Lincoln decided to try for a US Senate seat in late 1854, his relationship with David Davis had spanned more than seventeen years. Their association began when both were lawyers and Whigs traveling in the same professional and political circles from 1836 until Davis became a judge in 1848. After Davis assumed the bench, the bond between the two solidified into one of mutual trust and respect, permitting the judge to play a major role in Lincoln's unsuccessful first bid for a legislative appointment to the Senate.

Lawyer Lincoln and Lawyer Davis

After Davis purchased Jesse Fell's law practice in Bloomington in 1836 and joined his friend Wells Colton in a law partnership two years later, Davis's prospects for a successful legal career brightened. To develop enough business to make a living in central Illinois meant joining the troupe of lawyers traveling from county seat to county seat in the Eighth Judicial Circuit.[1] While suffering poor food, dismal accommodations, bad roads, and broken bridges, Davis enjoyed the "fun" and "excitement" of socializing with the other traveling lawyers, especially Lincoln. Davis relished the political speeches signaling the first day of each court session. The speakers often included Lincoln, who, in Davis's opinion, was "the best stump speaker in the State."[2]

Davis's reputation as a lawyer grew, and Davis, Lincoln, Stephen T. Logan, John Todd Stuart, and Edward D. Baker comprised "the 'big five' of the horseback circuit."[3] The five lawyers became close both personally and professionally. In 1846 Lincoln named his second son, Edward Baker Lincoln, after his circuit-riding friend. Baker and the others often stayed at the Davises' home during court days in McLean County. In Davis's first important contested case, he was opposed by former judge and now Lincoln law partner John Todd Stuart. Davis diligently prepared his case but had no idea how to make his arguments to the judge. Rather than taking advantage of the situation, Stuart instructed his inexperienced opponent on how to present his case in court. Stuart prevailed, but the experience demonstrated to Davis the camaraderie on the circuit. It also helped convince Davis to concentrate on transactional matters such as debt collection and probate rather than on litigation.[4] As further evidence of circuit fellowship, a year later Stuart handled Davis's cases when an "attack of fever and ague" delayed his return home from a trip to New York.[5]

Davis and Lincoln found themselves on opposite sides of cases involving debt collections, breaches of contract, and probate matters.[6] Occasionally, they represented competing parties in more interesting disputes. For example, Davis represented a client who rented his horse to Lincoln's client so that the latter could make the fourteen-mile trip from Money Creek, Illinois, to Bloomington, Illinois. The horse died during the excursion, and Davis sued Lincoln's client, claiming that the defendant's neglect caused the demise of the horse. The jury returned a verdict in the horse owner's favor for $70.25.[7] In another case, Davis's client (Boggs) sued Lincoln's client (Overton) for slander. Boggs claimed damage to his reputation when Overton spread a "false" rumor that Boggs had stolen a clevis pin, used to tow farm equipment. Lincoln won the case by producing witnesses who testified that Boggs did actually steal the clevis pin from a third party named Gideon Rathbone.[8]

Lincoln and Davis jointly represented litigants in state court and in the federal district court in Springfield. Some pleadings were signed "Davis & Lincoln," and while the men may have split fees, no formal partnership ever existed between the two.[9] The DeWitt County Circuit Court records show that Davis represented Lincoln in a lawsuit seeking to collect on a $200 promissory note signed by Spencer Turner and William Turner. The $200 represented Lincoln's fee for successfully defending Spencer in a murder case. An examination of the records, however, indicates that Lincoln and John Stuart did most of the work.[10] The close professional and personal relationship that developed between Lincoln and Davis as they traveled, lived, and worked together as circuit-riding lawyers was further enhanced by their joint activities as Whig politicians.

Two Whig Politicians

Just as Davis wasted no time joining the traveling troupe of law practitioners after moving to Illinois, neither did he delay joining the political fray. In the 1836 election, he supported Whig candidates, including Lincoln's soon-to-be law partner, John Stuart, in his unsuccessful run for Congress. But Davis's campaigning began in earnest two years later in Stuart's rematch against incumbent Stephen Douglas for the Third Congressional District seat, which included twenty-two counties in central and northern Illinois.[11] Davis and Lincoln attended many of the Stuart-Douglas joint appearances because the candidates campaigned in county seats during court sessions to take advantage of the large crowds. The 1838 congressional election was surprisingly close, with Stuart prevailing by thirty-six votes out of more than thirty-six thousand votes cast. Davis took some credit for helping Stuart to carry McLean County by about two hundred votes. Two days before the election, Davis attended a scheduled debate between the candidates in Bloomington. Stuart did not appear because he was home recovering from an inflamed bite to his thumb inflicted by Douglas a few days earlier. To be fair, Douglas could have argued self-defense, because he bit Stuart's thumb only after Stuart picked up Douglas during a Springfield debate and refused to put him down.[12] Taking advantage of his opponent's absence at the Bloomington appearance, Douglas made a false charge against his foe, which Davis "took the liberty of denying" on behalf of Stuart. Davis then promised "to have an authorized denial of the charge in every precinct of McLean County at the opening of the polls." According to Davis, he kept his word and helped Stuart to victory.[13] In early 1839, backed by Lincoln and the other Whig state legislators, Davis unsuccessfully sought appointment as district attorney for the Eighth Judicial Circuit. Instead, the Democrat-controlled Illinois General Assembly chose one of their own, David B. Campbell.[14]

During his first few years in Illinois, Davis was hindered from playing a greater role in Whig campaigns by a combination of factors, including a bout with malaria, teaching school to supplement a less than lucrative law practice, and the burden of convincing his future father-in-law to permit his marriage to Sarah.[15] But by 1840 Davis felt secure enough in his personal and financial life to run for a state senate seat and actively support the entire Whig ticket. In February 1840 a group from Bloomington led by Davis, Jesse Fell, and fellow lawyer Asahel Gridley ventured to a "celebration" of William Henry Harrison's campaign for president in Peoria, where Lincoln was a featured speaker. On the way, the group stopped in Tremont, where Davis's speech received the loudest applause from the Tazewell County and Bloomington Whigs. On the trip home, the McLean County entourage made another stop in Tazewell County, this time in the town of Washington, where Davis again delivered remarks at a Whig gathering.[16] After speaking at another Harrison rally in Bloomington, Davis received the Whig nomination for state senator. He lost the race to a two-term Democratic state senator by a vote of 1,335 to 1,165 but won McLean County with 656 votes to Democrat John Moore's 590 votes.[17] The defeated state senatorial candidate summed up his loss: "I overshot the mark in running for the State

Senate last summer—I could have been easily elected to the lower house—but by aiming too high, I lost all."[18]

In 1844 Davis lowered his sights and successfully campaigned for state representative, serving one term. A month before the election, Lincoln, Stephen Logan, and Davis addressed a Whig mass meeting and barbeque in Decatur.[19] During his two years in the state capital as a member of the assembly, Davis paid social visits to Springfield lawyers, including Lincoln, Stuart, and Baker; attended lectures, dances, balls, weddings, and a reception for the Illinois Supreme Court justices; and frequented other formal and informal gatherings.[20] After leaving the state legislature, Davis won an uncontested delegate seat to the 1847 state constitutional convention. Arriving at the convention in Springfield in June of that year, the Bloomington delegate was surprised by how many of the convention members he knew. While in Springfield, he often consulted with Lincoln, joined gatherings at Lincoln's home, and took trips with Lincoln. Further building on his statewide contacts, Davis attended dinners, concerts, parties, and other social events while he was a state constitutional convention delegate.[21]

In September 1848 the voters of the Eighth Judicial Circuit elected Davis to a judgeship created by the new state constitution. Benjamin S. Edwards, a Springfield lawyer and the brother-in-law of Mary Lincoln's sister Elizabeth, considered but ultimately chose not to run for the Whig nomination for the same judgeship. During the time that Edwards was considering entering the race, Lincoln withheld any endorsement of Davis. In the end, Edwards explained that he would step aside and sacrifice his personal advancement in favor of his well-qualified, personal, and political friend from Bloomington. Davis, however, believed that Edwards withdrew because he knew he would lose in a head-to-head contest. According to Davis, although Edwards had been endorsed by the Sangamon County Whig convention, he "had never traveled the eastern counties of the circuit—Champaign, Vermilion and Edgar," and overall had fewer friends in the fourteen counties comprising the Eighth Circuit. On August 23 the *Illinois State Journal* endorsed the unopposed Davis for the judicial seat.[22]

Lincoln and Davis's association as lawyers and politicians laid the groundwork for what would become a personal, professional, and political relationship of confidence, trust, and respect. The time the two spent together beginning when Davis became a judge in December 1848 until Lincoln decided to run for the US Senate in late 1854 was pivotal in solidifying that relationship.

Judge Davis and Lawyer Lincoln

When Davis assumed the bench in December 1848, Lincoln's single term in Congress was quickly coming to a close. Reflecting on his experience in Washington, DC, Lincoln thought about old friends. He appreciated that Davis's friendship included a heartfelt concern about the congressman as a person. In February of the next year Lincoln wrote to Davis, thanking the new judge for his personal interest in Lincoln's well-being: "Your letter of the 24th Jany. is received; and I have more cause to thank you for it, than you would suppose. Out of more than three hundred letters received this session, yours is the second one manifesting the least interest for me personally."[23] Davis worried about Lincoln's physical and mental health but also was concerned with practical matters, including what his friend would do after leaving Congress. Looking to the future, the ex-congressman sought an appointment as commissioner of the General Land Office of the Department of the Interior. The judge, of course, supported Lincoln. After losing out to Justin Butterfield, Lincoln wrote to Davis that while he could not give the particulars of the defeat in a letter, he would tell the judge all when they met in person.[24] Fortunately, Lincoln had the law practice he had formed in 1844 with his third partner, William Herndon, to fall back on. So he seamlessly returned to the Eighth Circuit, now with Judge Davis in charge.

For three months in the spring and three months in the fall, Judge Davis led the small band of traveling lawyers around the Eighth Judicial Circuit like a schoolmaster leading his pupils.[25] Davis's role had changed, but his approach to the law remained the same. Like Lincoln, Davis relied on common sense rather than a strict application of legal precedent. It was in both men's natures to do so, although, as a practical matter, "the traveling library consisted at most of a book or two, easily carried in the saddlebags."[26] Both cut to the chase of a dispute, quickly separating the controlling issues and facts from interesting but irrelevant considerations. Both exhibited an independence of judgment, seldom relying on the advice of others. And, most importantly, each practiced his trade with "rock-ribbed integrity."[27] They joined in advocating mediation and arbitration as alternative methods to resolve civil disputes. Leonard Swett gives the example of a case in which two sets of heirs contested a decedent's estate. Davis mediated the matter and suggested a fair distribution of the assets, benefiting all the claimed heirs. By accepting the judge's recommendation, the parties avoided a trial. The judge also suggested that the litigants forgive their deceased father for marrying two women.[28] In another case, Lincoln arranged for a settlement conference in his hotel room. The parties presented their sides of the story to Davis until midnight. At the end of the informal presentations the judge "ruled" for the winning party, creating more of a binding arbitration than a mediation.[29]

Under Davis's leadership, court days continued as "gala" events drawing lawyers, litigants, witnesses, jurors, politicians, and others who simply wanted to join in the high point of the county's social calendar. People without legal business attended court sessions to be entertained by the witnesses' testimony and lawyers' arguments.[30] Davis welcomed the social value of court days as a means to maximize his visibility among courtgoers. For instance, at an "exciting" trial in Danville, Judge Davis made sure to relay his wife's respects to the great number of ladies who attended the trial as observers.[31] The judge embraced the fact that his new role also placed him in full charge of the proceedings and festivities before court, during court, and after court recessed for the day. Before court, the lawyers often informally gathered for study and conversation in the clerk's office or other room where the judge had his desk.[32] Once court began the judge permitted some informal give-and-take between the lawyers, but there was never a question of who was in charge of the proceedings.

After dinner, the judge invited a few attorneys to adjourn to his room for storytelling, political talk, and mock trials. At one such trial Lincoln was accused and "convicted" of charging unacceptably low fees. Because people crowded the county seats on court days, some evenings the circuit riders returned to the courtroom and, joined by witnesses and townspeople, listened to Lincoln's stories. Davis presided over all judicial and social activities. If necessary, he imposed extrajudicial discipline on lawyers when their after-hours conduct breached expected standards of decorum.[33]

The fraternity-type association between the bar and the bench was very close and personal. As the judge observed, "It was impossible for a body of intelligent gentlemen to associate together, day by day, for six months of the year, without becoming attached to each other, and without mutual benefit."[34] Davis spent a lot of time with Lincoln not only because Davis preferred Lincoln's company but also because Lincoln traveled the entire circuit rather than limiting his practice to a few counties like most lawyers did. In addition, unlike other attorneys, Lincoln often did not return home on the weekends, so Lincoln was always there for court, meals, and the judge's invitation-only nighttime gatherings.[35] Davis usually shared a room with his favorite. When in McLean County Lincoln often stayed at the judge's house. They traveled from county to county together, went to church together, dined at mutual friends' homes together, engaged in long walks and in pillow fights, attended the same social and political events, and discussed books.[36] On one occasion, it befell Lincoln and Davis as an act of "charity" to escort the sisters of a tavern keeper's wife to a concert by the Newhall Family singers, a popular choir that toured Illinois, Michigan, and Indiana in the 1850s.[37] Sometimes Davis had to persuade a reluctant Lincoln to attend social events.[38] The cohorts also discussed books. The judge bragged to his wife that after reading a biography of John Randolph, he and Lincoln put the clues together and figured out why Randolph never married his "lady friend."[39] The two circuit-riding companions not only laughed together but also shared tragedies together. When Davis's infant daughter Lucy died in August 1850, Sarah accompanied the judge while he finished his circuit duties. Sarah traveled with her husband, and their son George rode with Lincoln for the remaining two months of the court session.[40] The special relationship extended to professional activities. Davis retained Lincoln to represent him in lawsuits, referred clients to him, and "appointed" Lincoln as a substitute judge to fill in when Davis was away from court.[41] It did not take any special powers of observation for the clerk of the Champaign County Court to describe Davis and Lincoln as constant companions.[42]

Although Lincoln held most personal matters close to the vest, he felt comfortable discussing intimate family matters with Judge Davis during their long periods together. Unfortunately, the judge's letters do not detail his discussions with Lincoln. Davis's letters to his wife, however, contain references to discussions concerning private matters. For example, Lincoln told the judge that he and Mary had hoped for a girl when their third son, Willie, was born in December 1850. Eighteen months later Lincoln shared the news that Mary had developed nursing sore mouth. (Davis was less than sympathetic to a mother nursing an eighteen-month-old child.) Lincoln also discussed the frequency or, more accurately, the infrequency of letters from Mary and the escapades of his in-laws.[43] The judge reported that Lincoln spoke "very affectionately of his wife & children."[44] Lincoln became fond of Davis's son George in their travels together after the death of George's infant sister Lucy. During one stop, George measured Lincoln at six feet, four and one-half inches, making him half an inch taller than he maintained. After the trip, the future president took an interest in George, affectionately inquiring after him and reminiscing about their journey in the cart pulled by old Buck. In 1858 Lincoln was the first to sign George's autograph book.[45]

On Tuesday, October 24, 1854, Davis shared a room with Lincoln in the Pennsylvania House in Urbana during the fall court session. In the evening, Henry Whitney, a fellow traveling lawyer, joined the two in their room for some Lincoln stories until it was time to walk to the courthouse for one of Lincoln's speeches in opposition to the Kansas-Nebraska Act. Upon returning to the Pennsylvania House, Davis, Lincoln, and Whitney continued their conversation until midnight. A likely topic was the upcoming election on November 7, in which Lincoln was on the ballot for state representative. One wonders if there was any mention of a possible Lincoln bid for US senator. The Illinois legislature would appoint the senator early the next year. About two weeks after leaving Urbana, Lincoln began soliciting commitments from state representatives and state senators for their votes for the Senate seat.[46]

The 1855 Senatorial Campaign Begins

On November 7, 1854, the Sangamon County voters elected Abraham Lincoln to the Illinois House of Representatives. He had previously served in the state house from 1834 until 1842 and had no desire to return. Lincoln agreed to run again for the Illinois General Assembly at the behest of party leaders who knew that his popularity would guarantee the seat for the Whigs. But Lincoln's sights were set on Washington, not Springfield. He held high hopes that enough Whigs, abolitionists, and anti-Nebraska Democrats would be elected to the state legislature in November 1854 to allow a Whig to oust Democratic US senator James Shields. At the time, US senators were elected by state legislatures rather than by popular vote.

Lincoln's hope to buck the consistently Democrat-controlled Illinois legislature rested on the split in the Democratic Party caused by the passage of the Kansas-Nebraska Act in 1854. Senator Stephen Douglas introduced and championed the act, which created the Kansas and Nebraska Territories, a large area including the present-day states of Kansas, Nebraska, Montana, North Dakota, and South Dakota. Under Douglas's doctrine of popular sovereignty, which Congress incorporated into the act, the residents of the territories would determine whether to allow or prohibit slavery. Many in the North, including some Democrats, despised the act and its sponsor because it repealed and replaced the well-established Missouri Compromise. The compromise admitted Maine as a free state and Missouri as a slave state and otherwise prohibited slavery in the lands of the Louisiana Purchase north of the 36°30' parallel, which included the Kansas and Nebraska Territories. Aspirants for the Illinois state legislature in 1854 ran as either for or against the Kansas-Nebraska Act.[47]

Although the state election returns were not yet complete, Lincoln believed that his hope had become a reality and that there would be enough legislators against the act to elect a Whig to replace Senator Shields.[48] Deciding to seek the US Senate seat, Lincoln began the task of securing commitments from legislators both by directly contacting state representatives and senators and by asking clients, lawyers, and officeholders to solicit support from their friends in the legislature. In an early campaign letter written on November 10, 1854, Lincoln asked Charles Hoyt, a former client and wealthy merchant from Aurora in the northern part of the state, for his support and for the names, addresses, and political offices of the legislators in his area. The next day, Lincoln wrote to lawyer Jacob Harding asking him to "make a mark" with the new representative from Edgar County if, in fact, a Whig had been elected. Among many other letters, the senatorial aspirant wrote Springfield state representative Thomas J. Henderson asking him to think the Senate race over "and see whether you can do better than to go for me."[49] In response to Lincoln's request, Congressman Elihu B. Washburne prepared a list of the state legislators in his congressional district with comments on their political leanings and likely support or opposition to Lincoln's senatorial bid.[50] Lincoln was fully committed to convincing enough state representatives and senators to vote to unseat Senator James Shields when the legislature met in January.

One historian has described David Davis as Lincoln's "unofficial campaign manager" in the 1855 senatorial campaign.[51] But while Davis and other loyal friends served as important lieutenants, Lincoln personally managed his bid for the United States Senate. As observed by David Herbert Donald, "There is little reason to believe that at this [1855 Senate race] or any other time Lincoln placed the direction of his political career in another man's hands."[52] Even Davis, who was born to give orders and who took matters into his own hands during the 1860 Republican National Convention, deferred to Lincoln on significant and insignificant matters of campaign strategy in the Senate race. For example, the judge offered to contact a legislator from Kane County with whom he served in the 1847 state constitutional convention if Lincoln approved. Davis also asked permission before sending lawyer Leonard Swett to solicit votes in Joliet and before sending Swett to Peru, Illinois, to seek the support of Whig lawyer Churchill Coffing.[53]

Lincoln did reasonably well in managing his own campaign, considering that he was maintaining an active law practice while canvassing for legislators' votes. Unfortunately, his practice took valuable time away from campaigning, especially in November. At dawn the day after the November 7 legislative election, Lincoln was on his way to court in DeWitt County.[54] During the remainder of the month, Lincoln was tied up in court or otherwise attending to legal matters on November 9, 11, 13, 14, 15, 16, 17, 21, 22, 23, 24, 25, 28, and 29. With the Sangamon County Court term ending on December 5, Lincoln could devote more time to his Senate campaign.[55] During the months of November and December, Lincoln formulated a campaign strategy that included compiling a detailed list of legislators and their likely votes in the senatorial contest early the next year.[56] He continuously solicited support and coordinated efforts with his field managers.[57] Chief among Lincoln's loyal lieutenants, David Davis commenced work immediately to promote his favorite Eighth Circuit lawyer for the United States Senate.

Davis's Campaign Role

Judge Davis not only set out to secure commitments from legislators in his own backyard, the counties of the Eighth Judicial Circuit of central Illinois, but also worked to build Lincoln support in the abolitionist-controlled northern part of the state. The backing of northern legislators was essential for Lincoln to have any chance at replacing Senator Shields. And the abolitionist vote was anything but assured. In December 1854 Lincoln complained that his "most intimate friends" in Chicago ignored his letters seeking support in the Senate fight.[58] Lincoln faced an uphill battle in gaining the trust of abolitionists, who now called themselves Republicans, because many abolitionists questioned the

Springfield lawyer's commitment to ending slavery.[59] By declining an appoint-ment to the new Illinois Republican Party's central committee, Lincoln further fueled the fear that he lacked commitment to the antislavery cause. Making mat-ters worse, northerners mistrusted what they viewed as Springfield's domination of state government and politics.[60] Congressman Elihu B. Washburne, from the northernmost part of Illinois, explained the regional jealousy to Lincoln: "The objection to you is that it is alleged that the Springfield influence has always been against us in the north, and that if you should be elected the north would be overlooked for the center and south part of the State."[61]

Recognizing the importance of the abolitionist vote, Davis successfully solic-ited support for Lincoln in the northern part of the state by contacting legisla-tors and friends of legislators.[62] Davis took care whom he contacted, because it was well known that he was no abolitionist and disliked the methods and rhetoric of the abolitionists. So Davis focused on contacting legislators whom he knew well and close friends of other legislators who might be favorable to Lincoln. Those legislators included state representatives Daniel J. Pinckney of Ogle County, Reverend Luther W. Lawrence of Boone County, and Hurlbut Swan of Lake County and state senators Wait Talcott of Winnebago County, George Gage of McHenry County, and Augustus Adams of Kane County.[63] In his effort to secure northern votes, Davis enlisted his protégé, Leonard Swett, who had recently moved from Clinton, Illinois, to Bloomington. Davis had befriended Swett in 1848 when Swett was walking through Bloomington on his way back home to Maine after serving in the Mexican War. Admitted to practice law in June 1849, Swett considered Davis his mentor on the Eighth Circuit.[64] At Davis's suggestion and expense, Swett made two trips to the northern part of the state in December 1854 visiting political operatives, including a newspaper editor, Postmaster James F. McDougall of Joliet, Whig state representative John Strunk of Kankakee, and anti-Nebraska Democrat Gavion D. A. Parks, a representative from Will County. Swett spoke with numerous Whigs in Joliet and recruited Judge T. Lyle Dickey to solicit votes in Kendall and LaSalle Counties.[65] The day after Christmas, Davis wrote to Lincoln that managing the trip with "discreet discretion," Swett had "done good" in the northern counties.[66]

Besides soliciting the votes of legislators, Davis served as a conduit of informa-tion to Lincoln. The judge relayed information gleaned from both Republican and Democratic sources, including friends, lawyers, newspaper editors, and newspaper articles that cast light on how support was coalescing around the senatorial candidates. Davis also forwarded responses to his letters soliciting support for Lincoln. The judge either summarized the response, quoted from it, or reproduced the entire reply.[67] From his intelligence-gathering efforts and knowledge of the political landscape, Davis suggested approaches designed to win the votes of undecided and doubtful legislators.[68]

Raising Lincoln's Spirits

Often overlooked is the role Davis played in helping the future president maintain a positive outlook in the face of repeated political setbacks. The 1855 senatorial campaign was no exception. The candidate's spirits needed a boost as a result of a double whammy that clobbered Lincoln at the very outset of the campaign.

In the middle of November Lincoln realized that the 1848 Illinois Constitution prohibited a member of the state legislature from accepting an appointment to the United States Senate. This was a problem, because Lincoln had been elected to the statehouse on November 7. Apparently, Whig lawyer Elihu N. Powell of Peoria brought the problem to Lincoln's attention. In replying to a letter seeking his support, Powell warned of the conflict and suggested a way in which the senatorial candidate could save his "bacon":

> Allow me to call your attention to the 7th Section of the 3rd Article of our new Constitution which makes you ineligible for the Senate of the U.S. Now if you decline accepting the seat in the legislature and so notify the Governor and have a new election this will save your bacon. I merely suggest this as worthy of your immediate consideration. It has been talked of here amongst some of us as your being the choice for Senator and the fact of your ineligibility has been mentioned which will have a tendency to injure your prospects unless it is removed immediately.[69]

To avoid further embarrassment, Lincoln followed Powell's advice and resigned from the legislature less than a month after his election. The resignation generated the need for a special election to fill the vacated Sangamon County state representative seat. That special election resulted in a second political humiliation.[70]

For unexplained reasons, the Sangamon County Whigs nominated Norman M. Broadwell for the seat vacated by Lincoln. Broadwell was a strange choice, since he was not a Lincoln supporter, was a Know-Nothing, and had filed against Lincoln's law partner, William Herndon, for the position of prosecuting attorney of the Eighth Judicial Circuit in 1852. Apparently, Lincoln and his advisors (except for the unexpressed reservations of Davis) were satisfied with the selection. Pretending to concede the election to Broadwell, the Democrats did not publicly nominate a candidate for the vacancy. But a few days before the election, "tickets" (sample ballots) were distributed to the Democratic "faithful" with instructions to vote for Jonathan McDaniel for state representative. On special election day, December 23, 1854, there was a huge Democrat turnout for McDaniel, who won Lincoln's vacated seat in a close race.[71]

Lincoln complained that the stealth candidacy of McDaniel combined with a rainy election day beat Whig Broadwell: "Our special election here is plain enough when understood. Our adversaries pretended to be naming running no candidate, secretly notified all their men to [be] on hand; and, favored by a very rainy day got a complete snap judgement on us."[72] In a letter to Lincoln after the election, Davis maintained that he had reservations about Broadwell's selection as the Whig candidate from the start, since he suspected that Broadwell preferred Richard Yates over Lincoln to replace Shields in the US Senate. The judge related that he did not register any objection to Broadwell because Lincoln and others seemed satisfied with him. In the letter Davis further claimed to have received information about the Democrats' secret plan to elect McDaniel, but it was too late to notify Lincoln or to institute any countermeasures.[73]

Knowing that the Democrats would "crow" over the election of a "Nebraska" man in Springfield, Davis undertook to console Lincoln on the humiliation inflicted on the Whig Party and on Lincoln personally. The judge tried to ease his friend's mind by minimizing the effect of McDaniel's vote on the outcome of the senatorial contest. Davis rationalized that it was better that a Democrat was elected to the Sangamon County seat, because Whig Broadwell would have voted for Richard Yates for senator. Davis continued by explaining that a Whig defection would have been even worse than Democrat McDaniel's election.[74] While the desire to ease Lincoln's anxiety and possible guilt over the lost legislative seat is commendable, the judge's dismissive explanation is almost certainly wrong. Even if Broadwell favored Yates over Lincoln, there was a much better chance that Lincoln's friends, including Davis, Swett, and Logan, together with other Whig and Republican backers, could have convinced Broadwell to come around to support Lincoln. One can almost picture Davis in a room, surrounded by Lincoln supporters, "discussing" Broadwell's vote. With Broadwell there was a chance to secure a vote for Lincoln; with McDaniel there was none.

The next day, still concerned about Lincoln's reaction to the loss of the crucial legislative seat, Davis wrote another letter imploring the defeated candidate to maintain a positive mindset, keep up his spirits, focus on the mission, and not "let Broadwell's defeat ex discourage you." But even in comforting Lincoln, the judge could not put aside one of his essential traits: absolute frankness. In reassuring Lincoln and predicting his ultimate victory over Shields, Davis wrote, "But keep up spirits & courage—& you will go through, *I think*." Even though it was equivocal, the letter helped convince Lincoln that the lost state representative seat was "not of the least consequence."[75]

The Legislative Floor Fight

Davis joined Lincoln and Stephen T. Logan in Springfield on January 2, 1855, to help "get things arranged for Lincoln" by soliciting vote commitments and developing a floor fight strategy.[76] Of course, Leonard Swett accompanied his professional and political mentor to the state capital. Danville lawyer and Lincoln loyalist Ward Hill Lamon was present to help. Davis would later describe Lamon as "one of the dearest friends I have in the world."[77] Judge T. Lyle Dickey came to Springfield to assist in securing votes for Lincoln. Dickey was first elected to the bench in 1848 and served in a judicial circuit adjoining the Eighth Judicial Circuit. The two judges substituted for each other in court and were good friends and loyal Whigs until Dickey joined the Democrats in 1857. At least until his conversion, Dickey respected Davis's opinion and followed his advice. Davis knew Logan well not only as Lincoln's former partner but also from having served with him in the state general assembly. They also served together as delegates to the 1847 state constitutional convention.[78] The judge secured other Lincoln operatives to help gather votes in Springfield, including close friend and former state representative John H. Murphy.[79]

Stephen Logan was the natural choice to direct Lincoln's floor fight. In addition to possessing one of the sharpest legal minds in the state, Logan was Lincoln's longtime political supporter, served three terms in the general assembly in the 1840s, and was reelected to the Illinois House of Representatives in 1854.[80] Logan did have shortcomings, however. Most importantly, he had poor political instincts and was a bungling campaigner. William Herndon described Logan's attempt to succeed Lincoln in Congress in 1848 as "a failure—and a fizzle."[81] Judge Davis agreed with Herndon's assessment attributing Logan's loss in a congressional election to his "own folly" by committing the political cardinal sin of telling "his friends . . . that his Election was sure—That they need not go to the polls."[82] Lincoln gave an even less flattering appraisal of his former partner's campaign acumen. After Logan lost an election for a state supreme court seat in 1855, Lincoln observed, "Logan is worse beaten than any other man ever was since elections were invented."[83] Davis noted Logan's main limitation in acting as Lincoln's floor manager: he "was not the kind of a man to go to men and order—Command or Coax Men to do what he wanted them to do. . . . [It] was not in his nature." He simply was not the man to convince reluctant or conflicted legislators to vote for Lincoln.[84]

The Floor Fight Begins

At the joint state legislative session held on January 2, 1855, Logan made a motion that the clerk of the Illinois House of Representatives call each legislative district so that members could present their credentials. Front and center on the house floor was Judge Davis performing the ministerial task of "qualifying" the legislators, who then officially took their seats. Certification of the members was immediately followed by Logan's motions to elect a Speaker of the House and to appoint nonlegislators to other state house offices.[85] Logan cut a deal whereby offices in the Illinois House of Representatives would be filled by persons selected by the Republicans. In return, the Republicans would vote for Whig Lincoln for senator. A week earlier, Davis had suggested this strategy to Lincoln: "Had you not better urge your friends to elect Say [Thomas J.] Turner Speaker—It would be well enough—I think to let the Republicans as they call themselves, have all the offices of the house, if they would agree to let the Whigs have the Senator."[86] Davis's suggestion that Whig legislators vote for Thomas J. Turner of Freeport for Speaker of the state House of Representatives was important because Turner had refused to support Lincoln until, as Turner put it, he determined how he could use his vote most effectively to defeat "those who are seeking to extend the era of slavery." Turner was very influential in the northernmost part of central Illinois, having served as congressman, state's attorney, editor of the first weekly newspaper in Stephenson County, and featured speaker at the Rockford Republican Convention held earlier that year.[87] Pursuant to the deal, the state house elected Turner Speaker, and he voted for Lincoln on the first two ballots. After that, Turner abstained until the final ballot, when he voted for anti-Nebraska Democrat Lyman Trumbull.[88]

Also consistent with the deal suggested by Davis, anti-Nebraskans filled the Illinois House of Representatives offices held by nonlegislators.[89] Edwin T. Bridges of LaSalle County, an active Republican associated with the *Chicago Evening Journal*, was elected state house clerk.[90] Twenty-year-old John Wickliffe Kitchell, a strong anti-Nebraska man from Montgomery County, was elected assistant clerk.[91] H. S. Thomas of Fulton County received the doorkeeper's post. Gershom Martin of Naperville, the former editor and publisher of the *DuPage County Observer*, became assistant doorkeeper.[92] The enrolling and engrossing position went to Alexander Sympson, a lifelong friend of Lincoln and a Republican leader in Hancock County.[93] Finally, the state house elected Benjamin J. F. Hanna, a newspaperman, farmer, and abolitionist from "Little Egypt," as Sympson's assistant.[94]

The deal with the state house Republicans, Lincoln's personal meetings with legislators, the efforts of his supporters, and the lobbying of card-carrying abolitionists such as Congressman Elihu Washburne, Congressman Jesse Norton, and law partner William Herndon combined to catapult Lincoln to the lead as the selection day approached. On January 6, 1855, Lincoln legitimately claimed that he led the pack of senatorial candidates, enjoying twenty-six pledged votes, with the next highest candidate enjoying no more than ten commitments. According to Davis, in January "it was supposed that [Lincoln's] election was certain."[95] On the first senatorial ballot, delayed by a snowstorm until February 8, Lincoln led with forty-five votes. But that was the highest total he would muster on any of the ten ballots needed to select a US senator.

The Legislators Vote

Lincoln and seven other candidates had been nominated for the Senate seat. The Illinois House of Representatives and Senate combined consisted of ninety-nine members, so that fifty votes were needed to select a senator. On the first ballot, Lincoln led with forty-five votes. Incumbent Democrat senator James Shields had forty-one votes, anti-Nebraska Democrat Lyman Trumbull tallied five votes, and Gustave Koerner, the anti-Nebraska lieutenant governor, received two votes. Six other candidates, including Governor Joel A. Matteson, received one vote each. Trumbull's votes came from his die-hard supporters, whose votes would have put Lincoln over the top. Davis blamed the five, especially their leader, Norman Judd, for Lincoln's eventual loss.[96] On the second ballot, Lincoln's lead over Shields slipped to two votes, forty-three to forty-one. Trumbull had six votes, three candidates had two votes each, and three candidates, including Governor Matteson, garnered one vote each.[97] The third ballot showed Lincoln and Shields tied with forty-one votes. Trumbull remained at six votes, two candidates had three votes each, and two candidates had two votes each. Matteson recorded no votes on the third ballot.[98]

At this point, Logan's motion to adjourn the joint session was defeated. Logan either wanted time to regroup or, more likely, saw the handwriting on the wall.[99] Lincoln's decline continued on the fourth ballot: he was now trailing Shields forty-one to thirty-eight votes, with Trumbull increasing to eleven votes. Lieutenant Governor Koerner and Governor Matteson each had two votes, and four candidates recorded a single vote each.[100] The vote total on the fifth ballot was Shields forty-two, Lincoln thirty-four, Trumbull ten, former Chicago mayor William Ogden five, Koerner and Orville Browning two each, and three candidates, including Governor Matteson, with one vote each.[101] Lincoln improved slightly on the sixth ballot, trailing Shields forty-one to thirty-six votes, with other candidates remaining about the same. On the sixth ballot Matteson had no votes.[102] On the next ballot, the Democrats' plan went into effect. Matteson went from no votes on the sixth ballot to top man on the seventh ballot with forty-four votes. Lincoln followed with thirty-eight votes, and Lyman Trumbull received support from nine legislators. The implementation of the Matteson plan left Senator Shields with one vote.[103] The eighth ballot found Matteson with forty-six, Lincoln twenty-seven, and Trumbull eighteen votes.[104] If it was not already clear, the ninth ballot definitively showed that Lincoln's chance to succeed Shields was gone. With only fifteen votes Lincoln now trailed both Matteson with forty-seven and Trumbull with thirty-five votes. At this point Lincoln feared that Matteson would "buy" the votes necessary to reach fifty and so directed his faithful supporters to vote for Trumbull. Lincoln put Trumbull over the top on the tenth and final ballot with fifty-one votes to Matteson's forty-seven votes.[105]

Debriefing the Defeat

Lincoln should not have been caught off guard by the Matteson stealth candidacy any more than he should have been surprised by Democrat Jonathan McDaniel's candidacy for state representative from Sangamon County. By the end of 1854, Lincoln had been forewarned of a possible Matteson plot to replace Shields as US senator. On December 22, 1854, Swett wrote Lincoln that during his campaign trip to the northern counties, State Representative Gavion D. A. Parks from Joliet reported that he had been "solicited in favor of Matteson." The editor of the *True Democrat*, a Will County newspaper, told Swett that Matteson was "secretly" working for himself and hoped to be a compromise candidate. It goes without saying that if Swett had information about a possible covert candidacy, so did Davis. But the judge did not mention a Matteson candidacy in his letters to Lincoln of December 26 and December 27.[106]

Swett's warning notwithstanding, Lincoln said that he first became aware of Matteson's secret candidacy about ten days before the election, "but with every possible effort, could not head it off." The defeated senatorial candidate squarely blamed Matteson's subterfuge for his defeat. Lincoln believed that he "could have headed off every combination and been elected, had it not been for Matteson's double game."[107]

For some unexplained reason, Davis was "necessarily" absent from Springfield on the day of the legislature's vote.[108] The day after the selection of Trumbull as senator, the judge returned to the capital to commiserate with Lincoln. Totally in character, Davis told Lincoln that if he were present for the election, "he never would have consented to the 47 men being controlled by the 5."[109] Writing to Julius Rockwell two months after the election, Davis explained the unfairness of the five legislators obstinately committed to Trumbull dictating the senatorial result:

> Mr Lincoln ought to have been elected—There were 51 anti Nebraska members of the Legislature—30 Whigs (being every Whig in the Legislature but one) 16 elected as republicans—and 5 men elected as anti Nebraska Democrats—Now—the republicans & Whigs were all for Lincoln—and but 5 men, wanted Trumbull—The 5 would not yield, and the Whigs & Republicans rather than let the election pass over and a Nebraska man be elected voted for Trumbull—The members would not do until Lincoln urged them to do so. . . . I reckon that Trumbulls election is better than that the matter should have passed over—But if I had been there—there were ten members of the Legislature, who would have fully appreciated—the fact—that 46 men should not yield their preferences to 5—But let it pass.[110]

One reason that the judge decided to "let it pass" was that although he distrusted Trumbull's Democrat "antecedents," he believed that Trumbull could be counted on to oppose the Kansas-Nebraska Act.[111] And Davis's protestations aside, the result of the 1855 senatorial contest would have been no different had he been in Springfield for the vote. The Democrats simply outsmarted the Republicans. Lincoln saw the inevitability of defeat and used his loyal legislator friends to ensure that double-dealing Matteson would not become Senator Shields's successor. And nothing Davis said would have changed Lincoln's mind.

Lessons Learned

Davis learned much from Lincoln's first Senate campaign. Those lessons would inform his later efforts to secure the presidency for his circuit-riding friend.

The result of the 1855 senatorial selection reinforced both Davis's and Lincoln's understanding that frontrunner status or tallying the most votes on the first ballot does not ensure victory. Lincoln acknowledged this fact of electoral politics when, prior to the vote, he told Congressman Washburne that although he had more senatorial preelection commitments than any other candidate, he did "not know that it is much advantage to have the largest number of votes at the start."[112] Lincoln and Davis learned from Governor Matteson's stealth campaign that sometimes it is advantageous to be the second or compromise choice of the delegates. Matteson also taught the judge how to execute a second-choice strategy. Exhibit A in the tutorial was Matteson's approach to Lincoln supporter John Strunk, a Kankakee Whig who early on pledged his support to Lincoln. Matteson convinced Strunk that Lincoln had no chance of winning and received Strunk's promise to support Matteson as Strunk's "second choice" after casting a vote or two for Lincoln. Matteson lined up anti-Nebraska Democrats in the same manner. This second-choice strategy would have given Matteson enough votes to become senator had not Lincoln directed his steadfast supporters to vote for Trumbull.[113] In 1860 Davis would perfectly execute the second-choice strategy on behalf of Lincoln at the Republican National Convention in Chicago.

The Senate loss also forced Davis to face the fact that the Democrats outmaneuvered Lincoln on two fronts. First, by feigning a lack of interest in the special election to fill the state representative seat vacated by Lincoln, the Democrats defeated Whig candidate Norman Broadwell by eighty-two votes.[114] It must have grated on Davis that the Whigs had been caught napping. To personalize the humiliation caused by losing the legislative seat, the judge surely regretted failing to voice his objection to Broadwell before he was slated by the Sangamon County Whigs. Moreover, at some point before the special election, Davis had word from William Herndon's brother, Elliott Herndon, that "the democrats would make great effort to beat Broadwell." Apparently, Davis did nothing to investigate the rumor and only gained specifics of the plan on the day of the special election.[115] On the second front, Matteson outmaneuvered the Lincoln forces.

Although Lincoln said that he learned of Matteson's plan only ten days before the senatorial vote, Swett had written Lincoln on December 22 that Matteson had solicited the support of Gavion D. A. Parks, an anti-Nebraska legislator from Will County.[116] In his dual roles as candidate and statewide campaign manager, Lincoln was bound to miss things. His lieutenants relied on him to control and direct campaign activities. No one else had the independent decision-making power or the authority to investigate or counter the opposition's moves. Davis knew that that situation must change if Lincoln was to ever obtain higher office. And it did change five years later at the Republican National Convention when Davis took matters into his own hands and exercised complete and uncontested authority in directing the fight for delegates. That included giving Lincoln orders. Lincoln remained in Springfield during the Chicago convention at least in part because of a telegram sent by Davis two days before the start of the convention instructing Lincoln, "Dont come unless we send for you."[117]

In some ways, the most stinging part of the defeat to Davis was that Norman Judd, Trumbull's floor leader, bested the Lincoln men. The judge would not forget Judd's role in Lincoln's defeat. And he was not the only one. Samuel C. Parks, speaking for himself and other Lincoln stalwart legislators, considered that "the conduct of Judd and Co. in compelling us to vote for Mr. Trumbull was ungenerous and selfish."[118]

The senatorial contest also brought home with stark clarity that sometimes deals must be cut to achieve desired political ends. Neither Lincoln nor Davis would ever cut the kind of vote-buying deals in which Matteson was apparently willing to engage. But some political deals were necessary and acceptable. Davis pointed out Logan's weakness in this particular political maneuvering skill and doubtlessly considered himself a master of cajoling, convincing, and persuading others to take a particular course of action. The judge's negotiating abilities were due to his strong personality coupled with the everyday necessity of maintaining order and discipline in court and ensuring the fair and timely disposition of legal matters. Simply put, Davis was an expert at getting things done. In the 1855 Senate race, the best deal that Lincoln could cut was transferring his hard-core votes to Trumbull not only as a matter of principle but also in hope of Trumbull's support against Douglas in 1858.[119] At the 1860 Republican nominating convention, Davis would remember the lessons of the 1855 race and do what was required, including exchanging promises when necessary to secure votes and outmaneuver the opposition.[120]

2 Lincoln's Second Senate Defeat

The Eighth Judicial Circuit changed in significant ways in the early 1850s. When Lincoln returned from Congress to practice law in 1849, the Eighth Circuit encompassed fourteen counties. In 1853, at the behest of Davis and Lincoln and because of the increased population and caseloads, the legislature eliminated six counties from the circuit: Piatt, Edgar, Shelby, Moultrie, Macon, and Christian. Davis now sat only in Sangamon, Tazewell, Woodford, McLean, Logan, DeWitt, Champaign, and Vermilion Counties. Since all circuit courts met at the same time, Lincoln's practice in state courts was largely limited to the counties remaining in the Eighth Judicial Circuit, although he continued to handle some cases in other counties and in federal court.[1]

At about the same time, railroad service arrived in the major cities traveled by Davis and the circuit lawyers. On September 9, 1852, the first train reached Springfield. Bloomington received service from the Illinois Central Railroad in the spring of 1853 and from the Alton and Sangamon Railroad (later renamed the Chicago and Alton Railroad) in October.[2] As Davis told his wife and son, the railroads reduced the need to travel to court in buggies and greatly improved Illinois by increasing the population, economic prosperity, and land values.[3] The railroads also facilitated travel for stump speakers and attendees at political rallies and conventions. Along with passengers, the railroads brought new litigation to the courts. Lincoln tried 133 cases for and against fourteen railroad companies during his circuit days.[4] His most lucrative client was the Illinois Central Railroad. In fact, Lincoln earned the largest fee of his career, $5,000, representing the Illinois Central in a case challenging McLean County's right to tax the railroad's property. By agreement of the parties, Judge Davis dismissed the case so that the issue of a county's right to tax a railroad would go directly to the Illinois Supreme Court. The state supreme court upheld Lincoln's argument that a state statute exempted railroad property from county taxation.[5] The railroad was pleased with the win but not so pleased with the amount of Lincoln's bill, and so Lincoln had to sue to recover his fee. The railroad did not seriously contest the suit, and a jury empaneled before Judge Jesse O. Norton returned a verdict for the full amount requested by Lincoln.[6] In an earlier fee dispute with the Illinois Central, Davis took the extremely unusual step of vouching for the reasonableness of Lincoln's bill. Lincoln's invoice contained the judge's endorsement that Lincoln rendered the services claimed and that his fee was "very reasonable."[7]

After his first Senate defeat in February 1855, Lincoln concentrated on practicing law rather than on politics. Nonetheless, according to Davis, Lincoln found time in the fall to make "a few very able speeches" against the Kansas-Nebraska Act.[8] Lincoln reengaged in politics during the presidential election year of 1856. In May Lincoln, Henry Whitney, Archibald Williams, and T. Lyle Dickey stayed at Davis's home while they attended the first Republican State Convention in Bloomington. Davis was holding court in Danville at the time and did not participate in the gathering.[9] Lincoln left the state convention as the leader of the new Republican Party. Both he and Davis hoped that Supreme Court justice John McLean of Ohio would be selected as the party's presidential candidate at the first Republican National Convention, scheduled for June in Philadelphia. Instead, the convention chose military man and former governor of California John C. Frémont. But Lincoln recognized his duty and beginning in July delivered more than fifty speeches throughout Illinois in support of Frémont and the Republican ticket.[10] Frémont lost, in no small part due to the third-party candidate, Millard Fillmore. Fillmore ran on the anti-immigrant Know-Nothing ticket and drew votes away from the Republicans. Lincoln and Davis knew that future Republican success depended on attracting Know-Nothing supporters, including old-line conservative Whigs.[11]

Lincoln's sacrifice of his law practice in favor of politics during the presidential canvass of 1856 distressed his financial condition, necessitating a refocus on earning a living in 1857 and the beginning of 1858.[12] And that is what Lincoln did up until it was time to start the canvass in the 1858 fall election.

A New Approach to Gain a Senate Seat

In his first bid for a US Senate seat, Lincoln waited until after the November election to declare his candidacy and begin campaigning for the state legislators' votes. Reviewing the preliminary results of the 1854 election, Lincoln believed that a sufficient number of Whigs, abolitionists, and anti-Nebraska Democrats had been elected to secure the state senate and house votes needed to defeat Democrat senator James Shields. In his second US Senate campaign,

Lincoln adopted a different and unheard-of strategy. Instead of waiting to see who was elected to the legislature, as he did in 1854, he worked to elect enough Republican legislators in the November 1858 election to assure his selection as senator by the legislature in early 1859. As a necessary part of the plan Lincoln needed to position himself as the favorite of the Republicans to oust Senator Stephen Douglas. So, months before the November 1858 election, Lincoln declared for the US Senate seat, secured county Republican convention support, obtained an endorsement from the statewide Republican convention, helped slate Republican candidates for the legislature, and campaigned against Douglas throughout the state.[13]

On February 18, 1858, Lincoln met with Chicago state senator Norman Judd, who also served as the chairman of the Illinois Republican central committee. Both agreed to the obvious: control of the state legislature would be won or lost in the counties of central Illinois. The northern counties would vote Republican, and the southern counties would go just as solidly for the Democratic candidates. Because it was the old Whig counties of central Illinois that held the balance, Judd told Lincoln that if he wanted to be a senator, he must personally canvass the center of the state.[14] Judd himself did not offer to help in the central counties, admitting that others would be much more helpful in the middle and southern parts of the state. In addition, as a former Democrat who led Lyman Trumbull's successful effort over Lincoln in the 1855 senatorial campaign, Judd had many detractors in the old Whig counties.[15]

On the evening of April 21, when the Democratic State Convention in Springfield ended in a walkout by President James Buchanan's supporters, Lincoln met with a group of Republican leaders in the Illinois State Library. They gathered not only to celebrate the disarray of the Democrats but also to formulate a campaign strategy to enhance the chances of a Republican victory in the fall election. It was agreed that a state Republican convention would be held on June 16, 1858, to nominate candidates for state offices and, in an unusual move for the time, to endorse Lincoln for the US Senate. To lay the groundwork for a statewide endorsement, the group of Republican leaders encouraged each county Republican convention to pass a resolution backing Lincoln.[16]

County and State Republican Endorsements

Interestingly, Lincoln did not necessarily encourage counties to endorse him for the Senate and on occasion discouraged endorsements. On May 29 State Representative Stephen A. Hurlbut wrote Lincoln that a full Boone County delegation planned to attend the Republican State Convention on June 16 and that "if it is desirable that any expression should be formally given of the feeling of the party upon the Senatorial Question we at this end of the state are fully prepared so to do."[17] Whether because of an overdeveloped sense of humility, or because he did not think county endorsements mattered, or because he thought he might not win the endorsement of some counties, Lincoln declined the offer: "I suppose it is hardly necessary that any expression of preference for U.S. Senator, should be given at the county, or other local conventions and meetings. When the Republicans of the whole State get together at the State convention, the thing will then be thought of, and something will or will not be done, according as the united judgment may dictate."[18]

Notwithstanding Lincoln's hesitancy to personally seek resolutions supporting his candidacy, by the time the Republican State Convention convened, ninety-four counties had endorsed Lincoln as their choice for US Senate.[19] The county resolutions took several forms. Grundy County resolved that "in Hon. Abram [*sic*] Lincoln, we recognize the true patriot and statesman, and an able indicator of Republican principles, and that we most earnestly desire to see him occupy the place in the U.S. Senate now filled by S. A. Douglas." Washington County simply announced that Lincoln was its "first choice" for senator.[20] But no county could top Davis's home county. The McLean County Republicans' resolution proclaimed that "the Hon. A. Lincoln is our first, last and only choice for the vacancy soon to occur in the United States Senate; and that, despite all influence at home or abroad, domestic or foreign, the Republicans of Illinois, as with the voice of one man, are unalterably so resolved, to the end that we may have a big man with a big mind and a big heart to represent our big State."[21]

Meeting in Springfield on June 16, the Republican State Convention unanimously adopted a resolution offered by Charles L. Wilson of Cook County proclaiming that "Abraham Lincoln is the first and only choice of the Republicans of Illinois for the United States Senate, as the successor of Stephen A. Douglas." After reconvening the convention that evening, Lincoln delivered his famous "House Divided" speech.[22]

Responding to Douglas

On July 9, 1858, Douglas commenced his reelection campaign in earnest with a blistering attack against Lincoln delivered from the north veranda of the Tremont House in downtown Chicago. The next day Lincoln replied to the Little Giant from the same location but to a smaller crowd that included members of the German Republican Club of Chicago's Seventh Ward. In Henry Whitney's opinion, Lincoln's reply to Douglas in Chicago "was the poorest effort I ever heard Lincoln make."[23] After that, Lincoln followed Douglas on the train for stops in Joliet, Bloomington, and the main event in Springfield.[24] The Republican state central committee did not like the fact that its candidate's main campaign strategy was to trail Douglas around the state. The committee members agreed that the strategy left Lincoln open to criticism for taking advantage of the large crowds drawn by Douglas and made Lincoln appear subordinate and inferior to a truly great statesman. Making matters worse, Lincoln was perpetually on the defensive. Something had to change if the Republican senatorial candidate was to be considered Douglas's equal.

On July 22, 1858, Lincoln met with the central committee in Chicago to address these campaign shortcomings. It did not take much to convince Lincoln that he needed to go on the offensive, since Lincoln had been receiving this same advice from others, including Davis.[25] Moreover, the Springfield lawyer felt somewhat self-conscious following at Douglas's coattails. So at the committee's direction Lincoln wrote to Douglas asking if it was agreeable for the two candidates "to divide time, and address the same audiences during the present canvass."[26] Judd delivered the note, and Douglas accepted, suggesting seven venues: Ottawa, Freeport, Jonesboro, Charleston, Galesburg, Quincy, and Alton.[27] Chicago and Springfield were not included because the candidates had spoken in the two cities earlier in the month. Lincoln agreed to the suggested locations, and the debates took place from the end of August to the middle of October.[28] The statewide and national importance of the Lincoln-Douglas debates was not lost on Davis. He evaluated each debate, considering the comments of friends in attendance and the debate transcripts published in newspapers. He urged his son to save the issues of the *Chicago Daily Press and Tribune* that reported the debates. He sent copies of the debates to his brother-in-law in Massachusetts, advising that "the state of excitement in this state is greater than I have ever known."[29]

Davis's Campaign Role

As he did in the first US Senate campaign, Davis played multiple roles in Lincoln's second attempt for a seat in the upper chamber. As an advisor, the judge counseled the candidate on the necessity of slating "unexceptional" legislative candidates in certain districts; the essential role of Know-Nothings and methods to secure their votes; who should and should not speak on Lincoln's behalf; where Lincoln should speak; and how to counter T. Lyle Dickey's defection to the Douglas camp. Davis also suggested that starting in August Lincoln suspend his law practice and devote himself full time to the campaign because "the attempt to practice would only embarrass & worry [Lincoln]."[30] Davis likely considered that his most important advice to Lincoln was to "emphatically disavow *negro suffrage*,—negro holding office, serving on juries, & the like." Halting the expansion of slavery was one thing; equal social and political rights were quite another. In the judge's opinion, any implication that Lincoln supported the latter would crush his chances in central Illinois and ensure defeat. Lincoln took this advice from Davis and others and told the audience at the Charleston debate that "I am not, nor ever have been in favor of bringing about in any way the social and political equality of the white and black races."[31]

The judge agreed with State Chairman Norman Judd that Douglas consistently put Lincoln on the defensive and that Lincoln needed to turn the tables. In an August 25, 1858, letter, Davis was characteristically blunt: "Pour hot shot into Douglas all the time—Attack him—through his whole record.—In this way alone, can the people see through him."[32] The following night, Norman Judd and Republican leader Ebenezer Peck gave Lincoln the same advice: he must go on the offensive. Judd and Peck advocated for the "ugly questions" developed by Charles Wilson of the *Chicago Evening Journal* and Joseph Medill and Charles Ray of the *Chicago Tribune* to put Douglas on the defensive for a change. The questions were designed to pin Douglas down on his doctrine of popular sovereignty and thereby increase the already existing hostility between the supporters of Douglas and the supporters of President Buchanan. Lincoln adopted the strategy and less than twenty-four hours later peppered Douglas with the questions at the Freeport debate.[33] On August 9 Davis wrote Lincoln to continue to speak in every place visited by Douglas to refute the stream of misrepresentations coming from the Little Giant.[34]

According to Davis, he spent June putting out fires to maintain the loosely knit coalition of Republican factions, including abolitionists, old Whigs, former Democrats, and anti-immigrant Know-Nothings, to ensure Republican legislative victories in the fall and Lincoln's election to the Senate in January. Davis reported that he was working "to keep things quiet—and to prevent any hostile demonstration" and to suppress "a great deal of smothered wrath which it needed but little to explode."[35] Unfortunately, the judge was not immune from adding fuel to the smoldering embers of intraparty discontent. In 1856 Davis did not support Illinois abolitionist leader Owen Lovejoy for the Republican nomination for Congress from the Third Congressional District. The judge had no sympathy for the abolition movement and considered its leaders, like Lovejoy, "insincere demagogues striving for public office at the expense of the public weal."[36] Even worse in Davis's mind, Lovejoy's abolitionist credentials helped the Democrats define the Republicans as abolitionists, or abolitionists in disguise, thus chasing conservative and moderate old Whigs to the Democrats. And those lost votes meant disaster for the Republican Party. To keep the peace and at Lincoln's request, Davis talked his friend T. Lyle Dickey out of running against Lovejoy in 1856, thereby clearing the way for Lovejoy's election. But the judge never stopped speaking his mind on the disservice Lovejoy did to the party and the country.[37] Then in 1858, when county Republican organizations began endorsement sessions, Davis briefly flirted with challenging Lovejoy for the Republican congressional nomination. That effort was short-lived, since support could not be mustered for the judge or any other challenger.[38] This renewed conflict with Lovejoy resulted in the *Chicago Daily Tribune* printing a letter to the editor in early June 1858 that criticized Davis for not supporting Lovejoy's reelection and having "no more sympathy with the vitalizing principle of the Republican party than an Egyptian mummy." In answering the *Tribune*, Lincoln acknowledged that Davis did not vote for Lovejoy in 1856. But Lincoln defended the judge's right to prefer one candidate over another, adding that Davis expected Lovejoy's renomination, intended to vote for him in 1858, and disapproved of any "scheme" to deny Lovejoy another term in Congress. The letter also defended Davis's commitment to Republican principles even if they differed from the "radical and progressive views" advanced in *Tribune* editorials.[39] Davis was "much obliged" to Lincoln for his intervention with the important Chicago newspaper, telling Lincoln that "the letter was a manifestation of your friendship, which gratified me."[40]

Davis shied away from addressing rallies even for Lincoln but made an exception in his hometown. In the afternoon of September 4, 1858, a long procession from the McLean County Courthouse arrived at the judge's home, where Lincoln had stayed the night before. Two carriages traveled back to the courthouse, one carrying Lincoln, Davis, and Davis's son George. On the speakers' platform Lincoln was flanked on his right by Leonard Swett and on his left by Davis. The judge called the assembly to order and introduced Swett, who introduced the guest of honor in an "eloquent" and "beautiful" speech. Lincoln spoke for two hours, denouncing slavery but denying that he believed in Negro equality. The Republican demonstration continued into the night with more speeches and partisan celebrating.[41]

Davis made sure that the rally in Bloomington did not suffer the same lack of energy and enthusiasm that he witnessed at other Lincoln events.[42] The McLean County Courthouse was covered with streamers and banners proclaiming that McLean County was "for Abraham Lincoln—first, last and forever" and "Freedom is National—Slavery is Sectional." Over the courthouse door a ship was portrayed in a storm with the motto, "Don't give up the ship—give her a new pilot." The podium was covered with white cloth and festively decorated with leaves and flowers, and "flags streamed across the streets and waved from staffs." Of course, a proper Republican rally would be incomplete without caricatures of the enemy. Davis's firm conviction that Douglas was "the most arrogant demagogue that ever disgraced humanity" may have fueled the display of one portrayal of Douglas trampling on the Missouri Compromise and the Declaration of Independence. Another depicted Chief Justice Roger B. Taney, author of the infamous *Dred Scott* decision, urging Douglas on. A procession was composed of carriages, footmen, and bands and was led by "an imposing array of German Republicans, with an appropriate banner." To avoid a repeat of an earlier poorly attended event in Tazewell County, Davis, Fell, and the other organizers secured an attendance of at least six thousand people from Bloomington and the adjacent countryside.[43]

While not a member of the Republican state central committee, Davis attended meetings of the group and freely offered campaign advice. The judge canvassed individuals in person and by letter, provided intelligence to Lincoln, and sent Swett, Herndon, Ward Lamon, and others on campaign-related tasks.[44] As in the first Senate race, Davis helped elevate Lincoln's spirits this time by complimenting his debate performances. Even though Republican leaders were "dispirited" over Lincoln's performance in the first debate, Davis wrote to Lincoln that he had received a "glowing" report from Henry Whitney about the debate and that everyone in Bloomington was "delighted with the rencontre at Ottawa." A month later the judge told Lincoln that his "concluding speech on Douglas at Charleston was admirable."[45] After the election defeat, the compliments turned into reassurances that Lincoln had made a "noble canvass," had nothing to blame himself for, and had earned a national reputation and friends everywhere.[46]

Another Failed Senate Bid

During the campaign, Douglas and Lincoln traveled a combined total of nearly ten thousand miles traversing Illinois. Douglas delivered more speeches than Lincoln and spent at least $50,000 compared to Lincoln's expenditure, likely between $1,000 and $2,000.[47]

The popular vote propelled the statewide Republican candidates to victory. The Republican state treasurer candidate received about thirty-eight hundred more votes than the Democrat. A Republican was elected state superintendent of public instruction by slightly more than twenty-one hundred votes. The total vote for all Republican candidates for the state legislature exceeded the aggregate vote for all Democrats by more than thirty-five hundred votes.[48] But Republican losses in old Whig state representative districts, including Madison County, Sangamon County, and Tazewell County, and the state representative district composed of Mason and Logan Counties, together with the Democrats' gain of a state senate seat in the Twenty-First Senatorial District, comprised of Madison, Bond, and Montgomery Counties, gave the Democrats a fifty-four to forty-six legislative majority and sent Douglas back to Washington.[49]

Assigning the Blame for Lincoln's Loss

Davis blamed Lincoln's second US Senate loss on four factors: (1) the "colonization" of Irish voters, (2) the malapportionment of the state's legislative districts, (3) State Republican Chairman Norman Judd's "inept" management of the campaign, and (4) the meddling of out-of-state Republican politicians and newspapers.

Voter Colonization

In the 1850s it "was a common electoral strategy" for a political party to transport men from Illinois districts in which they were registered to vote into districts where the party needed extra votes to prevail.[50] The "colonized" voters would be relocated from electoral districts in which the party's success or loss was certain into hotly contested counties. William Herndon worried about voters being transported on the pretext of looking for work from the northern part of the state, where Democrat defeat was a foregone conclusion, to the doubtful counties of central Illinois. Also, according to Herndon, on occasion voters would be brought to Illinois from out of state.[51] Republicans were especially concerned about the movement of Irish voters into the swing counties of Illinois.[52] In October 1858 Lincoln claimed to have stumbled across some transplanted and reliably proslavery, pro-Democrat voters loitering about cheap saloons in Scott County in west-central Illinois. In a letter to Norman Judd, Lincoln explained:

> On alighting from the cars and walking three squares at Naples on Monday, I met about fifteen Celtic gentlemen, with black carpet-sacks in their hands.
>
> I learned that they had crossed over from the Rail-road in Brown county, but where they were going no one could tell. They dropped in about the doggeries, and were still hanging about when I left. At Brown County yesterday I was told that about four hundred of the same sort were to be brought into Schuyler, before the election, to work on some new Railroad; but on reaching here I find Bagby thinks that is not so.

Lincoln also described the difficulty in preventing fraudulent voting: "What I most dread is that they will introduce into the doubtful districts numbers of men who are legal voters in all respects except *residence* and who will swear to residence and thus put it beyond our power to exclude them. They can & I fear will swear falsely on that point, because they know it is next to impossible to convict them of Perjury upon it."[53] In the same letter, Lincoln suggested that the Democratic colonization efforts might be thwarted by introducing an undercover "detective" into the dishonest enterprise. But nothing indicates that the plan was taken seriously. After the election, Republican newspapers did not hesitate to attribute otherwise "inexplicable" legislative losses to voter colonization. The *Chicago Daily Press and Tribune* could not understand how the Republican state representative candidate lost in McDonough County "unless by wholesale importations."[54]

Davis had worried about illegal voting since at least the election of 1840.[55] In October 1858 he feared that eastern money would finance the relocation of voters in Illinois and steal the election from the Republican legislative candidates in the central counties. Davis wrote to his brother-in-law, Julius Rockwell, that Senator Douglas had borrowed $39,000 from Fernando Wood, the former mayor of New York, and $13,000 from a New York money lender to finance the colonization effort. The judge predicted that if colonization succeeded, the Democrats would win, and if that happened, he would rather "live under a Russian Despotism." After the election, the judge blamed the Republicans' loss in part on the predicted Democratic voter relocation effort but decided to stay in Bloomington rather than relocate to Czarist Russia.[56] In 1860 he would again sound the alarm about voter colonization.[57]

Malapportionment

The Republican newspapers were quick to blame Lincoln's defeat on the malapportionment of the legislative districts resulting from the great influx of people into the northern Republican counties since the census of 1850. The *Chicago Daily Press and Tribune* concluded that "an apportionment law giving a large advantage to that part of the State devoted to [Douglas] and his cause, has to this extent enabled him to come out of the contest victorious, although repudiated by a majority of the people whom he represents. A change of a few hundred votes in certain Representative and Senatorial Districts, would have given us a Legislature corresponding in sentiment with a majority of the people of the State."[58] The *Illinois State Journal* reprinted an article from the *Milwaukee Daily Free Democrat* drawing the same conclusion: "[Douglas] succeeds entirely by virtue of an apportionment which gives the southern portion of the State, a large preponderance over the northern, in the choice of the Legislature. He goes back to Washington, to misrepresent Illinois for the next six years."[59]

There certainly was a basis for the malapportionment grievance. The Republican candidates for state treasurer and superintendent of public instruction, the only two statewide offices on the ballot, received more votes than their Democratic opponents. The Republican legislative district comprised of LaSalle, Livingston, and Grundy Counties, with a combined population of 47,190 people, elected two state representatives. Morgan and Scott Counties, with a combined population of 25,672, sent two Democrats to the state house. Sangamon County, with a population of 25,604, sent two Democrats to the lower chamber, while Kane and DeKalb Counties elected the same number of Republicans with a population of 40,301.[60] Davis's McLean County cast forty-nine hundred votes and sent one Republican member to the state House of Representatives. Madison County cast six hundred fewer votes and elected two house members.[61] The *Illinois State Journal* claimed that 750 votes in Democratic portions of the state were the equivalent of 1,000 votes in Republican districts. The paper also argued that Republican state representative districts needed an average population of

19,635 to send a representative to Springfield, while in Democratic districts it only took a population of 15,675.[62]

Davis had long recognized the importance of apportionment in elections and knew that the legislative districts drawn in 1850 did not reflect the population realities of 1858. After the election of 1860, he rejoiced that the Republican majority in the Illinois legislature would control redistricting for state and federal offices.[63] But like colonization, malapportionment was a fact of life. Davis could plan for and deal with these roadblocks introduced by the enemy. But he could not forgive the chairman of the Illinois Republican Party for his inept management of the 1858 campaign. Nor could he accept the defections of the eastern Republicans and Kentucky senator John Crittenden from Lincoln's cause.

Mismanagement by Norman Judd

Davis did not wait for Lincoln's defeat in the senatorial contest to accuse Norman Judd of mismanaging the Republican canvass. On August 18, 1858, the judge wrote to Ozias M. Hatch, secretary of the Republican state central committee, complaining that "this campaign has not been managed right." Davis bemoaned the fact that the development of a campaign strategy, as haphazard as it was, was dictated by the ex-Democrats on the central committee. This criticism reflected the long-standing friction between the former Democratic and former Whig factions of the Republican Party. Each wing was jealous of the influence of the other in party affairs. Davis's letter to Hatch also suggested that the campaign should have been staffed by "men of intellect [who] were accustomed to a political campaign." The complaint was not meant to describe all members of the central committee. The criticism was a thinly veiled, if veiled at all, attack on Norman Judd, the committee chair. Davis had not trusted Judd ever since he coordinated Lyman Trumbull's Senate victory over Lincoln in 1855. Former Whigs believed that Judd became committee chair for the primary purpose of advancing his chance of becoming governor.[64] Believing that Judd was unwilling to sacrifice time from promoting his campaign for governor to develop a plan for Republican candidates throughout the state, Davis wrote to Lincoln on August 3, suggesting that a statewide campaign blueprint was needed immediately. Six days later, Davis reiterated his opinion that "the sooner the programme for the whole state is laid down the better."[65] As far as the judge was concerned, this was just one example of Judd's failure to perform his duties as leader of the statewide campaign effort.

Davis also believed that the campaign should have been headquartered in Springfield to concentrate efforts on the old Whigs in central Illinois. This seems like a sound strategy, since everyone, including Whigs, Republicans of all stripes,

Democrats, and Know-Nothings, agreed that the election would be won or lost not in the predetermined contests in the northern and southern parts of the state but in the midstate, doubtful counties.[66] Since Republican control of the Illinois General Assembly and thereby Lincoln's senatorial hopes rested in the center of the state, it would seem logical to coordinate the campaign from the same geographic region. In addition, Lincoln's most ardent supporters came from the fourteen counties of the original Eighth Judicial Circuit. Judd's focus, however, was on increasing the Republican vote statewide rather than in doubtful legislative districts. Judd was selfishly looking ahead to his planned gubernatorial campaign in 1860, which would be decided by the popular vote rather than by the party that controlled the legislature. Judd also knew that coordinating activities from Springfield would severely reduce his influence over the campaign not only because of the distance between Springfield and Chicago but also because of the concentration of Judd detractors in the middle counties.[67] All in all, Davis felt that Judd paid far too little attention to the section of the state that would dictate which party controlled the legislature and thus the outcome of the senatorial race.

Rumors also circulated that Judd mismanaged campaign funds. Davis was predisposed to believe these reports but most likely did not attribute fraud or misappropriation to Judd. Rather, the judge's suspicions centered on whether the funds were spent to benefit the party or only Judd, whether the central committee or Judd alone approved expenditures, accounting deficiencies, and the committee's debt following the election. To retire the committee's $2,500 debt, Judd requested a contribution from Lincoln and asked him to solicit other donations. Lincoln balked at the request but promised Judd that he would contribute $250, to be paid as soon as "you and I settle the private matter between us."[68] This was an allusion to the fact that Judd had borrowed $2,500 from Lincoln in 1857 and never paid it back. In fact, the debt was not repaid until September 1867, when Davis as administrator of Lincoln's estate recovered the principal and interest in the total sum of $5,400.[69] If Davis was the holder of the note instead of Lincoln, his response to Judd's request for funds to retire the campaign debt might have been something more direct, like "I will contribute $250 to help retire the campaign debt. Deduct it from what you owe me." Judd claimed that he donated $1,300 to the 1858 campaign fund, but it was never clear if that money was used to further party interests or Judd's individual interests, assuming there was a difference between the two in Judd's mind.[70]

Eastern Republican Interference

President James Buchanan decided that the best way to simultaneously end the violence in Kansas Territory and placate southern senators was to quickly admit

Kansas as a slave state. The strongly proslavery territorial legislature agreed and set the election of delegates to a state constitutional convention for June 1857. Antislavery voters, who were a majority in the territory, boycotted the election. Dominated by delegates who wished Kansas to enter the union as a slave state, the state convention adopted the Lecompton Constitution, which prohibited free Blacks from entering Kansas and assured the continued involuntary servitude of persons (and their descendants) held in slavery at the time the constitution was approved. The constitution did not provide whether persons held in slavery could be imported into the state but left that question to the voters in a separate referendum. Buchanan urged Congress to admit Kansas under the Lecompton Constitution. Senator Stephen Douglas emphatically opposed Buchanan on the issue. Douglas's motivation could have been purely political because he hoped to gain votes in his upcoming battle for reelection, or it may have been that the Lecompton Constitution did not fully embrace popular sovereignty. Under the Lecompton Constitution, even if the Kansas electorate voted to prohibit bringing new enslaved persons into the state, slavery would continue for those held in bondage at the time (and their descendants), contrary to the doctrine of popular sovereignty embodied in Douglas's Kansas-Nebraska Act.[71]

Douglas's public opposition to the Lecompton Constitution and rift with Buchanan endeared him to many eastern Republicans, old Whigs, and newspaper editors. A group led by Horace Greeley of the *New-York Daily Tribune* urged Republicans in Illinois to support Douglas's reelection bid. In his newspaper, "Greeley called on Illinois Republicans to cross party lines and endorse Douglas for senator in the upcoming race."[72] Old-line Whig senator John J. Crittenden of Kentucky was the most vocal senator backing Douglas. Lincoln and Davis were fully aware of the defections. In December 1857 Lincoln wrote to Senator Lyman Trumbull, complaining:

> What does the New-York Tribune mean by it's [*sic*] constant eulogising, and admiring, and magnifying [of] Douglas? Does it, in this, speak the sentiments of the republicans at Washington? Have they concluded that the republican cause, generally, can be best promoted by sacrificing us here in Illinois? If so we would like to know it soon; it will save us a great deal of labor to surrender at once.
>
> As yet I have heard of no republican here going over to Douglas; but if the Tribune continues to din his praises into the ears of it's [*sic*] five or ten thousand republican readers in Illinois, it is more than can be hoped that all will stand firm.[73]

Writing from Washington in early January, Senator Trumbull confirmed the "laudation" of Douglas by eastern Republicans, including New York senator William H. Seward and Massachusetts senator Henry Wilson. According to Trumbull, "Some of our friends here act like fools in running after & flattering Douglas—He encourages it & invites such men as Wilson, Seward, Burlingame,

Parrot &c to come & confer with him & they seem wonderfully pleased to go."
Seward was so delighted by Douglas's feud with Buchanan that he spoke at
length with Douglas immediately after Douglas's Senate speech denouncing
the Lecompton Constitution.[74] Trumbull promised Lincoln that he would try
to persuade Horace Greeley "to pursue a different course" in his newspaper.[75]
Adding to Lincoln's concern was a rumor that Greeley, Seward, and New York
political boss Thurlow Weed had cemented their support of Douglas's reelection
through a deal in which Douglas agreed to back Seward for the 1860 Republican
presidential nomination.[76]

By March 1858 William Herndon was concerned enough about Greeley's
promotion of Douglas to obtain permission from Lincoln to travel east and
investigate the situation. Arriving in Washington, DC, Herndon dined with
Senator Trumbull, who three months earlier had pledged to support Lincoln
for Douglas's Senate seat. Trumbull reiterated to Herndon what he told Lincoln
in January: eastern Republicans praised Senator Douglas, and many actively
supported his reelection. Herndon's talks with Seward and Wilson "confirmed
Trumbull's startling news." The news did not improve when Herndon arrived
in New York. After meeting with Greeley, Herndon concluded that the editor's
"feelings" were with Douglas and that he wanted Douglas returned to the Senate. Greeley also let Herndon know that the Illinois Republican newspapers
were "fools" for not supporting Douglas. Some eastern political leaders simply
gave Herndon the cold shoulder. Other easterners took it for granted that the
Republicans in Illinois would back Douglas's reelection bid. For example, the
governor of Massachusetts, Nathaniel P. Banks, pointedly asked Herndon, "You
will sustain Douglas in Illinois, won't you?" Herndon's answer, "*No, never*,"
caught Governor Banks by surprise, and the subject was dropped. Herndon
assumed that the many questions that he received similar to the one posed by
Governor Banks were inspired by the remarks of "Greeley, Steward [*sic*], et al."[77]

Herndon's visit east did little to moderate the praise that Greeley showered
upon Douglas. In an editorial in the *New-York Daily Tribune* on May 11, 1858,
Greeley conceded that Lincoln might be the Republican candidate for senator
and that he was "one of the truest and most effective advocates of Republican
principles." But Greeley did not stop there; he went on to speak highly of Douglas's principled opposition to the Lecompton Constitution. Greeley's tacit intent
was clear: to encourage Republican support of Douglas's candidacy.[78] Greeley
was more direct in a letter to Herndon following the Illinois Republican Convention's endorsement of Lincoln for the Senate. In the letter, Greeley said that
after the endorsement he would not cause dissension by supporting Douglas
over Lincoln but that the entire situation could have been avoided if the Illinois
Republicans had been "wise and farseeing" and endorsed Douglas.[79]

In early June Lincoln received a report from Ward Lamon that the eastern influence was having some effect on Illinois Republicans. Lamon reported that while the McLean County Republican Convention passed a resolution declaring their preference for Lincoln for the Senate, the convention also passed a resolution "endorsing" Douglas. Lamon suggested that the McLean County "impolitic" vote was not calculated to give Lincoln "strength" over Douglas. Similarly, a letter from State Representative Stephen Hurlbut of Boone County warned that some former Democrats turned Republican in the Second Congressional District leaned toward Douglas.[80]

Lincoln and Davis agreed that Greeley would be "rather pleased" to see Douglas reelected over any Republican, including Lincoln, and that Greeley's "feeling constantly manifests itself in his paper." They further agreed that Seward shared Greeley's opinion. Lincoln worried more about Greeley than Seward because of the editor's ability to "manifest" his opinion to the public, including the many *New-York Daily Tribune* subscribers in Illinois. As far as Lincoln knew, Seward was not broadcasting his opinion to Illinois Republicans.[81]

Lincoln legitimately worried about another senator who might announce his support of Douglas in the Illinois race. Kentucky Whig John J. Crittenden consistently praised Douglas "in many conversations, at Washington and elsewhere."[82] An endorsement of Douglas by a leading Whig like Crittenden would have little effect on northern Illinois Republicans or southern Illinois Democrats but could easily be the decisive factor in the old Whig battleground counties of central Illinois. In an attempt to ward off such an endorsement, on July 7, 1858, Lincoln wrote a deferential but direct letter asking Senator Crittenden to put to rest the "whispers" that he was eager to see Douglas returned to the Senate and planned to "write letters to that effect to [his] friends . . . in Illinois." Lincoln suggested that Crittenden keep his hands off the election and not endorse either candidate. The letter concluded by assuring the Kentucky senator that regardless of what he did, Lincoln would remain his "friend and admirer."[83]

Crittenden pulled no punches in his response to Lincoln. He emphasized that Douglas's opposition to Lecompton was "highly gratifying" and "full of sacrifice" and that Douglas's reelection was necessary as a rebuke to the Buchanan administration. Crittenden readily admitted that he expressed his opinion "openly & ardently." He told Lincoln that he had written several letters endorsing Douglas and had recently received letters from Illinoisans seeking written confirmation of his praise and endorsement of the Little Giant. The Kentucky senator said he would answer the letters honestly to avoid any "imputations of insincerity or timidity."[84] One of the letters Crittenden received was from T. Lyle Dickey, a former Lincoln backer and Davis confidant turned Democrat. True to his word, on August 1, 1858, Crittenden answered Dickey and granted him permission to privately and publicly repeat the praise that Crittenden heaped upon Douglas for his "courage," "patriotism," and "heroism," which subjected Douglas to fierce, unwarranted attacks on his honor and on his life.[85] Dickey turned the letter into an "October surprise" by unveiling it about a week and a half before the election as part of Dickey's assault on Lincoln for abandoning Whig principles.[86] Some Republican newspapers tried to downplay the Crittenden missive but to little avail. For example, the *Illinois State Journal* took a shotgun approach to discrediting the letter by arguing that the letter had been concealed since August likely because it was a forgery; even if the letter was genuine, Crittenden had been deceived by Douglas; the letter was too old to express Crittenden's current opinion; and the letter did not expressly advocate for Douglas's reelection.[87]

Consistent with his nature, Lincoln was able to avoid taking the eastern defections personally. Soon after the election Lincoln explained that it never occurred to him to blame Crittenden for merely expressing his opinion. And while the use of the Kentucky Whig's name by Dickey and others "contributed largely" to Lincoln's defeat, Lincoln did not "for a moment suspect [Crittenden] of anything dishonorable."[88]

Davis was another story. To the judge, loyalty was an essential trait of an honorable man. A breach of loyalty or fidelity should seldom be forgiven. While Davis could never excuse Senator Crittenden for his "outrageous" act of interfering in Illinois's election, he reserved his greatest scorn for Dickey. Crittenden violated loyalty to Whig and Republican principles. By abandoning the Republican Party, joining the Democrats, and promoting Douglas, Dickey similarly deserted political loyalties. But much worse, Dickey betrayed a personal loyalty owed to Lincoln and Davis. So Davis blamed Dickey more for drawing the letter out of Crittenden than he blamed Crittenden for writing it. "The lever of Judge Dickey's influence" was felt not only in his soliciting the letter but also in his equally "shameful" act of concealing the letter until shortly before the election. To Davis, Dickey's breach of personal loyalty was inexcusable.[89]

In addition to Crittenden and Dickey, Davis included Senator Seward, his political manager, Thurlow Weed, and Horace Greeley on his list of deserters. The judge told Lincoln that while others might forgive Crittenden, Dickey, Seward, and Greeley for "throwing cold water" on Lincoln's election prospects, he could not.[90] Davis's mistrust of Greeley and Weed was not new. He hesitated to support the first Republican presidential nominee, John C. Frémont, in 1856 because Davis agreed with Justice McLean's remark that "money and corruption had been freely used to procure [Frémont's] nomination" and that if elected, he would have been controlled by corrupt individuals such as Greeley and Weed.[91] It was personal with Judge Davis, and he would seize his chance to even the score in Chicago in May 1860.

Davis Shares the Blame

Davis accepted a small part of the responsibility for the Senate loss. In late October he expressed regret for failing to resign his judicial post and campaign full time for Lincoln and the Republican legislative candidates. The judge believed that "in certain sections of the State, [he] could have done good." After the election, Davis voiced the same regret directly to Lincoln, lamenting that he had not freed himself from his judicial chains by resigning his office and committing himself to the "fight" for the Senate seat.[92] But would the "ex-judge's" full-time efforts have made a difference in the outcome of the election?

Whether or not Davis could have changed enough votes to put Lincoln in the Senate, a full-time effort by the judge likely would have increased support for Republican legislative candidates in central Illinois. Republicans and Democrats alike knew that the election would be won or lost in the middle counties; in Davis's words, "The central portion of Illinois is the fight."[93] Herndon described the political geography more fully:

> Our state is a peculiar one politically: first, we have a north which is all intelligence, all for freedom. Secondly, we have a South, people from the sand hills of the South, poor white folks. These are pro-slavery and ignorant "up to the hub." And thirdly, we have a belt of land, seventy-five miles in width, running from the east bank of the Mississippi to the Wabash—to Indiana; and running north and south, from Bloomington to Alton. In or upon this strip or belt of land this "great battle" between Lincoln and Douglas is to be fought and victory won.[94]

Davis's position as a well-known professional and political figure in the counties described by Herndon may have itself added votes to the Republican column if the judge spent all his time on the campaign trail. His decades-long presence on the circuit led one traveling lawyer to conclude that "almost every man, woman, and child in the fourteen counties of his circuit knew Judge Davis, and he undoubtedly was personally acquainted with a greater number of the residents than any other one man in the district."[95] In addition, Davis could have put his canvassing skills to more complete use if he had been unencumbered by court duties.

Davis's Canvassing Skills

The skills Davis would have employed to increase the Republican vote are easily pinpointed: organization and persuasion.

The judge possessed superior management and organizational talents, which were sorely needed in the legislative races in the doubtful counties. As in 1854,

Lincoln had no full-time campaign staff and no designated campaign coordinator for raising funds, recruiting volunteers, placing favorable articles in newspapers, or planning and scheduling events. Lincoln served as his own campaign manager, which burdened him with decisions concerning every detail of the campaign, including coordination with local Republican organizations and candidates.[96] Because of his personality and the disparate ideologies of the state's voters, Lincoln may not have appointed any single person as his campaign manager. But he certainly would have recognized the advantage in designating Davis full-time coordinator for the central counties where Whigs and Know-Nothings, often referred to as "Fillmore men," would control the outcomes in the legislative districts. Even Davis's detractors acknowledged his leadership abilities, management skills, work ethic, and loyalty to Lincoln. He could have relieved Lincoln of some of the minor campaign coordination tasks. For example, instead of trying to track down Lincoln to suggest that Lincoln arrange for the circulation of his Springfield speech to the voters in Tazewell County, the judge could have done it himself or, more likely, assigned the task to a "volunteer" such as Leonard Swett. On a larger scale, instead of twice urging Lincoln in early August to "plan out now the campaign for the entire state," Davis could have helped Lincoln accomplish that task or at least could have prepared a campaign blueprint for central Illinois.[97]

The judge's greatest assets in a full-time campaign role would have been his unimpeachable credentials as a moderate old-line Whig and his intimate relationship with Lincoln. At the time, Davis was the principal strategist and spokesman for both the midstate Whigs who had joined the Republican Party and the Whigs who were sitting on the fence.[98] Moreover, the personal, political, and professional association and confidential relationship between Lincoln and Davis were accepted facts. Their special relationship made Davis the perfect person to counter the Democrats' complaint against Lincoln that most damaged his chances with the old Whigs and Fillmore voters: the claim that Lincoln not only opposed the extension of slavery but also advocated the abolition of slavery in the states where it existed. The Democrats based this attack on Lincoln's June "House Divided" speech, in which he stated that "this government cannot endure, permanently half slave and half free."[99] For good measure, the Democrats added that Lincoln supported equality for Blacks, including the right to vote and serve on juries. This claim was extrapolated from statements Lincoln made during his speech in Chicago in July 1858 when he emphasized that all men are created equal.[100] Douglas supporters quickly transformed Lincoln's acknowledgment of the principle found in the Declaration of Independence into proof that Lincoln supported full citizenship rights for Blacks and intermarriage of the races.

Davis fully recognized that the main difficulty in carrying Tazewell and other midstate counties for Republican legislative candidates was the Democrats' charge of abolitionism and equality. That is why the judge helped convince Lincoln to clearly and unequivocally state at the Charleston debate that he did not support the social or political equality of the races.[101] Lincoln put it bluntly:

> While I was at the hotel to-day an elderly gentleman called upon me to know whether I was really in favor of producing a perfect equality between the negroes and white people. [Great laughter.] While I had not proposed to myself on this occasion to say much on that subject, yet as the question was asked me I thought I would occupy perhaps five minutes in saying something in regard to it. I will say then that I am not, nor ever have been in favor of bringing about in any way the social and political equality of the white and black races, [applause]—that I am not nor ever have been in favor of making voters or jurors of negroes, nor of qualifying them to hold office, nor to intermarry with white people; and I will say in addition to this that there is a physical difference between the white and black races which I believe will for ever forbid the two races living together on terms of social and political equality.[102]

Knowing that this unflinching statement was what many central county voters wanted to hear, Davis sent Lincoln a letter complimenting him on the speech.[103] Campaigning full-time, Davis could have reinforced Lincoln's declaration with Davis's own guarantee that he knew from conversations with Lincoln that he did not promote abolition or full equality. And there was no better person to persuade old Whigs and Know-Nothings, because the judge's own antiabolitionist credentials were unassailable and well known. He spoke and voted against the leading Illinois abolitionist, Owen Lovejoy, when Lovejoy ran for Congress in 1856. Davis's opposition to Lovejoy was no secret.[104] Two years later, when Lovejoy was seeking renomination to Congress, the abolitionists believed that "all the Lawyers of the circuit with judge Davis . . . are in a conspiracy to defeat Lovejoy."[105] And the abolitionists' belief was not without basis.[106] Regardless of whether seeking to deny Lovejoy renomination was a smart political move, it enhanced the judge's credibility and influence among the Whigs. The close relationship between Davis and Lincoln, the judge's reputation for brutal honesty, and his antiabolitionist credentials would have made his word good for at least a portion of the old Whigs and Know-Nothings who both feared equality for Blacks and controlled the election outcomes in the swing counties.

Moreover, Davis could have persuasively countered what some historians consider the turning point of the election: longtime supporter T. Lyle Dickey's endorsement of Douglas and his publication of Senator Crittenden's letter praising Douglas.[107] Dickey turned on his former friend because in Dickey's mind Lincoln had surrendered to the abolitionists. No one was in a better position to refute Dickey's charge by emphasizing Lincoln's repeated public and private statements that he did not support the abolition of slavery or equal political rights for Blacks.[108] The judge might also have mentioned that Dickey once wrote to Lincoln, "*I love you* & want you to be a U.S. Senator from Illinois."[109] To dispel any hint of a personal animosity toward Dickey, Davis could have reminded voters that when Dickey's wife died in December 1855, the Dickey children lived with the judge and Sarah for the winter.[110]

Finally, the judge had answers to arguments that Democrats put "to good and earnest Republicans" soliciting their support for Douglas. The *Chicago Daily Press and Tribune* reported that such appeals from the Democrats included the following:

> [Douglas] is as much opposed to the extension of slavery as you can be.
> [Douglas] is not willing that the South should ride "rough-shod" over the North any longer.
> [Douglas] will cooperate with those who seek the curtailment of the undue influence of slave power.[111]

Davis's rejoinder to these talking points would have emphasized that desperation and expediency rather a change of heart propelled Douglas's recent insincere and illusory statements on the slavery issue. The judge could quote the *Chicago Daily Press and Tribune* in pointing out that Douglas never dismounted from the "pro-slavery horse which he has ridden so furiously for the last four years" to cement the "domination of the Slavery Oligarchy."[112]

During the campaign Davis refuted Douglas's claim that Lincoln supported the abolition of slavery and Black citizenship, and Davis also refuted the importance of Crittenden's letter. He even challenged Douglas's antislavery credentials.[113] But these ad hoc, stopgap, spur-of-the-moment efforts could not produce the same results as Davis's coordinated efforts as a full-time campaigner and organizer.

The judge's approach to defeat Douglas and Democratic legislative candidates would have been simple: "old fashioned canvassing." The mainstay of old-fashioned canvassing was personal contact with the voters, whether at their homes, their businesses, gathering places, or local political events. Davis wrote letters if in-person contact was not feasible. And Davis certainly made use of letter writing even in his part-time campaign role, spending the "whole afternoon" of August 3, 1858, sending correspondence to residents of Tazewell County.[114]

Targeted Counties

In letters to his brother-in-law and Lincoln, Davis failed to specify the counties in which he "could have done good" and would have targeted for a full-time campaign effort. There is no doubt, however, that Tazewell County was on top of the list.

TAZEWELL COUNTY   Davis's first law office was in the town of Pekin in Tazewell County. One of his first Whig campaign speeches was at a rally for presidential candidate William Henry Harrison in Tazewell County in 1840. Davis possessed an intricate knowledge of the county's election history and the social and political leanings of its residents. The judge was convinced that Tazewell could be won by introducing some organization, enthusiasm, energy, and old-fashioned canvassing to gain Fillmore votes and dispel charges of abolitionism against Lincoln. As Benjamin F. James, a leading lawyer and Whig of Tazewell County, told Lincoln, Davis was needed in the county because "there is no one in Tazewell, that can do this work as it ought to be done."[115]

Davis's fixation on Tazewell is evidenced by the four letters that he sent to Lincoln about the difficulties facing the Republican candidate for state representative in the district. The judge wrote the first letter on July 30, 1858, after conferring with a former Tazewell County sheriff. Bemoaning the fact that in contrast to the well-organized and managed Democrats there were no Whig or Republican "political managers, or tacticians" in the county, Davis advised Lincoln that Tazewell "ought to be especially attended to . . . and a great deal of electioneering put on it." The judge suggested that Richard N. Cullom, who had previously served as a state representative and state senator from Tazewell, might be the only person who could beat the "talented" Democratic candidate. Davis further suggested that Cullom's son, Shelby M. Cullom, who was elected to the state legislature in 1856 as a Know-Nothing, be assigned to explore an alliance with the other Fillmore men of the county. Pursuant to the proposed alliance, the Fillmore men would support the Republican candidate for state representative in return for Republican support of the Fillmore candidate for county sheriff. Even though Davis believed that no self-respecting Whig would join the "mean narrow and selfish" Know-Nothing Party, he urged the deal to avoid losing the swing county to the Democrats. He further suggested that James H. Matheny, a Millard Fillmore supporter in 1856 and the best man at Lincoln's wedding, could help establish the coalition, which would benefit Republicans not only in Tazewell but also in DeWitt and Piatt Counties.[116]

Anxious for a response to his correspondence, Davis wrote to Lincoln three days later asking if he had received the letter about Tazewell County.[117] Twenty-four hours after that, the judge sent a third letter further detailing the situation in Tazewell. He reminded Lincoln that in 1856 the Democratic congressional candidate beat the Republican, William Kellogg, in the county because many voters, including Know-Nothings, voted against Kellogg when he voiced "extremist abolition opinions." Davis renewed his suggestion for a union with the Fillmore men supplemented by a rally attended by Lincoln and other moderate Republicans. The judge also advised that the speakers at the rally should "distinctly &

emphatically disavow *negro suffrage*—negro holding office, serving on juries, & the like." Talk of such rights would automatically lose the Kentucky-born Fillmore voters in "the Mackinaw Town Precinct & on Little Mackinaw." His last bit of advice implored, "For God's sake dont let [Owen] Lovejoy go into Tazewell."[118]

Davis's campaign work in Tazewell did not proceed flawlessly. On August 9, 1858, Davis desperately wrote Lincoln in an attempt to soothe potential bad feelings caused by Davis's suggestion that Republicans slate Richard Cullom for state representative. When the judge made the suggestion, he did not realize that others were interested in running for the seat and might take the endorsement as coming from Lincoln himself. David Kyes, another former sheriff of the county, wrote to Davis, advising him that the Tazewell Republicans planned to select a candidate for state representative at the Lincoln rally on August 14. Kyes said that many people had urged him to be the candidate but that he would decline, "knowing as I do that Lincoln wishes & desires that Major Cullom shall be the man."[119] The judge immediately responded to Kyes, disclaiming that Lincoln had any preference in the race: "I think that you are in error, in supposing that Mr Lincoln, desires Major Cullom's nomination for Representative in your county in preference to any other person—I know, that personally, he has no feeling on the subject.—He has so many friends in all parts of Tazewell, that he cannot possibly have any choice—whoever, on consultation is thought to be the most likely, to unite the Fillmore & Fremont vote should be the man."[120] Davis sent a copy of the letter to Lincoln and urged him to write a similar letter to Kyes.[121]

The judge was anxious enough about Tazewell to attend the Lincoln rally on Saturday, August 14, and stay through Sunday to campaign, arrange speaking engagements for Lincoln surrogates, and personally gauge the mood of the voters. He played no role in organizing the Saturday rally and was distressed by the poor attendance, since no more than fifty persons from out of town were present.[122] The trip confirmed that the Democrats bought the Pekin newspaper and heightened Davis's fear that Tazewell was far from "safe" and actually might be leaning Democratic. The judge, however, believed that Tazewell could "be carried, by prudence, energy & work," and after returning home, he desperately tried to locate Lincoln to convey the details of his Tazewell visit.[123]

While attending the August 14 Tazewell meeting, Davis recruited Samuel C. Parks, who was a hit speaking on behalf of Lincoln and the Republicans that day, to speak in "3 old Whig precincts" in the county.[124] Two of the precincts were Mackinaw Township and Little Mackinaw Township in the eastern part of the county bordering McLean County. Later, the judge reported to Lincoln that the visits by Parks, Bloomington lawyer William H. Hanna, newspaper publisher Thomas J. Pickett, and Major Richard Cullom, the Republican candidate for state representative, greatly advanced the Republican cause in the targeted precincts. Davis noted that "Major Cullom can get all the votes in the Mackinaw country—& that many will vote for him that will vote for nobody else."[125]

Davis arranged for Lincoln to speak from the steps of the old Tazewell County Courthouse on the afternoon of August 30. Lincoln's remarks were clearly directed to the Whigs. He reminisced about his campaign appearances on behalf of the Whigs in Tazewell County in the 1840s and told the fifteen hundred people in attendance that there was no difference between Henry Clay Whigs and Republicans: both opposed the expansion of slavery. Recognizing the importance of this legislative district, Lincoln returned to Tazewell on October 5 to rebut claims made by Senator Douglas three days earlier in Pekin that the Republicans were not Whigs but abolitionists and believed in Negro equality.[126]

Richard Cullom, the Republican candidate for the legislature in Tazewell County, the sole county in the thirty-ninth state representative district, lost by 177 votes.[127] Whether a full-time effort by Davis could have changed the minds of 89 voters or brought another 178 Republicans to the polls is open to question. Davis may very well have thought that he had the influence and arguments to do it. And the judge's best chance to make a difference certainly lay in Tazewell County. But turning the Tazewell seat from Democrat to Republican by itself would not have changed the outcome of the senatorial contest. Republicans would have needed to prevail in other state legislative districts that went Democratic.

SANGAMON, MORGAN, AND SCOTT COUNTIES   Sangamon County could have boosted Lincoln's chances to win a majority in the legislature. But Democrats James W. Barrett and Daniel Short won the state representative seats. According to Lincoln, the Democrats were elected because "nearly all the old exclusive silk-stocking whiggery" in Sangamon County voted against the Republicans. He was not complaining about all old Whigs, just "the nice exclusive sort."[128] If Lincoln was correct, then maybe a full-time effort by Davis, who could pass when necessary for "the nice exclusive sort" of old Whig, might have cut into the two-hundred-vote advantage enjoyed by the Democratic candidates. But it is difficult to see how Davis could have changed minds in Lincoln's home county. Indeed, Lincoln himself fared no better in the 1860 head-to-head presidential contest, losing Sangamon County to Douglas by more than four hundred votes. In 1864 he lost the county again, this time to Democratic presidential nominee George McClellan.[129]

Morgan County bordered Sangamon County on the west. Scott County bordered Morgan County on the west. Together the two counties made up the twenty-seventh state representative district and were considered old Whig counties. But the district went heavily Democratic, reelecting representatives

Cyrus Epler and Elisha B. Hitt over their Republican opponents by margins of slightly more than six hundred votes.[130] Davis's efforts could not have made up such large deficits.

SHELBY, CHRISTIAN, AND FULTON COUNTIES   Shelby County comprised the nineteenth state representative district, and Christian County formed the twentieth. Although both counties were in the Eighth Judicial Circuit until 1853, they were so heavily Democratic that Davis would have written them off, just as Lincoln did. Shelby and Christian were the only counties of the Eighth Judicial Circuit in which Lincoln made no campaign appearances in his second senatorial bid.[131] In Fulton County, just west of Tazewell County, the Republicans were "probably as well organized as any county in the State" but still could do no more than reduce the usual Democrat margin of eight hundred votes to three hundred votes, resulting in the election of two Democrats to the state house.[132]

LOGAN AND MASON COUNTIES   Davis may have believed that his full-time efforts would have turned the tide in the thirty-fifth state representative district, made up of Logan and Mason Counties. Douglas's forces were making "desperate efforts" in the district. After receiving information from Sam Parks that Republican success in the representative race was "a little doubtful," the judge successfully recruited Lincoln to make a personal appearance in the county seat of Logan County. Davis also convinced Lincoln to speak in Bath in Mason County on August 12 in an attempt to draw back some of the Whig voters who had deserted to the American Party and Millard Fillmore in 1856. Bath had always been the strongest Whig precinct in the county.[133] The Republican state representative candidate, William Walker, won Logan County by 122 votes (1,302 to 1,180) but lost Mason County to Democrat George H. Campbell by 200 votes. So the Democrat narrowly prevailed in the thirty-fifth district by a total of 2,208 votes to 2,130 votes.[134]

Possibly, Davis could have increased the Republican vote in Logan County or Mason County enough to make up the district-wide loss of seventy-eight votes. If he had, it would not have been because of his circuit-riding contacts in Mason County. The county had not been in the Eighth Judicial Circuit since 1845. Besides, court sessions were brief, because the county's small population did not create much court business.[135] Although Whig candidates won in the county in the 1840s, Democrats usually prevailed thereafter. In addition, George Campbell was a strong candidate, having served as a judge and treasurer for Mason County. A Whig until he ran as a Democrat in 1858, Campbell enjoyed support among his old Whig friends.[136]

MACON COUNTY   Davis enjoyed visiting Decatur, the county seat of Macon County, during his circuit travels to dine with old friends and check on the property that he owned in the town. Notwithstanding his general aversion to speaking at political rallies, the judge felt comfortable enough to join Senator Lyman Trumbull and Leonard Swett as a speaker at a rally in Macon County on July 7, 1860.[137] But Macon County was too tied to the Democracy for Davis to make a difference in the 1858 election. The county had enough Democrats to support two newspapers, the *Gazette* and the *Magnet*, both of which outsold the county's only Republican newspaper, the *Illinois State Chronicle*.[138] Macon County was Democrat when it was formed in 1830 and with few exceptions remained so through the election of 1860, when its electorate gave Douglas 1,541 votes and Lincoln 1,501 votes.[139] The 1858 state representative race was no exception: Macon County gave a 179-vote margin to the Democratic candidate. But the other counties of the thirty-sixth state representative district, DeWitt, Piatt, and Champaign, carried the Republican, Daniel Stickel, to victory.[140] In the state senate race in the sixteenth state senatorial district, where Moultrie, Christian, Shelby, and McLean Counties joined the counties of the thirty-sixth state representative district, Democrat Joel S. Post of Decatur was elected.[141] Whatever difference Davis could have made in Macon County in the state senatorial race would have been offset by the inclusion in the district of the Democratic strongholds of Moultrie, Christian, and Shelby Counties.[142]

Would Davis's full-time canvassing efforts have changed the vote in enough districts to give the Republicans a majority in the legislature? It is not beyond the realm of possibility, because the Democratic majorities in key legislative districts were razor-thin. Realistically speaking, however, increased election-eering by the judge probably would not have flipped control of the legislature to the Republicans. Davis acknowledged this unfortunate fact. After the election Davis told Lincoln that trading Davis's judicial job for a larger role in the canvass would not have brought victory because of the lack of support of the "Pharisaical old Whigs in the Central counties."[143] What the judge concluded from his unsuccessful campaign for state senator eighteen years before might have held equally true for the 1858 election: "I tried by personal interviews & public addresses to turn them from the error of their ways—but you might as well attempt to stem the Mississippi with a bulrush."[144]

Lessons Learned from the Second Senate Defeat

The battle for the legislature in 1858 reinforced Davis's view of the essential components of successful political campaigns, most of which he believed were absent from the Republican Party's playbook under Judd's leadership. First, an outpouring of enthusiasm, excitement, and energy, spontaneous or manufac-tured, must accompany political campaign events. Davis complained about the lack of enthusiasm of the "generally dispirited" group that attended Lincoln's August campaign event in Tremont.[145] Second, after seeing Douglas outspend

Lincoln in the US Senate campaign by at least fifty to one, the judge knew that no future Lincoln candidacy would prevail because Lincoln outspent his opponent. Third, a comprehensive game plan must be developed early in the election cycle. Davis complained to Lincoln in the late summer of 1858 that no statewide program had been established by the Republican state central committee.[146] Fourth, it was inexcusable that in 1854 and again in 1858 the Democrats outworked the Republicans. If Lincoln was lucky enough to get another shot at a federal office, someone had to make sure that Lincoln's men worked harder, longer, and smarter than their opponents. Fifth, while mass campaign meetings are important, changing votes comes down to good old-fashioned canvassing. And old-fashioned canvassing puts a premium on one-on-one and small group sit-downs with the electorate, whether the electorate consists of voters or convention delegates. Sixth, just as the 1858 Illinois election was decided by old Whigs and not abolitionists, so would the upcoming presidential nomination be controlled by moderates rather than extremists known as "ultra men." Seventh, campaign strategy must be dictated by the overarching reality, as Davis put it, that the Republican Party was a confederated, not a consolidated, party.[147] That might mean creating "unions" with the objectionable Know-Nothings in Tazewell County or making deals with otherwise distasteful persons or factions in the future. Eighth, and most importantly for Davis, the 1858 election proved what he already knew: someone with experience, political skills, and loyalty to Lincoln had to be in charge. Judd arguably possessed the first two traits, and Logan certainly possessed the third. But neither could get the job done. Davis knew that only he could.

Davis, Lincoln, and the Presidency

3 Davis Secures Lincoln's 1860 Presidential Nomination

The first Republican National Convention met in Philadelphia in 1856. Like most Whigs, Lincoln and Davis backed Supreme Court justice John McLean for the presidential nomination, but the convention chose former California senator John C. Frémont instead. Another former senator, New Jersey's William L. Dayton, was selected as Frémont's running mate. Surprisingly, Abraham Lincoln finished second in the balloting for vice president. On the advice of Thurlow Weed, New York senator William H. Seward chose to forgo seeking the presidential nomination in 1856 because his strong antislavery views and opposition to the Know-Nothings would ensure his defeat.[1] Weed was convinced that the party and the country would be ready for Seward four years later.

William H. Seward: The Prohibitive Favorite

Everyone in America, including Frederick Douglass, assumed that William H. Seward would receive the Republican presidential nomination in 1860. Seward led the Republican Party not only in the Senate but also in the nation. David Davis himself referred to the New York senator as "the father of the Republican party."[2] According to an article in the *Morning Courier and New-York Enquirer* in February 1860, Seward's nomination was "demanded" by a large majority of the party faithful for three compelling reasons. First, he best represented the principles of the Republican Party. Second, no one could match his past service to the party. Third, the Democratic candidate, whoever he was, would defeat any other Republican.[3] True believers considered Seward the "prophet, priest, and oracle" of the Republican movement. There was no second choice. Seward devotees "sneer[ed] at the idea that any one but [Seward would] receive the nomination."[4] Few inside or outside of the party thought that Seward would be denied what he had rightfully earned.

Seward's confidence in the nomination matched that of his supporters. The senator believed that the Republican Party owed its existence to his hard work and sacrifice. Seward represented the true Republican principles, unlike the "fickle and timid" Republicans, among which he most likely would have included Lincoln.[5] Less than three months before the Chicago convention, Seward spoke in the Senate, backtracking from his famous "irrepressible conflict" speech for the purpose of satisfying party conservatives and removing any scintilla of doubt about his nomination. The presumptive nominee believed that the Senate speech assured his place in presidential "posterity."[6] Upon learning of the *Chicago Press and Tribune*'s endorsement of Lincoln in early 1860, Seward blew up at the paper's editor and questioned how anyone could prefer a "prairie statesman" to the "chief teacher" of Republican principles. The *Tribune*'s snub infuriated Seward to such an extent that he threatened to retire from the "ungrateful party" unless he was nominated.[7]

Seward's confidence in the nomination had a solid foundation. To start, New York had 70 of the 233 delegate votes needed at the convention, and all were irrevocably committed to their favorite son. Adding to this advantage, in April 1859 Pennsylvania senator Simon Cameron wined and dined Seward at his home in Harrisburg, inviting all members of the state legislature to the meet-and-greet gathering. That evening Cameron assured Seward that while the state's delegates might vote for Cameron on the first ballot, all fifty-four Pennsylvania delegates would vote for Senator Seward on succeeding ballots.[8]

As the convention approached, Seward swiftly dismissed the viability of other likely candidates. Edward Bates, from the slave state of Missouri, would never receive the votes of true Republicans. Senator Salmon P. Chase had impeccable Republican credentials but was battling two other Ohioans, perennial candidate and Supreme Court justice John McLean and Senator Benjamin Wade, for the support of the Ohio delegates. William L. Dayton of New Jersey, Jacob Collamer of Vermont, William P. Fessenden of Maine, and Massachusetts governor Nathaniel P. Banks would never achieve more than favorite son status. Seward also knew that until shortly before the convention, Abraham Lincoln could not even count on unanimous support from his own delegation.[9] When Lincoln's name did surface it was usually as a possible running mate for Seward, Chase, or Cameron. In August 1859 the *Illinois State Journal* reported that a Kansas newspaper had urged the nomination of Seward for president and Lincoln for vice president. Three months later a Lancaster, Pennsylvania, newspaper recommended a ticket of Cameron and Lincoln. The next month the *Chicago Press and Tribune* ran a front-page article listing the officers and ward representatives of a Chicago-based C & L Club, which passed a resolution supporting a Cameron-

Lincoln ticket. Early the next year the *Chicago Press and Tribune* reproduced an article from the *Newton Star* declaring that the Newton Township (Iowa) Republicans endorsed Chase for president and Lincoln as his running mate.[10] Lincoln scholar Dr. Louis A. Warren correctly described Lincoln's popularity as a vice presidential candidate this way: "It is doubtful if, ever before or since, one political aspirant has been the first choice as a running mate by so many different candidates for the Presidential nomination."[11]

And by no means was it only Seward and the newspapers that placed Lincoln out of the presidential running. In early 1860 Norman Judd, chairman of the Illinois Republican Party, was the guest speaker at a meeting of one of the Cameron-Lincoln clubs in Chicago. In late February 1860 even David Davis privately conceded that Seward and Edward Bates had decidedly better chances at the nomination than Lincoln.[12]

Seward had another reason to be confident: Thurlow Weed. "The most powerful political boss in the country," Weed was the premier political strategist and manager of his day. He was especially adept "at the backroom politics of conventions."[13] Weed had cut his teeth on political campaigns in New York, and his influence then spread nationwide. He was highly sought after as a campaign advisor. He used his skills and power to help secure presidential nominations for William Henry Harrison, Zachary Taylor, and John C. Frémont.[14]

Weed had devoted himself to Seward's political advancement since 1830, when he engineered the nomination and election of Seward to the New York state senate as a Whig. Weed would now command Seward's forces at the presidential nominating convention.[15] Lincoln had no one who even approached Weed's experience, power, money, and successful history in securing party nominations. But Lincoln did have a secret weapon: his old circuit-riding friend Judge David Davis.

Davis Directs the Lincoln Convention Team

While historians agree that David Davis directed and managed the Lincoln loyalists at the Chicago convention, little has been said about how he became the head of the nomination effort.[16] One theory is that he automatically assumed the leadership role as he had during court sessions and after-court festivities while riding the circuit. This view is supported by Leonard Swett's observation that "without anyone electing [Davis] to the position, he at once became the leader of all the Illinois men." But circumstantial evidence suggests that Lincoln either expressly picked the judge as his convention leader or assumed that Davis would command his forces. At the Illinois Republican Convention in early May, Lincoln made it clear to Norman Judd that "he wished but one thing done, and that was that Judge Davis should be sent as one of the delegates." In the same conversation, Judd minimized expectations for what he could accomplish at the convention by telling Lincoln that Judd would have no influence at the Chicago gathering. It is also clear that Davis requested appointment as a delegate and sought the post for one reason: he believed that he could do more than any other man to secure Lincoln's nomination.[17] Consistent with an assigned leadership role for Davis, a week before the Chicago convention Lincoln advised Indiana delegate Cyrus M. Allen that State Auditor Jesse K. Dubois and Davis would meet and consult with Allen when he arrived in Chicago on May 12. On May 2 Lincoln sent a similar letter to Richard M. Corwine of Ohio, naming the judge and Dubois as the Illinois delegation's contact persons.[18] As would be expected of the designated floor manager, Davis was "first on the ground" in Chicago, arriving on the Saturday before the convention began the following Wednesday.[19]

Logic suggests that Lincoln either appointed Davis as floor leader or simply assumed that Davis would direct efforts to secure the nomination. Lincoln understood that the judge would accept nothing less than head of convention operations. He was not about to take orders from Norman Judd or anyone else who had failed Lincoln in his Senate campaigns. Davis firmly believed that no Lincoln supporter was better suited for management responsibilities. And he was right. As Harry Pratt concluded, Davis "did more than any man or group of men to bring about Lincoln's nomination for the Presidency."[20]

Judge Davis: Tailor-Made to Lead the Lincoln Forces

Davis's personality, skills, perseverance, experience, and loyalty were tailor-made for leadership roles inside and outside of politics.

No one ever doubted the judge's great energy and solid work ethic.[21] While riding the circuit, he often held court late into the night and on weekends. Unlike many trial judges of his day, Davis took some cases under advisement to allow time to research "nice law questions [that] arise every day in Court." His recordkeeping as a lawyer and judge was meticulous, detailed, and methodical.[22] Although not a gifted public speaker, the judge possessed good conversational and listening skills, "was punctilious in his courtesy," and could turn on the charm when necessary. His ability to negotiate settlements, honed when hearing cases on the circuit, would serve him well in dealings with the delegates at the convention. Further, Davis's capacity to form and execute a plan would work to Lincoln's advantage. Although not possessing a "tame" nature and demonstrating a "headstrong temperament" on occasion, Davis recognized and controlled these shortcomings when necessary to achieve important goals. His "incorruptible integrity" served as a nice counterpoint to Thurlow Weed's reputation for heavy-handed tactics and outright corruption.[23] In addition to social, organizational, and operational skills, Davis had a long-standing working relationship with the Illinoisans who would be the most active Lincoln supporters at the convention.

The vast majority of the boots on the ground in Chicago belonged to lawyers from the Eighth Judicial Circuit, all of whom were accustomed to taking orders from Davis without debate. On the circuit, no one questioned his authority in court or out of court. For example, when Lincoln stole the dinner gong at a hotel, Davis ordered Lincoln to return it immediately.[24] Davis dictated which lawyers were permitted to attend the after-hours entertainment sessions in the judge's room. Others were "frozen out" by the judge. When lawyers got wild or drunk, the judge ordered them to bed.[25] No one questioned the judge's authority on the circuit, and no one would question his decisions and orders at the convention. Appointing another lawyer from the Eighth Circuit to manage the convention effort would have flown in the face of decades of circuit-wide accepted practice. No one but Judge Davis could have commanded unquestioned obedience.

Besides the long-standing judge-lawyer relationships on the circuit, the judge had other professional and personal associations with many of the Lincoln stalwarts at the convention. Ward Lamon was one of Davis's "dearest friends . . . in the world."[26] Leonard Swett served as Davis's right-hand man in many personal and political endeavors, including Lincoln's US Senate bids in 1855 and 1859. Swett told William Herndon that he "had grown up leaning in hours of weakness on [Davis and Lincoln's] own great arms for support."[27] DeWitt County lawyer Clifton H. Moore and the judge had been real estate partners for more than a decade. In 1855 Davis conveyed eighty acres to Moore for his homestead.[28] When Lincoln was not available as a substitute judge, Davis appointed Moore and fellow Bloomington lawyer and convention worker Oliver Davis to preside in court. Lawrence Weldon, the judge's old traveling and rooming companion during circuit days, also served under Davis's direction at the nominating convention.[29] William W. Orme, Swett's law partner in Bloomington, relied on Davis for advice and favors.[30] Samuel C. Parks worked closely with the judge on Lincoln's behalf in Logan and Tazewell Counties in 1858.[31] In addition to their personal relationship, Stephen Logan, Herndon, and Davis regularly shared campaign duties on Lincoln's behalf.

Most importantly, the judge's support for Lincoln throughout his political career was not fueled by either a hope for his own advancement or agreement with Lincoln on the issues. It was simply a matter of personal loyalty. A campaign manager driven by loyalty might make mistakes, but those missteps would not result from self-promotion, double dealing, or a diminishing interest in the ultimate goal. Like Weed's relationship with Seward, this was personal loyalty politics; positions on issues were secondary at best.[32] Davis's unyielding loyalty to Lincoln was well known. As Jesse Fell told Lincoln in 1861, "Of all *living men* you have no truer more devoted friend and admirer than in the person of Judge

Davis."[33] No one other than Mary Lincoln could equal Davis's fidelity or personal and unqualified commitment to Lincoln's political advancement.

The lawyers, delegates, and other members of the convention team were well aware of the special relationship between Davis and Lincoln. According to Ward Lamon, "It was well understood that no man enjoyed more confidential relations with [Lincoln] than Judge Davis." Lamon, who had been a close associate of the two as a member of the Eighth Judicial Circuit bar and later as US marshal for the District of Columbia, never knew Lincoln and Davis to have a quarrel.[34] Lieutenant Governor Gustave Koerner, another circuit lawyer and important member of the team, shared Lamon's view: "Lincoln was, I believe, more intimate with [Davis] than with any other man." Koerner understood that the individuals for whom Lincoln "really entertained strong feelings of friendship could be counted on the fingers of one hand," and that list definitely included Davis.[35] Even Henry Clay Whitney, who was no fan of the judge, admitted that Lincoln was more intimate with Davis than he was with Whitney, Ward Lamon, or other travelers of the Eighth Circuit. Whitney referred to Davis, Lincoln, and Swett as the "great triumvirate" of the traveling troupe of lawyers.[36] Mary Lincoln told Leonard Swett and David Davis that they were "the two friends whom my dearly beloved husband most loved."[37] The close relationship extended to Robert Lincoln, who came to look upon Davis as a second father.[38] Lincoln confirmed what everyone knew in describing the judge as one of his "confidential friends," his "very good personal and political friend."[39] He assured President Buchanan's secretary of war that he was "never associated with a better man."[40] Lincoln did not hesitate to admit that he kept no secrets from Davis.[41] This generally acknowledged special relationship between Lincoln and Davis added to the judge's authority over other convention workers.

The judge had an extra incentive for leading his friend's nomination effort at the 1860 Republican Convention: assuaging guilt for Lincoln's two US Senate losses. Davis was not in Springfield for the 1855 senatorial selection floor fight, which he believed was ineptly managed by Stephen Logan. After the defeat, Davis claimed that if he had been present for the vote, "he never would have consented to the 47 men being controlled by the 5."[42] After Douglas won the Senate seat in 1859, Davis lamented that he might have made a difference had he resigned his judgeship and campaigned full time for Lincoln. The Chicago convention offered a chance of redemption and an opportunity to achieve the ultimate prize. Davis did not resign from the judiciary in 1860 to campaign for Lincoln, but he did the next best thing by suspending court to come to the convention. And he did not come to Chicago to be an observer or minion of some less qualified and less dedicated floor leader. Besides being Lincoln's "strongest political backer" and his "most trusted advisor," the judge had a personal score to settle with Seward, Weed, and Greeley because of their failure to support Lincoln for the Senate in 1858.[43]

If Not Davis, Who?

From a practical standpoint, there was no viable alternative to Davis as floor leader. According to Jesse William Weik, who with William Herndon authored the first significant Lincoln biography, "The two men in that convention on whose counsel and judgment Lincoln probably placed the most implicit reliance were David Davis and Stephen T. Logan."[44] Logan's loyalty notwithstanding, Lincoln knew from past experience that his former law partner did not have the political skill necessary to orchestrate a dark horse victory in Chicago. Other possible managers also suffered from disqualifying flaws.

STEPHEN T. LOGAN   While Lincoln's former partner was the logical choice to manage the legislative floor fight for the Illinois senatorial seat in 1855, his proven political ineptitude, tendency to say the wrong thing at the wrong time, and inability to cut deals kept him from consideration for the top spot at the 1860 convention. Based on Logan's own campaigns for Congress and the Illinois Supreme Court, both Lincoln and Davis considered Logan ineffective at best and incompetent at worst as a political strategist and tactician (see chapter 1). And Logan would unwittingly confirm that judgment with a bonehead move on the floor of the Chicago convention during the nomination of the presidential contenders. Being caught up in the "unearthly" and prolonged cheering, dancing, and stomping after the unexpected seconding of Lincoln's nomination by an Ohio delegate, Logan made the faux pas of taking the floor and proclaiming that whether "in order or out of order, I propose this Convention and audience give three cheers for the man who is evidently their nominee." As almost anyone else would have foreseen, the ill-timed and offensive proposal was voted down in a chorus of hisses.[45]

WILLIAM BUTLER   Illinois state treasurer William Butler would appear to have been a potential choice to lead the Lincoln men in Chicago. He was a Republican state officeholder, had befriended Lincoln upon his arrival in Springfield and paid some of Lincoln's debts, and had shared his home with Lincoln for five years preceding Lincoln's marriage. The state treasurer served as one of Lincoln's seconds in a planned duel with James Shields in 1842 and was disappointed when the contest was called off.[46] Butler, however, had a well-deserved reputation for being ill-tempered. He was a sore loser when Congressman Lincoln recommended Turner R. King rather than Butler to fill the post of register of the Springfield land office.[47] In retaliation for the slight, Butler circulated petitions opposing Lincoln's attempt to become commissioner of the General Land Office after he left Congress in 1849. Butler supported Justin Butterfield for the job. David Davis, of course, supported Lincoln, complaining that "the appointment of old Butterfield, would be outrageous." According to William Herndon, the dispute between Lincoln and Butler became so bitter that the two did not speak for years, and "Butler opposed Lincoln in all his aspirations for office from 1847 till about 1858."[48] Maybe these past difficulties explain why on May 15 Seward men chose Butler as the recipient of their offer that if Illinois supported Seward, Lincoln could be vice president and New York would supply $100,000 to carry Illinois and Indiana in November.[49]

ORVILLE H. BROWNING   Orville Browning's loyalty to the Lincoln cause was always in question. A convention delegate and longtime friend of Lincoln, Browning had spent the later months of 1859 and the early part of 1860 rounding up support for former Missouri congressman Edward Bates's bid for the nomination. While traveling the court circuit, Browning promoted Bates to Illinois party officials such as Judd and anyone else who would listen. Upon his arrival at the Chicago convention, Rufus Wilson asked Browning who would receive the presidential nomination. Browning responded, "Oh, if Lincoln would withdraw, as he should do, we could nominate that great statesman, Edward Bates, of Missouri. But as it is, of course Seward will be nominated."[50] Browning also assured Bates that after providing the mandatory unit vote for Lincoln, the Illinois delegates would switch allegiance to Bates.[51]

The expressed preference for Bates led many of Lincoln's advisors, including Davis and Richard J. Oglesby, to oppose naming Browning as an Illinois delegate. Browning's support of Bates was well known by Lincoln. But Lincoln trusted that Browning would abide by the Illinois delegation's decision to vote as a unit for its favorite son at least while Lincoln remained a viable candidate. Besides, it was probably best to have Browning in a position where Davis could keep an eye on him during the convention. And Davis did just that. For all or at least most of Browning's visits to state delegations he was accompanied by Davis, Swett, or both.[52]

Even after Ohio put Lincoln over the top on the convention's third ballot, the crowd went into an uncontrollable frenzy, and Davis wept, Browning could do no better than make a "rather dull speech" in support of a motion to make the nomination unanimous.[53] That may have been because Browning still believed Bates was the best candidate and voted for Lincoln only because all members of the delegation were instructed to do so. After the convention, Browning complained that Bates would have been nominated if only the proceedings had dragged on longer.[54] It was only at the urging of David Davis and others that Browning undertook the task of convincing Bates to endorse Lincoln in the general election. Browning summed up his opinion of Lincoln in late 1864: "You know, strange as it may seem to you, that I am personally attached to the President, and have faithfully tried to uphold him, and make him respectable; tho' I never have been able to persuade myself that he was big enough for his position. Still, I thought he might get through, as many a boy through college, without disgrace, and without knowledge and I fear he is a failure."[55] Apart from the loyalty question, Browning did not want a managerial post in the nomination effort. According to his diary, the Illinois delegates "designated" Browning to be vice president of the delegation, but he declined. David Davis took the job instead. And Browning was not eager to get to the convention; he arrived in Chicago three days after Davis.[56]

NORMAN B. JUDD   Lincoln credited Norman Judd with contributing more to the success of the Illinois Republican Party than anyone else, in part because Judd was "the best organizer we have." But, like that of Browning, Judd's loyalty was always in doubt. While campaigning for the Republican nomination for governor a few months before the Chicago convention, Judd told a Lincoln supporter in a "sneering tone," "I am astonished that any one should think of [Lincoln's] nomination when we have first class statesmen in our party like Lyman Trumbull, Salmon P. Chase and John M. Palmer."[57] Contrary to Davis's vehement request that Lincoln appoint John Wentworth, mayor of Chicago, as a delegate to the convention, Lincoln shunned Wentworth and instead named Judd as an at-large delegate. Judd and Wentworth were bitter enemies, and appointing both to the delegation was out of the question. Lincoln felt that Judd's organizational skills and positions as chairperson of the Illinois Republican Party and member of the Republican National Committee outweighed doubts about his commitment to Lincoln's cause.[58] Subsequent events proved that Lincoln was right and that Davis's support of Wentworth was sorely misplaced.

Moreover, the number of Lincoln supporters who did not trust Judd was far too extensive to permit him to effectively direct the convention workers. Judd's detractors included the most ardent and long-standing Lincoln devotees: Davis, Swett, Lamon, Herndon, Dubois, Samuel L. Baker, Richard Yates, Stephen Logan, and Mary Lincoln.[59] Even Judd's friends, such as Jesse Fell, admitted the "bitter feeling" against Judd "throughout the state," especially among the former Whigs. This bitter feeling arose from a series of real and imagined injuries inflicted by Judd on Lincoln.[60]

As a state senator, Judd led four other anti-Nebraska Democrats in refusing to vote for Lincoln for US senator in 1855. This single episode was enough reason for Davis and many Lincoln confidants to dislike and distrust Judd.[61] Some, including Davis, also placed part of the blame for Lincoln's 1858 senatorial defeat at the feet of Judd, claiming that he used his chairmanship of the Republican State Central Committee to advance his own political interests rather than those of the party and Lincoln.[62] As usual, the Rail Splitter was more magnanimous than Davis. Lincoln did not accuse Judd of a lack of support in 1855 or find any mismanagement or self-dealing on Judd's part in 1858.[63] He considered the allegations against Judd unfair and unfounded. By the time of the 1860 convention, Lincoln felt that Judd could be trusted to promote Lincoln's candidacy. Besides, Judd was the state party chairman and a member of the Republican National Committee. Leaving him off the delegate list would raise eyebrows. Making him a delegate, however, was a far cry from assigning Judd to captain the team.

OTHER POTENTIAL CONVENTION MANAGERS   There were others in addition to Logan, Butler, Browning, and Judd whom Lincoln could have chosen to manage the convention effort. Swett and Lamon demonstrated complete loyalty to Lincoln, but both were accustomed to taking direction from Judge Davis. Besides, "life-of-the-party" Lamon was more of a host and entertainer than a political strategist.[64] Lyman Trumbull was out of consideration for two reasons. Lincoln stalwarts blamed Trumbull, together with Judd, for the Senate loss in 1855. Second, a week before the national convention Lincoln had to direct Trumbull to stop writing letters opposing or appearing to oppose Lincoln's candidacy.[65]

Illinois Republican gubernatorial candidate Richard Yates was available at the convention to lead the fight. But Yates drank heavily even when he had important duties to perform. The most embarrassing illustration of his alcohol problem occurred in January 1861, when newly elected Governor Yates appeared before the legislature too drunk to read his inaugural message. The clerk of the House read the address instead.[66] Illinois Secretary of State Ozias Hatch, an outspoken abolitionist, probably was not the best person to lobby the conservative and moderate delegates who would form the backbone of Lincoln's support.[67] Lincoln trusted conservative Republican Jesse K. Dubois, who was elected state auditor in 1856. Dubois, however, sometimes exhibited a tendency toward timidity. Attending the Republican State Convention in 1856 as a delegate from Lawrence County, Dubois was either intimidated or disgusted by the presence of abolitionist delegates to such an extent that he temporarily left the convention. Henry Whitney described the incident:

> When Lawrence County was called, no response came. The secretary was proceeding with the call when Lincoln arose and exclaimed, anxiously looking all around: "Mr. Chairman, let Lawrence be called again; there is a delegate in town from there, and a very good man he is, too." The call was repeated, but no reply came. The delegate, whose courage failed him at the last moment, in the presence of the Abolitionist contingent, was Jesse K. Dubois; he came, indeed, as a delegate; but, seeing Lovejoy and other Abolitionists there as cherished delegates, he, through indignation or timidity, stayed away for the time being.[68]

Lincoln friend and loyal supporter Richard Oglesby possessed many of the attributes of a solid convention manager. He demonstrated his savvy as a political strategist by flawlessly orchestrating the "rail-splitter" image and the unit vote for Lincoln at the state Republican convention held in Decatur a week before the national convention. He certainly could cut deals, such as his pact with party leaders when he successfully ran for governor in 1872. Immediately after being installed as governor, he resigned, thereby turning the office over to the lieutenant governor. In return, Oglesby was appointed to the United States Senate. But Oglesby was never "one of the inner circle of Lincoln's supporters" and did not command instant respect and obedience from the convention ground forces, as did Davis.[69] All things considered, Judge Davis was the only choice to lead the Lincoln forces in Chicago.

Chicago as the Convention Site

Davis and Swett saw the obvious advantage to Chicago hosting the presidential nominating convention.[70] At his friends' urging, Lincoln wrote to Norman Judd a week before the Republican National Committee meeting at which the location of the 1860 gathering would be determined. In his letter, Lincoln discussed the place and date of the upcoming Republican convention. Lincoln believed that the meeting should be held after the Democratic convention in Charleston, South Carolina, set for April 23, 1860. But he was curiously indifferent to the benefits of a venue in Chicago: "Some of our friends here, attach more consequence to getting the National convention into our State than I did, or do."[71] Unless Lincoln had some unexpressed reason to downplay the importance of the site, it would seem elementary politics to play the game on one's home field if possible.

Fortunately, Davis and others convinced Lincoln to bring the matter of the convention location to Judd's attention ahead of the Republican National Committee meeting in New York. Judd took Lincoln's hint and adroitly maneuvered the national party executive committee, by a single vote, to choose Chicago over St. Louis as the host city. The Seward supporters had argued for New York, Chase men advocated for Cleveland or Columbus, and Bates's backers wanted St. Louis. Ironically, Chicago won out because it was considered a neutral site, Illinois at that point not having a horse in the presidential race. Holding the convention in Chicago had one clear advantage and one hidden advantage. Obviously, Lincoln supporters could more easily access the site than could devotees of out-of-state candidates. Less obviously, Judd would be in charge of seating arrangements for the delegates.[72]

Outnumbering and Outshouting Seward Men

Arrangements had been made to ensure a good turnout of Lincoln enthusiasts from day one of the convention. But after the arrival of thirteen train cars of

Seward men with their band, marching formations, banners, and bellowing voices, Davis and Judd worried that the New Yorkers might outnumber and out-shout the Lincoln stalwarts. The fears crystallized when late on the second day of the convention, Seward "roughs," led by pugilist Tom Hyer, poured into the Wigwam, the structure especially built for the delegate gathering. "Determined to call a check to that game," Lincoln's lieutenants devoted the entire evening to summoning what Ward Lamon described as "loose fellows" to take command of the Wigwam. And with help from the chair of the Indiana Republican Central Committee, Alexander Conner, the effort was a huge success, bringing thou-sands from downstate Illinois and Indiana to Chicago.[73] Transporting the new recruits to Chicago was easily handled through Judd's railroad connections, but getting them into the convention center proved to be more difficult. Admission tickets had long been distributed, and none were left. More accurately stated, the original tickets had been allocated. Fell, Lamon, and Conner could see no harm in hiring a printer to produce "duplicate" tickets, or, as some less philanthropi-cally inclined persons might say, "forged" tickets. The Lincoln supporters used their freshly stamped tickets to pack the Wigwam early the next morning while Seward fans leisurely paraded to the convention site. Ward Lamon admitted that the new ticket holders filled every available space of the Wigwam, much of which "they had no business to fill." As a result, the Seward men were unable to get in "and were forced to content themselves with curbstone enthusiasm."[74]

Of course, the right type of Lincoln supporter was needed to fill the spectator seats. Prior service to the Republican Party was not necessary. Former Whigs, former Democrats, Know-Nothings, young, old, residents of northern, south-ern, or central Illinois and Indiana were all welcome. The only qualification was the ability and willingness to outcheer, outscream, and outstomp the Seward faction. So Davis directed Richard Oglesby, who was known for his "very stout lungs," to fill the public areas of the Wigwam "with a strong-voiced brigade of shouters," which Oglesby delighted in doing.[75] The result was an "uproar beyond description . . . a concentrated shriek that was positively awful" when Lincoln's name was mentioned.[76]

Delegate Seating

The Republican National Committee designated Judge David Wilmot of Penn-sylvania as temporary president of the convention. As a member of the arrange-ments committee Judd took charge of seating the delegations.[77]

Seating chairman may not seem like a powerful position, but in the hands of an old "trimmer" like Judd it became exactly that. A large raised platform at the front of the 100-by-180-foot wooden Wigwam accommodated six to seven hundred people, including the delegates and the press. The entire facility, including a balcony running along three sides of the building, held ten thousand people. Shortly before the convention, Judd configured the location of the state delegations by placing the New York men to the right of the podium in the front of the hall. He then encapsulated the Empire State delegation by surrounding it with other staunchly Seward states. On the left side of the stage he stationed Illinois and Indiana, with Pennsylvania and Missouri nearby. To the extent possible, Judd assigned the border states, the undecided delegations, and states supporting candidates other than Seward to the rear of the platform in close proximity to the Illinois and Indiana delegations and as far away as possible from the New York delegates. The advantage to the seating arrangement was unmistakable: "When the active excitement and canvassing in the Convention came on, the Seward men couldn't get over among the doubtful delegations at all to log-roll with them, being absolutely hemmed in by their own followers who were not likely to be swerved from their set preference for Seward."[78] The jampacked overflow crowd in the Wigwam benefited Judd's isolation scheme by adding to the difficulty of moving around in the hall.[79]

During the convention, news reporter Murat Halstead observed that hosting the meeting in his "own stamping ground" was an "immense advantage" for Lincoln. Gustave Koerner agreed saying that he was "pretty certain" that Lincoln's nomination rested in large part on the fact that Chicago hosted the convention.[80]

Davis Arrives in Chicago

Four things were clear to Davis when he arrived in Chicago on May 12, 1860. First, Seward was by far the odds-on favorite for the presidential nomination. If Seward unexpectedly failed, Bates was the likely benefactor.[81] Second, on Davis's arrival Lincoln could not claim first- or even second-tier candidate status. Norman Judd was able to convince the National Republican Committee to hold the convention in Chicago because Illinois was considered neutral ground for the presidential aspirants.[82] Third, Judge Davis was disappointed but not surprised to find that Judd was too consumed with his unsuccessful campaign for the gubernatorial nomination a week earlier to rent a headquarters for the Lincoln team in Chicago. Fourth, Davis knew that only by outworking other contenders would Lincoln have a chance at the nomination.[83]

Setting Up Headquarters

Judge Davis adjourned court in Danville to attend the Republican National Convention in Chicago as an at-large Lincoln delegate.[84] He arrived in time for the grand opening festivities of the Wigwam on Saturday, May 12, 1860, four days before the convention began. Davis quickly learned that except for Lincoln, all presidential contenders had established headquarters and deployed operatives. The judge was disappointed that Judd had been so obsessed with his pursuit of the governorship that he forgot to rent hotel rooms for a headquarters.[85] But Davis took Judd's blunder in stride. He had little faith in Judd's political abilities and even less trust in the Chicago state senator's loyalty to the Lincoln cause. But the enormity of the task at hand did not permit the luxury of complaining to Lincoln or calling out Judd for his oversight. Compounding Judd's mistake, the Chicago hotels were filled beyond capacity. Even Supreme Court justice John McLean's son could not find a room and wound up sleeping with three strangers.[86] In his usual direct manner, Davis "sent for" John B. Drake, proprietor of the Tremont House, and paid $300 for rooms on the third floor plus a "bonus" to private families to evacuate adjoining rooms at the booked-solid hotel. He adorned the suite with a sign designating the "Illinois Headquarters."[87]

Davis chose the Tremont because it was "the focus of political excitement" and because it housed many of the moderate and conservative delegates (including Edward Bates's supporters) whom the judge hoped to recruit for Lincoln. The judge and his team would concentrate their efforts on anti-Seward delegates rather than try to convert the Seward men, who were "true as steel to their champion, and [who would] cling to 'Old Irrepressible' . . . until the last gun is fired and the big bell rings."[88]

The Strategy

First and foremost, Davis had to hold the Illinois delegation as a unit for Lincoln. But a unanimous vote from his home state delegates by itself would not raise Lincoln to the second tier of presidential candidates. Davis needed to secure the support of another state on the first ballot to avoid the "favorite son" oblivion that would befall other candidates such as William Dayton of New Jersey and Jacob Collamer of Vermont. In addition to thwarting Seward's nomination on the first ballot, Lincoln needed a respectable total of about one hundred votes, which would ideally put the Rail Splitter in second place in the balloting and separate Seward and Lincoln from the rest of the field. Stealing a few votes in the New England states on the opening ballot would also help demonstrate the presumptive nominee's potential vulnerability. On subsequent ballots Davis had to show increasing strength, and the best way to achieve that was to make Lincoln the second choice of delegations committed to other candidates on the first ballot. The judge had to coalesce those unalterably opposed to Seward behind Lincoln rather than the front-running "moderate" candidate, Edward Bates. He could do so by demonstrating that Bates had fatal flaws rendering him unelectable, thereby positioning Lincoln as the most available alternative to Seward. Next, Davis had to convince those on the fence between supporting a moderate candidate and supporting Seward that the New York senator at the top of the ticket would bring defeat to state and local candidates. Fortunately, these arguments found fertile ground in the "doubtful" but absolutely essential states of Indiana, Pennsylvania, and New Jersey, all of which were lost to Democrat James Buchanan in the 1856 presidential election. Davis knew that to make this long-shot strategy work, he needed a group of delegates and nondelegates determined to outwork and outmaneuver the teams of the other candidates. Of course, during all the frantic dealings care had to be taken to treat all delegates "tenderly" and with respect, giving no offense and "making no fuss."[89]

Courting State Delegations

A Unit Vote by the Illinois Delegation

In preparation for the national convention, Lincoln had to first achieve favorite son status by obtaining a unit vote of the Illinois delegation. Accomplishing that, Lincoln could claim an advantage that eluded Chase of Ohio and Simon Cameron of Pennsylvania, who would arrive at the convention with split state delegations.[90] A majority of Illinois county Republican conventions had instructed their delegates to vote for Lincoln at the state convention in early May, but some northern county delegates continued to favor Seward, and some delegates from southern Illinois remained Bates supporters. In fact, about 30 percent of the counties sent noncommitted delegates to the state convention in Decatur.[91] It would take some showmanship to secure a unit vote commitment for Lincoln at the Illinois state convention not only because some delegates favored Seward and others Bates but also because some hard feelings existed between the supporters of the three candidates seeking the Republican nomination for governor. The gubernatorial candidacy of Norman Judd was, as usual, bitterly opposed by the mayor of Chicago, "Long John" Wentworth. Leonard Swett and Richard Yates also sought Republican slating for the governor's race. Davis busily campaigned for Swett. The nomination finally went to Richard Yates, however, when Swett dropped out of contention and urged his supporters to vote for Yates rather than Judd.[92]

Davis arrived in Decatur on Tuesday, May 8, and stayed at the Revere House. Although not a delegate, the judge "was one of the leading men" at the state convention. He attended the convention to help secure support for Swett's gubernatorial bid and to help assure a unanimous delegate vote for Lincoln. Davis, Oglesby, Fell, and John M. Palmer "wanted the endorsement of [Lincoln's] candidacy by the Illinois convention as the first essential step in his campaign."[93] But it was a state senate candidate and self-appointed convention organizer,

Richard Oglesby, who planned and executed the maneuvers that resulted in a block vote for Lincoln at least on the first national convention ballot.

Immediately after Joseph Gillespie accepted the position of president of the convention on the opening day of the Decatur meeting, Oglesby took center stage to invite "a distinguished citizen of Illinois" to come up to the dais. After a perfectly timed pause, Oglesby bellowed out the magic name of the honored guest, "Abraham Lincoln." Conveniently located in the very rear of the convention center, Lincoln could not maneuver his way through the throng of three thousand Republican partisans. So a flailing Lincoln was passed hand to hand over the heads of the roaring, delighted, hat-throwing crowd until he reached the speakers' platform, where he "acknowledged the cheers and sank into a chair."[94]

After the three candidates for governor were nominated but before the first ballot could be taken, Oglesby rose again to orchestrate the second demonstration for Lincoln. Oglesby surprised the delegates with the revelation that an "old Democrat" had a gift for them. On cue, Lincoln's cousin John Hanks and his friend Isaac Jennings carried in two rails supposedly split by Lincoln and Hanks. Dangling between the rails was a banner reading in part "ABRAHAM LINCOLN. The Rail Candidate FOR PRESIDENT IN 1860." Hysteria followed. According to Ward Lamon, the whole scene was "simply tempestuous and bewildering."[95] The next day the delegates approved a resolution requiring that all delegates to the national convention vote for Lincoln for president, in other words, vote as a unit for the Rail Splitter. Some of the Seward supporters, led by Thomas Turner of Freeport, whom Lincoln and Davis made Speaker of the House in 1855, objected to a unit vote. John Palmer countered with the obvious: the unbridled, spontaneous enthusiasm demonstrated by the two outbursts for Lincoln proved beyond any doubt the unanimity of the delegates. The Seward holdouts finally consented to abide by the Illinois state convention's instruction for a unanimous vote for Lincoln.[96]

It would be up to Davis to keep this diverse group of delegates together for Lincoln in Chicago. By accepting the unit resolution, the delegates agreed that Lincoln was "the first choice of Illinois for the Presidency." The resolution did not state or imply that Lincoln was the state's only choice or that the delegates could not switch to other candidates as the balloting progressed. Since many delegates believed that Lincoln's candidacy would not survive to the second ballot, there was discussion in Decatur about delegates moving to other candidates if Lincoln's bid fizzled early. The Illinois delegates favoring Seward promised to vote for Lincoln on the initial ballot but "really wanted and expected finally to vote" for Seward.[97] Davis identified at least eight delegates "who would gladly have gone to Seward."[98] It would make the judge's job of holding the Illinois delegation together easier if he could convince another state to also vote as a block for Lincoln.

A Unit Vote by the Indiana Delegation

The united vote of the Illinois delegates made Lincoln no more than a favorite son. Lincoln needed the vote of another state to move beyond that dead-end status. States bordering Illinois should have been natural allies, but most were unlikely to offer substantial support. No influential Republican leader in Wisconsin was committed to Lincoln. His speeches in Milwaukee, Beloit, and Janesville in late September and early October 1859 did not garner him any significant backing. His speech in Milwaukee concerned nonpolitical topics, and one historian described his visits to the other two southern Wisconsin cities as "brief and unspectacular."[99] Wisconsin was solidly for Seward.

Nor were the bordering states of Missouri, Iowa, and Kentucky fertile ground for Davis to cultivate. Missouri was solidly for Bates. Iowa's eight delegates were divided among six candidates on the first ballot. Kentucky with twenty-three votes would have significantly boosted Lincoln's candidacy, but there was no hope of unifying the delegation for any single candidate. No fewer than five of Kentucky's delegates voted for Seward on all three ballots, and Chase held four of Kentucky's votes all the way through the third and final ballot.[100] Indiana remained as the only possibility for a unit vote for Lincoln.

Indiana, where Lincoln spent most of his youth, had no favorite son candidate. Like Illinois, the Hoosier State had a large contingent of old Whigs who now were anti-Seward Republicans in search of a moderate presidential nominee. John D. Defrees, chair of the Indiana Republican Central Committee, spoke for the majority of state Republicans when he told Iowa senator James Harlan that the Democrats would prevail in the 1860 elections "if ultra men are permitted to dictate our policy, and name our candidate." Defrees backed Bates but was amenable to supporting most any candidate who did not espouse abolitionism.[101] Indiana gubernatorial candidate and convention delegate Henry Lane was of a like mind, believing that "with Seward he [Lane] and his party will inevitably be defeated; but with Bates, McLean, or Lincoln, and perhaps others, he can sweep the state."[102] A strong contingent supported Bates at the February Indiana State Republican Convention, but any thought of a unit vote for him was illusory because of the strong German American hostility toward Bates.[103] Supreme Court justice John McLean also boasted support among both the Indiana delegation and the Indiana press. On April 19, 1860, an editorial in the state's premier Republican newspaper, the *Indianapolis Daily Journal*, favored the nomination of Justice McLean. The editorial, however, also heartened Lincoln's team by concluding that "next to Judge McLean, we believe Abram [*sic*] Lincoln of Illinois presents the best combination of qualities as a candidate and officer." Thus, an editorial of the most influential Republican newspaper in Indiana played right into the "second choice" strategy of Lincoln and Davis.[104]

Entitled to twenty-six votes, Indiana tied Massachusetts for the fifth largest number of delegates. Making the Hoosier State even more valued, the delegation had early on agreed to vote as a block.[105] Most important, Indiana, together with Illinois, New Jersey, and Pennsylvania, were viewed as pivotal states that Republicans had to carry in 1860 to win the presidency. If Indiana could be convinced to join Illinois in unanimously endorsing Lincoln on the first ballot, then Lincoln would be halfway to securing the four essential states. Locking up Indiana would also permit the chairman of the state's delegation, Caleb B. Smith, to second Lincoln's nomination, thereby broadcasting to all the delegates, especially those from New Jersey and Pennsylvania, that Indiana was solidly behind Lincoln.[106]

Davis's attempt to sway the Hoosiers was aided by several other factors, including that Lincoln and Davis knew some of the neighboring state's delegates from court sessions held in Illinois counties bordering Indiana.[107] In addition, Lincoln had served in Congress with fellow Whig Caleb B. Smith, who headed the Indiana delegation. The two were good friends in part because of their shared opposition to the Mexican War.[108] Lincoln had sporadically campaigned in Indiana for himself and others. He campaigned for Whig presidential candidate Henry Clay in southern Indiana from October 24 until November 4, 1844. His speech in Indianapolis on September 19, 1859, helped to solidify his relationships with important state Republicans, including John D. Defrees, who headed the city's welcoming committee that day, and Smith, who introduced Lincoln to the large audience assembled at Masonic Hall. Lincoln's Hoosier antecedents permitted him to address the crowd as "Fellow Citizens of the State of Indiana" and to remind the attendees that he grew up along the Ohio River in Spencer County.[109]

Immediately upon arriving in Chicago, Davis made courting Indiana delegates a top priority. The urgency of the task intensified when Davis heard the speech given by Indiana gubernatorial candidate Henry Lane at the dedication of the Wigwam on May 12. In his welcoming speech Lane mentioned several presidential contenders, including Seward, Chase, McLean, and even Nathaniel Banks of Massachusetts. Lane's failure to mention Lincoln with the others must have concerned Davis.[110] So "as soon as Davis came to the city he launched into private meetings with the Indiana delegation, intensive talks that continued day after day." It was not necessary for Davis to persuade the Indiana delegates that a Seward candidacy would bring defeat to Republicans running for state and local offices. The delegates were already convinced of that. Davis's job was to satisfy the delegation that Lincoln was the best alternative to Seward. The judge's work was cut out for him, because while a few Indiana delegates leaned toward Lincoln, most of the delegation was split between Bates and McLean.[111] Addressing the Indiana delegation on behalf of McLean, Pennsylvania congressman Thaddeus Stevens assured the Hoosiers that McLean could carry the Keystone State.[112] Davis surely responded to Congressman Stevens by indirectly reminding the Indiana delegates of McLean's advanced age, an "objection [that seemed] to occur to every one." In promoting Lincoln over McLean, Davis was also aided by the admission of McLean's supporters that he would "not show any strength on the first few ballots" and that his nomination hopes depended on a deadlocked convention. With a grand total of twelve votes on the first ballot, McLean was never in contention.[113]

Francis P. Blair, Francis P. Blair Jr., and New York newspaper publisher Horace Greeley were lobbying Indiana on Bates's behalf. Davis countered with plenty of ammunition against Bates. Bates was not even a Republican, he would certainly lose his home state to the Democrats, and German Republicans had vowed to boycott the Republican Party if Bates led the ticket.[114] Davis underscored Bates's anti-German sentiment at each meeting with the Indiana people. At some undetermined point before the convention began, Davis secured at least a tentative commitment from the Indiana delegation to provide Lincoln a unit vote on the first ballot.[115] But some Indiana delegates were still wavering as late as the day before the convention's first vote. Because of the fluidity of the situation, the Indiana contingent agreed to a joint meeting with the Pennsylvania delegates at the Cook County Courthouse to try "to work out a common position." When Davis received intelligence that Francis Blair Jr. and other Bates delegates from Missouri, including two delegates of German descent, were going to speak at the meeting, the judge dispatched Orville Browning and former Illinois lieutenant governor Gustave Koerner to counter the pitch for Bates.

Davis's strategy for the courthouse meeting was a simple one-two punch. Koerner would unequivocally tell the Indiana and Pennsylvania delegates that a ticket led by Bates meant no German votes for the presidential nominee or local Republican candidates in any state. Most Germans had distrusted Bates since 1856, when he presided over the Whig presidential convention. Millard Fillmore was nominated at that convention. The anti-immigrant Know-Nothing Party also nominated Fillmore as its presidential candidate that year. Adding fuel to the fire, Bates had backed Know-Nothing candidates in municipal elections in St. Louis. Based on Bates's record, Koerner told the crowd that he was "astonished" that some German Republicans from Missouri talked of supporting Bates. Koerner pledged that if Bates was nominated by the Republicans, he and other prominent Germans would campaign against Bates. The second prong of Davis's one-two punch came from Orville Browning. Everyone knew that Browning had long supported Bates and that Browning came to the convention hoping that Lincoln would withdraw, paving the way for the nomination of Bates.[116] Who better than Browning to stand before the delegates and admit that Bates could not win. According to Koerner, after the speeches, the Indiana delegates decided to vote for Lincoln on the first ballot, and a "large majority" of Pennsylvania delegates decided to support Lincoln after fulfilling their commitment to vote for favorite son Simon Cameron on the first ballot. As it turned out, Indiana voted for Lincoln on the first ballot, and Pennsylvania gave Lincoln forty-eight votes on the second ballot and fifty-two votes on the third ballot.[117]

Of course, rumors freely circulated after Lincoln's nomination that a deal had been cut to secure Indiana's support. As the years passed, the rumors became more and more outlandish. Joseph Medill stated that his coeditor on the *Chicago Press and Tribune*, Charles H. Ray, visited the Indiana delegation on the day before the convention opened and promised a cabinet post to Caleb Smith and the position of commissioner of Indian Affairs to William P. Dole in return for a first-ballot unit vote for Lincoln. According to Medill, when Indiana accepted the proposal, Ray "hurried back to Lincoln headquarters," burst into a crowded room, and announced to Davis and the others, "We are going to have Indiana for Old Abe, sure." Medill asked Ray how he had obtained the vote, and Ray responded, "By the Lord, we promised them everything they asked."[118]

The story is undoubtedly fabricated. To accept that Davis ceded control of Lincoln's campaign to freelancers like Ray, permitting them to flit around, freely trading governmental posts to delegations of their choosing, runs counter to Davis's obsession to control everything. To believe that Davis would have sat quietly through Ray's "news flash" is absurd. If Ray had traded two high-level government jobs for Indiana's commitment before the convention began, then why did the Indiana delegates meet at the courthouse the day before the vote to confer with the Pennsylvania delegates about selecting a candidate to jointly support and listen to a pitch from Bates supporters? And if Ray thought he had authority to cut deals, why did he later send a note to Lincoln suggesting that Judd, Davis, or, if no one else was better, Ray be authorized to cut deals, because "a pledge or two may be necessary when the pinch comes."[119] Finally, prior to arriving at the convention, Lincoln had advised Indiana delegate Cyrus M. Allen that he would be dealing with Davis and Dubois, not Ray. As Caleb Smith would later explain, rather than cutting a deal, the Indiana Republicans "generally supposed that Mr. L. would select some man from this state for a place in his cabinet." Indiana felt entitled to a reward for being the only state besides Illinois that committed to Lincoln on the first ballot. It was a tribute to Davis and his team that Indiana was persuaded to come over to Lincoln without the promise of a cabinet position.[120]

Virginia and Kentucky

Davis's delegate success in Virginia and Kentucky is another testament to the planning and execution of the Lincoln strategy. Going into the convention, both states were considered Seward strongholds. At the organizational meeting of the Virginia delegation in Chicago on May 15, Seward, Bates, and Lincoln had support, but a preliminary poll showed that Seward led the other candidates.[121]

Virginia delegate John C. Underwood was one of the solid Seward supporters. Underwood organized and led what little there was of a Republican Party in Virginia. A strong abolitionist, he admired Seward for his unwavering opposition to slavery. In 1858, with financial support from Seward, Underwood and his friends, including pro-Seward delegate Archibald Campbell, organized the fledgling Republican Party in northwestern Virginia and purchased the *Wheeling Intelligencer* and three smaller newspapers.[122] The *Wheeling Daily Intelligencer* became the leading Republican newspaper in the slaveholding states. As a delegate to the 1856 Republican National Convention, Underwood planned to vote for Seward if his name was placed in nomination. Underwood traveled to New England promoting Seward's nomination in 1860.[123] That is not to say that Underwood disliked Lincoln. In fact, in 1858 he wrote Lyman Trumbull, offering to support Lincoln if he chose to run for Congress. But Seward was the clear leader among Virginia delegates before the convention maneuvering began.[124]

Davis was the first candidate's manager to request a meeting with the Virginia delegation. He approached Virginia as he had approached other states by sending Illinois representatives who had roots or contacts in the targeted state to confer with the delegates. Davis assigned Ward Hill Lamon, who had grown up in Virginia, studied medicine there, and married a woman from a prominent landowning family in Virginia, to the delegation.[125] With a group of four or five others, Lamon visited the Virginia men shortly after they arrived on May 15. Lamon most likely took a soft-sell approach, reminiscing about family, friends, and acquaintances and sympathizing with the woes of being a Republican in a slave state. He then would have moved to his personal and professional relationship with Lincoln; Lamon would have outlined his firsthand knowledge of the candidate's honesty, integrity, qualifications, and solid Republican credentials. Lamon and his associates described "gallant Abe" as the man "whose first act was to maul rails and whose last act was to maul Douglas." Mention of Lincoln's humble origins and rise to a prominent position in the Republican Party would also have fit nicely in Lamon's remarks. No doubt Lamon and the others introduced the issue of Lincoln's availability but would have done so gently so as not to offend the many Seward supporters in the room. According to Seward delegate Archibald Campbell, by the close of the presentation there was "a decided good feeling for Lincoln." At nine o'clock the next morning the Old Dominion delegation was visited by the Maryland men, a majority of whom supported Bates, with the rest for Seward. For the remainder of the morning the Virginians heard speeches on behalf of Bates and Seward. Montgomery Blair, the older brother of Francis P. Blair

Jr., spoke on behalf of Bates, and a slew of Seward supporters, including William Evarts, presented the New York senator's case.[126]

After the first session of the convention concluded, Davis visited the Virginians, arguing the availability issue and Seward's inability to carry the doubtful states. Davis found that the chair of the delegation, Alfred Caldwell, although an abolitionist, supported Lincoln over the "courtly and distinguished" Seward because, as Davis argued, Lincoln would have a better chance of election.[127] Greeley also addressed the Virginia group, arguing for Bates and just as vehemently denouncing Seward as unelectable.[128] Davis's approach with Virginia and the other delegations was having an effect. By the end of the day, delegate Archibald Campbell reported that "he should not be a bit surprised to see Lincoln [become] the nominee of the Convention."[129]

On the evening before the convention vote, Davis's forces from Illinois and friends from other states worked nonstop to prevent Seward's nomination and to gain votes for Lincoln. At one o'clock in the morning a pale and haggard Henry Lane of Indiana was still making the rounds from one delegation to another. He "pleaded" with the Virginia men that party success was more important than any individual candidate and that Lincoln could win and Seward could not. Lane explained that Seward would lose the vote of the Know-Nothings, that he was too ultra for many conservative Republicans, and that his political managers, led by Weed, had been implicated in corrupt practices in New York. The constant warning of the Illinois team, reinforced by out-of-state backers such as Henry Lane, worried the Virginians. The proof came in the voting. Lincoln outpolled Seward fourteen votes to eight votes on all three convention ballots.[130]

Lincoln's nomination took the *Wheeling Daily Intelligencer* by surprise. On May 19 the Virginia paper reported, "We certainly had not the most remote idea that Mr. Lincoln would be chosen over so many prominent candidates." But the paper accepted Lincoln's old Whig and conservative credentials over the ultra views of others and acknowledged his full commitment to the principles of the Republican Party.[131] The number of delegates awarded Virginia at the convention helped Lincoln but certainly did not reflect the Republican strength in the state. In the November election, Lincoln received just 1.1 percent of the votes cast in Virginia.[132]

Davis's approach to the uncommitted delegation of Kentucky mirrored his approach to Virginia. He assigned Richard Yates, who spent the first sixteen years of his life in Kentucky, and Stephen Logan, another native Kentuckian who taught, married, and practiced law in the state, to visit the delegation. In addition to discussing and vouching for Lincoln's character and availability, Logan and Yates would have stressed Lincoln's close ties with the Blue Grass State. Lincoln and his wife were born there, Henry Clay was his political idol, and all three of Lincoln's law partners came from Kentucky.[133]

Meeting in November 1859, the Kentucky State Republican Convention was the first state caucus to select delegates to the national convention. As in all things Republican in Kentucky, Cassius Marcellus Clay was the main attraction and, according to the *Pittsburgh Gazette*, was chosen as an at-large delegate. But Clay did not attend the national convention. Maybe his absence was due to the unsupported belief that he was the second choice of many delegates and that he could be nominated if Seward and Chase faltered.[134] Clay's favorite candidate, other than himself, is unclear. According to Clay, at first he stayed neutral because Chase and Seward were his friends and were equally qualified for the presidency. After dining with Seward, however, he rejected supporting the New Yorker and made Chase his "first choice." But because the Ohio delegation was divided and so Chase could not be nominated, Clay was left with either Bates or Lincoln. After the convention, Clay claimed that he chose Lincoln. While this account is inconsistent with Clay's more contemporaneous letter to Seward in which Clay claimed that he had been working for Seward all along, Clay's shifting between favored candidates symbolizes the division among the Kentucky delegates.[135] On the first ballot, six candidates received votes from Kentucky delegates: Chase had eight, Lincoln six, Seward five, Benjamin Wade two, and Justice McLean and Charles Sumner one vote each.[136] Without doubt, visits by the Blairs and Horace Greeley to the Kentucky delegation hurt Seward. Seward's manager, Thurlow Weed, agreed that the Blairs were effective against Seward in the slave states, including Kentucky and Virginia.[137] While the Blairs and Greeley diminished Seward's prospects, they did nothing to advance the candidacy of their candidate, Bates. Bates did not receive a single vote from Kentucky on any ballot. The Illinois men, led by Kentucky-born Stephen Logan, Richard Yates, and John M. Palmer, together with indispensable backup from Henry Lane and Andrew G. Curtin, plus Horace Greeley's nonstop attack on Seward all worked to weaken the front runner. Lincoln went from six Kentucky votes on the first ballot to nine votes on the second ballot and to thirteen votes on the final ballot.[138]

The New England States

Davis knew that Seward had strength in the New England states. Indeed, the day before the convention began, Thurlow Weed was certain that he had Maine, New Hampshire, Vermont, and Massachusetts "in his pocket."[139] But regardless of Weed's belief, the delegations from those states plus the delegations from Rhode Island and Connecticut came to convention without instructions from their state conventions to vote for any particular candidate. Davis also knew that some New England delegates harbored doubts of Seward's electability and feared that his nomination would bring down Republicans running for state offices in the fall elections. So Davis immediately contacted the northeasterners as they arrived in Chicago both personally and through emissaries. Gathering even a few votes from the New England states early in the balloting would prove that Lincoln was more than a regional candidate and reveal Seward's vulnerability in his own backyard. So, starting on the Saturday before the convention, Davis sent Illinois men to the New England states in which they had roots to reminisce and to point out Lincoln's superior availability.

MAINE From the very beginning, Davis paid close attention to Maine. He wanted badly to break into the New England states, especially Maine, since it would be the first state called in the balloting. So Leonard Swett and three others of his choosing were deployed to visit the Maine delegation. Swett was born in Maine, attended school there, read law in Portland, and maintained contacts in the state. On Tuesday, when Browning finally arrived in Chicago, Davis took Browning to speak with the Pine Tree State delegates. Browning spoke to the group and then, together with Davis, "moved among the delegates." Davis and Swett later told Lincoln that they were "entirely indebted" to Maine delegate George Lawrence in bringing over some Maine and Pennsylvania votes to the successful nominee.[140] Davis's and delegate Lawrence's efforts were reinforced by Maine senator Hannibal Hamlin's advice to the delegation to be guided by the Illinois and Indiana men because Seward could not be elected.[141] As a result, Lincoln captured a surprising six Maine votes on the first ballot. Seward received ten votes.[142]

NEW HAMPSHIRE Lincoln's travels through New England following his Cooper Union speech in New York helped him gain support in New Hampshire. In March 1860 Lincoln gave well-attended speeches in Concord, Manchester, Dover, and finally Exeter near Phillips Exeter Academy, where Robert Lincoln attended school. The substance of Lincoln's remarks impressed State Republican chair Edward H. Rollins and other party leaders.[143] Success with the New Hampshire delegation was also fostered by Davis's intelligence network, which fed him information on the ever-changing preferences of the Granite State representatives. Based on what he learned, Davis initiated repeated visits to the delegation. On Tuesday, May 15, the judge and Browning visited New Hampshire, with Browning giving a speech to the entire group, followed by Davis's and Browning's usual practice of talking to delegates individually. This visit may have turned the tide from Seward to Lincoln.[144] And while it has been claimed that New Hampshire chairperson Amos Tuck, who served with Lincoln in Congress, "led the New Hampshire delegation in favor of Lincoln," he actually voted for Chase on the first ballot.[145]

Even though Tuck realized that Chase had only a "slight following," Tuck's friendship with the Ohio senator dictated his initial vote. Other New Hampshire delegates, including George G. Fogg, who served as secretary of the national

party executive committee, probably had more to do with Lincoln's strong showing within the delegation.[146] Lincoln received seven of New Hampshire's ten
votes on the first ballot, with Seward, Chase, and Frémont receiving one vote
each. On the second ballot Tuck and another Granite State delegate switched
to Lincoln.[147] Davis's strategy of peeling off first-ballot votes from New England
and increasing Lincoln's total on subsequent ballots worked like a charm in
New Hampshire. Davis's success is especially impressive considering Thurlow
Weed's claim that New Hampshire "positively pledged" to Weed and to New
York Republican chairman William M. Evarts a unit vote for Seward on the
second ballot. Lincoln received nine votes and Seward one vote on both the
second and third ballots.[148]

CONNECTICUT   Davis assigned former Whig Gurdon Saltonstall Hubbard to
contact the Connecticut delegation. Hubbard's forebears hailed from Connecticut, including his namesake, who was considered the first elected governor of a
British colony in America.[149] Gideon Welles, head of the Connecticut delegation,
backed Chase on all three ballots. He liked Chase almost as much as he disliked
Seward. Welles's distaste for Seward did not arise from the New York senator's
political views or personality. It arose primarily because of Seward's association
with the "often profligate, unscrupulous, and always debauching and corrupting" political lobby run by Thurlow Weed. Welles could not envision promoting
Seward and his "special managing friends" from Albany to Washington, thereby
permitting them to contaminate the entire country.[150]

In March 1860 the chair of the Connecticut delegation spent a few hours
talking with Lincoln before Lincoln's speech in Hartford, Connecticut, and
came away with a favorable impression of the Rail Splitter. But that was not
enough to persuade Welles to abandon Chase. Believing that anyone was better
than Seward, the future secretary of the navy indirectly aided the Lincoln cause
by doing his best to persuade the New England delegates to back anyone but
Seward. In that endeavor, he was enormously successful with his home state
delegation. Seward's sole vote from Connecticut came on the third ballot. On
the first ballot Bates received seven votes, Lincoln and Chase two votes each,
and Benjamin Wade one vote. On the second ballot Lincoln and Bates tied with
four votes, and Chase and Cassius Clay had two votes each. On the third ballot
one Clay vote went to Seward, and the totals for the other candidates remained
the same. Just as important as his effort with his home state delegation, Welles
worked with the Rhode Island delegates to limit Seward to no votes on the first
two ballots and one vote on the third ballot.[151]

VERMONT   Vermont arrived at the convention with an uncommitted delegation. Some delegates favored Seward, and others favored Governor Nathaniel
P. Banks of Massachusetts. With the state's ten delegates up for grabs, lobbying

efforts were fierce. Pennsylvanian gubernatorial candidate Andrew Curtin and Alexander McClure, the Pennsylvania Republican chairman, initially spoke for Bates, and so did Horace Greeley. New York chair William M. Evarts, in his usual fashion, made a "forceful and impressive" case for Seward. After Evarts's speech most of the Vermont delegates favored Seward. But Seward's old nemesis of "availability" was bluntly argued by the Illinois team, including native Vermont-ers Sam Parks and Gurdon Saltonstall Hubbard. Presentations by representatives of Indiana and New Jersey reinforced the theme and convinced the Vermont delegates that Seward was unelectable. Believing that the first ballot would not be decisive, the Green Mountain men voted unanimously for favorite son Jacob Collamer, a moderate US senator. To the jaw-dropping surprise of the Seward men, Lincoln received all ten votes on the second and third ballots.[152]

RHODE ISLAND   The Rhode Island gubernatorial election of 1860 supplied exhibit A to Davis's contention that an extreme or "ultra man" such as Seward would ensure national and state defeat in the fall elections. On January 4, 1860, the delegates to the Rhode Island Republican State Convention met to name a slate of candidates for state offices. The convention delegates, dominated by the more "radical" element of the party, nominated Seth Padelford for governor. Regardless of whether Padelford actually deserved the ultra mantle placed on him by opposition delegates, the conservatives bolted from the convention and nominated William Sprague for governor. The Democrats also named Sprague as their candidate. At the general election on April 4, the conservative Republican and Democratic coalition elected Sprague with about 53 percent of the vote: "The unalterable fact was that the Republicans lost an election in their New England stronghold. And also incontestable was the reason for the defeat: the issue of radicalism had split the party and had driven off the conservatives. The Rhode Island election underscored the ease with which the frail political alliance between conservatives and Republicans could be sundered."[153]

The importance of the Rhode Island Republican defeat in advancing the Lincoln candidacy was not lost on his supporters. Mark W. Delahay, a Kansas backer and distant relative, wrote Lincoln three days after the Rhode Island election that while he regretted the loss, the outcome "argue[s] strongly against the availability of the Seward movement." Delahay considered the unexpectedly narrow victory of the Republican candidate for governor in Connecticut further evidence that an ultra like Seward could not be elected. Iowan Hawkins Taylor agreed, telling Lincoln that "the Elections in Connecticut and Rhode Island have been any thing but favourable to Seward." Three weeks later, Senator Lyman Trumbull wrote from Washington that the elections had the congressional delegations from Connecticut and Rhode Island worried that Seward would lose both states.[154] The *Chicago Press and Tribune* warned the members of the fast-approaching Chicago convention to heed the lesson taught by the Rhode Island defeat and the "close shave" victory in Connecticut. The lesson was clear: "The nomination of a Radical Republican for President may result in the loss of even New England States."[155] The results of state elections in Rhode Island and Connecticut could not have fit better into Davis's strategy.

The same "radical" element of the Rhode Island State Republican Convention that nominated Seth Padelford for governor elected its slate of delegates to the Chicago convention. But some conservatives, including Republican senator James F. Simmons, were also selected. Maybe it was the blatant hostility of Senator Simmons toward the Seward candidacy.[156] Or maybe the delegates were not as ultra as the conservatives painted them. Or maybe Davis convinced the delegates of Seward's unelectability. For whatever reason, Seward did not receive a single vote on the first or second ballot from the Rhode Island delegation and received only one vote on the third ballot. Lincoln went from no votes on the first ballot to three votes on the second ballot and five votes on the final ballot.[157]

MASSACHUSETTS   Like many New England states, the Massachusetts Republican Convention suffered from a radical-moderate split. Radicals succeeded in selecting nineteen of the twenty-six delegates to the national convention. Although the hearts of the radical delegates belonged to Chase, they backed Seward as the more electable candidate. Some of the moderates ostensibly supported Seward but hoped for a deadlocked convention that might nominate favorite son Governor Nathaniel Banks as a compromise.[158]

John A. Andrew chaired the Massachusetts delegation. He held passionate abolitionist views, and his antislavery speeches drew widespread attention. He also provided legal services to John Brown after the events at Harpers Ferry.[159] Notwithstanding his commitment to Seward, on the day before the convention, Andrew led a Massachusetts contingent in a visit with the four doubtful states Illinois, Indiana, New Jersey, and Pennsylvania. According to Thomas H. Dudley, Andrew confronted the four swing states with their own mantra that Seward could not win. But, Andrew continued, that opinion was pointless, because the four essential states could not unite behind a candidate instead of Seward. Most Indiana and Illinois delegates favored Lincoln. Pennsylvania gave the nod to Cameron, and New Jersey backed its favorite son, William Dayton. So Andrew told the combined delegations that unless they agreed on a candidate, the New England delegates would vote for Seward. Andrew added, however, that if the four states agreed on one man, Massachusetts and its friends would give that candidate enough votes to secure the nomination.[160] It is puzzling that even before the convention began, Andrew contemplated abandoning Seward in favor of a compromise candidate. Just as peculiar was the proposal of Massachusetts abolitionist and Seward stalwart Ensign Kellogg that Illinois, Pennsylvania, and New Jersey provide Massachusetts with the names of three candidates who they thought could carry their states. According to the *Springfield Republican*, New Jersey responded that Dayton, Lincoln, and Banks could carry the state. Pennsylvania countered with Cameron, McLean, and Lincoln. Quick-thinking David Davis responded with only one name, Lincoln, justified by the fact that no other Republican could beat the presumptive Democratic nominee and state legend, Stephen Douglas, in his home state.[161]

Maybe Davis's consistent and persistent message started to worry some of the Massachusetts members about Seward's electability. That would help explain the willingness of Seward supporters such as Andrew and Kellogg to seek a compromise candidate. The effect of a Seward nomination on candidates farther down the ballot certainly concerned Andrew and Kellogg, both of whom planned to seek the nomination for governor at the August 1860 Massachusetts Republican Convention.[162] Davis and his lieutenants pounded the unelectability theme into the Bay State delegates from the moment they stepped off the train. While all meetings are not documented, we know that Davis and Browning met with the Massachusetts delegates on May 15 and that Jesse Dubois was in constant communication with the chair of the convention, Massachusetts delegate George Ashmun. Butler and Dubois, along with Yates and Lane of Indiana, addressed the Bay State delegation on May 16.[163] Davis took a personal interest in Massachusetts because he maintained contact with family and friends in the state, visited there, and subscribed to at least one Massachusetts newspaper.[164]

National Republican committee member John Z. Goodrich of Massachusetts also worked to move his state's delegates from Seward to Lincoln by the third ballot. Goodrich spoke to his state's delegates, emphasizing that Lincoln could win Pennsylvania and Indiana. He also defended Lincoln against attacks by Seward supporters that Lincoln was not fit to be president. Goodrich, who had succeeded Davis's brother-in-law, Julius Rockwell, in Congress, was a close friend of Davis.[165] Massachusetts delegate and former Illinoisan Edward L. Pierce told William Herndon that he was for Lincoln from the start, but to "keep company" with his delegation he voted for Seward on the first two ballots.[166]

Considering the strong Seward bent of the Massachusetts delegates, Davis achieved all he could hope to. On the first ballot the Davis forces had limited success, obtaining four votes for Lincoln and convincing one Seward delegate to abstain. That gave Seward twenty-one votes. On the second ballot the abstaining delegate voted for Seward. But with the groundwork laid by Davis, Goodrich, and others, and after seeing the surge of Lincoln support on the second ballot, four Seward votes switched to Lincoln, giving him eight votes and Seward eighteen votes on the third ballot.[167]

Ohio

On March 1, 1860, the Ohio Republican Convention adopted the following resolution supporting Senator Salmon P. Chase for the presidential nomination: "*Resolved,* That while the Republicans of Ohio will give their united support to the nominee of the Chicago Convention, they would indicate as their first choice and recommend to said Convention the name of Salmon P. Chase, of Ohio." Although the resolution would seem to require a unit vote for Chase in Chicago, some of the delegates elected from Ohio districts believed that it only applied to Ohio's appointed at-large delegates. The elected delegates felt free to vote for other presidential candidates based on the preference of the voters in their districts. In addition, anti-Chase Republicans felt that the resolution was not "fairly obtained." The fact that the resolution was not unanimous also weakened its hold on the dissenting delegates. Sixty-five counties voted in favor of the Chase resolution, the delegates of seventeen counties divided on the proposition, four counties voted against it, and two counties abstained.[168] Adding to Chase's woes, according to Samuel Galloway, a former Ohio congressman, a significant segment of the Chase men had "but little fervent attachment" to him, and three-quarters of his delegates were likely to abandon his candidacy by the second or third ballot. In Galloway's view, the desertion would result from the recognition that a conservative candidate was needed.[169] Even before the convention began, some Ohio delegates believed Lincoln to be that man. Jesse Dubois wrote Lincoln on May 13, 1860, that "eight of the Ohio men are urging you on with great vigor."[170] An informal poll of the Ohio delegation on the afternoon of May 15 supports Dubois's assessment. The poll disclosed that Chase had the support of twenty-four state delegates, Lincoln had nine, Wade had five, McLean had three, and Seward and Bates had one each. Another internal poll taken under the assumption that Chase dropped out of the race gave Wade twenty-two votes, followed by Lincoln with sixteen, McLean three, Seward two, and Bates one vote. The *Maine Union and Journal* listed the top three choices of the Ohio delegates as Chase, Wade, and Lincoln, in that order.[171]

Lincoln rose to the top out-of-state choice among the Ohio delegates in part because of his debates with Douglas and in part because of his speeches in Columbus, Dayton, Hamilton, and Cincinnati in the middle of September 1859. On September 1, 1859, Lincoln was invited by the Ohio Republican central committee to give three or four speeches to rebut Stephen Douglas's expected remarks during the Little Giant's upcoming visit to the state. The committee believed that Lincoln would boost Republican chances in the October state elections, especially in the old Whigs sections of central and southern Ohio. The next day, Peter Zinn, a member of the committee, invited Lincoln to speak in Cincinnati. Zinn signed the invitation as chairman of the Hamilton County

"Opposition" executive committee because in some quarters "Republican" meant ultra men advocating abolition. "Opposition" to the Democracy was less inflammatory and permitted the inference that the party included old Whigs, former Democrats, and Know-Nothings.[172] Lincoln's five Ohio speeches, including two in Columbus, were a success from the standpoint of presenting the candidate to the Ohio public and, most importantly, presenting him to local and state Republican Party officials.[173] For the most part, the speaking events were low-key and not especially well attended. The Cincinnati event, however, which included brass bands, cannons, torches, a mounted escort, fireworks, bonfires, and a German brigade, would have met Davis's requirement that political rallies radiate confidence, enthusiasm, and excitement.[174] The speeches also gave Lincoln an opportunity to subtly define himself as the moderate alternative to Seward and Chase.[175]

Whether or not Lincoln's Ohio visit actually helped the Republicans win both houses of the legislature in 1859, state leaders thought that it did. Lincoln received letters from the Republican Party of Ohio and Samuel Galloway, each of which credited Lincoln's appearances with contributing to the victories. Republican leaders were impressed with Lincoln's "searching and thorough practical expose of the fallacies of [Douglas's] position" and statement of Republican principles in both his Ohio speeches and his debates with Douglas.[176] Before the state elections, the Buckeye Republican Party wrote to Lincoln requesting publication of the speeches and debates for use as campaign literature in Ohio and elsewhere. Even before Lincoln's visit to Ohio, the Republican candidate for governor, William Dennison, asked Illinois senator Lyman Trumbull if Dennison could obtain a copy of the Lincoln-Douglas debates to mine some "valuable material" for use in Dennison's campaign speeches.[177]

The Ohio visit helped Davis's team successfully execute their strategy by obtaining a respectable eight Ohio votes on the first ballot, increasing the total to fourteen on the second ballot, and receiving twenty-nine of forty-six votes on the third and final ballot.[178] Because Joseph Medill was raised in Ohio, published several papers in the state, and helped organize the Ohio Republican Party, Davis directed that he spend plenty of time with the Ohio delegates.[179] Jesse Dubois also met with the Buckeyes. The day before the balloting, William Butler wrote Lincoln that Benjamin Eggleston, a member of the Ohio Republican central committee, advised that as long as Lincoln remained a viable candidate, the Buckeye State would vote for him on the third ballot.[180] Indiana's role in converting Chase votes to Lincoln votes should not be underestimated and demonstrates the importance of making Indiana the top convention priority. Securing Governor Lane and at least a majority of Indiana delegates early on allowed Illinois and Indiana to work "hand in glove" in wooing uncommitted delegations.[181] Lane and other Hoosiers were lobbying long and hard for Lincoln and were largely responsible for the Ohio jump from its favorite son to Lincoln. For example, William Butler's informant, Benjamin Eggleston, was for Chase, with Seward as backup, and "did not become a friend of [Lincoln] until he fell in with the Indiana Delegation." Another Buckeye delegate, Robert Hosea, told Salmon Chase that Indiana, Illinois, and Pennsylvania representatives had visited Ohio "in force determined to accomplish the defeat of Seward."[182] The alliance between Davis and Indiana also paved the way for Governor Lane to impose upon his good friend Columbus Delano of Ohio to second Lincoln's nomination on behalf of some of the delegates of Chase's home state.

Joseph Medill claimed to have cut a deal with Ohio to clinch the nomination for Lincoln. In 1895 the *Chicago Tribune* published an article titled "Recollections of Lincoln Furnished by Joseph Medill." According to the article, after the second convention ballot was completed and before the third ballot vote was started, Medill whispered to Ohio chairman David K. Cartter that "if you can throw the Ohio vote for Lincoln, Chase can have anything he wants." Cartter asked how Medill knew that, and Medill responded, "I know, and you know I wouldn't say so if I didn't know." Medill added that Cartter could check with Davis, since "[Davis] holds the authority from Lincoln." Apparently, that was good enough for Cartter, and so, again according to Medill, Cartter rose and "announced eighteen or nineteen votes of Ohio for Lincoln" on the third ballot.[183] On the third ballot Lincoln actually received twenty-nine of Ohio's forty-six votes. If Medill's story is true, he deserves credit for keeping it a secret for thirty-five years. But the story is "so suspect as to be discounted."[184] Two days before Medill's spur-of-the-moment "deal" with Cartter, Butler wrote Lincoln that the majority of the Ohio delegation had agreed to turn to Lincoln on the third ballot if Illinois kept his name before the convention.[185] Some historians interpret Medill's claim differently. They suggest that Medill asked Cartter to change four delegate votes to Lincoln *after* the third ballot was taken but *before* the results were announced. It is true that after the third ballot Lincoln was only one and a half votes from the nomination. It is also true that before the results of the third ballot were announced, Cartter rose to change four Ohio votes to Lincoln, putting him over the top.[186] But at that point there was absolutely no need to trade anything for Ohio votes. Every person in the Wigwam knew that Lincoln was the "coming man." It was only a matter of which delegation the convention chair would recognize first to change their votes. Several delegations competed for the honor.[187] The convention chair called on Ohio, and so Ohio put Lincoln over the 233-delegate mark. As Frank B. Carpenter has explained, Ohio changed four votes at the suggestion of a New York delegate rather than Medill, and the motivation was simply to claim credit for Lincoln's inevitable nomination.[188]

New Jersey

Davis's dealings with New Jersey illustrate another piece of the Illinois strategy. For Lincoln to be considered a serious candidate for the presidential nomination, any talk of him as vice presidential timber had to be quashed. No one dared speak of second place on the ticket for true top-tier candidates such as Seward, Chase, and Bates. Flatly forsaking the vice presidential nomination was a risky but necessary tactic if the Rail Splitter was to be considered in the same league as the front-runners.

In one of his visits with the New Jersey contingent, Davis learned that some of the delegates favored a Seward nomination, with Lincoln filling the second spot on the ticket. According to Davis, delegate Joseph C. Hornblower, a "grave and venerable" retired New Jersey Supreme Court justice, led the charge, "insisting" on Seward for president with Lincoln as vice president. Unable to convince the retired judge of the error of his ways, Davis left the meeting and later returned with former Democrat and former county judge John M. Palmer.[189] After Davis introduced Palmer to the delegation, Hornblower praised Seward and "effusively" praised Lincoln but persisted in his opinion that Lincoln should be Seward's running mate. In response, Palmer played on the well-known friction between the old Whigs and former Democrats who now made up the Republican Party. Palmer told Hornblower that former Democrats would not support a presidential ticket consisting of two onetime Whigs: "You may nominate Mr. Lincoln for Vice President, if you please; but I want you to understand there are forty thousand Democrats in Illinois who will support this ticket if you will give them an opportunity; but we are not Whigs, and we never expect to be Whigs. We will never consent to support two old Whigs on this ticket. We are willing to vote for Mr. Lincoln with a Democrat on the ticket; but we will not consent to vote for two old Whigs."[190] Seeking confirmation of Palmer's dire declaration, Hornblower turned to Davis and indignantly asked if internal party conflicts in Illinois were of such a degree to support Palmer's point of view. Regardless of the validity of Palmer's belief, it was plausible and helped fuel the ultimate fear that the wrong Republican candidate would lose large segments of votes in the doubtful states. So, displaying some distress at the state of the conflict between Illinois's old Whigs and former Democrats, Davis confirmed that "not a d——d one of [the forty thousand Democrats] will vote for two Whigs" and added that the nomination for either the president or the vice president must go to a Democrat turned Republican. Davis capped the argument, playing on the old Whigs' mistrust of Democrats by saying that nobody could explain "the conduct of these old Locofocos." After the meeting, Palmer and Davis laughed about Davis's use of the derogatory term for Democrats in front of Palmer. But as Palmer acknowledged, the argument had to be made to bring Seward and Lincoln head-to-head for the nomination.[191]

Although the New Jersey delegates arrived in Chicago uncommitted to any candidate, they agreed to vote for their favorite son, former US senator William L. Dayton, on the first ballot. To cement the favorite son unit vote, Dayton's friend Thomas H. Dudley was picked to chair the delegation. It was no secret that the Dayton candidacy was intended as a roadblock to Seward's nomination. While Seward had at least five committed New Jersey delegates, the bent of the state party was decidedly conservative. Thomas Dudley and the majority of New Jersey delegates told the other delegations, including Massachusetts, that they could carry the Garden State for Dayton, Bates, Lincoln, or Banks but not for Seward. Dudley's leadership and the conservatism of the state party earned Dayton all fourteen votes on the first ballot and ten votes on the second ballot. After a meeting on May 17 of the Committee of Twelve, composed of three representatives from each of the doubtful states (Illinois, Indiana, New Jersey, and Pennsylvania), Dudley convinced eight of the fourteen New Jersey delegates to go for Lincoln on the third ballot.[192] While things were going nicely for Davis and his team in rounding up vote commitments prior to the balloting, everyone knew that Pennsylvania would dictate the outcome.

Pennsylvania

Together, New York and Pennsylvania controlled 124 of the 233 votes needed for the nomination. With New York impenetrable, Davis needed a significant portion of the Pennsylvania vote to have a legitimate chance of securing Lincoln's nomination. Davis would not get much help on the first ballot, since the Pennsylvania state convention had urged initial support for Senator Simon Cameron. But a few things were working in Davis's favor. Although not a delegate, the nominee for governor of Pennsylvania, Andrew Gregg Curtin, attended the convention "determined to do all in [his] power to prevent the nomination of Senator Seward." Curtin, a former Whig, and Simon Cameron, a former Democrat, vied for control of the state party. Like gubernatorial candidate Lane of Indiana, Curtin believed that a Seward-led ticket would mean Curtin's automatic defeat in the fall state election. So Curtin and Lane teamed up to visit every delegation that would listen with the message that their two states could carry majorities with Lincoln but not Seward.[193] The Republican press in Pennsylvania reinforced Curtin's message by admonishing the delegates to refrain from nominating a radical for president. A few days before the convention, the *North American*, published in Philadelphia, cautioned, "Chicago must understand that conservatism is necessary."[194] The *Bradford Reporter*, a self-described Pennsylvania radical Republican newspaper, stated that Seward would be its first choice for the nomination if it could be convinced of Seward's availability. But the newspaper acknowledged that the New York senator would be weak in the southern part of the state. So instead of Seward, the *Bradford Reporter* endorsed Simon Cameron because he was sensitive to the conservative faction of the party in Pennsylvania and New Jersey.[195]

Thurlow Weed's neglect of Simon Cameron and the Pennsylvania delegates also helped Davis. Two months before the convention, Cameron told Seward that he would like to meet with Weed. Although Seward conveyed the message, Weed ignored the request. Maybe, as suggested by Doris Kearns Goodwin, Weed was confident of Pennsylvania's support at least by the second ballot because Cameron had promised Seward as much when he lavishly entertained Seward the previous year in Harrisburg.[196] But Weed was too experienced and savvy as a political manager to rely on a "promise" that he was not privy to and that had been made months before it was to be executed. Failing to shore up the support in a face-to-face meeting with Cameron seems not only imprudent but also an act of political malpractice. Even if a meeting with Cameron resulted in Cameron denying the existence of the earlier commitment to Seward or resulted in Cameron retreating from the promise, Weed would have had the opportunity to adjust his strategy. There is simply no denying that Pennsylvania's vote for Seward on either the first or second ballot would have ended the contest. In a letter to Seward explaining the nomination of Lincoln, Weed said that Pennsylvania delegate Alexander Cummings came to Chicago with a confidential letter from Cameron and that Cameron's brother and son attended the convention. According to Weed, all three refused to say a word in favor of Seward. They did tell Weed, however, that before Cameron's name was withdrawn from the field, Weed would have the opportunity to address the delegation. That promise was not kept. Weed complained to Seward that other than delegate Cummings and Cameron's brother and son, the Cameron friends inside and outside the Pennsylvania delegation "were violent and denunciatory—all saying that [Seward] could not carry the state."[197] These problems potentially could have been avoided had Weed acceded to Cameron's request for a preconvention meeting.

Davis also knew of the testy circumstances surrounding Cameron's endorsement at his state's convention. A resolution was introduced at the Harrisburg meeting stating: "*Resolved*, That General Simon Cameron is hereby declared the candidate of the People's party of Pennsylvania for President of the United States." The resolution passed eighty-nine counties in favor, thirty-nine counties opposed, and two county delegations (Chester and Delaware Counties) refusing to vote.[198] Later in the state convention, Cameron supporters presented a unit vote resolution: "The delegates from the State to the National Convention are hereby instructed to cast the vote of the State as a unit, and to vote for General

Cameron while his name remains before that body." The proposed resolution was amended to require a unit vote only of the delegates selected at the convention. The form of the resolution that finally passed read: "The delegates from the State to the National Convention *appointed by this Convention* are hereby instructed to cast the vote of the State as a unit, and to vote for General Cameron while his name remains before that body."[199] The significance of the amendment was that the Pennsylvania State Convention only chose delegates in eleven of twenty-five districts. In two districts, the people had already elected delegates. The state convention delegates from the remaining twelve districts reserved the right to select or elect delegates to the national convention at a later date. Thus, the unit vote instruction only applied to delegates of the eleven districts appointed at the state convention. The amendment thwarted a unit vote for Cameron and permitted Judge Davis to obtain four first-ballot votes for Lincoln.[200]

Davis's Illinois men, with help from Lane, Curtin, and others, continuously lobbied for Lincoln with the Pennsylvania delegates. But three meetings on May 17 proved to be decisive. Worried that Seward's nomination might be imminent, delegates from the four doubtful states (Illinois, Indiana, New Jersey, and Pennsylvania) held a joint meeting in the afternoon of May 17. The meeting was convened to prevent the nomination of Seward by uniting the delegations behind one "moderate" candidate. Pennsylvania delegate and former Democrat Andrew Reeder chaired the meeting. The group turned out to be too large and unwieldly to make any progress, so Norman Judd suggested that three representatives from each state meet later in the day to settle on an alternative to Seward. Davis led the Illinois group, Thomas Dudley headed the New Jersey contingent, and Lincoln supporter Caleb Smith directed the Indiana trio.[201]

The selection of the three Pennsylvania representatives to the Committee of Twelve was not so easy. The choice was severely complicated by the vocal and sometimes bitter anti-Cameron forces within the delegation. The state delegation chair, Andrew Reeder, initially selected three pro-Cameron men: Judge David Wilmot, Henry D. Moore, and B. Rush Petrikin. One of the younger Pennsylvania delegates, S. Newton Pettis, approached Moore and convinced him that since the delegation was split two-thirds for Cameron and one-third for other candidates, it was only fair for Moore to decline the appointment so that another man could be chosen to represent the minority members of the delegation. Moore agreed. Pettis suggested that William B. Mann replace Moore, and the delegation approved Mann's appointment by a five-vote margin. Mann led the anti-Cameron, "Curtin-McClure combine" in Philadelphia and "was known to be violently hostile to Cameron."[202]

At 6:00 that evening the Committee of Twelve met. They talked and promoted their favorite candidates for four hours without any movement toward choosing a nominee to rally behind. At about 10:00 p.m., the ubiquitous Horace Greeley entered the room and asked if the committee had unified behind an alternative to Seward. Upon being informed that no agreement had been reached, Greeley left the room and reported to his newspaper that Seward would be nominated in the morning.[203] In an attempt to get off the dime, someone on the Committee of Twelve suggested that each state name three men who could carry their state. According to Herman Kreismann, Davis named, in order of preference, Lincoln, McLean, and Wade.[204] This list certainly differs from the Lincoln, Seward, and Bates presidential preferences of the Illinois delegates when they arrived in Chicago. But the question was premised on electability, not personal preference. And it is unlikely that Davis polled the Illinois delegation on the question; instead, he probably gave his own opinion. In any event, Illinois "choices" really came down to Lincoln, since everyone knew that McLean and Wade were out of the running. Lincoln was also first on Indiana's list. New Jersey said that discounting favorite son William Dayton, the state could be carried by Bates, Lincoln, or Banks but not Seward.[205] Naming three candidates who could carry Pennsylvania created another contest between the Cameron and anti-Cameron forces. The Pennsylvania delegates easily put Cameron first and McLean second. Third place was a battle between Lincoln and Bates. Many individuals claimed credit for securing the third and final spot for Lincoln. Most probably, the delegates from the western part of the state who were originally for Seward and Wade voted for Lincoln to defeat the pro-Cameron eastern delegates who supported Bates. Whoever gets the credit, Lincoln defeated Bates for third place by the slim margin of three votes. The third-place finisher in Pennsylvania was the only candidate who counted, because every Keystone State delegate knew that Cameron and Wade were defeated before the balloting began.[206] So, in effect, Lincoln was the only candidate all four states agreed could win. That same evening, the New Jersey representatives on the Committee of Twelve ostensibly convinced their entire delegation to move to Lincoln on the second ballot after a first-ballot complimentary vote for Dayton. However, the New Jersey agreement to vote for Lincoln after the first ballot was conditioned upon Pennsylvania also switching to Lincoln.[207] And while Pennsylvania named Lincoln over Bates as the third person who could carry the state, the Committee of Twelve meeting ended without any commitment from Pennsylvania to vote for Lincoln on any ballot. That commitment would take a lot more work by Davis and the Lincoln supporters within the Keystone State delegation.

At about the same time that the Committee of Twelve started its meeting, the main body of Pennsylvania delegates together with delegates from Indiana met at the Cook County Courthouse to discuss uniting behind a candidate. At this point in the convention, most Indiana delegates supported Lincoln, but everything was in a constant state of flux. Pennsylvania had discussed Lincoln as a third choice, but at the time of the courthouse meeting no definite decision had been made if and when the delegates would vote for Lincoln. Davis sent Browning and Koerner to the meeting, Browning to explain the reasons Bates could not win and Koerner to argue why no self-respecting German American would vote for Bates or any other candidate on a Bates ticket. According to Koerner, after the speakers concluded, a large majority of the Pennsylvania delegates agreed to vote for Lincoln after a first-ballot complimentary vote for Cameron.[208]

After the courthouse meeting and after the Committee of Twelve concluded its session, the Pennsylvania delegation met as a whole to see if the delegates could agree to deliver an initial unit vote for Cameron, a second-ballot vote for McLean, and a third-ballot vote for Lincoln. Old animosities prevailed, and some delegates absolutely refused to vote for Cameron on the first ballot. Finally, S. Newton Pettis again stepped in as a seemingly objective observer and made a motion that the delegation's vote "be cast as a *unit* for General Simon Cameron until a majority of the delegation direct otherwise, then, its vote to be continued *as a unit*, for the candidate so designated by such majority." The vote on Pettis's resolution was postponed until 9:00 the next morning supposedly due to the lateness of the hour. In reality, the delay was designed to give Pettis time to lobby for the passage of his resolution. And lobby he did, getting people out of bed until daybreak. Pettis first confirmed with the Cameron men that a vote on the initial ballot would keep them in good graces with their boss. He then moved on to the herculean task of convincing anti-Cameron forces to swallow their pride and principles and vote for Cameron on the first ballot. Pettis's resolution passed at the 9:00 a.m. meeting.[209]

After the Committee of Twelve broke up late in the evening of May 17 and while Pettis furiously promoted his unity resolution among the Pennsylvania delegates, Davis and Swett met directly and confidentially with Cameron men Joseph Casey, Alexander Cummings, Judge Samuel Purviance, and John P. Sanderson. Apparently, part of the meeting involved only Davis, Swett, and Casey.[210] Swett and Davis had decided to court the Cameron leaders instead of trying to procure the support of the anti-Cameron faction because they believed that "the Cameron influence was the controlling element" of the delegation.[211] Sanderson and the others wanted something for Cameron in return for providing votes for Lincoln. Davis and Swett were in a pinch because Pennsylvania, figuratively and literally, was a wild card. The Pennsylvania delegates had not yet ratified the agreement of the Committee of Twelve, and, considering the bitter division, they might never do so. Also, there was no question that Cameron still controlled two-thirds of his state's delegates.[212] New Jersey's agreement to vote for Lincoln after the first ballot only if Pennsylvania did likewise further increased the importance of the Keystone State.

Whether a deal was cut by Davis and Swett has been debated since May 17, 1860. Frank Carpenter in his detailed discussion of the Pennsylvania delegation's deliberations emphatically stated that no promise of any kind was made to secure the Cameron supporters' votes for Lincoln.[213] At the other end of the continuum, Pennsylvania Republican chair Alexander McClure claimed that Davis gave "positive assurance" that Lincoln would appoint Cameron secretary of the treasury.[214] If that is true, then Lincoln broke the promise by appointing Salmon Chase to the treasury post. Another version of the promise provided that Lincoln would appoint Cameron to an unspecified cabinet position.[215] Speaking generally on the topic of promises, Jesse Fell observed that "a disposition of favor was a great deal spoken of at Chicago, in a quiet way, tho' of course no improper pledges—so far as I know or believe—were asked—as I am very sure they were not, and could not be, given."[216]

Henry Whitney claimed that while Fell's statement "was probably the literal truth," there was an agreement of sorts between Davis and Casey. First, Davis and Swett told Casey that they had no "actual authority" to promise cabinet posts and that Lincoln specifically instructed them that he would not be bound by any bargain. Second, again according to Whitney, it was understood that if Lincoln was elected, he would appoint Cameron to a cabinet post. This "promise" was based on a "moral right" to pledge an appointment, notwithstanding Lincoln's declaration that he would not honor any deals.[217] If accurately reported by Whitney, the "agreement" was so obtruse and indefinite as to permit Casey's belief that Lincoln was bound to appoint Cameron and Davis's belief that no such promise had been made. Historian Edward Achorn takes a less flattering view of the negotiations, concluding that even "if Davis had no authorization from Lincoln to sell offices, he would lie to delegates that he did," because he knew that deals had to be made.[218]

The logical starting point in analyzing whether a bargain was made for the Pennsylvania vote is the written instruction that Lincoln sent Davis concerning convention deal making. Lincoln's sole instruction came to the Illinois men on Thursday, May 17: "*Make no contracts that will bind me.*"[219] According to Herndon, Davis reacted to the note by arguing that Lincoln was in Springfield and could "not appreciate the gravity of the situation" and so continued his negotiations.[220] Henry Whitney's version of the Lincoln team's reaction to the instruction demonstrates his capacity to manufacture events and conversations out of thin air.[221] Whitney wrote that when Lincoln's note was read, "The bluff Dubois said: 'Damn Lincoln!' The polished Swett said, in mellifluous accents: 'I am very sure if Lincoln was aware of the necessities—' The critical Logan expectorated viciously, and said: 'The main difficulty with Lincoln is—' Herndon ventured: 'Now, friend, I'll answer that.' But Davis cut the Gordian knot by brushing all aside with: 'Lincoln ain't here, and don't know what we have to meet, so we will go ahead, as if we hadn't heard from him, and he must ratify it.'"[222]

It is unclear what induced Lincoln to convey the directive prohibiting deals that bound him. Some believe it was in response to a letter that Charles Ray sent the preceding Monday suggesting that Lincoln authorize Judd, Davis, or Ray to make "a pledge or two" when the time came.[223] According to Whitney, Lincoln's note was in response to a telegram sent at Davis's direction earlier in the day advising Lincoln that a promise of a cabinet position for Cameron could secure the Pennsylvania vote.[224] Whatever triggered Lincoln's note, the instruction was concise and to the point, written by a lawyer to be interpreted and applied by lawyers. Lincoln did not say "make no promises" or "make no contracts." The precise instruction prohibited Davis from making pledges, promises, or contracts that bound Lincoln. There was no blanket prohibition against promises. Davis, Swett, Logan, Palmer, Judd, and others could bind themselves as they saw fit, but they could not commit Lincoln to any future act or appointment. Davis knew how to toe the line, notwithstanding that the line could become blurry in the heat of last-minute negotiations between exhausted partisans. So while Davis, Swett, and Logan pledged their personal support for Cameron and solicited commitments from other Lincoln supporters and delegates, the weight of the evidence contradicts the conclusion that Davis guaranteed that Lincoln would appoint Cameron to the cabinet. Davis bound himself, not Lincoln.[225] As Davis said four months after the convention, "Mr Lincoln is committed to no one on earth in relation to offices. He promised nothing to gain his nomination, and has promised nothing since. No one is authorized to speak for him." Swett concurred, writing to his former school-mate: "No pledges have been made, no mortgages executed, but Lincoln enters the field a free man." He later wrote to Thurlow Weed: "Of course nobody is authorized to speak for Mr. Lincoln."[226]

Swett's letter to Lincoln in November 1860 concerning the Cameron appointment supports the view that no convention promise bound Lincoln. In the November correspondence, Swett complained that rather than being sent directly to the president-elect, many letters urging a cabinet position for Cameron were sent to Davis and Swett to be forwarded to Lincoln. Swett acknowledged, however, that Cameron's friends had a right to use Davis and Swett as middlemen because of the negotiations with Casey and Sanderson at the convention. The use of Davis and Swett as conduits to Lincoln is consistent with an agreement to provide access to Lincoln and to personally lobby for Cameron's appointment, which is exactly what Swett does in the letter. If the convention agreement provided that Lincoln would appoint Cameron, there would be no need to convince the president to do so by way of hundreds of recommendation letters.[227]

Lincoln's understanding of the negotiations with Pennsylvania mirrored those of Davis and Swett. After receiving a letter expressing opposition to Simon Cameron's appointment, Lincoln told Herndon that "he felt himself under no promise or obligation to appoint anyone." Similarly, Lincoln told Thurlow Weed that "it was particularly pleasant to him to reflect that he was coming into office unembarrassed by promises."[228] Indeed, Lincoln's actions and vacillation on Cameron's appointment attest to the fact that he did not feel limited by any convention dealings. On December 31, 1860, Lincoln handed Cameron a letter stating that at the appropriate time Lincoln would present Cameron's name to the Senate for confirmation as either secretary of the treasury or secretary of war.[229] Shortly before making the offer, Lincoln had compiled two memoranda detailing the pros and cons of giving Cameron a cabinet post. One report outlined the charges of bribery against the Pennsylvania senator. The other report summarized the voluminous recommendations supporting the senator's appointment.[230] After a full and frank conversation with Alexander McClure, Lincoln wrote to Cameron on January 3, 1861, that new developments made it impossible to put him in the cabinet. In the letter Lincoln awkwardly asked Cameron to telegraph him immediately declining a cabinet position.[231] Cameron did not respond. A month later, Alexander McClure and Andrew Curtin, leaders of the anti-Cameron faction of the Pennsylvania party, withdrew their objections to the appointment.[232] Then, the day after his inauguration, Lincoln submitted Cameron's name to the Senate for confirmation as secretary of war. To say that Lincoln vacillated on the appointment is certainly an understatement. The president-elect offered a cabinet position, then withdrew the offer, then renewed the offer. He laboriously reduced to writing the advantages and disadvantages of appointing Cameron. He did not question Davis or Swett about alleged promises and never tried to distance himself from his team's dealings at the convention. Taken together, the facts indicate that Lincoln did not believe that his agents in Chicago bound him to appoint the Pennsylvania senator.[233]

Casey may have thought that the negotiations with Davis and Swett guaranteed more than mere access to Lincoln and a pledge of personal support for Cameron. A few days after the convention, Casey advised Cameron that the withdrawal of his candidacy in favor of Lincoln "was only done after everything was arranged carefully and unconditionally in reference to Yourself—to our satisfaction—and we *drove* the anti-Cameron men from this state into it."[234] That may have reflected Casey's understanding. Or Casey may have overstated the nature of the promise because he was afraid to inform his boss that he settled for anything less than an assured cabinet post. As expected, the postconvention correspondence from Casey to both Swett and Davis does not relate the precise nature of the agreement, but it does indicate that Casey believed that Cameron would have a place in the cabinet.[235]

Also routinely offered in support of a claimed promise to appoint Cameron are the comments made by Joseph Medill to journalist George Alfred Townsend on May 30, 1888. Townsend interviewed Medill to learn the *Chicago Tribune* editor's reasons for promoting Judge Walter Q. Gresham for the Republican presidential nomination in the upcoming election. In response to the reporter's first question asking why he favored Gresham, Medill launched into a blow-by-blow account of Abraham Lincoln's nomination in 1860. During the oration, Medill gave his version of how Davis acquired the Pennsylvania convention vote. The editor of the *Tribune* related that in the wee morning hours of May 17, Davis came down the stairs at the Tremont Hotel. Medill, relaxing in the lobby, asked the judge what Pennsylvania was going to do. Davis, apparently not hesitant to discuss the confidential negotiations in the hotel lobby, responded, "Damned if we haven't got them." To Medill's next question, "How did you get them?" Davis replied, "By paying them their price." Then Medill said that he saw Charles Ray, coeditor of the *Tribune*. Ray, who was not part of the negotiation team, stated that they had agreed to make Cameron secretary of the treasury.[236] Simply put, there is no more reason to trust Medill's version of the Pennsylvania negotiations than there is to trust Medill's account of how Ray promised governmental posts to Caleb Smith and William P. Dole in return for Indiana's convention vote. Indeed, Medill's description of his encounter with Davis in the lobby of the Tremont is remarkably similar to his description of Ray's announcement of his deal with Indiana. Medill claimed that on the day before the Chicago convention, Ray came to the Illinois delegation rooms and broadcast to Davis and the others, "We are going to have Indiana for Old Abe, sure." Medill asked Ray how he obtained the vote, and Ray responded, "We promised them everything they asked."[237] Medill's accounts of the two episodes are nearly identical. Medill's interview with George Townsend was published in the *Chicago Tribune* on June 2, 1888, and republished in the *Tribune* in 1909 as part of the celebration of Lincoln's one-hundredth birthday.[238]

Finally, proponents of the argument that Davis positively pledged cabinet positions rely on a purported admission from the judge that he not only made promises but also lied to obtain the nomination. At a dinner party at the Wisconsin summer home of Nathaniel K. Fairbank, a phenomenally successful Chicago businessman and philanthropist, Davis reportedly admitted that he made some "dubious promises" to secure convention votes. Guests at the dinner party included Wirt Dexter. Davis described Dexter, a prominent Chicago lawyer and friend of Leonard Swett, as "eccentric."[239]

According to a document prepared by Fairbank's son in 1926, Davis told the partygoers that he had made promises to delegates "to bring them into line," and "sometimes the promises overlapped a little." In response, Wirt Dexter suggested that Davis must have "prevaricated somewhat" on the promises, to which Davis purportedly replied, "Prevaricated, Brother Dexter? We lied, lied like hell."[240]

Assuming the conversation between Davis and Dexter took place and was accurately reported by Fairbank's son, who at most was seventeen years old at the time of the dinner party, it is difficult to pinpoint what Davis was referring to.[241] Even if the bargains allegedly made by Ray with Indiana, Davis with Pennsylvania, and Medill with Ohio occurred, they were not "lies," since they were honored. It is also challenging to identify the jurisdictions to which Davis could have made "overlapping promises." Certainly, Davis did not lie to "bring into line" any delegates of Minnesota, California, Wisconsin, Texas, Michigan, Missouri, or New York, since none of those states gave a single vote to Lincoln.[242] Massachusetts delegate Edward L. Pierce confirmed that no promises were made to Massachusetts.[243] New Jersey agreed to go for Lincoln on the second ballot if Pennsylvania did likewise. No consideration other than the good of the Republican Party prompted the votes of the Garden State.[244] There is no evidence of a deal with Maine, Vermont, Connecticut, Rhode Island, New Hampshire, Virginia, or Kentucky. Did Davis misrepresent Lincoln's stance on the issues? There is no hint of such deception. Besides, Davis was not selling political philosophy other than as it related to availability. Certainly, Davis did not "lie" by offering money to states to help elect Republicans. Davis did not have a penny to offer. Anyway, that was Weed's bailiwick. There is one statement attributed to Davis that, if accurately reported, was false. If, as his biographer and Henry Whitney say, Davis assured Casey and Sanderson that he would secure the recommendation of every Illinois delegate for Simon Cameron's cabinet appointment, then that was a misrepresentation. Indeed, Judd told Lincoln face-to-face that he objected to an appointment for Cameron.[245] Fairbank's son's report of dinner-party banter forty years after Davis's death makes another good tale but offers nothing of substance to prove deals or wholesale misrepresentations by Davis. Indeed, the facts reflect just the opposite.

A combination of factors rather than a convention promise by Davis resulted in Cameron's appointment. Those factors included Davis's and Swett's postconvention advocacy for Cameron, Seward's and Weed's backing, an avalanche of supporting letters, the withdrawal of the objection to the appointment by anti-Cameron forces in Pennsylvania, an overestimation of Cameron's abilities, and the prevailing view that if Pennsylvania was to be rewarded, then "Cameron alone deserved to be recognized [because] there was no one else in the Keystone State with an equal claim to an appointment."[246]

In the final analysis, the nomination came down to a delegate count, and Davis successfully secured more delegates than the manager of any other candidate. The planned strategy, as modified by Davis on the fly, worked perfectly. But there was one important unplanned dynamic that worked in Lincoln's favor in securing the nomination and then prevailing in the general election. Davis's and Thurlow Weed's differing reputations and approaches helped tilt the delegates in Lincoln's favor. At the same time, the shared characteristics of the two campaign managers helped Davis obtain the full support of Weed and Senator Seward in the general election campaign.

Davis versus Weed

David Davis and Thurlow Weed, two old conservative Whigs, were dissimilar in important respects. But they were also alike in several ways that permitted them to appreciate each other, work together in the 1860 general election, and become friends.[247]

Experience

When it came to managing nomination and election campaigns Weed and Davis had vastly different experience. Davis had never attended a national political convention. He had attended state conventions, but not in the role of convention organizer or floor manager. Weed, on the other hand, was a veteran of state and national political conventions, playing an important role, if not the most important role, in the presidential nominations of Whigs William Henry Harrison and Zachary Taylor and Republican John C. Frémont. Weed, not Seward, made the decision that Seward would not seek the Republican presidential nomination in 1856. Other than his own successful runs for state representative and state constitutional convention delegate, Davis had played an important role only in losing campaigns: Lincoln's two unsuccessful campaigns for the US Senate. On the other hand, Weed organized, directed, and controlled Seward's successful nomination and election efforts for state senator, governor, and US senator. One reason for Weed's success was his unmatched ability to maneuver convention delegates to his favored candidates.[248]

At the first New York Whig Convention in September 1834, Weed was everywhere, "advising, cajoling, [and] persuading" delegates to support Seward for governor. His efforts were rewarded with the unanimous nomination of his candidate.[249] After Seward's defeat in the general election, Weed had a more challenging task securing his friend's nomination for governor at the next state convention. The 1838 New York Whig Convention opened with a close race for the top spot on the state ticket. On the first ballot Seward had fifty-two delegate votes, Francis Granger thirty-nine votes, Luther Bradish twenty-nine votes, and Judge Edwards four votes. On the second ballot Seward rose to sixty votes, Granger had fifty-two votes, Bradish ten votes, and Judge Edwards retained three votes. The third ballot gave Granger a one-vote lead over Seward, sixty to fifty-nine, with Bradish holding eight votes. At that point the convention recessed for the evening. After a night of blistering canvassing and maneuvering by Weed, the next morning's ballot resulted in 121 votes for Seward, 1 vote each for Granger and Bradish, and 1 vote for "blank." Bradish received the unanimous nomination for lieutenant governor.[250]

Except for the 1860 national convention, when Lincoln was 180 miles from Chicago, he retained ultimate control and decision-making authority in each of his political campaigns.[251] Seward employed a different approach. He ceded control of nomination, convention, and canvassing strategies and tactics to Weed. "Weed's master-hand" directed election efforts, and Seward followed Weed's campaign advice "with unquestioning confidence."[252] The selection of delegates to the Chicago convention illustrates the differing mindsets of Seward and Lincoln when it came to the hands-on direction of campaign efforts. When a supporter contacted Seward and volunteered to serve as a national convention delegate in 1860, Seward relinquished all control over the matter to Weed, trusting him to "do what [was] wise."[253] On the other hand, when Davis pleaded that it was absolutely essential that "Long John" Wentworth, the mayor of Chicago and archenemy of Norman Judd, be named a delegate at large to the Chicago convention, Lincoln declined the suggestion and had Judd appointed instead. Even Davis's pleas that the failure to appoint Wentworth would be "suicidal" failed to move Lincoln to Davis's point of view.[254]

Contrasting Reputations

Contrasting Davis and Weed was easy for the delegates because of the Dictator's widespread reputation for corruption. The stain on Weed's character was long-standing and to some extent deserved. Fresh in the minds of the Chicago delegates were the New York state legislature's "Gridiron Bills." Shortly before the convention, the New York legislature passed six bills that authorized private rail line companies to divide up "fifty to sixty of [New York City's] finest streets." The bills "bestow[ed] gratuitously upon individuals representing . . . political and moneyed interests, unconditional and unlimited rights and franchises in the public streets." Legislators received bribes for their votes, and Weed used his influence to help pass the legislation. Part of the price for Weed's support was a promise that the beneficiaries of the legislation would contribute to Seward's campaign for president. Whether Weed personally received money or whether contributions to the Seward campaign were actually made is subject to question.[255] But appearances are often as damaging as reality, and the whole sleazy matter confirmed the Chicago delegates' opinions of Weed's signature method of operation. Delegates had no problem putting two and two together when Weed started offering $100,000 to delegations that agreed to support Seward.

But it was no single episode that compromised Weed's reputation. He repeatedly employed cloak-and-dagger intrigues even when they were unnecessary. One illustration is Weed's behavior in the 1839 New York state election.

After Seward's election as governor in the fall of 1838, the 1839 election in New York took on a special importance because the Democratic-controlled state senate refused to confirm Seward's appointments. Unexpectedly, three senate seats opened in the third senatorial district, which included the state capital. If the three Democrats holding the seats were defeated in the 1839 election, then the Whigs would take control of the state senate. A week before the election, Weed concluded that the chances of success in the third district were slim. But the Dictator did not give up. He reported the dismal outlook to his political backers in New York City. His friends got the message and hurried by chartered steamboat to Albany. In the early morning on the day of their arrival, they summoned Weed to the parlor of the Eagle Tavern, where they opened a trunk and removed a large bandana from it. The bandana was wrapped around "packages of bank notes of various denominations, amounting to $8,000." The travelers announced that there was more where that came from. Since the election commenced the next day, Monday, with the balloting continuing through Wednesday, Weed only took $3,000. He kept $1,500 for Albany and sent $1,500 to four neighboring counties in the same senatorial district.

For some reason, Weed could not simply accept the money and distribute it to further Whig election prospects. Instead, he concocted an elaborate cover story to deflect any interest in the strangers who arrived in the state capital. He directed that four of the five New Yorkers remain "incognito" at their hotel. The fifth visitor's father-in-law, Judge Wendell, lived in Albany, so his son-in-law could stay there under his real name. To explain the arrival of the steamer, Weed created the fable that it had arrived from England with news that crops had been destroyed and that the "flour speculators" aboard the ship sought to purchase flour to secure a monopoly. Weed then moved the steamboat to a new location, and the strangers were stealthily carried in closed carriages at sundown to the boat dock and transported back to New York City. This type of intrigue only added to Weed's reputation as deceptive, scheming, and corrupt.[256]

Weed's activities at the 1860 convention confirmed his reputation for reducing man's nature to a single factor: What is a man's price? And the "man of mysterious powers" was none too subtle or shy about offering money for delegates' support. Through Illinois state treasurer William Butler, Weed offered Lincoln the vice presidency and $100,000 to ensure victory in Illinois and Indiana.[257] According to Henry Lane's wife, Joanna, who was in Chicago with her husband, Weed pleaded with Lane to convince the Indiana delegation to back Seward in return for enough money to ensure Lane's election as governor. The proposal was "indignantly rejected," according to Joanna Lane, who added that there was not enough money or influence in New York to purchase her husband's support.[258]

Pennsylvania and other delegations were offered "oceans of money" to secure delegate votes. Always planning ahead, Weed supplied funds to states such as New Hampshire prior to the convention with the hope of return support for Seward.[259] But it was not only the proposed bargains of money for votes that concerned the delegates unfamiliar with East Coast politics. The character of many of Weed's enthusiasts further worried potential Seward supporters. As observed by contemporary journalist Murat Halstead, the New Yorkers at the convention were "of a class unknown to Western Republican politicians."[260] Idealistic Carl Schurz led the Wisconsin delegation to the New York headquarters to help in Seward's convention fight. Schurz hoped to meet the "distinguished members" of the Empire State's delegation, including state chair William M. Evarts, civil rights activist George William Curtis, and Governor Edwin Morgan. Instead, the Wisconsin devotees found Thurlow Weed surrounded by men who did not strike Schurz as "desirable companions" but rather as New York politicians of the "lower sort." Halstead described the crowd of New Yorkers as able to "drink as much whiskey, swear as loud and long, sing as bad songs, and 'get up and howl' as ferociously as any crowd of Democrats you ever heard, or heard of." The New York boys were simply opposed "to being too d——d virtuous."[261] Weed's group was led in spirit and in marches by Thomas Hyer, considered the first heavyweight boxing champion and "among the earliest New York City gangsters employed for political purposes." He provided tactical support for politicians by intimidating campaign contributors and voters, guarding the polls, capturing opposing ballots, and facilitating repeat voters. But the presence of New York's "rough fellows" at the convention simply did not further Weed's ultimate goal.[262]

Davis suffered no similar reputational handicap. Davis did not have a nationwide reputation of any sort, much less as a corrupt politician or judge. As a judicial officer and Honest Abe's campaign manager, he probably enjoyed at least a presumption of integrity and honesty among the delegates.[263] And that presumption would have been confirmed by any of the Illinois convention attendees whether they agreed politically with Davis, were former Democrats or Whigs, or personally liked or disliked Davis. The judge's personal and professional ethics were never questioned. And nothing Davis did at the convention adversely affected his image of uprightness and veracity. This is especially true when the judge's conduct is contrasted with Weed's activities, including offering cash for votes; entertaining delegates with unlimited dinners, cigars, and Champagne; and employing the "lower sort" from New York to work the convention. Lincoln's lobbying team consisted of lawyers, businesspeople, elected state officials, and newspaper editors, all of whom were personal friends of Lincoln. Lincoln supporters who might be characterized as slightly less respectable certainly filled the streets. And those with stout lungs got promoted to fill the spectator sections of the Wigwam. But Davis did not have them working the delegations in the hotels.

Unshakable Fidelity and Loyalty

The most crucial shared characteristic of the two campaign managers was an unshakable personal loyalty to their candidate. Weed and Seward, and Davis and Lincoln, embraced Whig and then Republican principles. But political philosophy was not the binding force in either relationship. Rather, it was fidelity. While both Weed and Davis had personal ambitions, support for their candidates was not a means to accomplish their private ends. Seward recognized this when he described Weed's "exciting principle" as a "personal friendship or opposition, and not self-interest." Similarly, Jesse Fell told Lincoln that he had "no truer more devoted friend and admirer than . . . Judge Davis."[264] Weed and Davis appreciated and respected what they considered the superior character of their political favorite, but in the end the controlling factor was an indestructible devotion.

Conservative Political Advisors

Both managers also shared a political tactician's cautious approach to promoting new or controversial governmental programs and political agendas. Often the overriding consideration to Davis and Weed was whether a proposal helped or hindered the prospects for election or reelection. The virtue of a new program and the morality of a new political or social stance taken by a candidate was important, but equally important was the electorate's readiness to accept the proposal.[265] Meritorious programs not popular with the voters meant only one thing: defeat at the polls. Davis's opposition to the Emancipation Proclamation illustrates his overriding concern with the political effect of a new initiative. The judge's opposition to the Emancipation Proclamation was not based on support of slavery. He vehemently and publicly opposed slavery. Davis's dominant concern was the proclamation's effect on the war effort and Lincoln's reelection prospects, especially in the western states.[266]

Weed also opposed issuance of the Emancipation Proclamation. Although he had no doubt of the "righteousness" of the proclamation, he worried that in many northern states the war effort and the Republicans would lose support because of significant voter opposition to emancipation. In Weed's view, the Republicans had to accept and accommodate the fact that "the normal proclivities of the American people are Democratic."[267] In each of Seward's campaigns for office, Weed counseled his candidate on policy pronouncements with an end to making Seward's positions acceptable to the voters. When Weed's advice was not taken, his fallback plan was to soften or "carefully explain away" Seward's pronouncements, as Weed did with the senator's "irrepressible conflict" oration of 1858.[268]

In the end, Davis's message ("If you do not nominate Lincoln, how will you win the election?") prevailed over Weed's message ("If you do not nominate Seward, where will you get your money?").[269] At the convention, Davis worked relentlessly to defeat Weed. But now Davis needed Weed's connections, experience, and money to help persuade the electorate in the northern states to provide the electoral votes necessary to defeat the other presidential contenders, Democrat Stephen Douglas, Southern Democrat and current vice president John Breckinridge, and the Constitutional Union Party candidate, former Tennessee senator John Bell.

4   Davis and the 1860 General Election

David Davis and Leonard Swett wasted no time securing an essential element of a successful canvass in November: Thurlow Weed's and William Seward's commitment to Lincoln's election.

After the convention adjourned and while Chicago remained in full celebration mode, Davis and Swett made their way to Seward headquarters at the Richmond Hotel to call on Thurlow Weed. The move had been suggested by a Mr. Humphreys, who, while not a delegate, accompanied the Seward troops to Chicago. Before moving to New York, Humphreys had lived in Illinois. Davis and Swett knew that they must approach Weed at some point, and the sooner the better. His full support, including his money, influence, nationwide contacts, and dominance in New York politics, was essential to the success of any Republican presidential nominee. Weed could also ensure the public participation of Senator William Seward in the campaign. The Lincoln forces had to prevent what the Democrats hoped for: Weed or Seward or both sitting out the election.[1]

Weed had just witnessed his "long-cherished hopes" for a Seward presidency crushed. He harbored a bitterness against those, including Horace Greeley and Simon Cameron, who powered the loss. Weed also felt a "sense of injustice" at the defeat of so deserving a candidate. But the Wizard of the Lobby showed no signs of anger or bitterness when approached by Davis and Swett. Nor did he cast blame on anyone. According to Swett, he merely lamented, "I hoped to make my friend, Mr. Seward, President, and I thought I could serve my country in so doing." In addition to paying their respects, Swett and Davis wanted to convince Weed to stop in Springfield on his way home from an Iowa decompression trip to meet Mr. Lincoln. It took some time to convince Weed, and even then, Weed accepted the invitation "very reluctantly."[2] Maybe his daughter's presence in the room helped Weed agree to the visit. Or it could have been the New York boss's hope to cement a place in the cabinet for Seward or simply his belief that the show must go on. New York congressman Elbridge G. Spaulding, also at the meeting, agreed that Weed should see Lincoln. Spaulding requested a letter from Davis assuring Senator Seward that his supporters would not be shut out from receiving federal appointments. Spaulding's request came as no surprise to Swett or Davis. Swett was confronted with this same concern by Cameron and Seward men during the convention. Weed agreed to telegraph when he was leaving Iowa to arrange a time when Swett and the judge could meet Weed and take him to see Lincoln. Swett was pleasantly surprised by the degree of intellect, gentleness, and "large humanity" demonstrated by Weed during the meeting.[3]

On Monday, May 21, Davis went to Springfield and stayed until Weed arrived on Wednesday. That Wednesday, Davis wrote to Lincoln reminding him that Elbridge Spaulding was expecting a letter that he could show Seward confirming that Lincoln would not discriminate against Seward supporters in the appointment process.[4] Weed met with Lincoln and Swett on Thursday, Davis having returned to Bloomington. Upon arriving home, the judge found a letter from Spaulding repeating his request for a pledge of equal treatment for New Yorkers. Recognizing the importance of the issue to the Weed group, Davis immediately wrote Lincoln again, urging a response to Spaulding. After Weed departed Springfield, Lincoln ghostwrote a letter for the judge to copy and send to Spaulding. The letter stated that after Weed left Springfield, Davis had "full, and frequent conversations with Mr. Lincoln" in which he said that if elected, "it will be his pleasure, and, in his view, the part of duty, and wisdom, to deal fairly with all. . . . [T]hat, even if he had friends to reward, or enemies to punish, as he has not, he could not afford to dispense with the best talent, nor to outrage the popular will in any locality."[5]

During their five-hour meeting on Thursday, Lincoln and Weed "freely" discussed election prospects by dividing the states into four categories. All or nearly all of the slave states were lost. That was already determined and "could neither be changed nor modified." Some states were safe and required no effort to put in the Republican column. A third group of states "required attention." Finally, there were a few states that "were sure to be vigorously contested." Without doubt, the two old political strategists put Pennsylvania, Illinois, and Indiana at the top of the hotly contested category. After discussing the means and methods of conducting the canvass, a campaign program was agreed upon. Weed found the nominee "sagacious and practical," with "so much good sense, such intuitive knowledge of human nature, and such familiarity with the virtues and infirmities of politicians" as to impart faith in his fitness to serve as president. The net effect of the interview was to instill confidence in Lincoln's "capacity and integrity" in order to permit Weed to work for Lincoln's election "as zealously and cheerfully" as he would have done for Seward.[6]

Lincoln also thought that the meeting went well. He told Davis that Weed asked for nothing, seemed most interested in merely getting a look at the party's nominee, and left the meeting "satisfied."[7] To allay the fears of Norman Judd and Lyman Trumbull about the ex-Whig's ulterior motives in coming to Springfield, Lincoln reassured the former Democrats that Weed "showed no signs whatever of the intriguer."[8] It is unlikely, however, that Lincoln's assurance convinced either Trumbull or Judd that New York's master manipulator was not plotting something to his and Seward's advantage.

The Road to Victory Passed through Pennsylvania

Democrat James Buchanan won the 1856 presidential election with 45 percent of the popular vote and 174 votes in the Electoral College. Runner-up and first Republican presidential candidate John C. Frémont finished with 33 percent of the vote and 114 electoral ballots. American Party candidate Millard Fillmore received almost 22 percent of the vote, winning only Maryland, with eight electors.

Frémont won the states of Iowa, Maine, Massachusetts, Michigan, New Hampshire, New York, Ohio, Rhode Island, Vermont, Connecticut, and Wisconsin.[9] Many, including Lincoln, considered the new state of Minnesota "as sure as such a thing can be" for the Republicans.[10] But that would only add four electors to Frémont's total. Assuming the Republicans held all of the Frémont states, adding Minnesota would give Lincoln 118 of the needed 152 electoral votes. Turning Pennsylvania to the Republican side of the ledger would add twenty-seven of the thirty-four additional electoral votes needed to bring a Republican to the White House. Winning Pennsylvania offered several paths to victory. For one, Illinois would ensure victory by adding eleven electors. So would Indiana with thirteen electors and New Jersey with seven electoral votes. Even adding Oregon with three electoral votes and California with four votes would put Lincoln over the top, assuming that Republicans prevailed in Pennsylvania and retained the states won by Frémont.

Just as it had in the nomination fight, Pennsylvania held the key to victory in the general election. From his dealings with the Pennsylvania delegates at the Chicago convention Davis feared that obtaining unified cooperation from the McClure and Cameron state Republican factions would be a monumental task. And even with their united support, winning the Keystone State would not be easy. In 1856 Democrat Buchanan received 50.1 percent of the Pennsylvania vote, Republican Frémont 32.1 percent, and American Party candidate Fillmore 17.8 percent.[11] Gaining support from a significant number of Fillmore voters in Pennsylvania would be necessary to take the state from the Democrats. In fact, many of the voters who in 1860 identified with the Pennsylvania People's Party (Republican Party) had previously been members of the American Party.[12] Davis also understood that while courting the anti-immigrant Know-Nothings, he needed a strong showing of the German American vote to win Pennsylvania and the other doubtful states.

The Decision to Send Davis East

In early July Davis and Swett considered suggesting to Lincoln that they make a campaign trip to Pennsylvania. Lincoln's top two lieutenants not only appreciated the importance of the state and the need to smooth over the intraparty squabble but also had received letters from important Keystone Republicans, including Joseph Casey, Joseph J. Lewis, and John Sanderson, suggesting such a visit.[13] Adding to their concern, on July 11 Thurlow Weed wrote to Swett that "it would be well" if Judge Davis and Swett came to Pennsylvania and New Jersey in early September or possibly sooner, if Weed's intelligence from the two states warranted.[14] A month earlier, Lincoln received word that the Simon Cameron wing of the Pennsylvania People's Party was planning to establish its own election committee because the state's central committee, headed by rival Alexander McClure, was bungling the campaign effort. Rumors also surfaced that McClure had pocketed campaign contributions meant for the municipal elections the previous spring.[15] Joseph Medill joined the chorus, suggesting that Lincoln send "some confidential sagacious man" to Pennsylvania for yet another reason: to evaluate the likelihood that the supporters of the other three presidential contenders (Democrat Stephen Douglas, Southern Democrat John Breckinridge, and Constitutional Union Party candidate John Bell) might unite behind the Democratic nominee for Pennsylvania governor.[16]

Lincoln became uneasy about the situation and wrote to Swett asking him and Davis to come to Springfield to discuss one or both traveling to Pennsylvania. Swett responded that he would come to Springfield as soon as the Republican convention in Shelbyville concluded. Signaling his support for the trip, Swett reminded Lincoln that Weed thought that the judge, Swett, or another campaign representative should visit Pennsylvania and New Jersey.[17]

Not wanting to appear to take sides in the Cameron-McClure struggle for state party leadership, Lincoln "reluctantly" decided at the end of July to send Davis and Swett to "survey the field" and investigate matters in the Keystone State.[18] If nothing else, Lincoln would benefit from an objective look at the situation by trusted friends rather than relying on conflicting reports from Cameron and anti-Cameron partisans. Further, the trip would provide an opportunity for Lincoln's surrogates to convince party leaders that the presidential nominee stood right on an issue foremost on the minds of Pennsylvania voters: protective tariffs.

Davis wished to devote his canvassing efforts to his home state but believed the trip east was necessary, so he agreed to go. Davis informed Lincoln that as long as he was going to Pennsylvania, he would check matters in New York and New Jersey.[19] Swett could not make the trip east because he was committed to a whirlwind campaign tour of southern Illinois during the first two weeks of August.[20] So Lincoln substituted "little Judge Davis," otherwise known as Oliver Davis, as "big Judge Davis's" traveling companion. Oliver Davis became ill, and so with Lincoln's permission, Davis asked John Logan to join him, but Logan could not make the trip either. Although not his preference, David Davis traveled east alone.[21]

Davis Arrives in Pittsburgh

Davis left for Pennsylvania on Thursday, August 2, arriving in Pittsburgh at 3:00 p.m. the next day. He met with Russell Errett, owner and editor of the *Daily Pittsburgh Gazette*, and D. F. Williams, also an editor at the *Gazette*. Both were strong Cameron supporters. Davis learned from Errett and others that "everything in Pittsburg [sic] and that region of the State, is just as we could desire it." The editors complained to Davis about the ineptness of the state's central committee, a refrain both Lincoln and Davis heard repeatedly from Cameron supporters. Errett promised, however, that notwithstanding the shortcomings of McClure's leadership, the Republican vote would be "immensely increased, in the West and Northwest" parts of the state from the vote totals received in 1858 and 1859.[22] Most probably, the tariff issue arose during the judge's visit because of its importance to the subscribers of the *Gazette* and because of its importance to editor D. F. Williams, who had repeatedly urged Cameron to "keep the tariff excitement up."[23]

   While the specifics of the conversation between Davis, Errett, and Williams were not recorded, one thing is certain: the judge made a highly favorable impression on the editors of the most important Republican newspaper in western Pennsylvania. After Lincoln's victory in November, Errett wrote a glowing editorial, singling out Davis as the "Napoleon" who conceived and executed the campaign plan that put Lincoln in office: "It is to [Davis's] skill in planning, to his ability in directing, to his clear-headed-ness in perceiving the whole scope of what was before him, to his coolness in the hour of danger, to his unyielding firmness and indomitable energy that the Republicans of Illinois owe their splendid victory, won against extraordinary odds." In support of his suggestion that "the leading man in Illinois politics" be appointed to a cabinet position, Errett explained: "Intellectually [Davis] stands in the front rank of our public men; possesses administrative ability of a rare order; is remarkable for coolness, clearness of judgment, unbending integrity and iron will; and these are qualities which eminently fit him for a cabinet place."[24] On the day the editorial appeared in the *Daily Pittsburgh Gazette*, Errett sent a copy to Lincoln and reiterated his recommendation of Davis for a cabinet post.[25]

After leaving Pittsburgh, Davis traveled to the state capital to consult with Republican officials. He spent August 4 with Simon Cameron at the senator's mansion on Front Street in Harrisburg.[26] Topping Cameron's list of discussion points was Lincoln's stance on protective tariffs.

Davis, Cameron, and Tariff Concerns in Pennsylvania

The Panic of 1857 hurt Pennsylvania's industrial and mining interests, and the Republicans jumped at the chance to blame the problem on the low tariff enacted by the Democrats. Republicans of both the Cameron stripe and the Curtin stripe advocated for a high protective tariff. But more than merely staking out a policy position, the state Republican campaign for a protective tariff "took on the tone of a crusade." The Pennsylvania delegation at the Chicago convention vigorously advocated for a strong protection policy plank in the platform but settled for a watered-down version palatable to both ex-Whigs and ex-Democrats. In addition, the protariff state politicians took their cause directly to the public. During the 1860 general election campaign the Philadelphia Wide Awakes marched side by side with the "Mercantile Tariff Men."[27]

The state Republicans and especially Senator Simon Cameron were "exceedingly anxious" to learn Lincoln's position on protective tariffs.[28] In late July Lincoln had shown Cameron's operative, James Lesley Jr., notes that he had jotted down in the late 1840s on the issue. Lesley reported to Cameron that the notes established that Lincoln's support of tariffs was consistent with old Whig policy and the current position of Pennsylvania Republicans. On August 1, 1860, in a letter belatedly congratulating Lincoln on his nomination, Cameron acknowledged receiving the information from Lesley and expressed faith in Lincoln's "good intentions" to stand by coal and iron interests. According to Cameron, beyond that commitment the state Republicans had "no desires."[29] But Cameron was unsure how to persuade others that the presidential nominee stood right on the tariff issue. State chairman Alexander McClure also wrote Lincoln about the controlling issue in Pennsylvania. Congressman Thaddeus Stevens wanted copies of speeches or some other proof of Lincoln's tariff stance.[30]

The *Daily Pittsburgh Gazette* described Cameron as "the recognized champion of a Protective Tariff" with a "bold fearless and manly devotion to the interests of the industrial classes." The reputation was well earned. "Simon Cameron tirelessly called for higher tariffs in the Senate and implored voters to send pro-tariff men to Congress."[31] Cameron's interest in confirming Lincoln's view on the issue was intensified by attacks such as that of Democratic gubernatorial candidate Henry D. Foster, who argued that no evidence supported the claim that Lincoln ever backed a protective tariff. In one stump speech Foster asserted: "There is no record of [Lincoln's] public life that affords any knowledge of his views upon this question. Mr. Lincoln is held up as the friend of the protective policy, yet you cannot find a vote he ever gave, or a speech he ever made, wherein he favored the doctrine of protection at all."[32] To counter attacks by the Democrats, Cameron wanted additional assurance from Lincoln on the tariff issue. At the suggestion of Davis and others, Lincoln did not take public positions on any issue or make public appearances or speeches. He did not publicly respond to charges made by Democrats or the Democratic press.[33]

Instead of inviting new controversies by making a public statement on the issue, Lincoln sent Davis to convince Cameron that Lincoln stood by old Whig principles in support of protective tariffs. As proof of Lincoln's tariff position, Davis brought with him "eleven foolscap halfsheets of notes and memoranda" written by Lincoln. Some of the notes were prepared in 1848 and set forth what Lincoln thought that General Zachary Taylor should say on the subject during his campaign for the presidency. The remaining pages were written slightly earlier, between Lincoln's election to Congress in November 1846 and his assuming office in March 1847.[34] Besides presenting the notes, Davis could assure Cameron that Lincoln stood by plank 12 of the 1860 Republican platform, which presented the party's tariff position. But anyone could have traveled to Pennsylvania to deliver the note scraps and affirm Lincoln's commitment to the Republican platform. Davis was much more than a messenger. He could personally attest that Lincoln gave protariff speeches in Illinois and Indiana in 1843 and 1844. He could also explain why the speeches were not printed in the newspapers.[35] Moreover, the judge was highly familiar with the tariff issue, which, as McClure noted, was a prerequisite for any representative Lincoln sent to Pennsylvania.[36] In a letter to his brother-in-law in 1844, Davis stated that "the tariff [was] discussed more than anything else" during the political speeches that dominated the first day of every court session in the Eighth Judicial Circuit. In late 1845 the judge wrote that "the interests of [Illinoisans] are on the side of a protective Tariff" and that "the repeal of the tariff will scourge Pennsylvania." Three years later, on a trip to Philadelphia, Davis concluded from his observations and discussions with merchants that the already depressed iron business would suffer further from the recent action of the Democrats lowering the tariff.[37] Most importantly, Davis was in a position as a former Whig and close associate of Lincoln to convince Cameron that he was intimately familiar with the issue and that Lincoln personally expressed his views in their long conversations on and off the circuit. No one could question Davis's familiarity with the tariff question or his firsthand knowledge of Lincoln's position on the issue.

Topics other than protective tariffs were discussed at the meeting with Cameron. Davis was in Pennsylvania in part to assess Lincoln's chances of winning the state, and the senator was happy to report that based on a statewide survey of his friends, Lincoln would "get this state, beyond the shadow of a doubt." Cameron adamantly held that victory in the state would be accomplished without outside help of any kind. As "the Czar of Pennsylvania" stressed to Lincoln in a letter sent three days before Davis's visit, "*We will take care of Pennsylvania.*" This emphatic declaration told the world that Philadelphia was the equal of New York and Boston and needed no outside money. In fact, like New York and Boston, Philadelphia could help finance candidates in other states. To prove the point, Cameron sent Davis $800 for use in legislative districts to ensure a Republican-controlled legislature in Illinois. Cameron's declaration that he needed no money from New York was pure fluff, since Weed had no intention of sending him any. Weed still blamed Seward's defeat on the Pennsylvania delegation generally and Cameron specifically. During the meeting with Davis, Cameron likely did more chest-thumping by repeating another of his favorite boasts: his regret that the Democrats were not united so that the Republicans "could beat their great man Douglas" with a united party behind him.[38]

Cameron's assurance that Pennsylvania would have more than enough local money to support the October and November canvasses was reinforced by a statement of Russell Errett "insist[ing] that the Campaign Committee could get all the money they wanted." In addition, Davis understood from John Sanderson's letter in late August that the Cameron campaign committee had already raised funds.[39] So the judge was astonished when he received reports from Cameron men complaining about the results of their fundraising efforts. About three weeks after returning from his eastern trip, Davis heard from Cameron operatives now claiming a lack of funds. Errett grumbled that the counties were "clamoring" for needed cash and that the Cameron campaign committee was having difficulty raising money. Unsurprisingly, Errett blamed the situation on state Republican chair Alexander McClure. According to Errett, McClure was telling prospective donors not to give money to the Cameron campaign committee because McClure was failing in his own solicitation efforts. Errett predicted that McClure's interference would be "suicidal" and if left unchecked would cause Curtin's defeat in the October gubernatorial election.[40] Similarly, Sanderson wrote Davis explaining that the interior counties needed $10,000 for the October election. Sanderson and other Cameron men assumed the responsibility for providing the needed funds because they believed that the inept central committee would not raise any money. Repeating Errett's claim, Sanderson accused McClure of sending his "minions" to persuade likely contributors not to give to Cameron's group. For good measure, Sanderson added a new twist to the constant recriminations of both factions. He told Davis that an "utterly unscrupulous" Curtin had sanctioned his "clique of bold, bad men who surround & control him" to negotiate a deal with the John Bell supporters. By the terms of the proposed bargain, if the Bell supporters voted for Curtin for governor, McClure would exert influence on the state's electors to cast their Electoral College votes for Bell if by doing so the presidential contest could be placed in Congress's hands.[41]

Davis spent the entire Saturday, August 4, with Cameron. At the end of the meeting Cameron asked if he could retain Lincoln's tariff notes overnight. Davis agreed, and the next day Cameron said that he had reviewed the notes and that they were "abundantly satisfactory." Cameron kept the notes so that he could convince other Republicans of Lincoln's tariff stance and convince friendly newspapers to defend Lincoln from Democrat attacks on the issue. He said he would return the notes to Davis a few days later when they met in Philadelphia. But he did not. Possibly, the Pennsylvania senator wanted possession of the papers to show his favored position with Lincoln or simply to keep them out of McClure's hands. On August 29 Cameron wrote Lincoln that he would return the notes at Lincoln's inauguration. But Davis intervened and asked Cameron to return them earlier, as "they might be needed elsewhere." Cameron finally returned the notes on September 10.[42]

Satisfied with Davis's explanation and Lincoln's notes on the tariff, Cameron solicited newspapers to publish defenses of Lincoln's tariff policy. The *Daily Pittsburgh Gazette* addressed the Democrats' criticism that there was no proof that the Republican nominee was "a Protective Tariff man": "Mr. Lincoln has been all his life a Tariff man. His record as a Whig is clear upon this point. In the campaign of '44 he stumped the State of Illinois, arguing the Tariff question in every speech, and his arguments in favor of Protection, at that time, have never yet been answered, by any one in Illinois or out of it."[43] The *Gazette* added that by accepting the nomination, Mr. Lincoln explicitly endorsed and pledged himself to the party platform, including the plank advocating a protective tariff.[44]

This first-ever meeting between Cameron and Davis left a positive impression on both politicians. Davis began his visit at the Harrisburg mansion with an unfavorable opinion of the senator's sincerity, integrity, and trustworthiness. But Cameron's charm allayed any of Davis's misgivings. The judge described the meeting as "pleasant & eminently satisfactory" and found his host to be such a "genial, pleasant, and kind hearted man" that he had removed the "many prejudices that [Davis] heretofore entertained."[45] Maybe, like Lincoln, Davis was swayed by Cameron's "soft-spoken amiability."[46] Or it simply may be that the judge was predisposed to a favorable impression because he had promised to advocate for a cabinet spot for the Pennsylvania senator. Cameron "was well pleased with the visit of Judge Davis" and told Weed that he would "go to work earnestly" on Lincoln's behalf. Weed was heartened by the results of the visit because Cameron was "by far the strongest man and best worker in the State."[47]

Davis planned to depart Harrisburg for Baltimore on the evening of August 5. But after learning that gubernatorial candidate Andrew Curtin would be speaking the next day in New Bloomfield, Davis decided to stay and travel the twenty-five miles to hear the speech. While in Harrisburg, Davis met with others and found Joseph Casey to be an effective speaker for the Republican state and national tickets.[48]

Cameron's Campaign Committee Meets in Philadelphia

Because of what he viewed as Alexander McClure's ineptness, Cameron planned to seize control of the state canvassing operation at the state central committee meeting on July 10. The main agenda item was "to make definite arrangements for the campaign."[49] But McClure got wind of the attempted coup and outsmarted the Cameron forces.

Knowing that Cameron supporters made up a majority of the state central committee, McClure arranged a festive gathering for the committeemen the evening before the July 10 meeting. The joviality, card playing, and liquor consumption went on until dawn. The Curtin men were forewarned to join in the festivities but to remain sober or, failing that, to at least show up on time for the business meeting at 10:00 a.m. Curtin's backers arrived at the appointed time, while the Cameron committeemen were slow to get out of bed. The meeting was promptly called to order by Chair McClure. All the Curtin men answered the roll call, but many of the Cameron men were absent. Some "innocent" resolutions were passed endorsing Lincoln, denouncing the Buchanan administration, and, most importantly, approving McClure and Curtin's campaign plan. After fifteen minutes, the group adjourned. Not enough Cameron supporters were present to carry out their plan to establish a special executive committee in charge of campaign efforts and campaign funds. Of course, Cameron men would have been in charge of the special committee. If successfully formed, the Cameron special committee would have left McClure as no more than an "ornamental chairman." State central committee meetings could only be called by the chair, and McClure saw no reason to call another meeting for the remainder of the election cycle.[50] So Cameron formed his own unofficial campaign organization.

Davis agreed with Weed that under the circumstances, Lincoln would have to work with both competing canvassing committees in Pennsylvania.[51] To facilitate that effort, Davis attended the organizational meeting of the Cameron campaign committee on August 7 in Philadelphia. About twenty Philadelphians, including Cameron and his chief Philadelphia organizer, John P. Sanderson, met to establish a committee independent of the state central committee. The meeting was no secret to the McClure group. In fact, Cameron wrote to McClure and invited gubernatorial candidate Curtin to attend.[52] The Philadelphia members of the campaign group were chosen on August 7. The initial committee membership demonstrated Cameron's influence and broad-based support and included William H. Kern, the "High Sheriff" of Philadelphia; wealthy businessman William B. Thomas, who had been a delegate to the Chicago convention; John M. Butler, another delegate to the convention and congressional candidate;[53] Peter Fasel, a leading German Republican;[54] George Inman Riche, lawyer, academic, and president of the Republican Invincibles;[55] Samuel Lloyd, a prosperous brick manufacturer;[56] Peter C. Ellmaker, who was active in Philadelphia Republican affairs and who would help lead the procession when the president-elect arrived in the city in February 1861;[57] John M. Coleman, an importer; and John P. Sanderson, an editor, delegate to the 1860 convention, and most ardent and confidential advisor to Cameron. The committee appointed Sheriff Kern chair, Sanderson secretary, and William B. Thomas treasurer.[58]

After the meeting, another nine strategically selected Philadelphians were added to the committee's roster. In addition to Charles Gilpin, the former mayor of Philadelphia, Dr. David Jayne, who had built a fortune in the patent medicinal tonic business, joined the group.[59] So did Robert P. King, an extremely successful printer who received his share of government printing jobs.[60] King and new committee member Robert M. Foust were on the November ballot as Lincoln electors.[61] George R. Smith, a candidate for the state senate from Philadelphia, was added to the group.[62] James Freeborn, another new member, had held multiple government jobs, including tax office clerk, doorkeeper for the Pennsylvania State Senate, and at the time of his appointment to the committee deputy sheriff under Sheriff Kern.[63] Also added was William Elliott, who had served as a Philadelphia city prison inspector and delegate to the 1860 convention.[64]

After Davis left Philadelphia, nineteen representatives from the "interior" counties were selected to serve on the Cameron campaign committee. Loyal to Cameron, new members were distributed pretty much evenly throughout the geographic regions of the state and included residents of the cities of Bedford, Bellefonte, Danville, Doylestown, Easton, Greensburg, Harrisburg, Hollidaysburg, Lock Haven, Mauch Chunk, Meadville, Pittsburgh, Reading, Scranton, Towanda, and Union Town.[65] Davis knew some of the interior county appointees, such as former congressman and 1860 convention delegate David Wilmot, who would later succeed Cameron in the US Senate. In addition to Wilmot, another six committee members had served as delegates to the 1860 National Republican Convention.[66] Davis certainly had dealings with some of those delegates, including Joseph Casey, with whom he and Swett had negotiated for the Cameron delegates' support, and Andrew Reeder, the chair of the Pennsylvania delegation. Davis likely met others during presentations to the delegation. Davis may have known other interior members from his travels to Pennsylvania in the late 1840s and early 1850s and because of his in-laws' business interests in Scranton and his friends in Harrisburg.[67] Two weeks after the organizational meeting, John Sanderson wrote to Davis with an update on the progress of Cameron's campaign committee.[68]

Alexander McClure: Leader of the Anti-Cameron Faction

Most of the names on the list of people that Lincoln directed Davis to see in Pennsylvania were Cameron supporters. Alexander McClure was not on the list.[69] But either Lincoln orally instructed Davis to visit McClure or Davis took

it upon himself to do so. As state committee chair, McClure was responsible for
the organization and execution of the Republican canvass in both the October
gubernatorial election and the November presidential election. It was important
for Davis to meet with McClure in light of the letters that Lincoln, Swett, and
Davis had received from Pennsylvanians questioning whether the state central
committee's canvass was effectively structured. Davis also needed to assess if
there was any chance of consolidating or at least coordinating the Cameron and
anti-Cameron campaign machinery. The judge met with McClure probably on
August 8 or August 9. McClure's detailed description of the meeting suffers from
a few infirmities. First, his recollections were recorded thirty years after the event.
Second, he describes the meeting as including Leonard Swett, who did not make
the trip to Pennsylvania. McClure's more contemporaneous letter to Lincoln
on August 11, 1860, refers only to the presence of Judge Davis at the meeting.[70]
Third, and to be expected, McClure's recollections lean toward the self-serving.

According to his three-decade-old reconstruction of the meeting, Davis (and
Swett), upon arriving at the state central committee's headquarters, told Mc-
Clure that they were traveling through the eastern states on behalf of Lincoln to
determine the progress of the Republican and Democratic canvasses. McClure
remembered that he was shown a letter signed by Lincoln asking McClure to
"furnish [Davis] every facility to ascertain the condition of affairs in the State."[71]
McClure no doubt was referring to the letter of introduction that Lincoln furnished Davis before he left Illinois.

> Springfield, Ills. Aug. 2, 1860
>
> Whom it may concern:
> The bearer of this, Hon. David Davis, is my very good personal and political friend;
> and I shall be greatly obliged by any kind attention shown him.
>
> A. Lincoln[72]

McClure was "glad" to provide Davis with detailed information concerning
the state central committee's strategy, plan, methods, and organization because
he was proud of the fact that "for the first time in the history of Pennsylvania
politics the new party had been organized by the State Committee in every election district of the State." And this was no small task, since the Keystone State
had two thousand precincts.[73] McClure's boast was slightly exaggerated, because
while at the time of McClure's meeting with Davis the state central committee
was in direct contact with all the counties and many of the precincts, it would
not be until August 21, 1860, that half the precincts would be organized and
reporting directly to the central committee. A week later, 70 percent of the election districts would be covered.[74] McClure stressed that the county and precinct
captains were serving without compensation and were "thoroughly competent
and prompt and reliable men."[75] McClure and Davis would have discussed other
campaign matters, including planned rallies, the scheduling of in-state and

out-of-state speakers, and the gains and foibles of the opposition.[76] As part of his ongoing complaint about a lack of campaign funds, McClure might have dropped a hint similar to his later lament to Lincoln: "Here we are very poor. Our merchants are against us, & our Manufacturers are bankrupt."[77]

The tariff issue certainly found its way into the discussion. Two months before the meeting, McClure suggested to Lincoln that if he sent representatives to Pennsylvania, they should be thoroughly familiar with the tariff issue, because in "the Eastern, Southern & Central counties especially, the Tariff will be the overshadowing question in this contest." Like he did with Cameron, Davis could convincingly represent Lincoln's long-held position on the issue. But with McClure the judge would have done so without the "tariff notes," which remained in Cameron's possession.[78]

McClure's reconstruction of the meeting included a dinner after Davis completed a "very exhaustive examination" of the campaign blueprint and the progress made in carrying it out. According to McClure, during the private dinner Swett confessed that the real reason for the trip to Pennsylvania was that Lincoln had received letters alleging that the state's "organization was imperfect and the management incompetent." Swett purportedly continued that they found the complaints unsupported and that Pennsylvania had "the best organization that we have seen in any State."[79] It is likely that a conversation similar to what McClure reported took place, assuming that Davis is substituted for Swett. The judge did make it a point to compliment important Republican leaders during his trip. Besides, McClure's plan was impressive. In addition to blanketing the state with campaign coordinators, the plan featured a stellar list of out-of-state speakers, including William Seward, Francis Blair, Cassius Clay, Thomas Corwin, Benjamin Wade, Joshua Giddings of Ohio, Congressman Anson Burlingame of Massachusetts, Archibald W. Campbell and Alfred Caldwell of western Virginia, Charles Lee Armour of Maryland, Carl Schurz, and former American and Know-Nothing gubernatorial candidates Isaac Hazelhurst of Pennsylvania and Daniel Ullman from New York.[80] Statewide officeholders and candidates, including Simon Cameron, were in abundance, and so were dozens of local favorite stump speakers such as Judge Francis Jordan and local lawyer and newspaper editor Seth T. Hurd. The state central committee also helped establish clubs for Lincoln and vice presidential choice Hannibal Hamlin across the state, with forty clubs in Philadelphia.[81] McClure took seriously his duty as state chairman to run an effective campaign. As he wrote to Cameron, "No man can live long enough to survive the suspicion of losing the election by bad management."[82]

As the election results proved, no complaint could be lodged against the state Republicans' management of the campaign. Curtin prevailed in the gubernatorial race by more than thirty thousand votes, and Lincoln garnered fifty-nine thousand more votes than all his challengers combined.[83]

McClure and Campaign Financing

According to Alexander McClure, the Pennsylvania Republican Central Committee was continually pressed for campaign cash. Even though the committee received rent-free headquarters in Philadelphia and volunteers paid their own expenses, McClure complained that there was little money for printing, mailing, and other campaign necessities.[84] To remedy the financial difficulties, the chair of the state committee tried to raise money in New York during July and August. Of course, whatever McClure did, Cameron opposed. Cameron and his supporters unequivocally objected to receiving funds from "abroad." In July Russell Errett wrote to Joseph Medill protesting the state committee's solicitation of New Yorkers. In October Cameron renewed the objection in a letter to Davis.[85] But the complaints did not deter McClure's out-of-state fundraising efforts. In August he wrote twice to Thurlow Weed asking Governor Edwin Morgan and Weed for contributions to ensure success of the Republican state ticket in the October election. McClure should not have been surprised when Weed failed to answer either letter because the Dictator never forgave Pennsylvania for its part in Seward's failed nomination bid. McClure then personally visited Governor Morgan, who was "listless and indifferent" during the Pennsylvanian's sales pitch. According to McClure, the meeting resulted in "not one dollar of money [being] contributed from New York State to aid the Curtin contest in Pennsylvania." McClure admitted that the Republican National Committee contributed $12,000 to the Pennsylvania state committee but added that the paltry sum came only after November success was assured by the October election victory. In early September McClure tried New York again. This time he met with Morgan, Moses Taylor, and one or two other wealthy businessmen to solicit money for tight congressional races in Pennsylvania. The group raised $4,300 and sent it directly to the candidates in a half dozen targeted districts.[86]

McClure's claim of an impoverished state central committee is suspect. The *New York Herald* reported that the Republican National Committee donated $5,000 to Curtin and paid for two hundred thousand campaign documents for the October election. The *Herald* also reported that "the republican financial clubs of Boston, Providence and other New England cities . . . have been sending on their remittances to Philadelphia by hundreds and thousands of dollars . . . to make good the election of Curtin as Governor."[87] In September the *Daily Pittsburgh Gazette* claimed that "*one hundred thousand dollars* has been raised from merchants in New York city, and has been scattered broadcast over the State to operate on the October election."[88] In June National Republican Committee member and Davis's friend John Goodrich wrote to Congressman Henry Dawes that he "intend[ed] to devote pretty much the whole of [his] time to the Election," including soliciting contributions from Massachusetts residents "toward discharging such expenses as must necessarily be incurred" in the pivotal state of Pennsylvania.[89] The urgency to fund the Pennsylvania campaign, however, ebbed in Goodrich's mind when he met with Cameron, Joseph Casey, and Andrew Curtin in Philadelphia in July. At the meeting, Goodrich offered funds from the Republican National Committee to help finance the Pennsylvania campaign. Consistent with the position expressed to Lincoln and Davis, Cameron and Casey declined the offer, suggesting that Goodrich direct the money to other states. Surprisingly, Curtin, on whose behalf McClure had been begging for money, agreed with or at least did not object to Cameron's rejection of the national committee's offer of funds. So if McClure was short of funds, at least part of the blame belonged to Curtin.[90]

McClure's letters to Lincoln describing the state committee's massive literature distribution further undermine McClure's claim that little money was received from New York and his claim that what was received came after the October election. On August 1 the state chair wrote to Lincoln that in August alone his committee would "send out a full quarter of a million [campaign] documents." Three weeks later, McClure confirmed that they were "sending out over 5000 documents per day."[91]

After meeting with McClure, Davis stopped at Easton, Pennsylvania, to see Andrew H. Reeder, the former governor of the Kansas Territory. Reeder was not home.[92]

The Outcome of Davis's Pennsylvania Trip

The trip to Pennsylvania was vital and delicate. Simon Cameron was the most influential and knowledgeable politician in the state. He expected his importance to be acknowledged and his preeminent position praised no less by Lincoln supporters than by his in-state followers. Alexander McClure, who was powerful, albeit less powerful, than Cameron, held the Republican Party state chairmanship and controlled the official party campaign machinery and funds. While Cameron expected adulation, McClure searched for respect and appreciation. A month before Davis's visit, McClure tried to explain Pennsylvania's political situation to the Republican National Committee, and, in McClure's mind, the committee laughed at him.[93] Davis was familiar with the movers and shakers of both state party factions, having worked with them at the Chicago convention. That familiarity, together with the ability, when necessary, to flatter, praise, and foster the appearance of a special relationship, permitted Davis to meet the expectations of both Cameron and McClure without insulting or demeaning either. The judge came to Cameron's home just as Seward had done a year before. Davis entrusted Lincoln's private tariff notes to Cameron and no one else and allowed Cameron to show off Lincoln's confidential friend at the Cameron organizational campaign committee meeting in Philadelphia. Davis complimented McClure's organization and took him into his confidence by sharing that the real reason for the trip was to investigate claims that McClure was mismanaging the campaign. Davis was more than willing to let Cameron and McClure be the authorities. The judge permitted McClure to take him by the hand and show him the ins and outs of campaign strategy and organization.[94] Lawyers of the Eighth Circuit would probably have difficulty picturing the judge tagging along a few steps behind McClure and receiving an education on electioneering. Davis played it down the middle, satisfying both competing factions of Pennsylvania Republicans.

The tariff notes, supplemented by Davis's pitch, put an end to worries about Lincoln's stance on protective tariffs. Satisfying Cameron on the issue allowed the publication of friendly newspaper articles rebutting Democratic attacks that no evidence supported Lincoln's claim that he was protariff. The trip allowed Davis to gather intelligence on the Republican and Democratic canvasses, including opinions from both factions of the state Republican Party. Further, it fostered an open and frank line of communication between Pennsylvania Republicans and Davis, Swett, and Lincoln. For example, McClure sent multiple monthly correspondence to Lincoln advising, among other things, of the distribution of campaign documents, the progress of precinct organizations, the recruitment of speakers, the activities of gubernatorial candidates, the progress of the Democrats in constructing a fusion ticket, and county vote total predictions for Curtin and Lincoln.[95]

Judge Davis in New York

Davis left Scranton, his last stop in Pennsylvania, and arrived in New York to meet his cousin Henry Winter Davis on the evening of August 13, 1860. Davis had spent four of the first eleven years of his life living with Winter, Winter's father, the Reverend Henry Lyon Davis, and Winter's mother, Jane Brown Winter Davis. Winter graduated from Kenyon College five years after his cousin. They maintained a close relationship throughout their lives.[96]

At the time of their August meeting, Congressman Winter Davis and his family resided at West Point, about fifty miles north of New York City. He was serving on a commission evaluating the course of instruction and system of discipline at the United States Military Academy.[97] Winter had served as a Maryland congressman since 1856. Although he was elected to Congress as a Know-Nothing under the American Party label, Winter was held in high esteem by national Republican Party leaders. This was because in early 1860 he convinced another American Party congressman to join him in voting for the Republican candidate for Speaker of the House. The Republican, William Pennington, won by a single vote. Winter did not attend the Republican National Convention in Chicago, but when his name was mentioned before the assembly, he received "loud cheers." On the last day of the convention, he garnered eight votes for the vice presidential nomination.[98] His prestige as a political strategist was enhanced by the fact that he supported Know-Nothing Millard Fillmore in the 1856 presidential election, and Maryland was the only state that Fillmore carried.

Winter Davis wrote to his cousin on July 27, 1860, suggesting that they meet if David planned to be in New York for the campaign.[99] Even without the invitation David would have visited his cousin to get the views of a leading Know-Nothing and to draw upon the information gathered by Winter from his congressional and other political contacts. Open and frank conversations between the two were the norm because of a shared dominant trait: no hesitancy to express fixed opinions. In addition, they both intensely disliked the Democrats. A month before the election, Winter urged Maryland voters to "smite fearlessly the Democratic party," because the death of the Democrats would confer more strength upon the country "than the death of *all* other political organizations that have ever existed."[100]

Partly because Maryland had no chance of going Republican, Winter Davis supported the Constitutional Union ticket of former Tennessee senator John Bell for president and former Massachusetts senator Edward Everett for vice president. In June Winter wrote Davis suggesting that Republicans not even place Lincoln and Hamlin on the Maryland ballot and instead support the Constitutional Union candidates to ensure the defeat of Douglas. Winter believed that running Republican candidates in Maryland would "embitter" the adherents of the Constitutional Union Party who would view the Republicans just as they viewed the Democrats—as enemies. Winter thought that once elected, all opponents of the Democracy in Maryland would rally behind Lincoln. This would help ensure the success of legislative and congressional candidates running in the 1861 Maryland elections. Of course, those candidates would run under the Constitutional Union Party label, as the "Republican" brand meant automatic defeat. As requested by Winter, Davis forwarded a copy of the letter containing this suggestion to Lincoln. Not really expecting an answer, the judge included a noncommittal notation asking Lincoln if anything could be done to prevent the problem forecast by Winter.[101] Lincoln knew that although national Republican leaders lauded Winter for voting to put a Republican in the Speaker's seat, the extremely small but dedicated group of Maryland Republicans detested Winter's attempt to undermine their efforts in the state. Nevertheless, his standing with the American Party members, hate of the Democrats, and opposition to a fusion ticket made Winter a valuable Lincoln ally.[102]

Winter Davis made several suggestions that Judge Davis promised to convey to Lincoln when he returned home. One piece of advice was that Congressman William Alanson Howard of Detroit, Michigan, would be an important supporter of a Lincoln administration and that Howard needed help to ensure his reelection. A week after their meeting, Winter wrote Davis to remind him of the importance of Howard's election, adding that Howard had been beaten by fraud at the last election and had to file an election contest to retain his seat.[103] Winter also emphasized the importance of another Lincoln supporter, Congressman John Sherman of Ohio.[104] Winter believed that Sherman's moderate campaign speeches for Lincoln in Ohio, Pennsylvania, Indiana, New Jersey, and Delaware helped offset Democrat attacks on Lincoln's radicalism and "enabled & induced the great mass of Fillmores friends & of the old whigs to join Mr Lincoln."[105]

The judge's cousin sincerely believed that Lincoln would win and just as sincerely hoped that his administration would be successful.[106] At their meeting, Congressman Davis gave Judge Davis some advice on cabinet selections. First and foremost, Winter said that William Seward should not be appointed secretary of state. The congressman thought that the safest position for the New York senator was across the Atlantic as minister to England. The appointment of Seward to a cabinet post, especially secretary of state, would only inflame the South and alienate moderates and conservatives who voted for Lincoln. Winter's choice for the important cabinet post was Ohio congressman Thomas Corwin, known by many as the "peacemaker of the House." Winter believed that Corwin's "wise and moderate speeches" in the House of Representatives spoke the real views of the "masses of the north" rather than the abolitionist views associated with Seward. Congressman Winter argued that Corwin would give the public confidence in the Lincoln administration and unite the anti-Democrat forces. It may be that the judge pushed back on this suggestion, because a few weeks later Winter told Davis that since their meeting in New York he had "reflected much on our conversation about Seward & the Cabinet" and sought the opinions of others on the subject. Winter found that all agreed that England was the place for Seward and that Corwin was the man for secretary of state.[107]

Winter also explained to his cousin some of the key points that he intended to make in a major September address to the voters of Maryland. In the address, Winter would affirm his support for the Constitutional Union candidates Bell and Everett, severely criticize the Democrats, and defend Lincoln as a legitimate and safe alternative to Douglas and Breckinridge.[108] Although Judge Davis would have preferred that his cousin endorse Lincoln, he could appreciate the salutary effect of Winter's planned speech on Lincoln's chances. It was reminiscent of Greeley's role at the nomination convention. Greeley was for Bates but spent most of the time attacking Seward. Winter's speech would do the same by attacking the Democrats and then go one better by defending Lincoln. Winter gave the speech on September 27, 1860, at an American Party meeting in Baltimore. Immediately afterward, he sent a copy of the speech to his cousin.[109] In the speech, Winter admitted that his first choice was the Bell ticket but quickly added that where Bell was not viable, a vote for Lincoln was required. Lincoln was not an abolitionist, he stood by the Fugitive Slave Law, and his election would not result in dissolution of the Union. According to the American Party congressman, Lincoln's stance on slavery mimicked that of Bell: leave it alone where it existed and prevent its spread to new territories. Winter considered Lincoln's position identical to that of the Constitutional Unionists, who advocated leaving the slavery issue as it stood. Winter explained that American Party members could not countenance a fusion ticket because no Democrat-controlled state would vote for Bell if the election went to the House of Representatives.[110]

After the speech, Winter was "perpetually bothered" by invitations to speak at Republican meetings. The congressman responded that his speech before an American Party audience in support of Bell was "worth a thousand" speeches before Republican groups. Winter told his cousin that Republicans would be better off distributing copies of his Baltimore speech.[111] And in short order, Republican newspapers used the speech to Lincoln's advantage by reprinting it, summarizing it, or simply highlighting the favorable comments about Lincoln and the criticisms of the Democrats.[112] In reporting the speech, the *Lewistown Gazette* emphasized that although Winter supported Bell, "he denounced all coalition with Democrats, whether of the Breckinridge or Douglas school." According to the *Gazette*, Congressman Davis also demonstrated that the Republican Party was not an abolitionist party and merely desired to return the slavery question to where it stood before repeal of the Missouri Compromise.[113] The *Cleveland Morning Leader* underscored Winter's call to block fusion attempts and his characterization of Lincoln as a conservative. Referring to Winter's speech, the *Philadelphia Press* simply put it, "His First Choice Bell, his Second Lincoln."[114] Republican stump speakers referred to Winter's speech and often received three cheers in return.[115]

While in New York City Davis visited some Republicans, although probably not as many as he wished. On his first day in the city, he complained that it was hard to find anyone to speak with. In the morning Davis stopped by the *New-York Daily Tribune* office to see publisher Horace Greeley but learned that Greeley did not usually come to work until late afternoon.[116] The judge was no fan of Greeley, since he failed to support Lincoln over Douglas in the senatorial race of 1858. But Greeley was the owner and editor of the most influential Republican newspaper in the country, claiming nearly 290,000 subscribers and "probably" 1.5 million readers. The paper's primary market was New York, but it had a circulation of at least ten thousand copies in each of the states of Pennsylvania, Ohio, Illinois, Indiana, Wisconsin, Iowa, Massachusetts, Michigan, and Maine.[117] The judge himself subscribed to the *Tribune*. Although he supported Bates during the convention, Greeley and his paper backed the eventual Republican nominee. At the time of Davis's visit, the *Tribune* had endorsed Lincoln, defended him from attacks, reproduced stump speeches by Lincoln surrogates, and advocated against a Democratic fusion ticket. The paper also sold a thirty-two-page campaign biography titled "Life of Abraham Lincoln." Greeley personally entered the fray, giving a speech directed at "Old-line Whigs" during a Lincoln-Hamlin rally in Union Square.[118] When the judge finally caught up with Greeley, he no doubt offered his unvarnished opinions about the campaign mechanisms and personalities in New York, New England, and Pennsylvania. Because Greeley considered himself an expert on protective tariffs, he and Davis most likely discussed that topic. And without doubt, Davis assured the editor, just as he assured everyone else, that "the popular vote of Illinois [was] secure beyond peradventure."[119]

While in New York Davis saw Benjamin Welch Jr. Welch had started as a Democrat and then transferred allegiance to the Know-Nothings before he finally became a Republican.[120] Davis wanted to see George G. Fogg, the secretary of the Republican National Committee, rather than Welch, but Fogg was absent from New York for several days during the middle of August. Welch sometimes stood in for Fogg when the Republican Party secretary was out of town. Welch probably repeated to Davis what he had written to Lincoln: "Information from all quarters . . . [was] of the most satisfactory character." Although Welch expressed fear concerning isolated congressional districts in Maine and Pennsylvania, the success of the Republican ticket as a whole was certain. Predictably, Welch believed that Douglas's attempt to woo "the debris" of the Know-Nothing vote would not save the Little Giant.[121] Davis saw others in addition to Winter, Greeley, and Welch in New York but did not record their names in correspondence to Lincoln. Indeed, the letters sent to Lincoln during his eastern trip were bare boned. The judge saved the most important information for a personal meeting when he returned to Illinois.[122]

From New York City Davis traveled to Albany to see Thurlow Weed and Governor Edwin Morgan. It was especially important to touch base with Morgan, since his first meeting with Lincoln had left the governor less than impressed.[123] Weed confirmed the information received by Davis earlier in the trip that Rhode Island might be in trouble. Weed was quick to add, however, that Rhode Island was the only Eastern Seaboard state that was in doubt. To obtain firsthand information, Weed convinced Davis to stay an extra day in Albany to accompany Weed on the forty-five-mile trip to Saratoga to see some Rhode Island "politicians" who were in the city. Whatever the judge learned from the Ocean State visitors did not put his mind at ease. Returning to Bloomington, he wrote Weed, "I trust that you will not forget to look in on Rhode Island speedily." Either the potential problem was overstated or Weed fixed it, because Lincoln won 61 percent of the "Little Rhody" vote.[124]

Weed probably discussed the state's campaign structure with Davis to demonstrate that the Seward-Weed-Morgan triad was fully behind Lincoln. Besides, the Wizard of the Lobby enjoyed sharing the sophisticated nature of his canvassing network. Weed could have shown Davis an August letter from Starr

Clark, an abolitionist from Mexico, New York (forty miles north of Syracuse), detailing how his town committee solicited votes and ensured the appearance of right-thinking voters at the polls. In his letter, Starr also predicted the size of the Republican majority in Mexico and compared that with the majority secured for Republicans in 1856. Finally, Clark provided a projected vote total for Oswego County, the county in which Mexico was located.[125]

Davis was not in Albany to tell Weed how to run the state campaign any more than he went to Pennsylvania to direct the efforts of the McClure and Cameron forces. The judge appreciated that the state leaders knew what was best for their states as he knew what was best for Illinois. In addition, Davis and top lieutenant Leonard Swett employed a very deferential approach when dealing with leading party men such as Weed and Cameron. For example, a month before Davis's visit Swett assured Weed that the Lincoln team needed his advice because of his superior experience and that Weed's views "would have controlling influence."[126]

While out east Davis met his friend John Z. Goodrich, a national committee-man from Massachusetts and Republican financier who had helped during the presidential nominating convention. The top agenda item at the meeting would have been campaign fundraising efforts. Later, in the dog days of the campaign, Goodrich supplied much-needed money to Indiana. Davis also visited the chair of the New Jersey Republican State Committee, Thomas Dudley, whom Davis had met at the Chicago convention.[127]

The Campaign in the Prairie State

During the Republican State Convention in Decatur and in accordance with Lincoln's wishes, Davis was named an at-large delegate to the National Repub-lican Nominating Convention. At the same time, Davis was selected to serve on the Illinois Republican Central Committee, chaired by Norman Judd. On paper, the state central committee bore the responsibility of coordinating statewide election efforts for both state and federal candidates. And to some extent the committee served that function. But most of its influence was in recommend-ing rather than in commanding. Shortly after Lincoln's nomination, the state committee urged the formation of local Republican and Lincoln clubs. The committee sent a letter to the Republican faithful stressing the need for active clubs and committees and coordination with the state committee. The letter, in part, stated:

> The importance of the campaign upon which we have entered and the fact that the favorite son of Illinois has been made the standard-bearer of the Republican hosts of the nation—by which the *obligations of honor* are added to the promptings of duty—are, we trust, sufficient to call forth the utmost efforts of the Republicans

of the State from now till the day of election. Careful and systematic ORGANI-
ZATION is our safety. We take it for granted that you have an active and efficient
County Committee. If there is a town or a precinct in your county in which there is
not a local club or committee, cooperating with the central organization, it should
be attended to forthwith. May we request you as a zealous and working Republican
to give your personal attention to this all-important matter.[128]

In an attempt to synchronize campaign efforts, the letter included blank forms
for committees to complete and return to the state committee with the name,
location, and officers of each local Republican organization.[129]

But structuring a campaign in a state of the size and diversity of Illinois was
nearly impossible. This was especially true in the 1860 campaign, which drew
"unusual activity among the Republican masses." As Leonard Swett observed in
July, "There is not so much order and method as I might wish. Our meetings are
the result of independent action by men in the various counties not ordinarily
called politicians."[130]

Besides encouraging and coordinating local campaign efforts, the state
central committee had fundraising responsibilities. Judd established a refined
process for soliciting funds to support statewide canvassing activities. The
central committee assessed a fixed contribution for each county. The committee then appointed a respected individual in the county to make sure that
the fundraising goal was met. These overseers of fundraising efforts received
a letter directing them to take certain steps to ensure that they did not fall
short of their predetermined contribution amount. The letter urged the fundraising overseers to (1) notify the county central committee, executive committee, or other prominent Republican group of the assessment amount; (2)
"circulate immediately a subscription, and get the [assessment] reliably and
distinctly pledged"; (3) name a county treasurer, "upon whom the Treasurer
of the State Central Committee may make requisitions, as the money may be
needed in the progress of the campaign"; and (4) notify the state committee
when these steps had been taken. In the letter, Judd stressed that printing and
other campaign expenses must be paid and that the state committee needed
the money sooner rather than later. He suggested remittance of 10 percent of
the assessment without delay.[131]

Precisely how effective this procedure was in collecting money is unclear.
Judd's dismal fundraising effort in the 1858 senatorial election does not speak
well for the success of the system. According to Ozias Hatch, Illinois secretary
of state and member of the Republican State Central Committee, the central
committee raised little or no money for the 1858 campaign. In fact, he "never
heard that *anybody* received money in '58."[132] It appears that the difficulty in
raising funds carried over to the 1860 campaign. Judd's letter to Lincoln on
August 1, 1860, complained that "the great trouble" in executing the game plan

was a "want of funds." Judd specifically called out Springfield, Jacksonville, and Bloomington for failing to supply money for speakers and to distribute campaign flyers. A few months before Judd's letter, Davis complained to Lincoln, "It is very difficult to raise money."[133] And fundraising became no easier as the election neared. On September 5 Davis sent a letter (probably the form fundraising letter used by the state central committee) to Ezekiel Boyden, past chair of the Champaign County Republican Committee, seeking a commitment from the county Republican organization to raise funds for the presidential campaign. Boyden wrote back that while the county would answer Davis's expectations as far as votes for Lincoln in November were concerned, it was "exceeding doubtful" that local Republicans would meet expectations as far as fundraising. Boyden made it clear that there was little hope for money from the county committee or Republican officials or their friends.[134] That is not to say that county Republican groups were averse to contributing money to the party's efforts. But most counties, such as Whiteside County, preferred their money to remain at home to ensure the success of local events.[135]

Exactly where the money came from to finance Lincoln's presidential campaign in not at all clear.[136] The large contributions came from the Republican National Committee through the efforts or pockets of Weed, Goodrich, and other wealthy easterners. The Illinois Republican Central Committee through Judd and Davis and other members raised some funds to pay for speakers, postage, and campaign documents. Davis on his own raised money, although his ability to do so was hampered by Lincoln's failure to supply Davis with a promised letter to aid his fundraising effort. Davis paid the room expenses at the Tremont during the convention, and Ward Lamon and Ozias Hatch covered the costs of alcohol and cigars. Davis paid his own expenses during the campaign and probably paid some or all of Swett's expenses, as he had in Lincoln's senatorial campaigns. The judge most likely raised other funds and underwrote other expenses.[137]

Lincoln did receive a few large donations from Illinois benefactors. Wealthy businessman and friend John Bunn donated at least $3,500 toward Lincoln's election. Five hundred dollars of Bunn's donation came at the beginning of the campaign when he was asked by Stephen Logan to act as treasurer for an effort to raise $5,000 from donors in and around Springfield. Logan gave John Bunn a list of ten persons (including Logan) who would likely contribute to the fund. Among others, the list included John Bunn and his brother Jacob, Colonel John Williams, Ozias Hatch, Thomas Condell, and Robert Irwin. Each of the ten contributed $500 to meet the $5,000 goal. Some of the money from the fund was used to finance the Springfield rally on August 8. The expenses of the rally drained the account, so the ten contributors each donated another $500. When Lincoln was elected, the fund was overdrawn by $2,500, which John

Bunn covered.[138] A former law clerk at the law office of Asahel Gridley claimed that Gridley contributed "considerably over 100,000 dollars."[139] In the unlikely event that Gridley made such a contribution, he was apparently able to hide it from Lincoln's Springfield finance committee, Lincoln, Judd, and Davis.

When in Illinois, Davis faithfully attended the weekly meetings of the state central committee and participated in its activities. As a member of the committee and independently, he solicited in-state and out-of-state speakers.[140]

Speakers in Illinois

The State Republican Central Committee successfully solicited out-of-state personalities to speak at Illinois rallies. For example, on August 13, 1860, the committee invited former Ohio congressman and foreign diplomat Robert C. Schenck to speak in Illinois as his schedule permitted. A year before, Schenck took the stage with Lincoln at a Republican meeting in Dayton, Ohio. In his remarks, Schenck was one of the first to publicly suggest Lincoln for the presidential nomination.[141] The committee's letter to Schenck stated:

> Hon. R. Schenck
> Dear Sir
> I am instructed by the State Central Committee to invite you to address the Republicans of Illinois during the present Canvass—If consistent with your engagements so to do—I would like to be advised at which time and for how long you can devote your Services to Illinois. I will make your appointments on consultation with Mr. Lincoln.
>
> > Respectly [*sic*]
> > Yours
> > N. B. Judd[142]

Some Illinois communities relied on the state central committee to secure national speakers for their local gatherings. But Judd and the other committee members simply could not supply speakers for the hundreds upon hundreds of meetings in Illinois. In fact, the *Chicago Press and Tribune* suggested that local clubs not wait for the central committee to send speakers "whom they cannot command" and who would be busy in their own states until the fall elections were over. Instead, the *Tribune* encouraged Illinois counties and towns to use local speaking talent, glee clubs, and Wide Awakes to generate enthusiasm. But such suggestions did not satisfy all local leaders. Robert Wilson, clerk of the court in Whiteside County, wrote to Lincoln in October mildly complaining that because the county was "so confirmedly Republican," no speakers, except for Leonard Swett, were sent to rallies in the county.[143]

As part of its election strategy, the Illinois Republican State Central Committee decided to send speakers to southern Illinois. In Lincoln's campaigns for the Senate in 1854 and 1858, these solidly Democratic counties were ignored as a waste of time and effort. But the nature of the election had changed. Illinois electoral votes for president would be determined by the popular vote of the state as a whole. The 1855 and 1859 senatorial contests had been decided by vote of the legislators. So in Lincoln's senatorial contests, increasing the Republican vote by a small amount in a heavily Democratic legislative district would not change the result of the election for the legislative seat or for US senator. For the presidential election, however, whether the Republicans or Democrats controlled the state legislature was irrelevant. Picking up a hundred votes here and there in the southernmost counties of Illinois (collectively known as "Egypt" or "Little Egypt") could swing the state's popular vote and electoral vote to Lincoln. The move to send speakers south was bolstered by the anecdotal evidence that Republicans could add the former Know-Nothing vote. Also, speakers were needed in Clay and other southern counties to refute the unrelenting refrain of Democrat stump speakers that "'Negro Equality' in every respect is the ultimate end of Republicanism."[144]

Lincoln planned to send Davis and Swett to the southern counties. They were safe choices because neither could be labeled as an abolitionist. Both had impeccable credentials as conservative old-line Whig Republicans and Lincoln confidants. But the duo had to be split up when a last-minute decision was made in early August to send a troubleshooter to the eastern states.[145] The division of labor was easy. Swett was the accomplished stump speaker and would go south. Davis would go east. Swett began a two-week speaking tour of southern Illinois on August 1 with a speech in Vandalia, moving the next day to Centralia and then to Fairfield and Burnt Prairie. On August 7 he debated Samuel S. Marshall in White County. Marshall was a former Democrat congressman, and some considered him to be "the greatest lawyer of his day in Southern Illinois."[146]

In the next four days Swett visited Grayville, Mount Carmel, Albion, and Olney, Illinois. The day after he spoke at Albion he also spoke at a large rally in Mattoon. Some of Swett's speeches ran three and a half hours, and on at least one occasion he brought audience members to tears.[147] Swett reported the results of the trip to Lincoln, including his estimate of the attendance at each event, which ranged from six hundred to twenty-five hundred people. He also relayed the glowing predictions of local Republicans on the number of votes that Lincoln could expect in Wayne, Edwards, White, Wabash, Richland, and Clay Counties. According to a resident of Edwards County, Swett's meetings at Albion and Olney were the largest gatherings of any kind ever held in the county.[148]

In August 1860 John Hay described the value of the trips made by Swett, Richard Oglesby, and others to the Democratic stronghold of Illinois: "Swett and [Richard] Oglesby are doing wonders down there [in Egypt] also, in removing prejudices and bringing over the wavering vote that has long been inclining the right way, and that is coming over in platoons when success becomes certain. The sight of gentlemen, speaking in a gentlemanlike way, is a new revelation in politics to the Egyptians, and is charming from its very novelty."[149]

Some members of the state central committee asked Owen Lovejoy to speak for the Republican ticket in central and southern Illinois. Davis certainly disagreed with this suggestion. He had vehemently opposed the state's most famous abolitionist touring central Illinois during the 1858 campaign because it would confirm the Democrat's claim that the Republicans were a party of abolitionists, thereby scaring away conservative Whig voters.[150] One proponent of Lovejoy's southern trip was Jesse Fell, who believed that Lovejoy could convince voters that he was not some two-headed monster and that the Republican Party did not intend to interfere with slavery where it existed.[151] Lovejoy did travel south into heavily Democratic areas repeating a conservative antislavery theme. In a speech at Rushville on September 25, he told an audience of ten to fifteen thousand people that "he did not now nor ever did favor interference with slavery in the States; that he never had stolen a negro nor persuaded one to escape."[152] Lovejoy made more than one hundred speeches during the campaign, many to audiences from central and southern Illinois counties, including Lawrence, Marion, Christian, Woodford, Jersey, Greene, Macoupin, Morgan, Sangamon, DeWitt, Ford, Iroquois, Champaign, and Vermillion.[153] Describing Lovejoy as "the king of Illinois stump speakers," an article in the *New York Times* reported that his speeches in Egypt converted some Democrats to the Republican cause by rebutting the claim that he and his party were "furiously ultra." The *Times* correspondent noted, however, Lovejoy's difficulty in masking his "ultra" position on slavery, which he had unambiguously set out year after year in sermons from the pulpit and speeches in Congress. For example, four months before his southern Illinois campaign tour, Lovejoy told Congress that slavery was a "relic of barbarism," "the sum of all villany [sic]," and it deserved to be dealt a "death blow."[154] Lovejoy did not mind backsliding on his slavery stance to benefit Lincoln's cause. Lovejoy considered his campaign journey a success and thanked Fell for advising him to make the trip.[155]

As Davis expected, the Democrats expressed appreciation to the Republicans for finally showing their true colors by naming Lovejoy, the foremost ultra abolitionist in the state, as their spokesperson. One Democratic newspaper reported that "Parson Lovejoy's" speech exceeded his own record for "lying and low dirty abuse." The paper then reprinted a resolution of the Morris Democratic Club thanking the Republicans for bringing Lovejoy to town: "*Resolved*, that the thanks of this Club are hereby tendered to our Republican friends for the speech of the Hon. Owen Lovejoy . . . believing as we do, that it has been of great benefit to the Democratic party. And we hope that Mr. Lovejoy may be induced to deliver another such speech in Grundy county previous to the election."[156]

It is difficult to determine whether Lovejoy helped or hurt Lincoln's cause in the central and southern portions of the state. Maybe it was Lovejoy and the other speakers, or the disarray of the Democrats, or the influx of new residents from northern states, or the winning over of Fillmore and German voters. Whatever the reason, the Republican presidential vote increased dramatically in southern Illinois in 1860. For example, in Marion County, one of Lovejoy's stump stops, Lincoln received 32 percent of the total vote compared to Republican presidential candidate John Frémont's 8.75 percent four years earlier.[157] In Christian County, another stop for Lovejoy, the Republican presidential vote increased from 17 percent in 1856 to 40 percent in 1860. Another Lovejoy venue, Greene County, gave Lincoln 30 percent of the vote, while four years earlier Frémont received only about 10 percent.[158] Richland County, visited by Swett, gave Frémont 39 votes (3 percent of the presidential vote total) and Lincoln 777 votes (42 percent of the presidential vote). In 1856 White County, another Swett stop, gave Frémont 27 votes (1 percent of the total vote). In 1860 Lincoln received 756 votes (32 percent of the total). Some deep southern counties, however, remained steadfastly Democratic. For example, in 1856 Johnson County gave Frémont 2 votes, Buchanan 1,144, and Fillmore 74 votes. In 1860 the county gave Lincoln 40 votes and Douglas 1,563 votes.[159]

Davis Takes to the Stump

Davis did not like to speak at political rallies. He was acutely aware of his limitations as a public speaker and recognized the superiority of many in-state and out-of-state Republicans who could better command an audience. But Davis did have experience as a stump speaker in his campaigns for the legislature in the 1840s and in campaigning for others especially in the 1858 election. During the canvass in 1860 Davis made a few public speeches at Republican gatherings where he felt at home and thought that he could influence the crowd. His speeches were designed as one old Whig telling other former Whigs why they should vote Republican. He spoke at a Macon County rally with Senator Trumbull and Leonard Swett on July 7. The friendly *Illinois State Journal* did not report the substance of his speech but kindly noted that "his speech was a perfect model in its way. It was as sound in argument as Judge Davis' legal decisions are in law; and that is saying a good deal."[160] Later in July, Davis made it a point to speak at a rally of thirty-five hundred people in Tazewell County. Two years before, the judge spent considerable time and energy in the same legislative district in furtherance of Lincoln's senatorial bid. Davis knew the county well and was convinced that with the right approach it would go for Lincoln.

Davis was the first speaker at the July Tazewell rally, followed by Senator Lyman Trumbull and Leonard Swett. Davis began by reminding the crowd of his long association with the people of the county, including a shared political philosophy. He continued by characterizing the county as a former stronghold for Whigs, just like Davis. Now the majority of its voters were Republican, just like Davis. According to the judge, no longer were Republicans fearful of the "foul epithets" hurled at them by the Democracy. That was because the Democrats knew that they deserved to be beaten, and the voters in Tazewell would help ensure that the Democrats received their just deserts.[161]

Davis argued that the Northwest Ordinance of 1787, which prohibited slavery in the territory, caused no uproar in the country and was supported by southern and northern senators and representatives alike. To Davis the explanation was simple: "All parties at that day believed that slavery was an evil, and that it should be kept out of all Territory from which it could be lawfully excluded. Our fathers were a law-abiding, freedom loving people. Are not Republicans the same today? [Applause.]" Davis built on the argument. Most of the original immigrants to the Northwest Territory were from the slaveholding states of Virginia, Maryland, and North Carolina. They raised no complaint when they were barred from bringing their slaves to the new territory. That was because "they thought [the] prohibition both constitutional and right." These were the same people who voted to adopt the US Constitution obviously with the understanding that Congress could prohibit the extension of slavery to the territories. Davis then challenged the audience: "Will my modern Democrat friends say that *they* know more about the meaning and the spirit of the Federal Constitution than the very men who made and adopted it, and passed the first laws under it? Are there any here who think so? [Silence.] Well, then, you must admit that the Republicans are right, and that your party is wrong. [Great applause.]" Davis concluded by directly addressing the former Whigs. Davis explained that Democrats asked old-line Whigs "to entertain the doctrine of free slave trade in the Territories." In answer, the judge "read copiously from the writings and speeches of Henry Clay, Daniel Webster, Thomas Corwin and other great lights of the Whig party," demonstrating beyond question that Whigs always opposed the extension of slavery. A *Chicago Press and Tribune* correspondent reported that former Whigs paid close attention to this part of the speech. The correspondent added that during the "thunders of applause" as Davis ended his remarks a former Fillmore voter told the reporter, "That speech is just as good as fifty votes in this county for Abe Lincoln."[162]

Three days before he left for his eastern trip, Davis spoke again with Trumbull in the central Illinois city of Monticello, located halfway between Decatur and Champaign. Monticello was the county seat of Piatt County, one of the counties in the Eighth Judicial Circuit. According to the same *Chicago Press and Tribune* reporter who covered Davis's speech in Tazewell County, the judge again spoke directly to the former Whigs who made up a majority of the voters in the county. The audience "seemed greatly pleased when he contrasted the manly course of Clay with the hypocritical shuffling of Douglas." The correspondent reported that everyone left the one-and-a-half-hour speech convinced that Clay and the old Whig Party favored prohibition of slavery in the territories. Even though the rally did not end until midnight, the newspaper man was pleased to note that he saw only two drunk men, both of whom, of course, were Douglasites.[163]

In September Davis ventured "north" for one of his few speaking engagements outside his home territory of central Illinois. On Friday, September 7, the judge spoke from the courthouse steps in Ottawa, Illinois. The county seat of LaSalle County, Ottawa sat about 115 miles southwest of Chicago and 70 miles north of Bloomington. Davis was not unfamiliar with the area, having filled in on occasion for the circuit judge of the Ninth Judicial Circuit. Judge Davis by no means was the featured speaker of the Republican festivities. That honor fell to Kentucky abolitionist Cassius Clay, who gave an afternoon speech in a grove along the banks of the Illinois River. Davis spoke in the evening with former Democrat Burton C. Cook, who had served as a delegate to the Republican National Convention earlier in the year. As always, the judge's role was to convince former Whigs that their new home was with the Republicans.[164]

The Springfield Ratification Meeting

A huge ratification meeting was scheduled for August 8 in Springfield.[165] The Springfield Committee of Arrangements was pulling out all the stops to ensure an inspiring and exciting spectacle in Lincoln's hometown. Davis explained to Lincoln that the event must signal overwhelming support for the Republicans. Although not a member of the events committee, Davis, true to his character, did not hesitate to make suggestions concerning the festivities, including that Chicago mayor John Wentworth should speak at one of the five speaker stands. The suggestion to invite Wentworth was made in an attempt to cement Long John's support of Lincoln, which was by no means certain. But the recommendation was less than enthusiastic. Davis told Lincoln that at a meeting like the one planned for Springfield, Wentworth "would make as acceptable a speech as any body."[166] The unenthusiastic request rested in part on the fact that Wentworth was persona non grata among many Republicans in Springfield and elsewhere.[167] That was because the Democrats distributed Wentworth's abolitionist-tinged editorials published in his paper, the *Chicago Democrat*, and claimed that they reflected Lincoln's views. In central Illinois it was commonly believed that the editorials damaged Lincoln with conservative voters. By the beginning of October even Davis reluctantly had become convinced that Wentworth's newspaper articles were intended to hurt both Lyman Trumbull's run for the Senate and Lincoln's campaign.[168] Like Davis, Lincoln wished to have Wentworth's help or at least avoid his open opposition, and so the Springfield Ratification Committee invited the Chicago mayor to speak in Springfield on August 8.[169] If Wentworth spoke at the rally, the *Illinois State Journal* failed to mention it. Wentworth was a more effective speaker in Illinois's abolitionist strongholds of Chicago, Aurora, and Waukegan and in southern Wisconsin cities such as Beloit.[170]

Davis also suggested that the committee invite John Wilson, the leader of the Illinois American Party, to speak at the Springfield rally. Two months before the rally, Davis wrote to Lincoln advising him that Henry Whitney's father, a Know-Nothing, had urged the judge to visit Wilson in Chicago to help bring him publicly on the Republican side. Instead, Lincoln asked Indiana American Party leader Richard W. Thompson to contact the Illinois American Party leader to try to ward off a movement to run a Bell presidential ticket in Illinois.[171] When the effort to prevent the Bell ticket failed, and the Know-Nothing vote became even more important, Davis took it upon himself to visit Wilson. On Sunday, July 22, he spent the day with Wilson and Henry Whitney's father in Chicago and confirmed that Wilson favored Lincoln and strongly opposed the Democrats. If invited, Wilson agreed to speak at the Springfield ratification meeting. Davis requested an invitation to the American Party leader in much stronger language than he had used in suggesting an invitation to Wentworth. The judge wrote to Lincoln, "Now, I want the Com[mittee] of Arrangements to invite [Wilson] to speak, & also I want it attended to that so that he can have a good opportunity to speak." Davis further suggested that Jesse Dubois and William Butler take Wilson under their wings, and if they found him to be an effective speaker, then they should arrange other speaking engagements for him. Davis added that the American Party organizer's ego required personal attention, including a mention in campaign documents advertising the gathering. Wilson spoke at the Springfield rally.[172]

The *Illinois State Journal* estimated that seventy-five thousand people attended the Springfield mass meeting on August 8. Democratic papers put the number much lower, the *State Democrat* estimating the attendance at thirty thousand.[173] The event began at sunrise with the firing of a national salute. The parade to the fairgrounds included nineteen Wide Awake clubs from Illinois and two clubs from Missouri, followed by "forty-one couples of ladies and gentlemen on horseback . . . hailing from Cotton Hill Precinct," a "full-rigged schooner with sailors aboard," and an immense wagon from the Springfield Woolen Mill making several yards of jeans cloth from which a pair of pantaloons were constructed for Lincoln. Then came the county delegations with banners, flags, rail splitters at work, wagons with young ladies, a log cabin on wheels, horsemen disguised as Indians participating in the Boston Tea Party, and wagons and carriages of every description. Tazewell County, where Davis had spoken two weeks earlier, displayed a claimed five hundred wagons, including one hundred from Delevan, where Davis would address a rally in September. Dozens of speakers regaled the crowd, including Lyman Trumbull, John Palmer, William Kellogg, Francis Blair, Richard Oglesby, Orville Browning, congressional candidates Henry Case and

David T. Linegar, Joseph Gillespie, John Wilson, Henry S. Baker, and Chicago abolitionist Dr. Charles V. Dyer.[174]

Lincoln made his only public campaign appearance at the rally. Arriving during the afternoon speeches, Lincoln's carriage was quickly engulfed by a cheering crowd. He declined to make a speech and only paused to let the "vast assembly" see him and to let him see them. He thanked the people for supporting the "truth on the questions that now agitate the public" and invited everyone to listen to the scheduled speakers. He then "escaped" on horseback from a makeshift platform. Still on his eastern trip, Davis was unable to attend the Springfield festivities.[175]

State Fair in Jacksonville

The judge traveled to Jacksonville on Tuesday, September 11, to attend the Illinois State Agricultural Fair. The visit afforded Davis the opportunity to consult with members of an important voting block, including the candidates for office of the Illinois State Agricultural Society. Springfield banker and merchant Jacob Bunn, a longtime Lincoln friend and financial backer, was elected treasurer of the society the next day.[176] Lincoln supporters in the farm community had invited him to speak at the Illinois State Fair in 1858. He also received invitations from various county agricultural societies to address county fair audiences.[177] In preparation for his presidential run, Lincoln spoke at the Wisconsin State Fair in September 1859.[178] Judge Davis was popular with the farm community and like other rich landowners who leased property out for farming was regarded as an "agriculturist." His half-brother Lyman Betts managed a farm for Davis east of Bloomington. The judge enjoyed attending agricultural fairs and considered himself a gentleman farmer, although he quickly added that he made no money in the venture.[179]

On the train trips to and from Jacksonville, Davis may have participated in one of the many informal presidential preference polls conducted in the rail cars. A survey on a September 13 morning train from Springfield to Jacksonville showed Lincoln with 167 votes, Douglas with 57, Bell with 14, and Breckinridge holding 7 votes. Another poll between Naples and Jacksonville gave Lincoln 61 votes, Douglas 34, Breckinridge 8, and Bell 6. The *Illinois State Journal* reported that even a train poll taken by a Democrat revealed Lincoln with 111 and Douglas with 63 votes.[180]

During the Jacksonville trip, Davis met Lincoln in Springfield to discuss the Pennsylvania situation. Davis also returned the tariff notes, which he had finally received back from Cameron. In addition, the judge delivered a letter to Lincoln from Thomas H. Dudley, chairman of the New Jersey State Republican Committee.[181]

German Speakers

Davis knew the importance of the German vote. Two weeks before the Republican National Convention in Chicago, Davis told Lincoln that the "5,000 dutch and Scandinavian voters in Chicago, . . . cannot & must not be lost."[182] At the Chicago convention, the judge brilliantly deployed former Illinois lieutenant governor Gustave Koerner to hammer home the importance of the German vote in his successful effort to defeat the nomination of Edward Bates. Koerner's presentation to the Hoosier delegates on the eve of the convention vote so impressed Hoosier John Defrees that in June he wrote Davis asking if Koerner could come to his state, because "he could do great good by speaking to the Germans in Indiana."[183] Davis conveyed the invitation to Koerner. Koerner, however, spent most of his campaign time in central and southern Illinois. The *Chicago Press and Tribune* listed his speaking engagements for the week of September 10, 1860, to include Peru, Bloomington, Lincoln, Springfield, Carlinville, and Alton, Illinois.[184]

Davis knew that many of the German delegates and visitors to the Chicago convention were "despondent" after the nomination because Seward or Chase had been their first choice. As a result, Republican leaders feared a lack of enthusiasm among German voters in the November election. But enthusiasm could be generated with the right speakers, preferably Germans who had initially supported Seward or Chase.[185]

When Davis advised Weed that "the first order of German speakers are needed in Indiana" he certainly put Carl Schurz at the top of the list. Schurz was an elegant and effective speaker in both English and German and in the view of the *Daily Pittsburgh Gazette* "the greatest orator upon the American continent."[186] Within a week after the Republican convention, Schurz presented Lincoln with a detailed plan to place friendly "Germans, Norwegians, [and] Hollanders" in "squads" to canvass, township by township, the doubtful states, especially Indiana and Pennsylvania. After the first squad finished in a state, it would move on to the next state, to be followed by another team of German speakers in the state just vacated. Schurz would personally supplement this tag-team effort by traveling "to all the principal points" in order to "do the heavy work" himself. He would survey the entire landscape and coordinate with the various state central committees to avoid a repeat of 1856, when "piles of money and much work was spent for no purpose, because it was done at random and without plan and direction."[187] Besides organizational skills, Schurz possessed a keen political sense. He understood that alienating the archenemy of the Germans, the Know-Nothings, would not advance Lincoln's cause. A speech in Evansville, Indiana, demonstrates how delicately he handled the conflict between the anti-immigrant Know-Nothings and the foreign-born.

Schurz began his Evansville speech by aligning himself with other Germans who strongly opposed the Know-Nothings. Yet he could not say that the American Party was useless or uncalled-for. To understand the American Party's outlook, he asked his fellow countrymen to put themselves in the shoes of their adversaries. How would the people of Germany feel if all of a sudden an "overwhelming American population should pour into Germany." These newcomers would have the right to vote after a short probation and would vote in ignorance of the institutions and traditions of Germany. Or they would vote without first studying the political situation. Even worse, their votes might be influenced by a pretty-sounding party name or controlled by an ecclesiastical authority. If the shoe were on the other foot, Schurz asked, would not a large party of German Know-Nothings rise up?

Schurz then answered his own question. While he understood the "provocation" that led to the formation of the American Party, the situation had dramatically changed, negating the need for such an organization. The "foreign vote" was not monolithic. Voters read, discussed, and thought for themselves, were governed by their own convictions, and surrendered to no person's or party's control. Schurz encouraged his fellow German immigrants to "Americanize" themselves by learning the language and studying the literature and political institutions of their new country. Once that was accomplished and they came to know and be known in America, they would be welcomed with open arms into "the warm American heart."[188]

His eloquence and his message, delivered in English and in German, put Schurz in demand all across the North. For long stretches Schurz traveled state to state, speaking daily and sometimes two or three times a day. He was one of the few speakers who could command compensation for his services. According to Alexander McClure, Schurz more than earned the $500 he received for a week's engagement in Pennsylvania.[189] Schurz traveled to Indiana in August, September, and October. In August Schurz's scheduled speaking appearances in northern, central, and southern Indiana included the cities of La Porte, Fort Wayne, Logansport, Lafayette, Terre Haute, Delphi, Vincennes, Evansville, Mount Vernon, Tell City, Corydon, New Albany, Seymour, and Columbus.[190]

Davis and the other Illinois Republican State Central Committee members arranged for Schurz to visit Illinois in July. After speaking in Chicago, Schurz headed downstate for an eleven-day excursion with scheduled speaking appointments in the cities of Quincy, Peoria, Pekin, Havana, Beardstown, Springfield, Alton, Marine, and Bellville.[191] Then after a speech on August 1 in St. Louis, Schurz returned home to Watertown, Wisconsin, to leave a week later for Indiana.[192] He arrived back home to make a speech on August 25 and then left for September engagements in Indiana, Pennsylvania, and New York.[193] On October 1 he departed on a train from Erie, Pennsylvania, to Indianapolis, delivering an impromptu whistle-stop speech in Painesville, Ohio.[194] He returned home from Indiana on October 9 and three days later left for New York State. Schurz was back in Milwaukee for a speech on October 24 and was scheduled to speak in his hometown on November 1.[195]

At the request of Lincoln, Davis, and the national and state central committees, other German Republicans traveled the Illinois speaking circuit. Friedrich Hassaurek from Ohio was popular in the Prairie State, making stops in central and southern Illinois, including Carlinville, Jacksonville, Petersburg, Springfield, Decatur, and Arenzville. Hassaurek's popularity arose in part from his reputation of confronting Democratic bullies. On one occasion, the story goes, when he was prevented from speaking by a constant barrage of stones and other "missiles," he drew out his gun, laid it in front of him, and threatened to shoot anyone who advanced toward him. After having taken care of the "rough element," he finished his speech.[196]

Indiana Campaign Efforts

While Davis intended to concentrate his efforts in Illinois, he also planned to help the canvass in Indiana. Davis had political and professional contacts in Indiana, it was relatively easy to travel from his home to Indiana, the state was vital to a Lincoln victory, and both Illinois and Indiana suffered from similar political divisions between the northern and southern parts of the states. The southern portions of Illinois and Indiana were primarily populated by transplants from the states of Kentucky, Virginia, North Carolina, and Tennessee. The southern counties were unique regions, culturally and politically different from the northern parts of the two states.[197] Most residents of the southern counties were Democrats and supported, or at least sympathized with, the peculiar institution. Indiana congressman George Julian put it bluntly by describing southern Illinois and southern Indiana as "outlying provinces of the empire of slavery."[198] The northern parts of the states, especially Illinois, voted Republican and became abolitionist strongholds populated by foreign-born immigrants and transplants from New England. The central counties represented a mix of North and South, with additional settlers from the mid-Atlantic states. Davis understood and appreciated the competing interests at play, including geographic jealousies; conflicting philosophies of the radical and moderate Republicans; and the importance of the voting blocs composed of German Americans, anti-Nebraska Democrats, old-line Whigs, and Fillmore men. His plans for winning Illinois and Indiana were the same: hold the Republican vote while attracting old Whigs, Fillmore men, and a few Democrats.[199]

On his way out east in August, Davis stopped at midnight on August 2 to meet his friend and Republican leader Jesse L. Williams at the train station in Fort Wayne, Indiana. Williams rode with Davis to the next station, and the two "talked over Indiana politics pretty thoroughly." They discussed the effect of the Breckinridge movement, which was headed by the state's two Democratic senators, Jesse D. Bright and Graham N. Fitch. Williams believed that Lincoln would be elected regardless of the result of the state election in October but was not "entirely hopeful" that Lane would be elected governor. Davis conveyed Williams's thoughts to Lincoln three days later.[200]

At the request of New York governor Edwin Morgan and the National Republican Committee, Davis stopped in Indiana on his return trip from the East.[201] He found that the state was "in a good deal of danger" because attempts to prevent the formation of a Bell presidential ticket had failed. Some of the old Fillmore men of southern Indiana were convinced by the politicians and newspapers of Kentucky to get behind Bell. State Republican leaders believed that Bell supporters would vote for the Democrat gubernatorial candidate, Thomas Hendricks, in the October election, because if the Republicans won the governor's seat, conventional wisdom held that a Lincoln victory would follow. In August Kentucky governor Charles S. Morehead spoke in support of the Bell-Everett ticket at the Constitutional Union Party Convention in Indianapolis. The Indianapolis Republicans told Davis that Morehead admitted that "the object of running Bell was to prevent Lincoln's carrying the state."[202] From the information gained during this Indiana visit Davis concluded that "a large portion of the Bell men" in Indiana would vote for the Democratic gubernatorial candidate and that the majority of the Breckinridge party would likewise support Hendricks. Davis, like Lincoln, abided by the accepted political perception that the party that won Indiana in October would also prevail in the state in November.[203] To counter the efforts of the opposition, Republicans told Davis that they needed $10,000 in out-of-state money.

Raising Funds for Indiana

After arriving home from his eastern trip in mid-August, Davis wasted no time contacting Thurlow Weed. The bottom line: the Hoosiers were in trouble unless they received $10,000 in "foreign aid" to supplement the measly $1,500 the "poor" state's central committee was able to raise. But as of August 25, a week after Davis wrote to Weed, Indiana had received only $2,000 from the Republican National Committee, and it had been spent on financing speakers such as Carl Schurz and supporting German newspapers.[204] To make matters worse, at the beginning of September Davis received a letter from trusted Indiana Republican leader Caleb Smith advising Davis that money was needed not only to finance speakers and German newspapers but also to combat the Democrats' "pipe-laying" efforts: bringing men from Kentucky to vote in Indiana.[205]

Smith did not explain how the "foreign aid" would be used to combat the recruitment of illegal voters by the Democrats. And it may be that the Hoosiers intended to fight fraud with fraud. Davis himself suggested less-than-honorable means to deal with the importation of voters. In September Davis wrote to the chair of the National Republican Committee complaining that the Democrats were moving voters residing in the Republican-dominated northern counties to swing counties in central Illinois in order to control the outcome of the legislative elections. Davis believed that such dishonesty could "only be counteracted by like means on [Republicans'] behalf."[206] In 1858, during his second senatorial campaign, Lincoln's suggested approach to combat pipe-laying was no more commendable than that of Davis. Lincoln thought that a Republican detective in disguise could infiltrate the nonresident voters and "at the nick of time, control their votes." To Lincoln, "it would be a great thing, when this trick is attempted upon us, to have the saddle come up on the other horse."[207]

In response to the letters from Caleb Smith and Jesse Williams, Davis wrote to Thurlow Weed and Governor Edwin Morgan in early September explaining that funds were needed to hire speakers, cover routine campaign expenses, and offset plans by the Democrats to send Kentuckians across the Ohio River to vote in Indiana's gubernatorial election. Since defeat in the October Indiana and Pennsylvania elections would be "disastrous," Davis frantically implored Weed, "For God's sake send them aid speedily." Davis recommended that "the National Committee should put their entire power and & force on Pennsylvania & Indiana until after the October elections."[208] Trusting Davis's assessment of the Indiana situation, Weed promised that he and Morgan would personally and through the Republican National Committee "bend all our strength upon [Pennsylvania] and Indiana." Morgan wrote back to Davis saying that he would see John Goodrich on September 12 about the funds.[209] Then on September 11, after Davis received another urgent letter from Caleb Smith advising Davis that a *Louisville Journal* editorial urging Bell supporters to vote for the Democrat in the October gubernatorial election would find adherents in southern Indiana, Davis again wrote to Weed. After advising Weed of the influence of the *Louisville Journal* editorial in southern Indiana, Davis renewed his request for $10,000 for Indiana:

> I hope the National Committee will do all they can for [Indiana]. The whole money they asked (& more if it can be raised) should be sent at once—*Men work better with money in hand*—The first order of German speakers are needed in Indiana.
>   I believe in God's Providence in this Election, but at the same time we should "keep our powder dry."[210]

As a backup plan, Davis contacted his friend John Goodrich, the Republican national committeeman from Massachusetts. Goodrich raised the money in Boston in sums of $100 to $500 and sent it to Indiana. After receiving the early gubernatorial election returns, Davis wrote to his wife that if the Republicans were victorious in Indiana, Goodrich would congratulate himself for helping to achieve the victory.[211]

Leonard Swett in Indiana

Like Illinois Republicans, Indiana leaders emphasized attracting voters in the heavily Democratic southern part of the state. Davis aided this effort by calling upon Leonard Swett to combine an information-gathering visit to Indiana with a week of speaking engagements in the southwestern counties bordering Illinois. Swett would help dispel the abolitionist tag the Democrats were pinning on Lincoln. Further, Swett had success speaking in central and southern Illinois to old Whigs and Fillmore men.

Swett arrived in Terre Haute, Indiana, on October 1, 1860. There he consulted with John P. Usher, a lawyer who practiced on both sides of the border and who was well known to Lincoln, Swett, and Davis; Richard W. Thompson, a Know-Nothing who helped organize the Constitutional Union Party and supported John Bell but who more than anything else wanted to defeat the Democrats; and Thomas H. Nelson, a member of the Indiana Republican State Central Committee and congressional candidate. Swett also talked to Daniel W. Voorhees, Nelson's Democratic opponent in the congressional race. The day he arrived in Terre Haute, Swett wrote to Davis that, as usual, all Republicans had glowing predictions about the upcoming victory. Always thinking like a lawyer, Swett complained that "our friends *argue* we will carry the state rather than state such facts as one can see it from." He did find, however, that Richard Thompson had a solid basis for forecasting a strong showing for Lincoln among Know-Nothings.[212] Davis forwarded Swett's letter to Lincoln.[213]

During the first week of October Swett had speaking engagements scheduled along a 110-mile stretch of border counties, including stops at the Indiana cities of Terre Haute, Sullivan, Carlisle, Vincennes, Princeton, and Evansville. The rallies drew participants from both Indiana and Illinois. After Swett's return home, he reported directly to Davis, who then reported to Lincoln on the success of the rallies, especially in Terre Haute and Vincennes.[214]

Know-Nothings in Indiana

Davis recognized the pivotal influence of the former Fillmore voters on the outcome of the October and November elections. Swett was good at what he did. So were the Indiana Republican speakers, such as gubernatorial candidate Henry Lane, who made more than eighty speeches in Indiana.[215] But of greater benefit in the targeted search for Know-Nothing votes would be a leader of the American Party hitting the campaign trail endorsing both Lincoln and Henry Lane. Falling short of outright endorsements, great benefit would accompany

American Party speakers attacking the Democrats and saying kind things about the Republicans. The need for Know-Nothing speakers in Indiana was especially acute, since Hoosier Republicans had not always welcomed Fillmore voters with open arms. At their state convention in February 1860, the Republicans shut out Know-Nothing adherents from leadership roles in the party. No Fillmore man was made an officer of the convention, placed on the convention's resolutions committee, included on the state ticket, sent as a delegate to the national convention, made a presidential elector, or appointed to the state central committee.[216] The best way to woo Fillmore voters was to secure speakers identified with the American Party or former Know-Nothings who could advance the Republican cause either directly or indirectly. Davis, Lincoln, and the Indiana Republican leaders knew that Terre Haute resident Richard Thompson was perfect for the task. Indeed, two weeks after Lincoln's nomination, Indiana congressman and future vice president Schuyler Colfax believed that Thompson "held the fate of Ind[iana] in his hands."[217]

Born in Virginia, Thompson lived briefly in Kentucky. Before moving to Terre Haute he resided for a decade in Lawrence County, Indiana, seventy miles from Louisville. He served as a Whig in Congress with Lincoln and later transferred allegiance to the American Party. He was one of the few important "Americans" at the Constitutional Union Party's convention in Indianapolis, which nominated former Tennessee senator John Bell for president.[218] Lincoln maintained friendly relations with Thompson, holding on to the possibility of receiving his backing.[219]

Similar to Maryland congressman Henry Winter Davis, Thompson remained loyal to Bell but devoted much of his campaign rhetoric to denouncing the Democrats and promoting Lincoln as an acceptable alternative to Douglas. While Thompson consistently declared that he would vote for Bell, he did not hesitate to add that Lincoln was a conservative and if elected would make an excellent president. Judge Davis understood that Thompson, as a leader of the Constitutional Union Party, could not endorse Lincoln and appreciated all that Thompson was doing short of an actual endorsement.[220] But Davis saw no reason why Thompson could not endorse the Republican candidate for governor since the Constitutional Union Party had no candidate for that office. So Davis wrote Lincoln on September 3, suggesting that it would "be a good thing to get Thompson to come out openly in a speech for *Lane*." Davis added that if Lincoln agreed, then Davis would be willing to travel to Terre Haute to see the American Party leader. Apparently, this suggestion was coordinated with Henry Lane, because on September 3 Lane wrote to Thompson asking him to consider saying a word publicly in favor of the Republican state ticket.[221] Thompson agreed, and by October 3 he had openly proclaimed his support for Lane over Democrat Thomas Hendricks. Five days before the state election, the *Evansville Daily Journal* reported that Thompson was "exerting all his influence and energy for his old Whig friend, Henry S. Lane."[222]

The majority of American Party members apparently followed Thompson's lead and cast their ballots for Lane.[223]

Davis Attends the Douglas Rally in Indianapolis

Davis's curiosity and information-gathering function took him to the Douglas mass meeting in Indianapolis on September 28, 1860. Democratic rallies followed the same formula as Republican rallies with a parade, slogan-covered banners, illuminated buildings, evening torchlight processions, speeches, and fireworks. Fan favorites at the events were the wagons filled with smartly dressed young women supporters. Douglas's Indianapolis rally was no exception. The most popular feature of the parade "was the young ladies' car, in the center of which stood a young lady attired as the Goddess of Liberty." The main difference between a Douglas and a Lincoln rally was the active participation of the Democratic presidential candidate. In Indianapolis Douglas greeted his admirers from a carriage drawn by four white horses. At the county fairgrounds, he gave his usual stump speech, including a lambasting of the Breckinridge candidacy. Davis's Hoosier hosts no doubt pointed out the numerous Kentucky residents attending the rally, many of whom, according to Republicans, would stay in Indiana as temporary laborers and fraudulently vote in the October state election.[224]

Estimates of the crowd size varied dramatically depending on the partisan leaning of the reporter. One Republican newspaper characterized the attendance as "respectable" at about 25,000 people. Another Republican newspaper put the size of the Douglas crowd and the size of the crowd at an earlier Lincoln Indianapolis rally at about the same. A Democratic paper reported estimates of between 75,000 and 150,000 people, settling on its own approximation of 100,000.[225] The editor of the *Indianapolis Journal* tried to depreciate the size of the turnout by claiming that he never attended "a political gathering contain[ing] as many women and children."[226] Whatever the actual number of attendees, the size of the gathering worried Davis. He wrote to his son that the demonstration "was very imposing [and] much larger than [he] liked to see."[227] After Douglas and vice presidential candidate Herschel V. Johnson spoke at the fairgrounds, other speakers, including Illinois congressman John A. Logan, spoke from the balcony of the Bates House in downtown Indianapolis. Davis reported that Douglas "look[ed] worn and very much dissipated" from his grueling speaking schedule. The judge's initial worries about the Hoosier state were not allayed by this late September visit to Indianapolis and actually confirmed what he already knew: "Indiana will be very hotly contested at the October Election—Both sides claim the victory."[228]

Davis campaigned full-time for Lincoln until October, when he had to return to court duties. His absence from the circuit during September led to heavy court calls and late court nights in October.[229] Although his canvassing time became limited, Davis continued to direct and participate in important campaign matters.[230] The judge kept close track of the October election returns as they trickled in from Pennsylvania and Indiana.[231] He attended and evaluated events. For example, on Saturday, October 13, he rode to the fairgrounds in Decatur with former Ohio governor Thomas Corwin to listen to Corwin's speech before an audience ten thousand strong. After the rally he dined with friends in Springfield and then joined a party Lincoln hosted for Governor Corwin in celebration of the October victories in Pennsylvania and Indiana.[232] The judge kept close track of meetings in central Illinois, including huge rallies in Danville and Bloomington. He took note of Democratic gatherings in the court towns and became weary from writing dozens of "essential" political letters.[233] He attended the State Central Committee meetings and consulted with other operatives locally and in Chicago.[234] Of course, he knew of all of Swett's activities.[235] But the demands and stress of the campaign wore on Davis. On November 4 Davis wrote to his son that he would be glad when the "long and laborious" election was over. He left court in Danville on November 5, arriving in Bloomington at 9:00 p.m., and voted the next day.[236]

Election Day to Inauguration Day

On Election Day Lincoln received 51.1 percent of the Indiana vote, which was four-tenths of a percent better than he did in Illinois. Forty-two percent of the Hoosier electorate voted for Douglas, with Breckinridge tallying 4.5 percent, and Bell trailing the field with 1.9 percent. That meant that of the 58 electoral votes controlled by the four "doubtful" states of Illinois, Indiana, Pennsylvania, and New Jersey, Lincoln received 55 and Douglas 3. The North provided all of Lincoln's 180 electoral votes. Breckinridge followed with 72 electoral votes, all from the South. Bell received 39 electoral ballots from Kentucky, Tennessee, and Virginia. Douglas finished with 3 electoral votes from New Jersey and 9 from Missouri.[237]

The day after the election, Davis went to Springfield and stayed until Saturday to join in the victory celebration. Surrounded by a "great crowd," he could only manage a short note to his wife. The throng celebrated both Lincoln's election and "the first time in the history of Illinois that the Democratic party [was] effectively beaten." The judge was especially proud that his home county provided Lincoln with a nearly thousand-vote margin and only slightly less delighted that his efforts in Tazewell County finally paid off with a majority vote for Lincoln.[238] But time for gloating and celebration was short-lived. The president-elect had work to do.

Davis was heavily involved in the top priority: the selection of cabinet members. As journalist and abolition leader Henry Stanton observed, Davis "took an active part in the construction of the Cabinet."[239] For ninety days following the election, the judge received dozens of letters endorsing and opposing candidates and asking him to use his influence with Mr. Lincoln in the appointment process.[240] The supplicants included Mary Lincoln, who requested the judge to convince Mr. Lincoln to not include Norman Judd in the cabinet.[241] A few of the letters suggested a post for Davis.[242] The judge was not shy about forwarding the letters to Lincoln or expressing his own preferences.[243] At Lincoln's request, Davis and Swett invited Thurlow Weed to Springfield to discuss cabinet appointments and general policy issues facing the new administration. On December 20 Lincoln spent the day with Weed, Davis, and Swett in confidential discussions. The men vetted candidates for each cabinet seat, and while the primary exchange was between Lincoln and Weed, Swett and Davis did not hesitate to express their views.[244] As it turned out, the president followed Davis's advice on many appointments, including making Simon Cameron secretary of war, Caleb B. Smith secretary of the interior, and William P. Dole commissioner of Indian affairs. The judge's influence was further felt in filling lesser offices, such as Archibald Williams's appointment to the Kansas judiciary, William Pitt Kellogg's appointment to the Nebraska Territory judiciary, Lawrence Weldon's choice as district attorney for southern Illinois, and Tazewell County Court clerk John A. Jones's selection as the State Department's superintendent of commercial statistics.[245]

The first significant postelection public event was the inaugural train trip to Washington, DC. Before leaving on the trip, Lincoln gave Davis a draft of his inaugural address for the judge's comments. The judge and John Nicolay were the first two people to review the speech.[246] The president-elect then invited Davis to join the train that left from Springfield on Monday, February 11, 1861, taking a meandering route of nearly two thousand miles to Washington. The unnecessarily long journey was designed to give Americans a chance to see their president and to coalesce support for Lincoln and the Union.[247] Mary Lincoln and the judge joined the convoy in Indianapolis on the afternoon it left Springfield. Davis complained that the throng of twelve thousand well-wishers made it difficult for him to get breakfast before the train departed Indianapolis the next morning.[248] On February 18 the troupe was in Albany, New York, where Thurlow Weed convinced Ward Lamon that until the inauguration the president should reside at a public house in Washington rather than rent a private dwelling. Weed wrote a letter to the owner of the Willard Hotel, advising him that Lincoln would be his "guest" and requesting Mr. Willard to "please reserve nearest him apartments for two of his friends, Judge Davis and Mr. Lamon."[249] Davis spent a lot of time with Lincoln on and off the inaugural train. There were speeches, ceremonies, and meet and greets at every stop. Davis dined with the president informally and at lavish dinner parties, including one hosted by Congressman Elbridge Spaulding of New York.[250] The president and vice president and cabinet members attended the Spaulding dinner together with the New York senators, the Speaker of the House, and Congressmen John Sherman, Thomas Corwin, and Elihu Washburne. The *New York Herald* described the affair as "very elegant and highly intellectual."[251] There were carriage rides with the president in Cleveland and New York.[252] Joining the president in the lead carriage for the procession from the train station to the hotel in New York were Davis, security officer Colonel Edwin Sumner, and the chair of the reception committee. Thirty carriages followed. During the trip Lincoln invited Davis to join in social events, including a night at the opera.[253]

The most stressful event on the trip occurred on February 22, when the caravan visited Harrisburg, Pennsylvania. The train was scheduled to travel through Baltimore and arrive in Washington the next day. After the president-elect addressed the Pennsylvania legislature, a meeting was called of Lincoln's "most trusted advisers" to evaluate reports from the Pinkerton National Detective Agency and William Seward's son that an assassination plot was brewing in Baltimore. The night before, Norman Judd and Allan Pinkerton advised Lincoln of the nature of the threats. The meeting included Judd, Lincoln, Ward Lamon, and Davis. Also present were three members of the regular army, Colonel Edwin Sumner, Captain John Pope, and Major David Hunter, all of whom had accompanied Lincoln from Illinois.[254]

For the group's benefit, Judd summarized the facts surrounding the alleged Baltimore conspiracy and the plan developed by Pinkerton and Judd to thwart any assassination attempt in the city. There were diverse opinions among the advisors, with Colonel Sumner arguing that any diversion from the set route would be a "damned piece of cowardice." He volunteered, if necessary, to "get a squad of cavalry . . . and *cut* our way to Washington."[255]

Although Davis did not express an opinion during the "warm discussion" that ensued, he probably doubted the seriousness of the threat.[256] A few days later, Allan Pinkerton complained that Lamon and Davis "were surely playing the Devil" with the plan that he and Judd devised to avoid the danger in Baltimore.[257] The judge, who was usually not shy about expressing opinions, knew that this was not an ordinary matter of policy or politics. Instead, this decision could literally have life-and-death consequences for Lincoln and his family, and so the final judgment must rest with Lincoln. But Davis also knew that the facts supporting the president-elect's decision needed testing, and so he conducted "a very rigid cross examination" of Judd with "rather pointed questions."[258]

When Judge Davis determined that the discussion had gone on long enough, he turned to Lincoln and said, "You personally heard the detective's story. You have heard this discussion. What is your judgment in the matter?"[259] With Mary's safety concerns in mind, the president-elect answered the judge's question: "I have thought over this matter considerably since I went over the ground with

Pinkerton last night. The appearance of Mr. Frederick Seward, with warning from another source, confirms my belief in Mr. Pinkerton's statement. Unless there are some other reasons, besides fear of ridicule, I am disposed to carry out Judd's plan."[260] Davis ended the meeting by saying, "That settles the matter, gentlemen."[261] As part of Judd's diversionary strategy, Lamon was to be Lincoln's bodyguard on the route devised to frustrate any assassination plot. When asked if he was prepared for the task, Lamon replied by exhibiting "a brace of fine pistols, a huge bowie-knife, a blackjack, a pair of brass knuckles and a hickory cudgel."[262] In accordance with Judd's plan, Lincoln left on a special train that night from Harrisburg to Philadelphia. In Philadelphia he transferred to a sleeper and arrived at the President Street Station in Baltimore at about 3:30 a.m. Lincoln traveled undetected from the President Street Station to the Camden train station to board a train that arrived in Washington at 6:00 a.m.[263]

When he reached Washington on February 23, Davis set up shop in the middle of the excitement at the Willard Hotel. Until the inauguration ten days later, the judge "stamped back and forth among the male and female politicians that crowded the corridors at Willard's, doing great and small errands for large and little people, with hat cocked awry on his head, in the free-and-easy fashion of the boundless West."[264] After the installation of President Lincoln, Davis unceremoniously returned to the bench in the Eighth Judicial Circuit.

Lincoln's election opened the door a sliver for state trial court judge David Davis to attain the highest office in the legal profession: justice of the United States Supreme Court. It would take the lobbying efforts and litigation skills of Leonard Swett to turn that slim possibility into a reality.

David Davis and his wife, Sarah Woodruff Walker Davis, in the 1840s. Abraham Lincoln Presidential Library and Museum.

Born on September 9, 1852, Sarah "Sallie" Worthington Davis was the daughter of David and Sarah Davis. Abraham Lincoln Presidential Library and Museum.

George Perrin Davis, born on June 3, 1842, was the son of David and Sarah Davis. Abraham Lincoln Presidential Library and Museum.

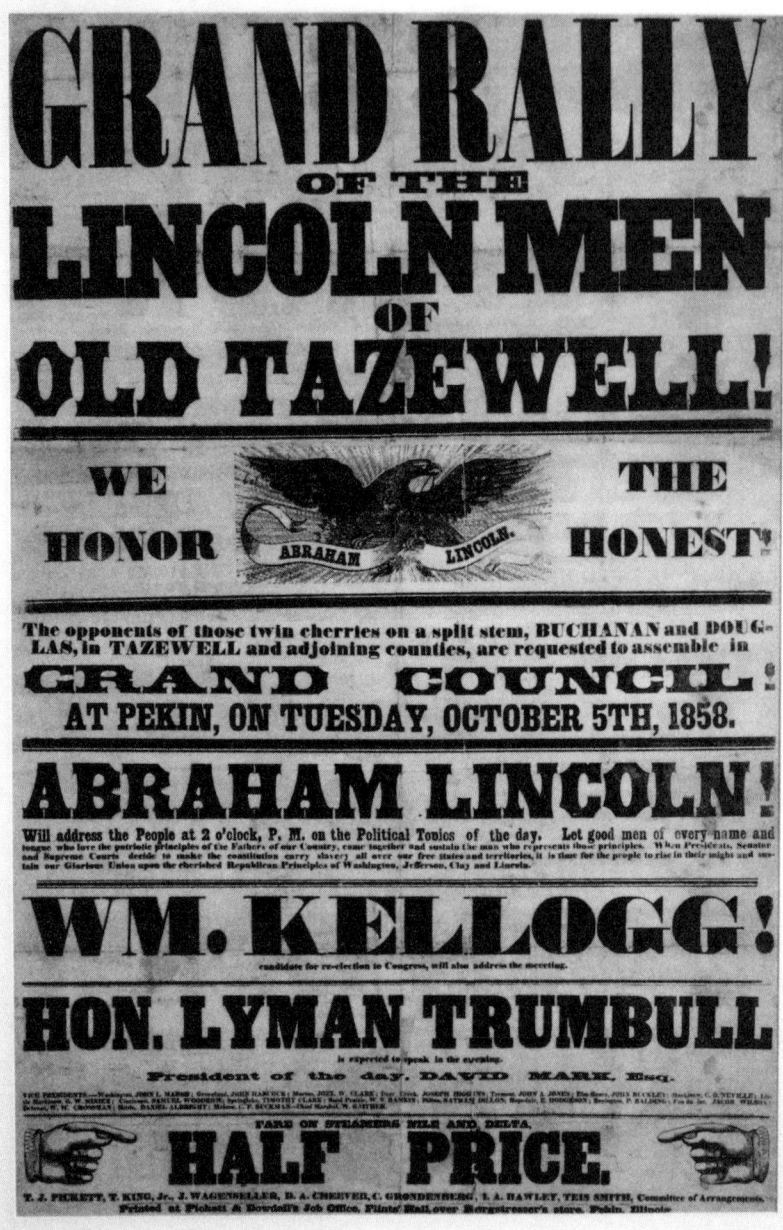

Broadside used to promote Abraham Lincoln's visit to all-important Tazewell County in October 1858 during his second attempt for a US Senate seat. Abraham Lincoln Presidential Library and Museum.

The "Wigwam" was constructed especially for the 1860 Republican National Convention at the southeastern corner of Market (now Wacker Drive) and Lake Streets in downtown Chicago. Chicago History Museum, ICHi-002001, Alexander Hesler, photographer.

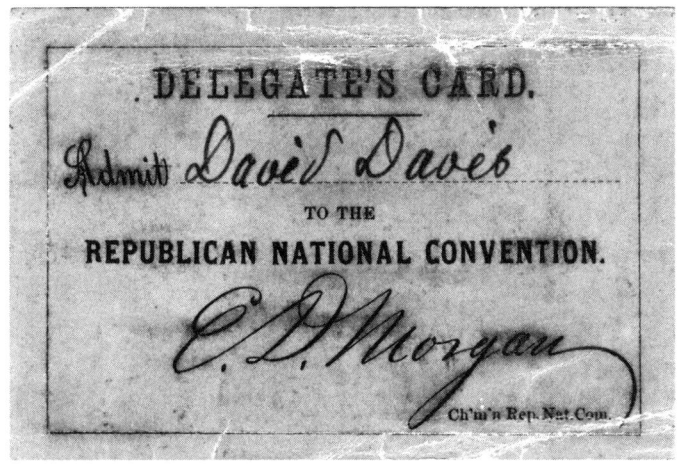

Delegate's card issued to David Davis for the 1860 Republican National Convention signed by Edwin D. Morgan, governor of New York and chairman of the Republican National Committee. Abraham Lincoln Presidential Library and Museum.

David Davis sometime between 1855 and 1865. Brady-Handy photograph collection, Library of Congress, Prints and Photographs Division.

Judge Davis while on the Supreme Court sometime between 1870 and 1877. Brady-Handy photograph collection, Library of Congress, Prints and Photographs Division.

The Chase Court, February 1867. *Left to right*: Clerk of the Supreme Court D. W. Middleton, Justices David Davis, Noah H. Swayne, Robert C. Grier, and James M. Wayne, Chief Justice Salmon P. Chase, and Justices Samuel Nelson, Nathan Clifford, Samuel F. Miller, and Stephen J. Field. Collection of the Supreme Court of the United States, Alexander Gardner, photographer.

Front page of the April 24, 1880, issue of *Frank Leslie's Illustrated Newspaper*. David Davis's possible presidential candidacy in 1880 was discussed as part of a series on contenders for the presidential nomination. US Senate Collection.

John S. Rock, the first African American lawyer admitted to practice before the US Supreme Court. Library of Congress, LOC Control Number 94502940.

JOEL A. MATTESON,
Governor of the State of Illinois,

To all to whom these presents shall come—GREETING:

Know Ye, That _David Davis_ having been duly elected to the office of _Judge of the Circuit Court_ for the county of _Eighth Judicial Circuit_, I, Joel A. Matteson, Governor of the State of Illinois, for and on behalf of the people of said State, do commission him _Judge of the Circuit Court_ for said county, and do authorize and empower him to execute and fulfil the duties of that office according to law.

And to Have and to Hold the said office, with all the rights and emoluments thereunto legally appertaining, until his successor shall be duly elected and qualified to office.

In Testimony Whereof, I have hereunto set my hand and caused the Great Seal of State to be hereunto affixed. Done at the city of Springfield, this _Twenty Sixth_ day of _June_ in the year of our Lord one thousand eight hundred and fifty-_Six_ and of the independence of the United States the _Seventy ninth_.

J. A. Matteson

BY THE GOVERNOR:

Alexander Starne Secretary of State.

In 1856 Illinois governor Joel A. Matteson certified the reelection of David Davis as judge of the Eighth Judicial Circuit. Three years later Lincoln directed his loyal followers in the legislature to vote for Lyman Trumbull for US senator to prevent Governor Matteson from gaining the office. Abraham Lincoln Presidential Library and Museum.

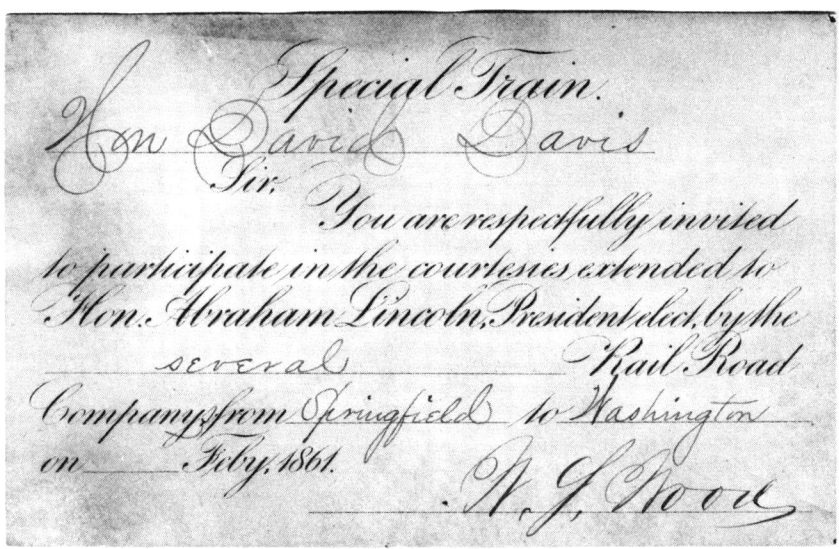

Davis Davis's inaugural train trip pass (front and back) signed by William S. Wood, who supervised the railroad journey from Springfield to Washington, DC, in February 1861. Abraham Lincoln Presidential Library and Museum.

III

Davis, Lincoln, and the US Supreme Court

5 Lincoln Puts Davis on the Supreme Court

Similar to Lincoln's low ranking in the Republican presidential nomination field in 1859 and early 1860, Davis was barely on the radar for a seat on the Supreme Court in 1861 and early 1862. But a series of events, including a whopping three vacant court seats, would catapult to the high court a judge who had never handled an appeal.

Three Court Vacancies

On May 31, 1860, Supreme Court justice Peter V. Daniel died. A year later, Justice John McLean succumbed to pneumonia, and Justice John A. Campbell of Alabama resigned. President Buchanan failed to nominate a replacement for Justice Daniel. So, early in his presidency, Lincoln had three Supreme Court seats to fill. While the new president took his time in bringing the court back to full strength, suitors for the openings commenced their efforts without delay.[1]

On March 6, 1861, two days after Lincoln assumed office, Henry Winter Davis wrote to the president suggesting that he choose Winter Davis's cousin David Davis to fill Justice Daniel's seat. On March 9 Secretary of State William Seward offered George W. Summers as a possible replacement because, like Daniel, he was from Virginia. Twenty-four hours later, Lincoln received a letter from three Virginia politicians asking him to appoint Senator John Crittenden to the vacancy.[2] The day that Justice McLean died, Ohio lawyer Noah H. Swayne asked fellow Buckeye senator Salmon Chase to support him for the McLean vacancy.[3] Shortly thereafter, Orville Browning, newly appointed to fill the US Senate vacancy created by the death of Senator Stephen Douglas, made an audacious direct appeal to Lincoln for the McLean opening. That was followed by an equally unprecedented letter from Browning's wife seeking the appointment for her husband. In her letter, Eliza Browning mentioned only one competitor for the appointment and that was to plead that no one, not even David Davis, had a stronger claim to the office than Mr. Browning.[4]

Lincoln nominated Noah Swayne to replace Justice McLean on January 21, 1862. Born in Virginia, Swayne was a well-respected lawyer from Ohio and an antislavery Democrat turned Republican. The *New York Evening Post* welcomed the nomination of such a leading member of the bar, describing Swayne as "a gentleman of fine personal appearance, of dignified and engaging address, of irreproachable private and professional character, of ample fortune" who would bring "industry, experience and integrity" to the Supreme Court. The Senate confirmed Swayne three days later, and he started work the following Monday.[5]

Filling the second court vacancy would wait until Congress reorganized the federal court circuits due to the southern states, in effect, leaving the Union and the admission of new western states. On July 15, 1862, the president signed the Judicial Reorganization Act, revamping the territory covered by each circuit court. In addition to court duties in Washington, Supreme Court justices shared responsibility with federal district court judges for hearing cases in their assigned circuits. Under the Judicial Reorganization Act, Missouri, Minnesota, Kansas, and Iowa became the new Ninth Judicial Circuit. Although Lincoln did not know Samuel F. Miller, Miller's managers had laid the groundwork for his appointment by leading the effort to construct a Ninth Circuit favorable to an Iowan.[6] A petition was presented to the president that supported Miller and that was signed by twenty-eight of the thirty-two US senators. Three-quarters of the House members signed another petition. Miller also had the advantage of being a former Whig and an "original Republican." Moving from Kentucky to Iowa when he was thirty years old, Miller opposed slavery but was not an abolitionist. He viewed the Republican Party as the middle ground between the Democrats who wanted to extend slavery everywhere and the abolitionists who wanted to abolish it everywhere. A day after signing the Judicial Reorganization Act, Lincoln nominated Miller to fill former Justice Daniel's seat. No one else really had a chance. The Senate confirmed Miller the day he was nominated.[7]

Davis versus Browning

That left one vacant court seat with two serious contenders, both from Illinois. Although Orville Browning had been the front runner for much of 1862, Lincoln finally offered the position to Davis on August 27, 1862.[8] While many forces combined to bring about the nomination, one stood out above all others: the lobbying effort of Leonard Swett. As Davis is legitimately credited with securing Lincoln's nomination for president, Swett's unrelenting efforts and trial lawyer logic undoubtedly secured his friend a spot on the high court.

Swett's loyalty to Davis matched Davis's loyalty to Lincoln. Davis served as Swett's mentor and personal confidant. They shared a common political philosophy and the same favorable and unfavorable opinions of Republican leaders and candidates. Throughout their relationship Swett was the judge's right-hand man in efforts to advance both Lincoln's and Davis's political careers. The judge reciprocated by supporting Swett when he ran for state office and for Congress. So it is no surprise that Swett was at the forefront of the "Davis for Supreme Court" movement. But Swett had an additional motivation in backing Davis: Orville Browning's support for the presidential nomination of Lincoln had been lukewarm at best. Browning promoted Edward Bates for the nomination right up to the start of the Republican National Convention. He was late getting to the convention and even then expressed the hope that Lincoln would withdraw in favor of Bates.[9] During the convention, Browning made presentations to other delegations in favor of Lincoln but was usually accompanied by Davis or Swett or other supporters whose loyalty was not in doubt (see chapter 3). Swett simply could not comprehend how Browning's opposition and then indifference to Lincoln's nomination could warrant the reward of a Supreme Court post. Browning's appointment would constitute an "injustice" that Swett could not let happen without a fight.[10]

Browning's initial advantage in the contest for the court opening had nothing to do with his political support or, more accurately, lack of support for Lincoln. It had nothing to do with his service as a senator, since he had held that post for only a brief time. Nor did it rest on his admitted legal ability. Senator Browning's advantage was that he was within easy reach of the White House and was a longtime friend with whom Lincoln felt comfortable discussing governmental, political, and personal matters.[11] Starting the day after he arrived in Washington on July 2, 1861, Browning made it a point to spend as much time as possible with the president. Browning's activities during his first two weeks in the capital illustrate how he benefited from his access to the Lincolns.

On the evening of July 3, 1861, Browning visited Mr. and Mrs. Lincoln at the Executive Mansion. The president discussed the Fort Sumner situation and the stress he was feeling. He also had Browning review a draft of his war message to Congress.[12] On July 6 Browning met with Lincoln and some cabinet members.[13] On the following Monday, July 8, the senator visited Lincoln twice, once in the morning to pay his respects and, at the president's request, again in the afternoon for a lengthy discussion of army matters, the "negro question," the war, and political events.[14] The next morning Browning spoke with the president.[15] On July 11 Browning only saw Lincoln briefly, but on July 13 the two had a long talk.[16] According to his diary, Browning did not see the president on July 15 but wrote him a note.[17] The Illinois senator attended the "levee at the Presidents" on the evening of July 16. The next day he had a three-hour discussion with Lincoln on Indian and railroad affairs. Browning visited again on July 19.[18]

The regular meetings between the friends included political and business discussions, dinners, parties, and many intimate personal conversations. When eleven-year-old Willie Lincoln died on the evening of February 20, 1862, the president sent his carriage to pick up Orville Browning and his wife, Eliza, and both spent the night with the Lincolns. The following day the senator left the Executive Mansion at noon, but Mrs. Lincoln would not allow Mrs. Browning to leave, so she remained. Browning returned that evening to sit up part of the night with an extremely ill Tad Lincoln. Browning helped check on funeral arrangements for Willie. After the funeral on the afternoon of February 24 and while Mary remained uncontrollably distraught at home, the senator rode with Lincoln, Robert Lincoln, and Senator Lyman Trumbull to the cemetery. That night Orville and Eliza Browning attended to Tad Lincoln until 2:00 a.m.[19]

The close relationship with the Brownings during the second half of 1861 led Lincoln to remark about the last court vacancy, "I do not know what I may do when the time comes, but there has never been a day when if I had to act I should not have appointed Browning." When Davis and Swett got wind of Lincoln's statement in August 1861, "glum" reigned, because it appeared the nomination was a fait accompli. But Swett would not permit such a travesty without at least one face-to-face meeting with the president. Over Davis's objection, Swett went to Washington. He met the president in the morning and afternoon on a day in August, probably August 15. In the morning session, Swett reminded Lincoln that he was brought to prominence by the lawyers of the Eighth Circuit, who were led by Judge Davis. And to Swett's argument that if Judge Davis had not lived and if all other things had remained as they were, Lincoln would not be sitting where he was, Lincoln admitted, "Yes, that is so." Having established the factual predicate, lawyer Swett presented the only conclusion to be drawn: that Lincoln needed to recognize the force that had raised him to his present position and do justice by appointing Davis. After spending most of the morning with the president, Swett returned to his hotel, where he thought of an additional argument in his friend's favor. He reduced the new argument to writing and personally delivered and read it to Lincoln that afternoon. The letter pledged that Swett would consider Davis's appointment a favor to Swett personally, thereby releasing Lincoln from any obligation to provide Swett with a governmental position.[20]

To offset Browning's nearly daily visits to the president, the backing of Attorney General Edward Bates, and congressional expressions of support, Swett solicited, secured, and sent Lincoln letters and petitions supporting Davis. In January and February 1862 he coordinated efforts to obtain recommendations from members of the Illinois Constitutional Convention, then in session; lawyers from the Eighth Circuit; bar associations; and, with the help of Judge Samuel H. Treat, now the federal judge in St. Louis, a petition of Missouri bar members.[21] One of the letters Swett transmitted to Lincoln was from the president's first law partner, John Stuart. In his cover letter forwarding Stuart's endorsement, Swett made another new argument for Davis's appointment.[22] Swett departed from his earlier appeals that Lincoln owed his job to Davis and that by appointing Davis Lincoln would negate any claim Swett had on the president. Swett had a new approach. Swett, like Lincoln, was a very accomplished trial lawyer. From trying cases with and against Lincoln, Swett knew how Lincoln approached the art of persuasion. So Swett's new strategy was to treat the president as a witness under cross-examination, albeit friendly cross-examination. Like any experienced cross-examiner, Swett would ask Lincoln questions that could only be answered yes or no. Moreover, Swett would only ask questions to which he already knew the answer. He presented his most effective pro-Davis argument by proposing a hypothetical situation to Lincoln: "Suppose your elevation had rested in the power of Judge Davis as his does now in yours?" Then Swett propounded his first question: "Would all the men in place, in the world, would pressure brought to bear from any source, have made [Davis] swerve or hesitate[?]" Then he asked the same question about Browning: "Suppose your elevation had rested in the power of Mr Browning as his does now in yours, would he have decided in your favor[?]"[23]

Anyone even vaguely familiar with relationship between Davis and Lincoln would immediately answer the first question with a resounding "no." Davis had unwaveringly backed Lincoln to the fullest whether Lincoln was seeking the post of commissioner of the Land Office, US senator, or president. Lincoln knew that Davis had worked harder for his nomination in Chicago than anyone else. The president remembered that after his Senate loss in 1855, Davis said that if he had been present at the legislature's vote, he would not have allowed Lincoln to relinquish his votes to Trumbull. In the 1858 campaign Davis wrote to both his brother-in-law and Lincoln that Davis should have resigned his judgeship to promote Lincoln full-time.[24] President Lincoln knew that if Davis had the power to appoint Lincoln to any office during their relationship, nothing in the world could have persuaded him not to do so.

As to the second question, if Browning had the power to appoint the president, would he have done so? The best answer an objective observer could offer on this question would be an ambivalent "maybe." Browning had never gone out of his way to help Lincoln unless he received a return benefit or was compelled by the circumstances to do so. Arriving at the Chicago convention, Browning still supported Bates and voted for Lincoln only because of the unit vote rule adopted at the Republican State Convention. He had so little interest in Lincoln's campaign for the nomination that he refused to serve as vice president of the

Illinois delegation.[25] And Browning's "strange indifference" to Lincoln's success or failure would culminate in his refusal to endorse the president in his reelection bid.[26]

Davis's Supreme Court prospects received an unexpected boost when Congressman Owen Lovejoy, whom Davis had opposed for years, "urged" the judge's appointment.[27] At the end of July, Mary Lincoln told Leonard Swett that she had been "fighting Davis's battles" by lobbying her husband to appoint the judge over Browning. Senator Browning had returned to Illinois after Congress adjourned, and the president's wife "was glad of it." Mrs. Lincoln had soured on Browning because he became "distressingly loving."[28] While Mary did not elaborate on what she meant, it may be that she distrusted the sincerity of the seemingly unrelenting attention Browning paid to her husband and to her. Or maybe Mrs. Lincoln sensed "Browning's implied claim of superiority."[29] Whatever the reason for his fall from grace, it was only temporary. By early 1863 Mary backed Browning's failed attempt to become secretary of the interior.[30]

The reason that Lincoln chose Davis for the third court vacancy is not recorded. As David Herbert Donald suggests, it may be that Browning and Lincoln began to drift apart in the summer of 1862, precisely when the president was making the final selection.[31] Possibly Browning's brash, blunt, beseeching request for the job, followed by his wife's pleading letter, hurt Browning in Lincoln's eyes. The tactics of the top contenders for the last spot on the court could not have been more different. Davis understood much better than Browning how to deal with Lincoln. The judge knew not to make a direct plea for the position. Indeed, Davis told Swett not to see the president about the appointment, but Swett went anyway and probably told Lincoln that he came over the judge's objection. Davis told Judge Treat that he disapproved of the signature-gathering effort in Missouri, knowing that almost certainly Treat would mention that fact, which he did, when he submitted the petition to the president. When John Usher, assistant to Secretary of the Interior Caleb Smith, wrote to Davis in May 1862 that Browning would most likely be appointed to the Supreme Court and suggested that Davis fill a newly added seat on the court of claims, the judge knew how to counter that move. Writing just as much to Lincoln as to Usher, Davis stated that the president should appoint those who could "most assist him in his great work" rather than base appointments on personal friendships. The judge added that the president knew him well and the capacity, if any, in which Davis could serve the country. While Davis would not be at liberty to decline a presidential request, he could not personally or through his friends "importune him for any position, whether humble or exalted." So that there would be no mistaking the judge's feelings about the court of claims as a consolation prize, Davis implicitly rejected Usher's offer by recommending another judge from central

Illinois for the court of claims position.[32] Another factor that may have helped influence the final selection was the flood of letters favoring Davis, although Browning had his own cadre of prestigious supporters, including US senators and congressmen.[33] Maybe Mary Lincoln's backing and the kindness that Davis showed Robert Lincoln figured into the decision.[34] It also has been suggested that Davis was selected to shore up support of the old Illinois Whigs in the 1862 congressional elections.[35] The judge's unwavering backing of Lincoln's election efforts over three decades, culminating in securing the presidential nomination in 1860, must have influenced the decision to some extent. But just maybe what tipped the scales was Leonard Swett's skillful cross-examination of Lincoln, comparing the respective willingness and likelihood of Davis and Browning appointing Lincoln if the shoe was on the other foot.

On August 27, 1862, Lincoln sent a letter to Davis offering him the court appointment. Lincoln stated that he was "anxious" that the clerk of the federal court in Chicago, William H. Bradley, be retained and asked Davis to confirm that he would not remove him.[36] Davis had not threatened Bradley's job or implied that he might replace the clerk. It was the possibility of Browning's appointment that made Bradley fear losing his job. Bradley was no fan of Browning and opposed his selection to the Supreme Court. Bradley believed that Browning only accepted the senatorial appointment to finagle his way to the high court. Of course, Bradley was hoping for the appointment of his boss, Judge Thomas Drummond, of the federal district court in Chicago.[37] Failing that, Bradley preferred Davis over Browning. Davis immediately wrote the president expressing his utmost "thankfulness and gratitude" and reassuring Lincoln that it never crossed his mind to replace Bradley as clerk of the court.[38]

Lincoln Gets What He Expects

Davis expressed "great trepidation" and "dread" in going on the Supreme Court. He knew that he fit better on the trial court bench, where he could depend on his common sense, sense of equity, and settlement skills in rendering justice. Members of the high court, on the other hand, were expected to rely on scholarly interpretations of laws and legal precedent to decide cases. Written judicial opinions were not required of circuit-riding judges but were expected of Supreme Court justices. And preparing opinions came hard to Davis. While he often researched questions of law in the Springfield library, he did not write with "facility." As lawyer and Chicago convention delegate John M. Palmer put it, "[Davis] had not been accustomed to the accuracy of judicial thought required in the preparation of written opinions."[39] The fact that as a lawyer Davis had never handled a case in a reviewing court and as a judge sat only in a trial court concerned both the new appointee and the president.[40] But Lincoln knew that Davis's work ethic together with his integrity and regard for the dignity of his new office would make him into a respectable, if not scholarly, high court judge.

The judge's affable nature allowed him to succeed in a "collaborative court" where the majority rather than Davis alone had the final say. He had a solid working relationship with the other justices, including Chief Justice Roger B. Taney and his successor, Salmon Chase, both of whom Davis disliked personally. Davis became friends with some of the justices, including Noah Swayne, whose son, Henry, married Davis's daughter.[41]

Lincoln did not expect Davis to change his style of judging when he moved to Washington. The judge continued to rely on his innate sense of fairness rather than on the scholarly analysis of authoritative legal opinions and texts. He proudly acknowledged that his opinions were shorter than those of any other justice.[42] His proclivity toward brevity and preference for the practical application of common sense rather than legal analysis led to many opinions in which Justice Davis failed to provide even a single citation to precedent in support of his decision.[43]

Unsurprisingly, Davis's "fixed beliefs" found their way into his opinions, including an absolute intolerance for corruption in any branch of government, especially the judiciary.[44] A just legal system demanded the honest and equal application of the law to all men at all times regardless of their station in life. So Davis was ready when the Supreme Court considered whether a judge should be immune from a civil lawsuit alleging that a judge's ruling was not based on the evidence but on the judge's malicious or corrupt motives. That precise issue came before Davis and the rest of the court in *Bradley v. Fisher*. Three years before *Bradley*, the court had decided that a litigant could not sue a judge to recover money damages for any judicial act, no matter how stupid or wrong, as long as the act came within the court's jurisdiction.[45] The justices left for the *Bradley* court whether the blanket rule of judicial immunity shielded judges from liability even when they acted not out of mere stupidity or an erroneous application of the law but out of a corrupt or malicious motive, like taking a bribe from a litigant. In *Bradley*, the majority of the court unwaveringly held that judicial immunity protected judges from civil lawsuits seeking money damages in all cases, even when the judge acted on the basis of bad faith, personal vengeance, or corrupt or malevolent motives. The majority reasoned that litigants often blame an adverse decision on the failings or improper motives of the judge rather than on the true reason for their loss: a lack of evidence or a faulty legal position. According to the majority of the Supreme Court justices, if a civil action could be maintained against judges by merely alleging judicial malice, bad faith, corruption, or partiality, disgruntled parties would not hesitate to make such claims regardless of the truth of the allegations. That "loophole" would effectively end judicial immunity and cause judges to expend time and energy defending one meritless lawsuit after another filed by disgruntled parties. The majority also feared that wealthy or influential litigants would use the threat of lawsuits to intimidate judges to rule in their favor.[46]

Davis dissented from the court's decision in his characteristically curt and commonsense manner. In a 167-word dissent, Davis asserted that the doctrine of judicial immunity, while generally sound, should not apply when a judge is alleged to have acted maliciously or corruptly in deciding a case. Davis had fought against judicial and legislative corruption his entire professional life and was not about to surrender now. The short and sweet dissent required no pontification on the origins of or philosophy behind the judicial immunity doctrine. In the judge's mind, the case rested on the foundational principle of equal treatment under the law. If a private person could be sued for actions taken in bad faith or for corrupt motives, so could a judge.[47] Davis's aversion to granting special privileges to judges or any other person or entity was well known and sometimes considered by Chief Justice Morrison R. Waite in assigning the opinion writing in cases. Thus, when the court voted to rule in favor of the railway in *United States v. Union Pacific Railroad*, the chief justice assigned the opinion to Davis to forestall any public perception that the court favored wealthy businesses. Waite reasoned that the public would say that if Davis ruled for the railroad, it must be because the law required it rather than because the justices kowtowed to corporate interests.[48]

Davis's decisions also reflected his life experiences. He was ever mindful that his inheritance had been stolen by his stepfather. This left Davis especially sensitive to the proper accounting of money and property held by guardians for the benefit of their wards. While many Illinois circuit court judges routinely allowed guardians to sell the real property of their wards, Davis did not. Instead, he held the property in trust until the ward reached majority and then turned the property, with its increased value, over to the ward. His interest in protecting inheritances did not change once he was in Washington. In an unusually long Supreme Court opinion, the judge made it clear that no one was going to cheat Myra Clark Gaines out of a rightful inheritance from her rich, philandering, and possibly bigamist father on account of an undocumented marriage or missing will.[49]

In placing Davis on the Supreme Court, Lincoln had to accept the inevitable: the appointment would only facilitate the judge's ability to provide a continuous stream of unsolicited advice to the president on an endless variety of subjects, including the Emancipation Proclamation and the effectiveness of cabinet members.[50] Lincoln also knew that once Davis was in Washington, he would continue to lobby on behalf of relatives, friends, and political supporters.[51] The judge's pressure on Lincoln for a military promotion and a leave of absence for William Orme demonstrates the insensitivity and borderline rudeness of Davis's approach. Orme was Leonard Swett's law partner and worked to help orchestrate Davis's appointment to the Supreme Court. A close friend of the Davis family, he ardently supported every one of Lincoln's bids for political office.[52] No measure was out of bounds to further the interests of a loyal friend like Orme. So Davis solicited another Supreme Court justice to lobby Lincoln on behalf of Orme. Even worse, Davis audaciously asked Lincoln for proof when the president told him that Orme's name had been submitted to the Senate on the military promotions list. Justice Davis admitted that his efforts on behalf of Orme were "incessant."[53] The judge was well aware that the number and tenor of his patronage requests could damage his influence with Lincoln. But for someone to whom personal loyalty trumped almost everything else, accepting the risk was easy. As the judge put it, "I don't care a straw about losing my influence with the administration when I want to aid one of my best friends."[54]

Lincoln did not ask any of his nominees how they would vote on issues that came before the court, but he believed that Justice Davis would back most of Lincoln's wartime decisions.[55] Yet the president understood that the new justice was no rubber stamp. Seeing his duty as scrupulously following the law and "fearlessly and honestly" deciding cases, Davis would not hesitate to strike down measures that he saw as contrary to the US Constitution. And that is exactly what he did in the most important war measure case to come before the Supreme Court, *Ex parte Milligan*.[56] If Lincoln had survived to see the *Milligan* decision, it would have come as no surprise. Davis had lectured Lincoln repeatedly on the unconstitutionality of military trials of citizens of nonseceding states in which civilian courts were open.[57]

6 Justice Davis and Wartime Presidential Edicts

Everyone expected the Supreme Court to be the final arbiter of the legal and constitutional questions raised by the president's unprecedented wartime actions. The right of a state to secede from the Union, the right to use military force to prevent secession, conscription, the legal tender acts, suspending the writ of habeas corpus, blockading Confederate ports, shuttering newspapers, the legality of the Emancipation Proclamation, and the trial of civilians in military tribunals were some of the monumental issues the justices awaited. Contemplating the day when the right of a state to withdraw from the Union came before the court, Justice Davis wrote to his brother-in-law Julius Rockwell that the law, and only the law, would dictate his decision. Displaying his customary confidence, Davis also assured Rockwell that he knew what the law required on the subject. Preparing for a challenge to the federal conscription law, Davis ordered a copy of the Civil War Military Draft Act (the Enrollment Act of 1863) shortly after its enactment.[1] Notwithstanding expectations, few war-related issues made it to the court during actual hostilities. The constitutionality of the blockade of Southern ports was one issue that did.

The *Prize Cases*

The *Prize Cases* were probably the most important matters to reach the Supreme Court while the war was in progress.[2] In April 1861, while Congress was in recess, Lincoln unilaterally issued a proclamation establishing a naval blockade of the ports of the seceding states. Not until three months later did Congress authorize the president to declare a state of insurrection. Then in August, Congress finally ratified Lincoln's previous military actions, including the military blockade. At issue in the *Prize Cases* were the blockade-running "prizes" seized by the United

States before the congressional actions. The owners of the seized ships claimed that the blockade exceeded the president's power in two ways. First, Congress had not yet declared war at the time Lincoln established the blockade. Second, blockades were authorized only against belligerent nations, and no belligerent nation was at war with the United States. A nation "closed" rather than "blockaded" its own ports. The argument made good use of Lincoln's adamant refusal to recognize the Confederacy as a separate nation. A majority of the Supreme Court took a commonsense approach to the issue, finding that a war is a war and that a president has a duty to defend a nation from external and internal enemies. While a civil war is never officially declared, it exists none-the-less with all the trappings of hostilities between nations, including destruction of property, loss of lives, invasion of territory, exchange of prisoners, and the closure of civil courts. According to Justice Robert C. Grier's majority opinion, the president cannot declare war but has a duty to accept its existence and suppress an insurrection through authorized means, including the blockade of the states in rebellion.[3] The court's decision was a slim five-to-four majority, with Justice Samuel Nelson arguing in dissent that seizure of the ships was illegal because the Civil War did not exist until Congress acted in July, and Lincoln had ordered the blockade much earlier, in April. As a result, Nelson and the other dissenting justices believed that the blockade and seizures were unconstitutional.[4] David Davis joined the majority along with Lincoln's two other appointees, Noah H. Swayne and Samuel F. Miller. Davis did not write a concurring opinion probably because his practical approach to resolving legal questions was fully voiced in the majority opinion. Without doubt, Grier expressed Davis's sentiments when he wrote: "The President was bound to meet [the war] in the shape it presented itself, without waiting for Congress to baptize it with a name; and no name given to it by him or them could change the fact."[5]

Ex parte Vallandigham

Similarly, Davis played little public part in the second significant war policy case to reach the Supreme Court during the rebellion: *Ex parte Vallandigham*.[6] Ohio congressman Clement L. Vallandigham worked hard to become Lincoln's most vocal and persistent critic outside of the Confederacy. If Lincoln proposed it, Vallandigham opposed it. The congressman campaigned against conscription laws, the Emancipation Proclamation, blockades, military tribunals, and the suspension of the writ of habeas corpus. He questioned the motives of "King Lincoln" in conducting the unnecessary and "wicked" war. As far as Vallandigham was concerned, the overarching issue was easily resolved: states possessed the power to secede from the Union. Vallandigham's eloquence and "exaggerated vehemence" drew big crowds, such as the twenty thousand people in his Mount Vernon, Ohio, audience on May 1, 1863.[7]

Recently demoted after his stunning defeat at Fredericksburg, Major General Ambrose E. Burnside was in no mood to tolerate the antics of Vallandigham.[8] As military commander of the Department of the Ohio, Burnside accused Vallandigham of expressing sympathies for those in arms against the US government. More specifically, Burnside formally charged Vallandigham with "having uttered, in a speech at a public meeting, disloyal sentiments and opinions, with the object and purpose of weakening the power of the Government in its efforts for the suppression of an unlawful rebellion."[9] Shortly before daybreak on May 5, 1863, after a few shots were fired from inside his residence, Vallandigham was arrested by the military. The next day, the military commission arraigned him on the charge filed by Burnside. The prisoner contested the jurisdiction of the military tribunal since he was not a member of the military. He claimed that he could only be tried in a civilian court for a crime established by state or federal law in accordance with procedures consistent with the Constitution. But, if nothing else, military justice is swift, and Vallandigham was tried and convicted two days after his arrest. The military commission "sentenced him to be placed in close confinement in some fortress of the United States, to be designated by the commanding officer of this department, there to be kept during the war." According to John Nicolay and John Hay, writing in 1889, the arrest of Vallandigham took Lincoln by surprise.[10] And while Lincoln admitted that he was unsure whether he would have ordered the Copperhead's arrest, he felt compelled to defer to those in the field and in a better position to evaluate the threat that Vallandigham posed. In defending Burnside's action, Lincoln asserted that while Vallandigham had a right to publicly criticize the war effort, he crossed the line by "laboring, with some effect, to prevent the raising of troops, to encourage desertions from the army, and to leave the rebellion without an adequate military force to suppress it."[11]

On May 11, 1863, Vallandigham's lawyer, former Ohio senator George E. Pugh, presented a petition for a writ of habeas corpus to the federal court for the Southern District of Ohio. The petition requested an order directing the military to bring Vallandigham into court and justify his detention. Judge Humphrey Leavitt, appointed by President Andrew Jackson, denied the petition. Judge Leavitt offered a litany of rationales for denying the writ: that Justice Noah Swayne had issued a prior decision denying a similar petition; that even if the writ was issued, the military would ignore the writ of habeas corpus; and that judges should not "embarrass or thwart the executive in his efforts to deliver the country from the dangers which press so heavily upon it." Finally, Leavitt ruled that in the face of a rebellion, "the president is guided solely by his own judgment and discretion, and is only amenable for an abuse of his authority by impeachment." Judge Leavitt did not hide his disdain for Copperheads such as Vallandigham who "disseminate their pestilent heresies among the masses of the people," an evil "of alarming magnitude." Leavitt made it crystal clear, however, that he was merely upholding Vallandigham's arrest and continued detention and was not deciding whether military commissions had jurisdiction to try civilians. He left that issue for the Supreme Court.[12]

After Judge Leavitt's decision, Vallandigham filed a petition for a writ of certiorari asking the US Supreme Court to vacate the judgment of the military commission and to release him from custody. The Supreme Court sidestepped the thorny substantive issues in the case by finding that it had no authority to hear the matter at all. The court reasoned that its constitutional and statutory appellate authority was limited to reviewing the actions of "courts" established by Congress under Article III of the Constitution, and military commissions were not "courts." The Supreme Court further found that neither the Constitution nor Congress had invested the court with original jurisdiction to issue a writ of certiorari or a writ of habeas corpus to review a military tribunal's proceedings.[13] Justice James M. Wayne authored the court's opinion, which refused to reach the issue of whether military commissions could try civilians. The opinion indicates that Justices Nelson, Grier, and Stephen J. Field "concurred in the result" and that Justice Miller was absent for the argument and took no part in the decision.[14] The opinion does not mention Justices John Catron, Nathan Clifford, Swayne, Roger B. Taney, or Davis. One would assume that if any of those five justices concurred with Justice Wayne's opinion, their names would be included with Justices Nelson, Grier, and Field as justices who "concurred in the result." Similarly, if any of the unnamed justices did not participate in the case, logic dictates that they would be listed along with Justice Miller as taking no part in the decision. Without such designations, the five unnamed justices seem to be in a state of judicial legal limbo, participating in the case but neither concurring in nor dissenting from the decision.

The fact of the matter is that Chief Justice Taney was very ill and most certainly took no part in the case.[15] If he had participated, he would have voted to issue a writ of habeas corpus and grant certiorari to review Vallandigham's conviction by the military tribunal. He had done just that in 1861 when he considered an emergency petition challenging the army's arrest of civilian John Merryman.[16] Justice Catron was also probably too ill to participate. If he participated, he likely would have had no problem with the court denying Vallandigham relief. Although he supported slavery, Catron was a "hard-line Unionist" who had previously refused to grant habeas relief to civilians held by military authorities while simultaneously "blister[ing] secessionists in his comments."[17] Justice Swayne would not have disagreed with the court's dismissal of the petition. Sitting as circuit judge in the Southern District of Ohio in a case predating *Vallandigham*, Swayne held that federal courts lacked authority to grant habeas relief to persons imprisoned by the military.[18] Justice Clifford probably acquiesced in the denial of the writ because he had discovered the hard way that courts have no means to enforce orders against the military. Presiding as a circuit judge in 1862, Clifford had issued a writ of habeas corpus commanding the military to produce civilian William H. Winder, who was held in a military installation in Boston Harbor on charges of conspiracy to overthrow the government. But issuing the writ was easier than executing the writ. The US marshal refused to serve the court order, and a deputy sheriff of Suffolk County Massachusetts was forcibly denied entry to the military fort when he attempted to serve the writ. Justice Clifford took the subjugation of legal process to military force stoically:

> The court does not perceive that anything more can now be done to effect service of this writ. The service appears to have been prevented by force. The court deeply regrets that officers of the United States should obstruct process out of a court of the United States, especially this process. But those officers are at present beyond the control of the law, and the court has not the command of the physical force needful to effect a service of this writ at the present time. Let the writ be placed on file, to be served when and where service may become practicable.[19]

That left Justice Davis, who, like Justices Catron, Clifford, Swayne, and Taney, is not mentioned in the court's opinion. After the war, Davis privately condemned the court's refusal to take jurisdiction in the case, grant the writ, and release Vallandigham from military custody. In 1866 Davis told William Herndon that "the Vallandigham was an Error—the decision an outrage—and I should have so decided."[20] Thus, from his statement, it appears that Davis felt that he took no part in the decision. But that fact, if it is fact, is not reflected in the court's opinion, and Davis authored no dissenting opinion. Moreover, Davis was in Washington for the December 1863 court term and joined in or authored other opinions issued by the court during that session.[21]

Not until the rebellion was suppressed would Davis write the Supreme Court's majority opinion in *Ex parte Milligan* declaring unconstitutional the trial of civilians by military tribunals in nonseceding states. Most probably, Davis stayed out of the court's decision in *Vallandigham* to avoid interfering with the Union's war efforts. It may also be that at the time the court considered the *Vallandigham* matter, Davis did not want to be linked to any court opinion on the military's authority to suppress opposition to the war because he was knee-deep in that issue in Illinois and Indiana both as a judge and as a political advisor to the president.

Suppression of the *Chicago Times*

General Burnside continued to drag the courts and Davis into the fight over the proper exercise of the president's war powers. Burnside not only despised individuals like Vallandigham but also detested Democratic newspapers that, in his view, undermined the war effort. High on Burnside's list of offending publications was the *Chicago Times*, known for its unrelenting attacks on the president and his war policies. By June 1, 1863, Burnside had had all of the newspaper that he could stomach, and he issued General Orders, No. 84, which suppressed the *Chicago Times* because of its "repeated expression of disloyal and incendiary sentiments." Burnside ordered Brigadier General Jacob Ammen to execute the suppression order.[22] Upon learning of the order, the editor of the *Chicago Times* hired a Republican law firm to visit federal district court judge Thomas Drummond at his Chicago home and request an injunction restraining the military from shutting down the newspaper until the matter could be heard in court. Shortly before midnight on June 2, Drummond granted the request and directed General Ammen "to take no steps or measures to carry into effect the said order of Major Gen. Burnside . . . until the application can be heard in open court to-morrow."[23] Judge Drummond's remarks in issuing the temporary injunction paralleled the views of Judge Davis:

> I may be pardoned for saying that, personally and officially, I desire to give every aid and assistance in my power to the Government, and to the Administration in restoring the Union, but I have always wished to treat the Government as a Government of law and a Government of the Constitution, and not a Government of mere physical force. I personally have contended and shall always contend for the right of free discussion and the right of commenting, under the law and under the Constitution, upon the acts of the officers of the Government.[24]

About the same time that Drummond issued the injunction, Judge Davis dined in Springfield with Senator Orville Browning, Judge Samuel Treat, US District Attorney Lawrence Weldon, and Springfield lawyer Antrim Campbell. The main topic of discussion was the suppression of the *Chicago Times*. According to Browning, all five agreed that Burnside's order was "despotic and unwarrantable . . . and calculated to produce civil war in the State." The diners also agreed that Judge Drummond "should, at once, grant an injunction to restrain the military authorities from interfering with the publication." Davis, never shy about expressing an opinion concerning a pending case, said that if he were presented with the application for the injunction, "he would not hesitate to grant it."[25] Davis would nearly get his wish.

That same day Judge Drummond telegraphed Davis requesting that he come to Chicago to join in presiding over the *Chicago Times* injunction hearing set for the next morning. Davis boarded a train that evening for Chicago.[26] No doubt Drummond extended the invitation in part to gain an influential cojudge if a ruling became necessary concerning the military's authority to shut down an opposition newspaper. But most likely the invitation was extended to gain Davis's extrajudicial influence with the president to resolve the matter short of litigation. Before leaving Springfield for Chicago, Davis and William Herndon telegraphed Lincoln that "we deem it of the highest importance that you revoke the order . . . suppressing the *Chicago Times*."[27] Six days earlier, Davis had telegraphed Secretary of War Edwin Stanton, advising him that the "honor and interests of the Government" demanded the immediate removal of General Milo Smith Hascall of Indianapolis because he had threatened to shut down several Indiana newspapers.[28] Davis and Herndon were not alone in communicating disapproval of the shutdown of the *Times*. On June 3, 1863, Illinois senator Lyman Trumbull and Republican congressman Isaac Newton Arnold sent a telegram signed by fourteen others, both Republicans and Democrats, urging the president to rescind the *Chicago Times* suppression order.[29]

Notwithstanding Judge Drummond's midnight order temporarily restraining the military from closing the *Chicago Times* and notwithstanding the pending court hearing set for later that day, at about 4:00 a.m. on June 4 two companies of Union soldiers seized the *Times*' office, halted the presses, and destroyed as many newspapers as they could. The hearing in Judge Drummond's courtroom began about six hours later with a presentation by the *Times*' lawyers contesting the constitutionality of General Burnside's order. The case was then continued to the next morning ostensibly to give the government time to prepare a response to the newspaper's arguments.[30]

The telegrams sent by Davis and Trumbull and the negative reaction of others to the seizure of the *Times*, together with Lincoln's own misgivings about the legality of the move, caused the president to order Secretary Stanton to revoke Burnside's suppression order.[31] Davis expected this result because he knew that Lincoln was too good of a lawyer not to realize that suppressing newspapers violated the First Amendment.[32] The editor of the *Chicago Times* received a message from General Burnside at 6:30 p.m. on June 4 advising him that the suppression order had been rescinded and that the paper was free to resume publication.[33]

In light of the rescission of the suppression order, the *Times* dismissed its lawsuit the next morning when the parties appeared in Judge Drummond's court. Davis's political connection with Lincoln helped avoid a legal battle that Lincoln was likely to lose and that would have added fuel to the antiwar movement already in full gear in the western states. And this was not the only time that Davis employed extrajudicial means to help influence the resolution of a potentially explosive wartime court case.

Judge Charles Constable

In March 1863 Indiana Union army officers tracked four deserters across the state line and arrested them in Illinois. Outspoken Lincoln critic and Illinois circuit court judge Charles Constable ordered the four deserters released. If that was not embarrassment enough for the military, Judge Constable directed that the two Indiana army sergeants who made the arrests be held on kidnapping charges.

Davis knew Constable very well. They had served together as delegates to the 1847 Illinois Constitutional Convention, and years later Davis broke up a heated argument between Lincoln and Constable while traveling the Eighth Circuit. In 1849, at Constable's request, Davis and Lincoln wrote letters recommending Constable for a diplomatic appointment with the Zachary Taylor administration. The next year, Davis and Lincoln backed Constable in his unsuccessful attempt to gain a federal judgeship in Washington, Oregon, or New Mexico Territory. But by 1856 Constable had moved from Whig allegiance to the Democrats. In 1861, now "a vociferous opponent of Lincoln's war policies," he was elected a judge of the judicial circuit that included Clark and Coles Counties and that bordered Davis's Eighth Judicial Circuit.[34]

During the kidnapping trial of the Indiana sergeants before Judge Constable, about three hundred Union soldiers surrounded the Clark County Courthouse, freed the defendants, and took the judge into custody for interfering with the military. Constable was transported to Springfield to stand trial in federal court. Federal judge Samuel H. Treat, a Democrat but a friend of Lincoln and Davis, presided over the trial of Judge Constable. On April 7, after both sides made less than vigorous presentations, Treat found Constable not guilty of enticing soldiers to desert in a terse fifty-seven-word order.[35] To neither Treat's nor Davis's surprise, the *Chicago Daily Tribune* disapproved of the decision, calling Treat a "malignant Copperhead."[36] Knowing the potential political and military significance of the case, it is likely that Treat conferred with Davis about the Constable situation, as they had communicated about military matters previously.[37] Davis could have sat with Treat during Constable's trial as part of his circuit-riding duties. The Supreme Court term had ended, and Davis was back in Bloomington.[38] But the need for Davis to join Treat on the bench was eliminated when the government and Constable's lawyers consented to Judge Treat hearing the case.[39] In any event, Davis and Treat would have agreed that the best resolution of the unfortunate matter was to end the court proceedings as quickly and painlessly as possible, just as Treat did by finding Judge Constable not guilty. It was only a matter of time before Judge Constable would enmesh himself in another incident that required Justice Davis to employ extrajudicial means to resolve a wartime legal issue.

The Charleston Riots

On March 28, 1864, furloughed members of the Fifty-Fourth Illinois Infantry were gathered outside the Coles County Courthouse in Charleston. Also present was a large contingent of antiwar Democrats from Edgar and Coles Counties attending a rally with Judge Constable as a featured speaker. The Democrats came prepared to resist the Union soldiers' favorite spectator sport of forcing Democrats to kneel and profess an oath of allegiance to Lincoln and all his past and future proclamations. Earlier that year Judge Constable was a victim of the oath brigade. Fueled by hostility and whiskey, the brief melee began in the courthouse square and spilled into Judge Constable's courtroom, where he was in the middle of the trial of a hog thief. At the end of the "Charleston Riot," six Union soldiers, two antiwar Democrats, and a Republican civilian were dead, with another twelve persons suffering nonfatal injuries.[40]

Of the more than fifty Copperheads initially rounded up by the Union army in the aftermath of the riot, sixteen were held and transferred to a military installation. In June 1864 the Coles County grand jury returned murder and riot indictments against fourteen defendants, four of whom were held by the military. The judge advocate general, Henry Burnett, and Lieutenant Colonel James Oakes, assistant provost marshal general for Illinois, recommended to Lincoln that the prisoners held by the military, including those indicted by the state grand jury, be tried by a military commission rather than by a civilian court. On June 22, 1864, the attorneys for the prisoners filed a petition for a writ of habeas corpus in federal circuit court in Springfield. District court judge Samuel H. Treat and David Davis, sitting with Treat as a circuit court judge, granted the petition and ordered the military to bring the prisoners to court and explain the authority under which they were being held. Lieutenant Colonel Oakes responded to the writ by advising Judge Treat that the president had suspended habeas corpus for the Coles County prisoners and that they had already been transferred out of the court's jurisdiction to Fort Delaware. Although Davis was in St. Louis when Oakes informed Treat of the military's refusal to bring the prisoners to court, the two judges had earlier agreed how to deal with the matter whether Oakes complied with the writ or disregarded the writ. To neither judge's surprise, Colonel Oakes continued the military's routine practice and refused to honor the writ of habeas corpus. There was nothing Davis or Treat could do about it—in court, that is. So the case was dismissed.[41]

Davis did not like the fact that the military held the civilians and planned to try them in a military tribunal, and he let Lincoln know about it. In a letter dated July 1, Davis told the president that the government "must have acted on wrong information" and that he was in the process of getting the "correct information" from an attorney defending the Coles County prisoners. Once he did, he would forward the accurate information to Lincoln.[42]

Before receiving Davis's letter, Lincoln had sent telegrams to Judge Davis and Judge Treat requesting a summary of the evidence and the judges' impressions concerning the Coles County riot cases. Two days later, Judge Treat telegraphed Lincoln and informed him that the certified court record of the proceeding was on its way to the president. Treat also wrote that he believed "the prisoners should have been surrendered to the civil authorities" and that Judge Davis shared his opinion. On July 5 Davis telegraphed the president, saying that he had replied to Lincoln's request for information by letter sent the previous day.[43] In his letter of July 4, Davis explained that the Charleston rioters violated no law of the United States or the military, did not resist governmental authority, did not interfere with conscription laws, and were not army deserters. According to the judge, the civilian offenders, although "bad men" and guilty of "the gravest offenses against the state," were subject only to prosecution in state court and could not be prosecuted in a military tribunal. In support of his opinion, Davis cited provisions of the Habeas Corpus Act of 1863 requiring that the military supply the local federal district court with the names of all prisoners in military custody other than actual prisoners of war. The Habeas Corpus Act further provided that civilians held by the military and indicted by a grand jury must be transferred to the custody of the civil authorities until their trial in civilian court. The act also stated that individuals held by the military but not indicted must be discharged from custody. On July 5 Davis sent another letter to Lincoln enclosing an abstract of the case prepared by the prisoners' lawyers. In the letter, the judge repeated his opinion that the Coles County prisoners held by the military should have been turned over to the civil authorities.[44]

In November 1864 Lincoln finally ordered the release of all the Charleston prisoners except George Washington Rardin and John Redmon, who were among the fourteen charged by the Coles County grand jury. Rardin and Redmon were the only two persons tried in connection with the riot in Charleston, and both were acquitted by state court juries.[45]

In their capacity as judges, Davis and Treat did not affect the fate of the civilians arrested by the military. But in their private dealings with the president, they helped convince Lincoln to reject military trials for the Charleston rioters. Davis made no effort to conceal his opinion on the constitutionality of military trials of civilians. But by communicating with Lincoln informally by way of letter and telegram, he was able to avoid rendering a judicial ruling on the issue during the war. After the war ended, Davis welcomed the opportunity to play the leading role in delimiting the jurisdiction of military tribunals.

Ex parte Milligan

On October 5, 1864, Lambdin P. Milligan was arrested by US Army officials in his home state of Indiana and charged with (1) conspiracy against the government, (2) affording aid and comfort to the rebels, (3) inciting insurrection, (4) disloyal practices, and (5) violations of the laws of war. Each charge was supported by specifications, including allegations that Milligan belonged to "a secret society known as the Order of American Knights or Sons of Liberty, for the purpose of overthrowing the Government," communicated with rebel forces, conspired to raid military arsenals and seize munitions, conspired to free Confederate prisoners, and conspired to resist the draft, all while Indiana was allegedly threatened with invasion by the enemy.[46] There never was much doubt about Milligan's guilt. He was one of four "major generals" of the Sons of Liberty and directed the group's operations in Northwest Indiana. In August 1864 the Sons of Liberty planned to storm Camp Morton in Indianapolis and liberate Confederate prisoners. Milligan was not shy in urging Democrats to organize and arm themselves "with pikes and scythes[,] with long guns, with short guns" in order to maintain their liberty against the transgressions of the Lincoln administration.[47]

Two months later, Milligan was tried, convicted, and sentenced to death by a military commission that "President Abraham Lincoln had unilaterally created."[48] Two weeks after Lincoln's death, President Andrew Johnson approved the sentence and set the execution date for May 19, 1865. On May 10 Milligan's lawyers filed a petition in the US Circuit Court for the District of Indiana seeking the discharge of Milligan and his codefendants. The petition alleged that the military commission lacked authority to arrest, try, or confine Milligan and his confederates. Local district court judge David McDonald and circuit justice David Davis jointly presided over the case in Indianapolis.[49]

At the time the petition was filed, Davis had not known Judge McDonald very long. The two first met on the evening of May 7, 1864, while Davis attended circuit duties with then district court judge Albert Smith White. McDonald and Davis took tea together. McDonald recognized that Davis possessed "good sense" but otherwise was unimpressed with the Supreme Court justice. McDonald saw "no mark of legal learning or any other kind of learning in him. Respectable general learning and literature he certainly has not. Indeed, there is no polish and no literature about him."[50] Davis was apparently more impressed with the Indiana lawyer, because when district court judge White died, Davis lobbied Lincoln to appoint McDonald to the vacancy. He wrote Lincoln that McDonald's qualifications included being "an admirable Lawyer & a pure upright man." Equally important to Davis, McDonald was poor, with three daughters and five grandchildren to support.[51] On September 24 McDonald noted in his diary that both Justice Davis and Justice Noah Swayne were determined to secure his appointment to the federal bench. And they did just that. On December 17, 1864, McDonald took the oath of office as a federal judge.[52] Over the next five years, Davis and McDonald became friends, sharing the bench as well as sharing home remedies for gastrointestinal disorders, including McDonald's prescription of "Wheat bran—Mixed in molasses or butter milk" for Davis's daughter's bowel ailment.[53]

In their petition filed on May 10, Milligan's lawyers requested that the federal court order the military to bring Milligan to the Indianapolis courthouse for a hearing on the legitimacy of his continued confinement.[54] The easy way out for McDonald and Davis would have been to simply issue the writ to bring Milligan into court. In response, the military would have refused to produce Milligan, just as it refused to produce the defendants in the Charleston riot cases. Milligan's case, like so many others, then would have been dismissed or continued generally with no hope that Milligan would ever be brought to a civilian court. But Milligan's situation was significantly different from that of most other Copperheads arrested by the military. Milligan had been sentenced to hang, and the execution date was ten days away.[55] This was not a matter of merely imprisoning another Copperhead until the end of the war.

Further augmenting the importance of the situation, Davis abhorred the death penalty. While he was on Illinois's Eighth Judicial Circuit he refused to pronounce a death sentence returned by a jury. As the court term wore on without the sentence being imposed, future judge Charles Constable finally wrote out what Davis needed to say and "nerved the Judge up" to pronounce the sentence, albeit in a shaky voice.[56] In another example of Davis's uneasiness with capital punishment, in June 1865 five defendants were convicted of murder before Davis and McDonald. Judge McDonald recorded in his diary that "if it were left to me, I would, at once, pronounce sentence of death on them all." But Judge Davis would not sign off on the death penalty until he checked with the other Supreme Court justices on "one legal point on which possibly some doubt may exist." When the justices failed to respond to Davis's inquiries, he and McDonald filed a certificate of division permitting the Supreme Court to hear the case. The Supreme Court reversed the defendants' convictions.[57]

Even before Milligan and his codefendants filed an application for a writ of habeas corpus, McDonald and Davis had discussed the case. They jointly concluded that the authority of a military tribunal to try and convict Milligan was in serious doubt. Because of the significance of the issue, the two judges agreed to advance the matter to the Supreme Court by once again filing a certificate of division stating that they were split on the correct answer to three questions that controlled the case.[58] Feigning disagreement on the questions was the only method by which jurisdiction could be invested in the Supreme Court.[59] The certificate of division of opinion was filed and forwarded to the Supreme Court. The three questions upon which McDonald and Davis claimed to be divided were the following:

I.   On the facts stated in the petition and exhibits, ought a writ of habeas corpus to be issued according to the prayer of said petitioner?
II.   On the facts stated in the petition and exhibits, ought the said Milligan to be discharged from custody as in said petition prayed?
III. Whether, upon the facts stated in the petition and exhibits, the military commission had jurisdiction legally to try and sentence said Milligan in manner and form, as in said petition and exhibit is stated?[60]

On the same day, the two judges "united in a strong letter to the President [Andrew Johnson] praying him to delay the execution till the Supreme Court should decide the case." In the letter the judges did not question the guilt of Milligan or his codefendants, Dr. William Bowles and Stephen Horsey. Rather, they questioned the wisdom of executing the defendants before the Supreme Court ruled on the jurisdiction of the military tribunal. They wanted to avoid the "stain on the national character" if the conspirators were executed, and the court later ruled that the convictions were unconstitutional. Davis and McDonald also feared making the Copperheads "political martyrs."[61] Judge Davis had "a long and earnest talk" with Indiana governor Oliver Morton and evidently convinced him to request that the president commute the sentences of Bowles, Horsey, and Milligan to life imprisonment.[62]

The pleas of Davis, McDonald, Morton, and others persuaded President Johnson to commute Horsey's death sentence to life imprisonment and delay the executions of Milligan and Bowles until June 2.[63] Then on May 30 the president ordered that the death sentences imposed by the military tribunal against all three defendants be commuted to life imprisonment at hard labor.[64]

The Davis Majority Opinion and the Chase Concurring Opinion

Oral arguments before the Supreme Court in *Ex parte Milligan* began on March 5 and ended on March 13, 1866. Three weeks later, on the final day of the court's term, Chief Justice Salmon Chase read an order directing that a writ of habeas corpus be issued, that Milligan be released from custody pursuant to the Habeas Corpus Act of 1863, and that the military commission "had no jurisdiction legally to try and sentence said Milligan." The chief justice also announced that the full opinion of the court and the statement of any dissenting justice would be read at the next court term.[65]

How the preparation of majority opinions was assigned to individual justices during Chase's reign as chief justice remains uncertain.[66] Thus, it is not clear how the task of writing the *Milligan* majority opinion fell to Davis. Generally, Chief Justice Chase assigned opinions to himself or another justice if Chase was part of the court's majority. If the chief justice was not in the majority, then some historians say that the senior associate justice in the majority assigned the opinion.[67] Other historians, based on Chase's diary entries and correspondence, convincingly argue that the assignment was made by agreement or "caucus" of the judges in the majority.[68] But whether the assignment power rested solely with Samuel Nelson, the senior justice in the majority, or with the majority justices collectively, the selection of Davis was a foregone conclusion. Not only was he an outspoken critic of the military trial of civilians in peaceful states but, more importantly, he was the sole Republican member of the court who voted to deny both the president's and Congress's authority to establish military tribunals to try civilians.

For the entire summer the judge worked on what would be his most important contribution to Supreme Court jurisprudence.[69] Without the present-day luxury of law clerks to assist in the research and writing of court decisions, Davis wrote the opinion himself. Justice Nelson helped by sending Davis a copy of his June 1866 decision in *In re Egan*. In that case, Justice Nelson, while sitting as a circuit court judge in New York, held that a military commission lacked authority to try a South Carolina civilian seven months after the war ended. While the lawyers arguing on behalf of Milligan relied on authorities cited in Nelson's opinion, Davis did not. Nelson's opinion relied on the narrow proposition that martial law ended when the war ended.[70] Davis's narrative rested on the broader foundational principal of the supremacy of the Constitution at all times for all men.

On December 17, 1866, the first day of the new Supreme Court term, Davis took his seat on the bench and read the majority opinion, joined by Democratic justices Nelson, Grier, Clifford, and Field. Davis began by declaring that the importance of the question before the court could not be overstated, because it involved "the very framework of the government and the fundamental principles of American liberty." According to Davis, "No graver question was ever considered by this court." It affected not only Milligan's rights but also the birthright of every American to receive constitutional protections against overzealous or unfair state actors. Those "plain and direct" constitutional protections included the Fourth Amendment protection against unreasonable searches and seizures, the Fifth Amendment right to be charged by grand jury indictment for capital and infamous crimes and to receive due process of law, and the Sixth Amendment guarantee "to a speedy and public trial by an impartial jury." At the time of the adoption of the US Constitution, Davis continued, the people knew that without fundamental safeguards they would be "at the mercy of wicked rulers, or the clamor of an excited people," and so Americans demanded these key amendments before ratifying the Constitution. The Founders knew the history of the struggle "to relieve those in civil life from military trials" and intended that every right secured by the Constitution would be shielded from intrusion by the executive and legislative branches.[71]

After spelling out the crucial interests at stake, Davis examined possible sources of authority for military courts to try and sentence civilians in disregard of constitutional protections. Certainly, military tribunals possessed no part of judicial power, since the Constitution conferred judicial power only in the Supreme Court and other inferior courts established by Congress. Military courts were established by the executive branch, not under Article III of the Constitution. The Fifth Amendment did except from the requirement of a grand jury indictment "cases arising in the land or naval forces, or in the militia, when in actual service in time of war or public danger." But on its face that exception had nothing to do with the charges against Milligan. Davis then explained why he did not examine the government's contention that the military commission had jurisdiction over Milligan under the "laws and usages of war": "It can serve no useful purpose to inquire what those laws and usages are, whence they originated, where found, and on whom they operate; they can never be applied to citizens in states which have upheld the authority of the government, and where the courts are open and their process unobstructed."[72]

Although later faulted for his conclusion, Davis took judicial notice that the federal authorities in Indiana were never opposed, and the "courts [were] always open to hear criminal accusations and redress grievances."[73] To support this finding, the judge noted that soon after Milligan's military trial ended, the federal court was open and peacefully conducting business without the need of "bayonets" for protection or the need of military assistance to enforce its judgments. Davis knew from personal knowledge and from the circuit court's records that the court "was constantly engaged in the trial of similar offences, and was never interrupted in its administration of criminal justice." For good measure, Justice Davis added that the Indiana courts could be counted on to conduct fair trials and render proper decisions and just punishment because the Hoosier State was "eminently distinguished for patriotism." To allay the fears of Unionists that Copperhead-tainted juries would refuse to convict fellow travelers, Davis observed that "upright" and "intelligent" jurors would be selected by a marshal appointed by the president.[74]

Davis conceded that military commissions could constitutionally operate in cases of foreign invasion or civil war but only when courts were closed, thereby making it impossible to administer criminal justice. Military tribunals could exercise authority only in the "theatre of active military operations, where war really prevails" in states such as Virginia, for example. Military control over the administration of justice might continue as long as the civil courts were obstructed in the exercise of their jurisdiction. But that was not the case in Indiana, since there was no "hostile foot" on Hoosier soil and the courts were open. To Davis, the Constitution reigned over all men at all times.[75]

> The Constitution of the United States is a law for rulers and people, equally in war and in peace, and covers with the shield of its protection all classes of men, at all times, and under all circumstances. No doctrine, involving more pernicious consequences, was ever invented by the wit of man than that any of its provisions can be suspended during any of the great exigencies of government. Such a doctrine leads directly to anarchy or despotism, but the theory of necessity on which it is based is false; for the government, within the Constitution, has all the powers granted to it, which are necessary to preserve its existence; as has been happily proved by the result of the great effort to throw off its just authority.[76]

Republican justices Swayne, Miller, and Wayne joined in a concurring opinion authored by their fellow Republican, Chief Justice Salmon Chase. While agreeing that Milligan's conviction was improper and that he was entitled to release, Chase took a much narrower view of the controlling question. To Chase the case did not involve monumental constitutional issues pitting the civil authority against military necessity. Instead, he saw the matter as simply applying a statute passed by Congress to Milligan's situation.

The Habeas Corpus Act of 1863 is most famous for its first section, which authorized the suspension of the writ of habeas corpus throughout the United States. The lesser-known second and third sections of the act limited the suspension of habeas corpus in states such as Indiana where the federal courts remained open. In states with functioning court systems, the privilege of habeas corpus could still be suspended for Copperheads and other civilians considered by the military as dangerous to the public safety. But those individuals could only be arrested and detained by the military until the local grand jury met. If the arrestee was indicted by a grand jury, the military was mandated to release the prisoner to the civil authorities for trial in civilian court. If the grand jury met and failed to indict, the act was clear: the military's authority to detain the prisoner ended, and he must be released. As Chase put it, "Indeed, the act seems to have been framed on purpose to secure the trial of all offences of citizens by civil tribunals, in states where these tribunals were not interrupted in the regular exercise of their functions." Since the Indiana grand jury had not indicted Milligan by the time it adjourned, the Habeas Corpus Act mandated Milligan's release. According to Chase, nothing more need be said. But, of course, Chase did say more, feeling compelled to rebut the majority's gratuitous conclusion that Congress had no more power than the president to authorize military commissions like the one in Indiana. The chief justice predicted that Davis's misguided opinion would subject members of the military commissions to lawsuits by civilians illegally detained by the military.[77]

Chase believed that Congress's power to raise, support, and govern armies, to declare war, and to enact legislation for carrying on a war necessarily included the authority to create military commissions to try civilian traitors like Milligan. Further, it would be up to Congress, not the Supreme Court, to decide which states faced sufficient danger to justify the use of military tribunals for civilians. Chase's description of the situation in Indiana countered that of Davis. The chief justice claimed that Indiana "had been actually invaded, and was constantly threatened with invasion." He further maintained that a powerful secret military association with a military structure cooperating with the Confederate forces conspired against the draft, plotted insurrection, and planned to free war prisoners and seize arsenals. The fact that Indiana courts were open meant little to Chase, because the courts might be operating normally but ineffectively, unable "to avert threatened danger, or to punish, with adequate promptitude and certainty, the guilty conspirators."[78]

Chase and the other concurring justices did not contest the majority's conclusion that the president lacked authority to establish the military commission in Indiana. They also agreed that Milligan was wrongfully convicted. But they vehemently disagreed with Davis's further finding that Congress had no authority to establish military commissions to try civilians. It was the disagreement on this final point that led Republicans to condemn Davis.

The Aftermath

Davis and his opinion were brutally attacked by Republicans. The Republican Party produced a pamphlet titled *Review of the Decision of the U.S. Supreme Court, in the Cases of Lambdin P. Milligan and Others, the Indiana Conspirators* that not only "condemn[ed] the opinion in scalding terms" but also attacked the integrity of Justice Davis.[79] The pamphlet characterized Davis's factual findings concerning the state of affairs in Indiana at the time of Milligan's arrest as "distorted," "erroneous," and "wholly misconceived and mistaken." According to the authors of the pamphlet, these were not innocent or negligent factual errors on Davis's part. Instead, the misstatements and omissions were the "the most striking instance of a judicial *suppressio veri* in our annals," and they should be "condemned by every patriotic citizen." Likewise, Davis's legal conclusions were called "feeble," "false," imbecilic, and monstrous if not criminal.[80] And the Republicans could not conclude their attack without comparing the heroic deeds of the martyred president with the cowardly dicta of a former collection lawyer:

[Davis] approaches the subject theoretically, with contracted vision and compre-
hension uninstructed by personal participation in the events of the war, treating
a gigantic rebellion as a provincial attorney is accustomed to treat an action of
assumpsit on a promissory note, . . . while Lincoln, sublimely presiding upon a
theatre to which the eyes of all mankind were turned, . . . keenly alive to the occasion, . . . approached the practical treatment of the same question with a courage
and intelligence that showed him adequate for the crisis. . . . While Davis's opinion
in effect lends judicial sanction to the escape of such criminals as the members of
the Northwestern conspiracy, and would seem to declare the faithful officers who
tried and punished the murderers of the President to be themselves murderers
for having done so.[81]

Republican newspapers joined the assault. Some, like the *Chicago Tribune*,
criticized the opinion in a toned-down version of the critique presented in the
pamphlet. The *Tribune* rebuked Davis's opinion for its faulty legal and factual
analysis without impugning the judge's integrity or engaging in name calling.[82]
The *New York Herald* was not so kind, comparing Davis's opinion to the infamous *Dred Scott* decision: "This two-faced opinion of Mr. Justice Davis of the
Supreme Court is, then, utterly inconsistent with the leading facts of the war, and
therefore utterly preposterous. This stultification of the Supreme Court we dare
say results from the great blunder of attempting to regulate the war by the old
exploded Taney and Buchanan notions of the constitution. . . . This constitutional
twaddle of Mr. Justice Davis will no more stand the fire of public opinion than
the *Dred Scott* decision."[83] In a not-so-subtle threat, the *Herald* warned that if
the Supreme Court remained "a hospital for invalid party politicians," Congress
had the duty to abolish the court and establish "a new court . . . with new judges,
from the Chief Justice down, and fewer or more in number, as Congress may
prescribe." Other newspapers endorsed the same drastic measures.[84]

The *Delaware (OH) Gazette* believed that the "infamous decision" authored
by members of the "old fogy junto of the Court" would give more "encouragement and consolation to the Copperhead party" than anything since the
first battle of Bull Run. The *New York Times* complained that the Copperhead
press gloated over the decision and renewed its attack against national unity
while "shelter[ing] themselves behind Mr. Justice Davis and his associates."[85] A
northern Indiana newspaper repeated the refrain by protesting that the opinion
"created great exultation among the rebels in Washington."[86] According to many
Republican papers, Davis's opinion shocked the common sense and sensibilities
of loyal citizens and warranted a severe rebuke.[87] After declaring that treason
"found a secure shelter in the bosom of the Supreme Court," the *Washington
Chronicle* observed that its editors had not "met a Republican who does not
speak with contempt of the language of Justice Davis." The *Philadelphia North
American* personalized the attack by claiming that Lincoln "made a mistake in

appointing a Judge of the fatal name of Davis," an unmistakable reference to Jefferson Davis.[88]

Not unexpectedly, Democratic papers celebrated the *Milligan* decision as "vindicat[ing] the sacred rights of the citizen against the exercise of arbitrary power by military authority."[89] Where the Republican papers saw the majority opinion as purely partisan and political, the papers of the Democracy viewed the decision as demonstrating the court's independence, uprightness, and freedom from partisan interests.[90] The *National Intelligencer*, President Johnson's messenger, defended the five justices in the majority by finding no evidence that they were "influenced by political or personal considerations" and by observing that the justices had "devoted themselves with dignity and with assiduity to their high duties."[91] But some Democrat newspapers, while praising the opinion as a savior of constitutional liberty, could not help but demean its Republican author. After describing Justice Davis as unknown to the judicial world, the *Louisiana Democrat* doubted that he was "distinguished for anything unless it be for 'rail splitting,' engineering a flatboat or some other Hoosier accomplishment for which 'the second Washington' and the 'people's martyr of [N——] liberty' was somewhat remarkable."[92]

Reconstructionists in Congress detested the *Milligan* opinion because they viewed it as jeopardizing the ability to replace civilian courts in the South with military tribunals.[93]

Congressman Thaddeus Stevens showed the depth of Republican hostility by classifying the opinion as "far more dangerous" than the *Dred Scott* decision and claiming that it "unsheathed the dagger of the assassin, and places the knife of the rebel at the throat of every man who dares proclaim himself . . . a loyal Union man." Republican congressman James F. Wilson of Iowa described Davis's decision as a "piece of judicial impertinence which we are not bound to respect." He further singled out Davis and his sidekicks as "manifest[ing] most singularly crude ideas of the great questions they are discussing." Although Wilson had no disagreement with Chase's concurring opinion, he predicted that if the majority opinion had been issued during the hostilities, the Union would have lost the war, "and the confederate States would to-day occupy a place among the nations of the earth."[94]

Secretary of War Edwin Stanton joined the outrage, claiming that *Milligan* threatened the Reconstruction plans of Congress. The *Chicago Tribune* reported Stanton's dire judgment that the *Milligan* decision emasculated the Freedmen's Bureau and rendered the army powerless in the South. Stanton joined with other "good lawyers" who believed that the opinion rendered the secretary of war, the judge advocate general, and the members of the military tribunal who tried the president's assassins liable to prosecution. Testifying before Congress, Stanton added for good measure, "I do not think that the decision in the Milligan case is justified by any principal of law recognized by any civil Government on earth."[95]

Davis's opinion did not escape criticism in legal circles. The *American Law Review* felt compelled to comment on the decision because of the hostile critique that it received, the abuse heaped on the justices, and, most importantly, the fact that many viewed the opinion as a political pronouncement rather than a judicial decree. The *American Law Review* found especially problematic the court's willingness to go beyond the precise question presented by the parties and gratuitously establish principles by which it would, in the future, decide questions "involving the gravest and highest powers of Congress." By doing so, the article continued, the court had abandoned its constitutional duty to stick to the issue before it. By failing in that duty, the decision aroused the jealousy of the other branches of government, thereby undermining public confidence in the impartiality of the court. According to the *American Law Review*, the majority should have stopped when they found that the president lacked authority to establish the military commission that sentenced Milligan and leave the issue of Congress's power to establish such commissions to a day when the issue was squarely before the court. The author of the law review article concluded that a minimalist approach would have resulted in a unanimous court opinion commanding universal respect.[96]

The article reserved some blame for the chief justice and the three justices joining in his concurring opinion. It faulted the concurring justices for presenting a wholesale attack on the majority opinion rather than merely noting their disagreement with the part of the opinion that went beyond the precise issue presented. The commentary reprimanded all the justices for failing to learn from the *Dred Scott* decision to stay clear of political controversies and to avoid the appearance that the judiciary was influenced by party loyalties.[97]

Davis's Reaction to the Criticism

Davis expected criticism for the decision, but he did not anticipate the vile and personal denunciations. When the *Milligan* case first came to the circuit court in Indianapolis, Davis and McDonald discussed the "public clamor" that would likely result when it became known that they had asked President Johnson to delay the execution of Milligan and his two confederates. But both judges were convinced that the executions would be "impolitic if not illegal" and so were willing to endure popular abuse for their action. In his diary, Judge McDonald acknowledged the tenor of the times by observing that "the mob about town are greatly exercised lest, Judge Davis and I release [Milligan, Bowles, and Horsey]."[98] So adverse reaction to the *Milligan* opinion came as no surprise to Davis.

Davis might even have foreseen a comparison to Jefferson Davis, since Lincoln suffered a similar fate, being described as a tyrant and "a worse traitor than Jeff Davis."[99] The judge did not expect, however, that his opinion would be placed in the same category as the infamous decision of Chief Justice Taney in the *Dred Scott* case. Nor did Davis anticipate the charge that political motives rather than the fair application of the law controlled his decision. He was disheartened when his hometown newspaper declared that the opinion gave comfort to "rebels and their sympathizers." Sarah Davis wrote to her husband, informing him of how "the *Pantagraph* talks so harshly of the 'Milligan case' and the decision of the five Judges." Attuned to her husband's sensibilities, however, Sarah declined to send the judge a copy of the newspaper article. Instead, she expressed her pride in the judge "standing firm against the attacks of editors and others." She knew that her husband was "a man to stand for the right—without flinching."[100]

Davis was further surprised when the Radical Republicans interpreted the decision as throwing cold water on their Reconstruction plans. In a letter to his brother-in-law Julius Rockwell, Davis pointed out that the opinion did not contain a single word about Reconstruction and that no one doubted the legitimate authority of military commissions in the "insurrectionary States."[101] Indeed, at least until 1868, a unanimous Supreme Court consistently refused to hear challenges to military governments and military trials of civilians in the South.[102] Davis's participation in those ruling is consistent with his pre-*Milligan* complaints to Lincoln that the military trials of civilians were unconstitutional in the Northern states and border states, omitting mention of the states in the Confederacy.[103]

In the same letter to Rockwell, Davis refuted the claim that the portion of the opinion finding that Congress could not authorize military trials for civilians was unnecessary dicta. Davis explained that the heart of the opinion was that the Constitution prohibited a military trial of Milligan. If the Constitution barred the trial, how could Congress authorize it? Neither the president nor Congress could repeal the Constitution. Davis further explained that restricting presidential authority to establish the commissions for the trials of civilians without imposing the same limitation on Congress would invite the claim that the omission was an implicit recognition of the power of Congress to authorize military tribunals. In structuring the majority opinion, Davis sought to avoid a "cowardly" escape from addressing a future threat by the legislative branch to civil liberties. As Davis told his brother-in-law, "The opinion wd have been worth nothing for future time, if we had cowardly toadied to the prevalent idea, that the legislative dept of the govt can override everything. Cowardice of all sorts is mean, but judicial cowardice is the meanest of all. . . . I abide the judgment of *time*. The people are mad now, and, if they dont recover soon, civil liberty will be entirely gone. During the war I was afraid it wd be all gone." Continuing to defend his decision, Davis acknowledged that "the Republican press every where has denounced the [*Milligan*] opinion as a second Dred Scott opinion." The judge's rebuttal was simple: "The Dred Scott opinion was in the interest of Slavery, & the Milligan opinion in the interest of liberty." Finally, Davis affirmed his ability to stand by his convictions in the face of public criticism: "This Court wd be a hell on earth to me, unless I can decide questions according to the light which God has given me. I hope that God will give me strength to utter my convictions & never to quail before any political tempest."[104]

The vile nature of the criticism took a toll on Davis, who greatly cherished his reputation as an impartial judge immune from political pressure and public clamor. Davis himself admitted that he was not "indifferent to criticism" concerning the *Milligan* decision. But the judge also knew that his spirit would not permit him to "wilt" under partisan or public bullying from a course dictated by the Constitution.[105] By April 1868 Chief Justice Chase had replaced Davis as the main target of the Radical Republicans for his rulings in the impeachment trial of President Andrew Johnson. According to Davis, the Republicans denounced "every impartial ruling" the chief justice made during the trial before the Senate and was "hated intensely by those in the lead of the Republican party." The judge took the opportunity to tell Chase that he was "getting a little taste" of what Davis endured after issuing the *Milligan* opinion.[106]

Ex parte Milligan: *A Reflection of Judicial Character*

Legal scholars and historians have described Justice Davis's opinion in *Milligan* "as one of the bulwarks of American liberty," "a milestone case for individual civil liberties," "a monument in the democratic tradition," an "eloquent and powerful opinion," and a decision that "burns brightly as a lighthouse on a rocky coast."[107] Justice Antonin Scalia agreed that the opinion endures as "one of the great landmarks" in the court's history.[108] Taking a different view, Professor Mark E. Neely Jr. described the opinion's legacy as "confined between the covers of the constitutional history books." Professor Aziz Rana more critically contends that the *Milligan* opinion was "employed to stymie a redemptive agenda" and "provide[d] a straitjacket for social transformation" in the South after the war.[109]

Whatever its long-term impact, *Milligan* demonstrates two facets of Davis's judicial character. First, he was acutely aware of the tension between the fundamental principles upon which the nation was founded and the demands of national security in time of war. He knew that the balance had unavoidably tipped in favor of military authority during the four years of the rebellion and that it was now time to realign priorities. The end of hostilities signaled the perfect time to make the adjustment. If an error was to be made, Davis's training as a lawyer and judge informed him that the overcompensation should favor constitutional principles.

Second, the *Milligan* opinion showcases Davis's predominant judicial attribute: an unwavering commitment to judicial impartiality. At the time he wrote the opinion, appearances belied any hope that Davis could impartially decide a case involving the legitimacy of Lincoln's military commissions. Not only had Davis and the deceased president maintained a long-standing personal, professional, and political alliance, but the judge actively and publicly promoted Lincoln at every turn. As Lincoln's law partner William Herndon recognized, "Davis had done more for Lincoln than any dozen other friends he had."[110] That included directing the floor fight that led to Lincoln's nomination for president. In return, Davis owed his Supreme Court appointment to Lincoln. Moreover, the judge had helped build the Republican Party, whose members passionately wanted an opinion clearly declaring Congress's authority to install military commissions in the South. He knew that he would take a beating from those Republicans for his decision. Justice Davis despised Copperheads like Milligan and had publicly rebuked organizations like the Knights of the Golden Circle and Sons of Liberty.[111] Davis also realized that he would be the only Republican member of the court voting to deny Congress the power to establish military commissions with jurisdiction over civilians. To top off all the apparent conflicts, Davis was serving as the administrator of the late president's estate and, at Robert Lincoln's insistence, would be appointed Tad Lincoln's guardian.[112] And last but not least, Davis was reviewing a lower court case that he had presided over with Judge McDonald. These vast personal and partisan considerations completely destroyed any appearance of impartiality. Today, the public's call for Davis to disqualify himself from the case would be deafening. But Davis, as he had throughout his entire judicial career, disregarded outside considerations and decided the case as he viewed the facts and law independent of personal, professional, and political considerations.[113]

IV

Judge Davis:
A Model of Judicial Impartiality

7 Impartiality on the Trial Court Bench

To the extent that David Davis is remembered at all, it is because of his relationship with Abraham Lincoln and his essential role in Lincoln's nomination and election as president. That is only natural, considering Lincoln's importance in American history. It is also true that except for his opinion in *Ex parte Milligan*, Davis has little claim to be remembered for scholarship or contributions to constitutional theory either as a trial judge or as a Supreme Court justice. Indeed, legal scholars classify Davis as a run-of-the-mill, average justice of the high court.[1] This less than superlative assessment of Davis's impact on the bench is not of recent origin. At the time of his death, the *Chicago Inter-Ocean* acknowledged that the judge could "hardly be ranked with [Justices] Marshall and Story as an expounder of constitutional law." The *Inter-Ocean* correctly observed that in neither of his judicial roles did Davis take a bare-bones legal proposition and through "critical erudition" transform it into some "admired abstraction."[2]

Contemporary commentators, however, did not define Davis's judicial worth solely in terms of his scholarly impact. The newspapers and the public recognized the judge's true contribution to the third branch of government: a devotion to judicial impartiality. So, after conceding that he was no Justice John Marshall or Justice Joseph Story, the *Inter-Ocean* went on to describe Davis as a model jurist because his commitment to fairness and impartiality permitted him to rise above prejudice and faithfully promote the ends of justice.[3] The *Bloomington Weekly Pantagraph* identified the judge's legacy as his unquestioned honesty, incorruptibility, "equity and judicial fairness," common sense, integrity, and sound judgment in the everyday responsibilities of a judge. The *Pantagraph* credited Davis's "sturdy integrity and honesty" with building public confidence in the courts: "The great point in Judge Davis' character was the implicit confidence reposed in him by the people. They honored him because they trusted him."[4]

Davis's career as a trial court judge and Supreme Court justice reflects his commitment to judicial impartiality. And that unheralded contribution to the third branch of government started in the fourteen counties of central Illinois known as the Eighth Judicial Circuit.

Public Recognition of Davis's Impartiality as a Trial Court Judge

On March 28, 1849, Davis finished his first court session as a judge in Sangamon County. Apprehensive about the state's experiment with an elected judiciary, the *Illinois State Journal* declared that the voters' first test under the new constitution was a success because "Judge Davis gave the best satisfaction as Judge." While Lincoln was not in town at the time, his partner, William Herndon, attended court and agreed with the *Journal*'s editors. Eight years later the *Journal* affirmed its initial assessment by reporting that Judge Davis was "long and favorably known as an honorable, impartial and pure-minded jurist," with no other judge "more popular or more highly respected."[5] Davis received similar accolades when substituting for judges outside the Eighth Judicial Circuit.

Before sitting in his own circuit, Davis filled in for Judge T. Lyle Dickey in Grundy County during the week of December 11, 1848. After making the seventy-five-mile trip to the county seat of Morris, Davis most likely stayed at the Grundy Hotel, where other traveling judges resided during court days. The hotel was owned by William E. Armstrong, the moving force behind the organization of the county. Court was conducted in a two-story frame "court-house" built by Mr. Armstrong. After returning home to Bloomington, Davis was pleased to hear from his friend and Eighth Circuit lawyer Kirby Benedict that Illinois Supreme Court justice John Caton spoke in "very commendatory terms" of the manner in which Davis discharged his duties while sitting for Judge Dickey. In 1862 Caton would "unreservedly" tell Lincoln that Davis's fitness for the US Supreme Court was "unsurpassed" by anyone in the Prairie State.[6]

After Davis's visit as a substitute judge in Champaign in 1850, a newspaper reported that the stand-in judge "was impartial in his decisions, firm in his integrity, had the confidence of the profession, and was deservedly popular with the masses."[7] The judge's popularity was regularly acknowledged and apparently extended to at least some defendants whom he sent to prison. While residing in the Illinois State Penitentiary, Edward Finegan wrote to the judge requesting a few words of encouragement because Davis was his only friend.[8]

In 1858 the *Joliet True Democrat* printed a resolution of the Will County Bar Association thanking Judge Davis for his "just decisions" and the "able, efficient and impartial manner in which he has discharged the duties of Judge of this court." The Will County resolution was signed by the bar's chairperson, Sylvester W. Randall, a prominent Democrat, and by its secretary, Gavion D. A. Parks, a Democrat turned Republican. Probably at Lincoln's request, the *Chicago Daily Tribune* reprinted the complimentary proclamation.[9] In the same year, the *Urbana Union* commented that "Judge Davis was as usual the personification of courtly dignity and impartiality."[10] In March 1855 Abraham Lincoln and twenty-three other members of the Springfield bar of all political persuasions signed a letter urging the judge to run for reelection because another six years of his demonstrated ability and impartiality "would give general satisfaction to the people, and meet with the approbation of the members of the bar in the circuit." Other county bar associations expressed similar sentiments.[11] Seven years later, letters from lawyers' associations and individual lawyers urging Davis's appointment to the Supreme Court emphasized the judge's character, his reputation for honesty and integrity, his high moral position, and his "wise, pure, and impartial" administration of justice.[12] Thomas Dent, who became president of the Illinois Bar Association four years after Davis served in that capacity, agreed with the local bars, stating that the judge discharged his trial court duties with such "firmness for the right" and "strong sense of equity" that "he gave satisfaction to the bar and to the people."[13]

Davis's impartiality led lawyers to submit cases to the court without a jury, and his decisions "evoked fewer appeals than those of any other judge in the state." His reputation for fairness in decision-making also meant that lawyers and litigants seldom exercised their statutory right to have a different judge hear their case simply by asking for a "change of venue."[14] The fact that he did not hesitate to remove himself from cases in which he harbored a doubt about his ability to remain neutral added to the judge's reputation for fairness.[15] His commitment to impartiality extended to the jury. Davis was a stickler for the right to a fair and impartial jury free from influence by outside forces, including influence from the judge himself. As Frederick Trevor Hill explained, because Davis knew so many residents of the Eight Judicial Circuit, "it naturally followed that he knew the jurors who were selected by the sheriff, and in some counties the same men composed the jury term after term. They were his friends, but the idea that they would be subservient to his wishes on this account, or that he would attempt to take advantage of their friendship to impose his authority upon them, never, apparently, entered any one's head."[16] In capturing the essence of his career as a trial judge, the *Chicago Tribune* put it succinctly: "For thirteen years Mr. Davis sat upon the Bench, amidst the universal silence of private and party passion."[17]

African American Litigants

African Americans suffered systemic discrimination in the Illinois courts during Davis's days as a trial judge. State law prohibited Blacks from serving as jurors and from testifying against a white person.[18] Most judges, most Republicans, and even some Democrats railed against the rule barring the testimony of Blacks.[19] Davis's friend Supreme Court justice Noah Swayne noted that the rule resulted in a denial of justice "where a white man was sued by a colored man, or was prosecuted for a crime against a colored man."[20] Newspapers reported the injustices caused by the rule and called for its repeal. In 1859 the *Chicago Press and Tribune* reported that a white defendant was tried in "Recorder's Court" for "robbing a colored man and woman of $20." According to the *Tribune*, the offender was acquitted because the race of the prosecuting witnesses precluded them from testifying. Since no white person witnessed the event, the defendant was acquitted.[21]

Whether Davis enforced this testimonial bar is unclear. Without doubt he shared Justice Swayne's unfavorable opinion of the rule. It would have grated against his sense of fairness and equity. Besides, his ego would not allow him to silently suffer legislators telling him what evidence he could consider. We do know that in 1862 Davis believed that Blacks were entitled to redress for injuries caused by whites. In the case of a white person's attack on an African American, Davis stated in court that "'negroes' have *just as good a right* to be secure in their property and persons as any other class of men." In effect, Davis rejected the Supreme Court's holding five years earlier in the *Dred Scott* case that Blacks were not included in the Declaration of Independence and that "they had no rights which the white man was bound to respect."[22]

Aside from the restraints on the fair treatment of African Americans imposed by state law, there is no indication that Davis treated Black litigants differently from white litigants in court proceedings. The procedures followed by Judge Davis and the case outcomes of lawsuits involving African Americans tracked the standard procedures and outcomes in cases involving white parties. For instance, Isabella Hill, an African American, was brought into Sangamon County Court charged with disturbing the peace. She was placed on a recognizance bond, meaning she did not have to post any money to guarantee her promise to "keep the peace." The case was later dismissed, with her husband paying the court costs. Davis imposed the same disposition on Lewis Tomlinson, who was likewise summoned to court for disturbing the peace. The white defendant posted a recognizance bond to keep the peace and paid the court costs. The state's attorney then dismissed the case. In another matter, the court awarded William Florville, Lincoln's African American barber, a judgment for $114.75

when the defendant, Joseph Stockdale, failed to make good on a promissory note executed in Florville's favor. The court procedure and outcome paralleled similar cases with white plaintiffs.[23]

Usher Linder Dissents

One contemporary who did question Davis's impartiality, at least in cases in which Lincoln appeared, was Usher F. Linder. Born in Kentucky in 1809, Linder moved to Illinois in 1835 and soon relocated to Coles County, where he practiced law. His practice took him to four counties of the Eighth Circuit: Vermillion, Edgar, Shelby, and Champaign. Linder was an accomplished trial lawyer with superior oratory skills and given to "the highest flights of eloquence," peppered with wit and humor. But even his friends acknowledged Linder's self-destructive nature caused in large part by his excessive use of alcohol and volatile temper.[24]

Linder began his criticism of Davis's impartiality in an unusual way by stating that "Judge Davis was a very impartial judge." Linder went on to say that while Davis did not intend to show a preference for one lawyer over another, "such was the marked difference he showed to Mr. Lincoln that Lincoln threw the rest of us into the shade." Linder hastened to add that Judge Davis always treated Linder "with great kindness and consideration." It seems clear that Linder was talking about deference shown to Lincoln in court rather than at social or political gatherings. It is less clear whether Linder intended to suggest that case outcomes were dictated by Davis's close friendship with Lincoln. For several reasons, that conclusion seems unlikely. First, Linder did not come right out and claim that personal considerations dictated the results of cases. To the contrary, Linder said that he was not at all damaged by the friendship between the judge and Lincoln. Second, Linder added that it was "quite likely" that if he had "been placed in the same relation to Mr. Lincoln as Judge Davis, [Linder would] have shown to [Lincoln] the same consideration as was shown by his Honor, Judge Davis." If Linder meant that Davis's deference to Lincoln dictated which party would win, then Linder in effect admitted that as a judge, he would have also thrown cases in Lincoln's favor—an unlikely admission. Third, Linder reminisced that some of the most pleasant days of his life were spent traveling and lodging with Lincoln and Davis between Danville, Paris, and Shelbyville.[25] It is improbable that a lawyer would consider some of the best days of his life traveling, lodging, and trying cases with a judge and lawyer who had stacked the deck against Linder and his clients.

Most likely, Linder was not commenting on partiality in the sense of ruling in favor of Lincoln's clients; instead, Linder was referring to the seemingly greater deference shown to Lincoln in court. To a degree that was true, because Lincoln had a more nuanced way of dealing with the judge than other attorneys did. Henry Clay Whitney, a fellow lawyer, furnished the example of Davis giving his close friend Leonard Swett a "terrible scathing" when Swett objected to a court's ruling. Similarly, Whitney described the judge's "expression of perfect contempt" when Whitney objected during the trial of a railway case. Whitney explained that Lincoln often avoided these caustic responses not because of favoritism but because "Lincoln had a way of excepting [objecting] with so much grace and deference, and so apologetically, that the Judge was rather flattered by it."[26] And while Lincoln was better than most at schmoozing with the judge, even he could not fully escape Davis's blunt rebukes. During jury selection in one case, Lincoln asked the prospective jurors if anyone knew his opposing counsel. The judge interrupted and in a severe tone chastised his friend: "Now, Mr. Lincoln . . . you are wasting time. The mere fact that a juror knows your opponent does not disqualify him."[27]

It also may be that when Linder described Lincoln's favored position with Davis, Linder was referring to the fact that Davis relied on Lincoln to provide comic relief and editorial comment on unusual courtroom occurrences. For example, Whitney told the story of an excellent but lazy lawyer who handed an extraordinarily lengthy legal document to the judge. Davis asked the lawyer how he got up enough energy to write such a long pleading. After the lawyer responded, "Dunno, Judge," Davis flipped through the pages of the document, turned to Lincoln, and said, "Astonishing, ain't it? Brother Snap did it. Wonderful, eh! Lincoln?" According to Whitney, Davis's comment to Lincoln amounted to an order for Lincoln to "heave a joke in at this point." Ready as always, Lincoln responded that it reminded him of the "lazy preacher . . . that used to write long sermons, and the explanation was, he got to writin,' and was too lazy to stop."[28] Admittedly, Linder did not share this same special space with Lincoln. No one did. In fact, when the judge singled out Linder in court it was usually to correct some indiscretion on Linder's part. So when Davis saw Linder enter the courtroom with a pipe in his mouth, the judge said, "Mr. Sheriff, you will permit no one to smoke in this room while court is in session except General Linder." Neither the judge's instruction to the sheriff nor the laughter it invoked deterred Linder from taking full advantage of his special privilege, and so he continued to smoke during the trial.[29] But tobacco was not the worst of Linder's addictions.

Although he delivered a well-received temperance lecture to the Sons of Temperance in Paris, Illinois, in 1848, Linder drank way too much.[30] And unlike some of the other hard-drinking lawyers of the circuit, he did not confine his alcohol consumption to the evenings. Linder often appeared in court drunk. His drinking caused at least one in-court confrontation with Davis. According to Davis's biographer, Linder had appeared at two consecutive terms of court under the influence of alcohol. As a result, Linder was in no condition to do more than ask to continue his cases. To avoid prejudice to Linder's clients, Davis granted the delays. But when Linder appeared in an intoxicated state at the next court session the judge warned: "Mr. Linder, I must give you some advice. You must drink less and work more, or you will roll in the gutter." Linder was not so drunk as to miss the tenor of the remark, and he singled out what he considered Davis's Achilles tendon by responding, "And I must give your Honor some advice. You must eat less and [in the flattest term] eliminate more or you will bust." Unfortunately, Davis's prediction came true. In 1874, two years before Linder's death, Orville Browning reported that he ran into Linder in Chicago and that he was meagerly dressed and looked broken, poor, and needy.[31]

Linder had a temper, which was inflamed by his excessive use of alcohol. In April 1859, during a court session in Charleston, Illinois, Linder attacked fellow attorney Elisha H. Starkweather. After the incident, a judge granted Starkweather's request that Linder post a $500 peace bond because of the beating and the fact that Linder carried a pistol. When dealing with Judge Davis, Linder was able to cast his anger into a more acceptable form: sarcasm. Examples are not hard to come by. When an inexperienced Danville attorney filed a pleading in court that was clearly insufficient on its face, Linder "demurred," meaning that he asked Judge Davis to dismiss the pleading because of its technical flaws. Davis knew the pleading was lacking but abhorred deciding cases on technicalities. So the judge granted the demur and offered suggestions to the young lawyer on how to fix the deficiencies. The lawyer's attempt to cure the defects fell short, so Linder demurred again. The judge granted the second demur but in the simplest and most explicit language instructed the lawyer what to write in the amended pleading. The young man still got it wrong. Taking matters into his own hands, Judge Davis grabbed the paper and rewrote it himself to satisfy formal pleading requirements. As a practical matter, when a judge writes a party's petition it is impossible for the opposing lawyer to claim that it is incorrect. So Linder "could demur no more." Linder's anger over the judge's intervention on behalf of Linder's adversary did not subside, and he let the judge know about it. That night Linder went to the judge's room and found him writing a letter. According to Leonard Swett, when Davis invited Linder into the room Linder responded, "O, no, . . . I see you are writing pleas in some of your numerous cases. I will not disturb you."[32] Linder's conduct did not ingratiate him with the judge.

While Davis may have had Linder in mind when he lamented, "Oh the evils of intemperance & the horrors of an ungovernable temper," there is no indication that personal feelings influenced the judge's decisions in Linder's cases.[33] In fact, one of Linder's illustrations of what he called the judge's "eccentricity" demonstrates just the opposite. In May 1852 Linder was in Edgar County representing a party in an appeal from a decision of a justice of the peace denying a claim that totaled three dollars. Justin Harlan, the judge in the circuit south of the Eighth Judicial Circuit, was visiting Paris, Illinois. So Davis invited Harlan to sit on the bench to better observe the proceedings. Linder supported his three-dollar claim by reading a decision from the Illinois Supreme Court. When Linder finished, he observed Davis lean over and whisper something to Harlan. According to Linder, he later learned that Davis, apparently thinking the citation to the supreme court case was overkill, whispered to Harlan, "Great God! . . . [F]or a lawyer of Linder's age and standing to read a decision of the Supreme Court in a little appeal case where there are only three dollars in dispute!" Notwithstanding Davis's personal opinion of Linder or the nature of his argument, the judge reversed the decision of the lower court and found in Linder's favor.[34]

As Michael Burlingame concluded, Linder's claim of partiality, if it was meant to include Davis's rulings in court cases, is not borne out by the record. Lincoln lost more cases than he won in trials heard before Judge Davis without a jury.[35]

Criticism from Abolitionists and Democratic Newspapers

Davis had other critics. Abolitionists attacked him, but usually for his conservative form of Republicanism rather than his judicial conduct. A good example is a letter to the editor titled "Opposition to Lovejoy" published in the *Chicago Daily Tribune* in 1858, when abolitionist Owen Lovejoy sought renomination to Congress. The letter's author, "Fair Play," lambasted Davis as leading the effort to deny Lovejoy another term, seeking the congressional job for himself, threatening voters who supported Lovejoy, possessing no allegiance to the Republican Party, and hurting Lincoln's chances of becoming a senator. About the only thing Fair Play failed to criticize was Davis's fairness and impartiality in court. In fact, Fair Play began his letter by conceding that "Judge D. is a very fair man in his way" before commencing his attack on the judge's politics.[36] Similarly, another of the judge's political opponents criticized how Davis made his money but conceded that he was "a great man on the bench."[37]

One might expect the local Springfield Democratic newspaper to attack or at least criticize the performance of the Republican judge presiding over the circuit. But the *Illinois State Register* stuck mainly to reporting the beginning of court terms and the convening of grand juries and then summarizing court proceedings.[38] With one exception, which was more of a dustup between the editors of the Democratic *State Register* and the Republican *State Journal*, the *Register* did not criticize Davis's performance as a trial court judge.

In February 1857, at the urging of Lincoln and Davis, Sangamon, Macoupin, and Christian Counties were removed from the Eighth Judicial Circuit and together with Montgomery County made into the new Eighteenth Judicial Circuit. (Davis still presided over the Eighth Judicial Circuit.) The new four-county circuit had its own judge, Edward Y. Rice. Pleased with the election of a "fierce Democrat," the *Illinois State Register* welcomed Rice to Sangamon County.[39] Two days into the Springfield court session the newspaper sang Rice's praises, noting that the new judge "has already grown into unmistakable favor with the bar and the public." The paper continued by highlighting the fact that Judge Rice possessed a quality that had been missing in the Sangamon County Court for some time: treating well-established lawyers and new lawyers equally. According to the *Register*, in the past, the court routinely accepted the opinions of seasoned lawyers as to what the law was while requiring young lawyers to back up their opinions with case or statutory authority, which the judge would then follow "rather reluctantly."[40] The newspaper did not mention Davis by name, but since he had been the Springfield judge for the preceding nine years, the implication was obvious.

The validity of the complaint aside, the criticism was indirect and mild at best. But it was still too much for the Republican newspaper to ignore. The next day, April 23, 1857, the *Illinois State Journal* ran a short article denouncing its Democratic competitor's meanness for unjustifiably attempting to cast a slur of "contemptible imputations upon Judge Davis."[41] That response got the *Register*'s ire up, and the newspaper wasted no time replying that by complimenting Judge Rice it did not denigrate Judge Davis. The *Register* added that it had no quarrel with Davis, and if someone would point out "the particular portion of the *Register* to which they take exception," the *Register* would "take back" anything that the "especial friends of Judge Davis" found offensive. But the editors of the *Register* could not pass up the chance for one more thinly disguised dig at Davis, stating that the newspaper did not blame lawyers just because a judge extended favors to some lawyers that he denied to others and that there was no reason to cast aspersions just because a judge liked Republican lawyers better than Democrat lawyers.[42] (The *Register* did not explain what the outcome would be if a seasoned Democratic lawyer faced off against a young Republican lawyer.) The amended accusation earned another response from the *State Journal* accusing the *Register* of a second unwarranted attack on Davis by "subterfuge and implication" in the guise of denying that it made any assault on Davis's character in the first place. The Republican *State Journal* was not worried, however, because no judge was ever more popular or highly respected than Judge Davis. The *Journal* ended the battle of the editors by uniting with the Democratic *Register* "in awarding praise to Judge Rice."[43] Other than this pointless squabble, the *State Register* did not challenge Davis's independence or impartiality as a trial judge. Commenting on the judge's appointment to the US Supreme Court, the *Register* noted that "Mr. Lincoln has made a good selection from his party friends."[44]

The Commission on War Claims at St. Louis

In late October 1861 Davis's honesty and impartiality led President Lincoln to name him to head the commission created to investigate the legitimacy of contacts entered into by General John C. Frémont while he commanded the US Army's Department of the West, headquartered in St. Louis. Former secretary of war Joseph Holt and lawyer Hugh Campbell of St. Louis joined Judge Davis as members of the commission. The three members were chosen for their unassailable reputations for fairness and incorruptibility. As the register of the US Treasury, Lucius E. Chittenden, explained, "These gentlemen, were eminently fitted for the stern duties they were required to perform. They were just men, who would as readily reduce to its true value the claim of the most influential citizen as of the most insignificant person."[45]

In November 1861 Davis's commission began reviewing thousands of claims. It received testimony from twelve hundred witnesses in sessions lasting nine or ten hours a day. The commission submitted a comprehensive report ahead of schedule on March 10, 1862.[46] A few weeks before the report was issued, legal counsel for the commission, Samuel Glover, and assistant counsel John Shepley sent separate letters to President Lincoln urging the appointment of the chair of the commission, Davis, to the Supreme Court. It had not taken Glover long to recognize Davis's "bold sincere industrious" nature. Similarly, Shepley stated that Davis's "vigorous truthful character" had led Shepley and his professional brethren in Missouri to back Davis for the open Supreme Court seat.[47]

Departing Bloomington for Washington

After leaving the Eighth Judicial Circuit, Davis faced new challenges in maintaining his reputation for impartiality while serving on the Supreme Court. No longer would Davis be judged by people with whom he had had long judicial and extrajudicial relationships. No longer would the county court docket consist solely of mundane cases involving noncontroversial and nonpartisan issues. In Washington, partisan interests rather than independent assessments of fairness and impartiality determined a judge's merit and the "correctness" of his decisions. The stakes were simply much higher. The Supreme Court's opinions impacted the entire country. A country judge's decisions only affected the litigants before the court.

8 Impartiality on the Supreme Court Bench

During circuit-riding days it was easy for impartial judges to maintain their reputation for integrity and fairness because lawyers and the public personally interacted with their local judges both in and out of court. Besides, trial court judges seldom handled cases with political overtones that might ferment partisan praise or resentment. Instead, the diet of circuit court judges consisted of routine cases, including the collection of debts, defamation, breach of promise to marry, and damage to private property. Even decisions in more serious cases involving sexual assault and murder did not evoke responses from members of the public colored by their Democratic or Republican leanings. And of course, decisions by state court judges such as Davis had no application outside resolving the disputes of parties before the court. Although Davis's stern independence and impartiality would be on full display while he was an associate Supreme Court justice, no longer was he evaluated primarily by the general public and practicing lawyers who knew him well. Now, it was mostly strictly partisan newspapers that rendered judgment on the judge's performance. The Supreme Court's opinions were not evaluated in terms of the author's fairness, impartiality, and faithfulness to the law but rather by the effect, or perceived effect, the decision would have on a political party's agenda. Davis learned this lesson the hard way after writing the majority opinion in *Ex parte Milligan*.

Ex parte Milligan

Justice Davis's majority opinion in *Ex parte Milligan* is the most well-known example of his ability to separate personal relationships and biases from the decision-making process. As detailed in chapter 6, it was difficult for anyone to claim that considerations other than Davis's independent assessment of the law's requirements dictated the outcome of the case. No one could claim that Davis's unbreakable personal loyalty to Lincoln interfered with his impartiality in the *Milligan* case because Davis ruled against the military commissions created by his longtime friend. Similarly, no one could argue that his personal hatred of Copperheads prejudiced his decision because he ruled in favor of Milligan, a leader of the Knights of the Golden Circle. No accusation could be made that the judge's affiliation with the Republican Party clouded his objectivity because, as far as the Republicans were concerned, Davis ruled against them and, appallingly, joined four Democrats to do so. Nor could criticism be levied against the judge's decision that Milligan had been wrongfully convicted. All nine Supreme Court justices agreed with that. A charge that Davis disingenuously changed his views to facilitate a desired partisan outcome was also off the board, since Davis had been speaking against the trial of civilians by military commissions for years. But judicial impartiality and independence were of no concern to the press or Congress in 1866. Rather, all that mattered to the warring factions was whether, in their partisan view, the *Milligan* decision facilitated or impeded the Republican Congress in its Reconstruction plans. The Republicans were convinced that Davis and his decision dealt a severe blow to Congress's strategy for restoring the Union and so trashed the opinion and its author (see chapter 6).[1]

A few individuals defended Davis's character when it came under relentless attack. His old friend the former mayor of Chicago, John Wentworth, now a congressman, defended the *Milligan* decision.[2] Senator Reverdy Johnson deplored the personal assault: "The opinion of the [*Milligan*] majority was given by a man whose character, public and private, stands beyond possible reproach." Johnson added that he knew that no senator would approve of the newspapers' attacks on Davis's loyalty and character.[3] And in a sense the Maryland senator's opinion was borne out a decade later when Congress could think of no one better than Davis to serve as the only independent member of a commission established to decide the disputed presidential election of 1876.

The Hayes-Tilden Electoral Commission

Notwithstanding the vicious attacks on Davis after the *Milligan* decision, Davis never lost his standing as an independent and impartial judge. That fact is fully demonstrated by his anticipated involvement in the electoral commission established to determine the outcome of the 1876 presidential election. Democrat Samuel J. Tilden won 50.9 percent of the popular vote and 184 of the 185 electoral votes needed for victory. Rutherford B. Hayes trailed with 47.9 percent of the popular vote and 165 uncontested electoral votes. Both candidates claimed the twenty combined electoral votes from the disputed states of Florida, Louisiana, Oregon, and South Carolina. So Congress established a fifteen-person electoral commission composed of five Republicans and five Democrats from each branch of the federal legislature and five Supreme Court justices to determine the winner of the twenty Electoral College votes still up for grabs. Justices Nathan Clifford and Stephen J. Field, Democrats, and Justices Samuel F. Miller and William Strong, Republicans, would represent the judiciary and pick a fifth justice to round out the commission. It was accepted that the four justices and the legislative representatives would vote strictly on party lines. Consequently, the fifth justice would decide the election.

The Democrats agreed to the arrangement only because they believed that Justice David Davis would be the fifth and deciding Supreme Court justice. While not sure of Davis's politics, the Democrats were sure of his "sterling honesty." Democratic representative William M. Springer from the deep southern Illinois Twelfth Congressional District told the joint House and Senate committee trying to work out the details of the electoral commission that although they were unsure of his political alignment, Illinois Democrats were certain that Justice Davis "was absolutely honest and fair." Both parties considered the judge a "genuine independent." Before Congress actually created the commission, however, the Democrats and Independents in the Illinois legislature joined on the fortieth ballot to elect Judge Davis to replace John A. Logan in the United States Senate. While Davis did not seek the office, he had let it be known through his friend Jesse Fell that he was tired of the Supreme Court and would welcome the change. The judge accepted the appointment and promptly announced that it would be improper for him to serve on the Hayes-Tilden Electoral Commission, since he planned to leave the court and join the Senate. Even before his selection as a US senator, Davis had privately expressed his belief that a congressional electoral commission was unconstitutional and that he would refuse to serve as a member if asked. Republican justice Joseph Bradley took Davis's place, and with his vote the electoral commission decided for Hayes.[4]

Many Democrats blamed Davis for the commission's decision in favor of President Hayes. In February 1877 F. E. Richards, a member of the Chicago Democratic City Executive Committee, complained that "if Davis had still been a Supreme Court Judge Samuel J. Tilden would have been the next President."[5] But Richards was mistaken. Even if the new Illinois senator agreed to serve on the commission, it would not have changed the result. Davis told his friends that he "heartily" approved of Justice Bradley's decision and that "no good lawyer, not a strict partisan, could decide otherwise."[6] But that did not prevent Democrats from denouncing Senator Davis just as the Republicans denounced Justice Davis for his *Milligan* decision. In each case, the political parties took turns condemning the judge for, in effect, his independence and his failure to represent partisan interests.

Davis's reputation for integrity, independence, and impartiality followed him into the Senate. A month before his retirement from the Supreme Court to assume his Senate seat, the *Quincy (IL) Weekly Whig* sarcastically noted that "it seems likely that by the time Judge Davis gets ready to retire from the bench he will be able to form some definite opinion as to whether he is a Democrat or a Republican." Another Quincy newspaper, the *Daily Quincy Herald*, thought that he would side with the Democrats because "an independent party of one is hardly worth figuring on."[7] But once Davis was in the Senate, the newspapers acknowledged that that is exactly what Davis became: a party of one.[8]

The *Chicago Daily Tribune* reported that the Republicans accepted Davis's election as senator because he was preferred over any other candidate of the "opposition" and because his popularity "extend[ed] far beyond mere party lines." A better prognosticator than the *Daily Quincy Herald*, the *Tribune* predicted that the new Illinois senator's "unblemished integrity," "great independence of character," and "pure personal and official character" would instruct him to represent all the people of the state rather than any political faction.[9]

Although elected by the Democrats, Davis took a seat on the Republican side of the Senate. He did not attend either party's caucus and voted his conscience on the basis of issues rather than party affiliation. By doing so, Davis felt that he "triumphed" in maintaining his independent status and made "'Independence in Politics' a success."[10] The newspapers tried in vain to pigeonhole Davis into one of the two political camps. For instance, the *Weekly Louisianian* proclaimed that Davis had finally shown his true colors as a Democrat and should "march into the Democratic caucus." But twenty months later, the paper admitted that the judge had voted with the Republicans during the legislative session.[11] In 1880 he supported the Democrat, Winfield S. Hancock, for president and in 1884 pivoted to the Republican presidential candidate, James G. Blaine.[12] After succeeding slain president James Garfield in September 1881, Chester Arthur called a special meeting of the Senate to elect a new presiding officer. On the motion of Senator John A. Logan, whom Davis had defeated in the Illinois race for senator four years earlier, a unanimous vote of the Republicans installed Davis as president pro tempore of the Senate.[13] Both political parties viewed Davis as above partisan rivalries in his role as presiding officer of the Senate. As Leonard Swett put it, the judge was the only person ever "to make a personal party, consisting solely of himself, respectable."[14] In accepting his new Senate office, Davis emphasized his lifelong approach to public service in both the judicial and legislative branches: "It will be my duty to administer the trust with impartiality and with entire fairness."[15]

But impartiality is neither expected nor valued in the legislative branch. Davis's refusal to take a partisan role in a partisan body prevented him from playing an instrumental part in the passage or defeat of legislation. As his biographer concluded, "His independence removed him from the main currents of political action."[16] Davis's dedication to independence and impartiality in his governmental duties did not have an on and off switch. He could not turn it on while a judge and turn it off when serving in a political branch of government.

Slavery and Race

Did Davis's views on slavery and the role of Blacks in society influence his decisions while he was on the Supreme Court? While the judge's words and actions present a mixed picture on slavery and race, the answer is no. Davis's ability to divorce personal feelings from court decisions included the capacity to separate his attitude on integrating African Americans into society from his judicial duty to render impartial decisions according to the law.

Inconsistent Signals

In many ways, Davis's words and actions concerning slavery and race were contradictory. On the one hand, he vocally and morally opposed slavery. He thought slavery was "evil" and proclaimed as much in a speech before Tazewell County voters in 1860.[17] Two years later he lamented to Leonard Swett that "outside of the New England States a large majority of the people care nothing about the moral aspects of slavery." Instead, most residents of the western states viewed slavery as only a "disturbing element."[18] Every trip back to Maryland confirmed Davis's "desire to live in a Free State." According to Davis, no one could be more opposed to the Kansas-Nebraska Act because the founding fathers and the members of the Confederated Congress who approved the Northwest Ordinance in 1787 "believed that slavery was an evil, and that it should be kept out of all Territory from which it could be lawfully excluded."[19] As a delegate to the 1847 Illinois Constitutional Convention, the judge opposed a provision that directed the legislature to enact laws prohibiting free Blacks from settling in Illinois and barring the transportation of enslaved persons to the state for the purpose of setting them free.[20] His opposition to the proposed state constitutional provision was consistent with his invitation to a formerly enslaved childhood playmate, Perry Vezey (also spelled Veazey), to move from Maryland to Illinois. Vezey declined, saying that Illinois "was too far out of the world, and there were no Ethiopians there."[21] Later, when Vezey and his wife fell on hard times, Davis had a house built for them in Delaware.[22] The judge was proud of the fact that he faithfully attended each Senate session as president pro tem except when he "went to Wilmington to see [his] old colored friend Perry Veazey," who was dying.[23] A newspaper described the deathbed visit as "very affecting."[24]

Some contemporaries criticized Davis for treating Black servants with too much dignity. One critic was Illinois lieutenant governor Gustave Koerner. While dining at a Springfield hotel, Davis said to a "colored" waiter, "Hand me the bill of fare, if you please." Koerner believed that Davis "carried his courtesy a little too far." Koerner was especially chagrined that Davis extended this degree of politeness to a Black servant even before the passage of the Fifteenth Amendment.[25] Koerner may also have disapproved of Sarah Davis referring to her farm and household staff, both Black and white, as part of the "family," to Sarah teaching a Black housekeeper to sew and read, and to the Davises permitting another African American housekeeper to be absent for two weeks to attend a religious gathering in Terre Haute, Indiana.[26] When David and Sarah first moved to Bloomington the only "colored man" in town was a member of the church attended by the Davises.[27] Forty-two years later, representatives of the Prince Hall Grand Lodge of Illinois, an organization of African American Freemasonry, met in Jacksonville and decided to incorporate and establish a permanent headquarters. Springfield, Peoria, and Bloomington were in the running until the Peoria advocates withdrew their city from consideration in favor of Bloomington because it was the home of David Davis. Of course, Springfield was chosen. But the actions of delegates indicate that David Davis was held in high regard by the members of the Grand Lodge.[28]

At the same time, some of Davis's statements do not support the equal treatment of African Americans. Davis tried to talk Lincoln out of issuing the Emancipation Proclamation. Further, and seemingly contrary to his vote as a delegate to the state constitutional convention, in 1862 Davis pleaded with Lincoln to postpone the movement of Black war refugees from the southernmost Illinois town of Cairo farther north into the state.[29] To the extent that opposition to the proclamation and opposition to moving the refugees north seems inconsistent with Davis's disapproval of slavery and hostility to laws prohibiting free Blacks from settling in the state, an explanation exists to reconcile the conflict. The judge's letters and statements to Orville Browning explain that his motivation for opposing the Emancipation Proclamation and the army's movement of Blacks from southern to northern Illinois did not rest on racial animus. Instead, it rested on Davis's conviction that those acts, especially unpopular in states such as Indiana and Illinois, would damage the war effort and harm Lincoln's bid for reelection in 1864.[30] And Davis's fear was not without foundation.

In 1860 Lincoln barely won Illinois with 50.69 percent of the vote and Indiana with 51.09 percent of the vote.[31] The October and November state elections following the issuance of the preliminary Emancipation Proclamation in September 1862 proved catastrophic for Republicans. Davis did not exaggerate when he described the results as "disastrous in the extreme."[32] Democrats won majorities in the congressional delegations from the crucial states of Ohio, Illinois, Indiana,

and New York. In Pennsylvania it was an even split. The Republican gubernatorial candidates in New York and New Jersey lost. Democrats dominated the
state legislatures in Illinois, Indiana, New Jersey, and New York. Winning the
popular vote in Wisconsin, Democrats elected representatives in three of the
state's six congressional districts. Davis knew that Lincoln could not afford to
lose any of these states in his reelection bid.[33]

Republican election losses in the fall of 1862 were blamed on the "illegally or
unwisely" issued Emancipation Proclamation and the suspension of the writ
of habeas corpus.[34] Thomas Ewing of Ohio told Orville Browning that "the
Presidents [*sic*] emancipation and Habeas Corpus proclamations had ruined
the Republican party in Ohio. That without them [we] would have carried
the state easily and that with them [we] were badly beaten in the elections."[35]
Democrat John T. Stuart, who defeated Leonard Swett for Congress in 1862,
went further, postulating that but for the Emancipation Proclamation and
the writ of habeas corpus "the democrats would steadily and earnestly have
supported the administration."[36] At first, Davis welcomed the preliminary
Emancipation Proclamation because he believed that it "took well" with the
people and could help Republicans in the upcoming election. But after the
devastating fall 1862 voting results, Davis, like many others, considered the
defeat as a referendum on the proclamation. The judge was also concerned
about the edict's harmful effect on the war effort. Success on the battlefield was
absolutely essential to keeping Lincoln in the White House.[37] In Davis's mind
the proclamation's adverse impact on the prosecution of the war and on the
voting preferences of old Whigs and Union Democrats was bad enough. But
making matters worse, at the time the proclamation was issued the government began moving Black war refugees into central Illinois. The Democrats
declared that the two acts were not coincidence. Moving African Americans
into Illinois, Democrats claimed, disclosed the Republicans' and the proclamation's true purpose: to ensure equality of the races.

General Ulysses Grant sent Black refugees to Cairo, the southernmost city
in Illinois, located at the confluence of the Ohio and Mississippi Rivers. On
September 18, 1862, four days before Lincoln issued the preliminary Emancipation Proclamation, Secretary of War Edwin Stanton authorized transporting the
evacuees farther north into Illinois to increase their prospects for employment.
Davis wrote Lincoln that moving the "Negroes" into central Illinois "would
work great harm in the upcoming election." Davis did not necessarily object to
bringing the refugees into the state or moving them north. But he "earnestly"
believed that the movement of Blacks from Cairo into central Illinois should
not take place "until after the election." To Davis, the Emancipation Proclamation, coupled with the simultaneous relocation of Blacks to Illinois, fueled the
Republican defeat in 1862. He was afraid it would do the same in 1864.[38]

Adding to Lincoln's dismal reelection chances in the Prairie State were the damaging attacks that the "anti-emancipation majority" thrust upon the Lincoln administration.[39] As early as the spring of 1861, long before Lincoln issued the Emancipation Proclamation, Pope County, which borders Kentucky, and neighboring Williamson County proposed a division of the state, with southern Illinois counties joining the Confederacy. Nine months later Republican governor Richard Yates warned the legislature that the secession movement in Illinois was "deeper and stronger" than the legislators knew. The announcement of the Emancipation Proclamation only further emboldened the Lincoln administration's adversaries. Legislators repeatedly offered resolutions condemning the Emancipation Proclamation as unconstitutional and vowing to "protest" against a war fought to achieve the goals of the proclamation.[40]

The razor-thin margins of victory in Indiana and Illinois in 1860, the magnitude of the Republican defeat in the fall 1862 elections, growing opposition to the emancipation movement, and the desire of southern Illinois counties to join the Confederacy convinced Davis that the Emancipation Proclamation would severely damage the war effort and destroy Lincoln's chances for reelection. That worry led the judge to visit the president on January 18, 1863, "describe the alarming condition of things," and urge the president to withdraw the proclamation to "save the country." And Davis was not the only one to do so. But Lincoln made it absolutely clear to Davis that the Emancipation Proclamation was a "fixed thing" regardless of the consequences.[41]

Five years later, in 1868, Davis wrote to Julius Rockwell concerning the "problem of Negro suffrage." The letter contains a stark statement of the judge's views toward racial equality. During a visit to South Carolina in April of that year, Davis's observation of "the degraded ignorance of the poor creatures" who voted at the insistence of politicians who cared only for their votes and cared nothing for the voters made Davis feel "sad." The letter continued: "The problem of negro suffrage—necessarily involving all political and social equality—may prove a measure of wisdom and good statesmanship, but I dont believe it—It seems to me that no candid man could believe it who saw the plantation hands voting & the kind of men fr[om] the North who solicit their votes." The solution, according to Davis, was "qualified, intelligent suffrage" rather than universal suffrage. And to be fair, the judge also believed that an intelligence or educational requirement should apply to whites. Lincoln similarly believed that the franchise should be limited to educated Blacks and those who fought for the Union.[42] Even leading Radical Republican Charles Sumner advised Congress that a state could limit the right to vote as long as restrictions were equally applicable to whites and Blacks. Sumner approved of "such regulations as the safety of society may require," including age, good character, residency, and registration. Sumner added that "education also, may, under certain circumstances, be a requirement of prudence, especially valuable in a Republic, where so much depends on the intelligence of the people."[43]

Like Lincoln, Davis further feared that the Radical Republicans in Congress were attempting to place too much power in a centralized federal government, including usurping control over voting that traditionally rested with the states. Both men most likely agreed with the provision of the 1868 Republican Platform that left the issue of African American male suffrage in the northern states up to each individual state.[44]

Clearly, Justice Davis held negative views on the right of members of what he called the "docile race" to full political and social rights.[45] The precise nature and evolution of Davis's opinions on race are worthy of further study but are not the point here. The issue is whether the judge's personal views on the political and social integration of African Americans into society were reflected in his decisions as a member of the Supreme Court. In that context, two matters warrant examination: (1) the admission of the first African American lawyer to practice before the Supreme Court and (2) Davis's Supreme Court opinion deciding whether a railroad company could maintain separate but equal cars for white and Black passengers.

The Admission of John S. Rock to the Supreme Court Bar

At 11:00 a.m. on February 1, 1865, the day after the House of Representatives passed the Thirteenth Amendment, Senator Charles Sumner made a motion to admit fellow Massachusetts lawyer John S. Rock to practice before the United States Supreme Court. Chief Justice Salmon Chase, with most of the associate justices present, granted the motion, making John Rock the first African American lawyer placed on the Supreme Court's roll of attorneys. According to Indiana congressman George W. Julian, who was present for the brief ceremony, "No objection was made, even by the old Dread [*sic*] Scott judges." That included associate justices Robert Grier and Samuel Nelson, who joined Chief Justice Roger B. Taney's decision in the *Dred Scott* case. It would have been difficult for anyone, except maybe former chief justice Taney, to object to Rock's admission because he was a man of "impressive attainments" and a scholar. Rock was a practicing medical doctor and dentist in Boston who turned to the law because of his failing health. He would survive only twenty months after his installation and would never practice before the court. But representing clients before the high court was never his or Senator Sumner's goal.[46]

The previous December, Rock sent a letter to Sumner asking whether Chief Justice Chase might be willing to admit him to practice before the Supreme Court. Sumner forwarded the letter to Chase with a note vouching for Rock's ability, reputation, and character. The senator recognized that the *Dred Scott* decision, which held that African Americans were not citizens, might pose a roadblock to Rock's admission. But Sumner saw Rock's admission as a way to nullify the *Dred Scott* opinion. He told Chase that "of course, the admission of a colored lawyer to the bar of the Supreme Court would make it difficult for any restriction on account of color to be maintained anywhere. Street cars would be open afterwards." Chase wrote back the same day, December 21, 1864, advising that he would discuss the matter with the other justices during their next regularly scheduled conference. The chief justice did not believe that "any, or any serious, objection will be made." Not hearing anything for three weeks, Sumner sent a brief follow-up note asking Chase if he had made a decision on Rock's admission. Chase replied that he had nothing else to report but that he had not forgotten about the matter. Then on January 23 the chief justice advised Sumner that he could move to admit Rock to practice before the Supreme Court at Sumner's convenience.[47]

The symbolic nature of the admission of Rock was obvious. In the same hallowed chamber where Chief Justice Taney declared that Blacks were not citizens, Chief Justice Chase proved otherwise by bestowing on Rock the highest status that any lawyer could achieve: admission to the Supreme Court bar. The *New-York Daily Tribune* made sure that no one missed the point. The lead paragraph of the *Tribune*'s article titled "The Dred Scott Decision Buried in the Supreme Court—a Negro Lawyer Admitted by Chief Justice Chase" solemnized the event: "Oh, augustly simple funeral cortège—oh, dead, wrapped in the cerements that the divine hand of revolution folds its victims with, augustly exciting in your stormy birth, transcendently mischievous in your little life—Senator Charles Sumner and Negro lawyer John S. Rock, the pall-bearers—the room of the Supreme Court of the United States the Potter's Field—the corpse the Dred Scott decision!"[48]

Davis was not present at the meeting Chase held with the other justices to discuss Sumner's letter requesting Rock's admission. Nor was he present at Rock's installation ceremony. Davis was sick at home in Bloomington.[49] But that did not prevent the judge from privately expressing his view on the matter. On February 19, 1865, Davis complained to his brother-in-law about Sumner's motive in arranging for Rock's admission: "Mr Sumner is running his radicalism athwart every body's prejudices. What object of swearing in the negro man, as an attorney of U.S. Supreme Court. He had no business there & never would. It was all for effect & cui bono?"[50] In Davis's mind, the admission of Rock had little to do with African Americans practicing before the court. Rock had no cases before the Supreme Court and never would. That was not because of a lack of legal skill but because Rock had no intention of representing clients in the high court. His health simply prevented it. Rock died less than two years after his historic admission to the court. Twenty-five years would pass before an African American lawyer actually argued a case before the court.[51]

Sumner's "object" in sponsoring the admission of Rock was not to initiate and promote the appearance of Black lawyers in the Supreme Court. His purpose was purely symbolic: to overrule sub silentio the *Dred Scott* decision, which declared that African Americans were not citizens. Davis did not miss the emblematic nature of the act but considered the move just another of the Radical Republicans' meaningless, grandstanding acts intended to stir up partisan vitriol, thereby making it more difficult to resolve postwar issues. To Davis, Sumner's move was designed not to advance the interests of Blacks but instead to advance Sumner's own political purposes. The judge simply failed to see the overlap between the two goals: "It was all for effect & cui bono." In other words, Sumner and not African Americans stood to gain from the admission of Rock. The irony was not lost on Davis that Rock had now joined the previously all-white Supreme Court bar but could not leave Washington and return to Boston without first obtaining permission from the provost marshal. Permission was required to comply with the rule that "colored men" could not leave Washington without a pass.[52]

If we take Davis's letter to Julius Rockwell at face value, it becomes clear that Davis objected to Sumner's motion to admit Rock because Sumner used the event to further his own political agenda and aggravate the hostility between the North and South. Davis did not denigrate Rock's competency as a lawyer, his intelligence, his accomplishment of graduating from an otherwise all-white medical school, or his right to practice law in Massachusetts. Nor does Davis suggest that the legal profession should remain all white or that Rock's race should preclude admission to the Supreme Court bar. Davis despised the ultra men on both sides, especially Sumner, who in the judge's mind was a "fanatic" who "crushed out" the more reasonable, middle-of-the-road plans for reuniting the country.[53] No doubt Davis considered Rock's statements praising insurrections, "especially those of the pen and of the sword," including "the insurrections of Nat Turner and John Brown," as unnecessarily fueling antagonisms.[54] Davis feared a return to bloodshed if the ultra men continued to provoke each other over voting and other issues. He had seen enough bloodshed and "want[ed] no more blood spilt in this Country."[55]

In the same letter to Rockwell, Davis made the seemingly categorical declaration that "the negro can never be elevated to social & political rights in this Country & all wise statesmen know it." The judge would backtrack somewhat from this statement three years later by supporting "qualified" suffrage for African Americans. And five years after that he wrote an opinion barring separate but equal cars on the train trip between Washington and Alexandria, Virginia.[56]

But even if we assume that Davis disapproved of the effort to admit Rock because of his race, the point is that Davis's personal belief did not influence the judge's official action in the matter. He communicated no objection to Rock's admission to the chief justice or any other member of the court.[57] He made no public criticism of the event. And it is certain that if Rock had had the opportunity to argue a case before the court, Davis would have ruled on the facts and law and not on the race of the attorney.

Social Equality for African Americans: Railroad Company v. Kate Brown (1873)

The second most important decision authored by Justice Davis, second only to *Ex parte Milligan*, involved the right of Blacks to ride in the same passenger cars as whites on the train trip between Washington, DC, and Alexandria, Virginia. The case presented the Supreme Court with its first opportunity to consider what would become known as the separate but equal doctrine. To the detriment of the country, Davis's opinion soundly rejecting the doctrine was ignored twenty-three years later when the court erroneously constitutionalized the separate but "equal" treatment of the races.

On February 8, 1868, Kate Brown took the 2:00 p.m. train for the seven-mile trip from Washington, DC, to Alexandria, Virginia. At the Washington station she boarded the "white people's" car and without incident arrived at her destination. At 3:00 p.m., as she was boarding the train at the Alexandria station for the return trip to Washington, a railroad security officer told her to change cars because the car that she had entered was for "ladies." Kate Brown responded that that was the very car she wanted. The security guard replied that "no damned n——r was allowed to ride in that car anyhow; never was and never would be." He then grabbed Mrs. Brown and tried to physically remove her from the train. She resisted, clasping onto the car door and railings. The guard then struck Mrs. Brown's knuckles, twisted her arm, and hit her in the back, stating that if she did not release her grip, he would beat her until she could not stand. But Kate had "made up [her] mind not to leave the car, unless they brought [her] off dead." She was then pulled from the train and dragged down the platform.[58]

Arriving shortly after the incident, passenger B. H. Hinds asked the conductor what had happened. The conductor answered that the woman could only ride the train back to Washington in the car for colored people. Mrs. Brown explained to Hinds that she did not want to go into the assigned car because some of the passengers were disorderly. Hinds offered to accompany her to ensure that she would not be molested. He later testified that Kate Brown could hardly walk and was injured so badly that he had to assist her in getting on and off the train.[59]

Unfortunately for the railroad, Kate Brown had connections. She was employed by the United States Senate as the manager of the retiring room for ladies, located in the Senate gallery. So, four days after the incident, Senator Lot M. Morrill of Maine presented a resolution directing the Senate Committee on the District of Columbia "to inquire into the facts connected with the forcible eject-ment from the cars of the Alexandria, Washington and Georgetown Railroad of one of the employees of the Senate, on account of race." The resolution also called upon the Senate committee to examine whether additional legislation was necessary "to protect the rights of the passengers" on the railway.[60] In support of the resolution, Senator Charles Sumner stated, "A whole race suffers in this wrong" and agreed with Senator William P. Fessenden that reparations needed to be paid by the railroad company. The resolution passed, and the Committee on the District of Columbia investigated the incident.[61]

The committee heard eight witnesses via live testimony and sworn deposi-tions. Kate Brown testified from her home because she had been bedridden since the attack. She described the incident and her injuries. Alexander T. Augusta, who was the army's first African American physician and who worked at the Freedmen's Hospital, also described Kate Brown's injuries and the care that he provided. Dr. Augusta had treated Mrs. Brown since the day after the assault.[62]

The general superintendent of the Washington, Alexandria and George-town Railroad, Oscar A. Stevens, testified that he had instructed the conduc-tor, brakeman, and security guard at the Alexandria station "to direct colored people to take one car and the white people another car." He further testified that the conductors had been "directed that where colored people were in the other car, to have no difficulty with them." He said the company's policy at the Washington and Alexandra stations for seating was the same. Stevens never envisioned an incident like the one involving Mrs. Brown because he assumed that passengers would go to the car designated by the conductor. The railroad company separated the races for the "convenience to the public [rather] than from a dictatorial spirit." It was meant to protect Blacks from the "annoyance" of white people complaining about "riding with colored people."[63]

The superintendent described the train cars as "all manufactured alike" with "no difference in them." In fact, the car designated for white ladies and their escorts on the trip from Alexandria to Washington became the passenger car assigned for Blacks on the return trip. So white and Black passengers were rid-ing in the same cars, just not at the same time.[64]

The Senate committee issued a report summarizing the incident, the inju-ries sustained by Kate Brown, and the railroad's policy to separate passengers by color. The committee determined that new legislation was not necessary to protect passengers like Brown because An Act to Extend the Charter of the Alexandria and Washington Railroad Company and for Other Purposes, approved by Congress on March 3, 1863, prohibited the segregation of passengers by color. The committee relied on Section 1 of the act: "That the Alexandria and Washington Railroad Company be, and the same is hereby, authorized to extend their said railroad from the south side of the Potomac across said river, to and along Maryland avenue, to the Capitol grounds, and across Pennsylvania avenue along First street to Indiana avenue, and thence to the Baltimore and Ohio depot. . . . *And provided, also*, That no person shall be excluded from the cars on account of color."[65]

Significantly, the Senate committee believed that the provision of the charter providing that "no person shall be excluded from the cars on account of color" barred any discrimination against travelers on the basis of race or color, including the use of separate but equal cars for train passengers. The committee also indicated that if Mrs. Brown's monetary recovery in her civil lawsuit against the railroad was insufficient, or if the railroad violated its charter again, Congress could revoke the company's right to run the railway.[66] The incident and investigation received widespread attention in the press.[67]

Before the Senate issued its report, Kate Brown filed a lawsuit in the District of Columbia against the Alexandria, Georgetown and Washington Railroad. She sought $20,000 for injuries sustained during the assault.[68] It took two years for the case to come to trial because of the defendant railroad's delaying tactics. David K. Cartter, chair of the Ohio delegation to the 1860 National Republican Convention and Lincoln appointee to the federal bench, presided over the trial. The trial before an all-white male jury involved notable witnesses, including the former mayor of Alexandria and Iowa senator James Harlan.[69]

At the close of the case, the railroad requested that the trial judge instruct the jury to find for the railroad and against the plaintiff if (1) all train cars were identical, (2) the separation of the races was standard in the rail industry, (3) the separation was necessary to retain passengers and maintain receipts, and (4) excessive force was not used to remove Mrs. Brown. The trial judge refused the defendant's instruction. On March 25, after a four-day trial, the jury returned a verdict in Kate Brown's favor for $1,500.[70] The railroad appealed to the United States Supreme Court, claiming that it had the authority "to make the regulation separating the colored from the white passengers." To answer the controlling question, the court examined the history and terms of the railroad's congressional charter.[71]

In February 1854 the Virginia legislature incorporated the Alexandria and Washington Railroad Company for the purpose of providing rail service from Alexandria, Virginia, to Washington, DC. Five months later Congress authorized the company to expand its service area. In 1863 Congress further authorized the company to extend its line northward, following a defined route to the Baltimore and Ohio Railroad depot.[72] The 1863 act placed restrictions on the Alexandria and Washington charter, including a limit on fees for transporting passengers and goods. The act granted "no authority or right to interfere with the United States military use or possession of said road or contemplated extension during the present rebellion, or to any claim for damages or indemnification therefor." The mood of the times, however, dictated that Congress was concerned not only with fair rates and facilitating the war effort but also with the treatment of Black passengers. Thus, the 1863 act also directed that "no person shall be excluded from the cars on account of color."[73] In 1866 the Washington, Alexandria and Georgetown Railroad Company, which had succeeded to the rights of the Alexandria and Washington Railroad Company, obtained an amendment to the 1863 charter permitting a change in the railway's route. That amendment continued to bind the successor railroad company to all conditions previously imposed by Congress, including the prohibition against excluding passengers from the cars on account of color.[74]

The railroad was firmly convinced that it had honored the terms of its charter, notwithstanding its policy requiring separate cars for whites and Blacks. After all, the railroad argued, no one was excluded from the train. Whites and Blacks alike were welcome. At most there was assigned seating, which did not violate the charter's proviso. Foreshadowing the separate but equal doctrine, the railroad argued that "all the cars were equally safe, clean, and comfortable." In fact, the cars were not only identical but also used interchangeably to transport whites and Blacks. The races were separated, but the accommodations were undeniably equal.[75]

Justice Davis disagreed with the railroad's contentions. Writing for a unanimous court, Davis acknowledged that a literal reading of the antidiscrimination provision of the charter might bear the interpretation suggested by the railroad. But Davis characterized the defendant's argument as "an ingenious attempt to evade a compliance with the obvious meaning of the requirement." The court needed no citation to legal precedent and only a single paragraph to reject a separate but equal interpretation of the charter. According to Davis, it was obvious to everyone that Congress did not intend such a narrow reading of the provision of the railroad's charter. When amending the charter in 1863 and 1866, Congress was concerned with discrimination in assigning cars on the basis of race. Congress was not concerned with the railroad barring Blacks from riding altogether, because it had never excluded riders on the basis of race, and the company's financial interests would prevent it from doing so in the future. Davis went on to say that Congress believed that the discriminatory use of the passenger cars was unjust and must end and that whites and Blacks should be "placed on an equality" in the use of the cars. That was simply "the temper of Congress at the time."[76]

In *Railroad Company v. Brown*, the Supreme Court interpreted the provisions of a statute passed by Congress. The Thirteenth and Fourteenth Amendments played no role in the decision. But in speaking for the court, Davis linked the use of segregated cars to the prohibitions of the two amendments by characterizing the separate but equal doctrine as a remnant of slavery: "It was the discrimination in the use of the cars on account of color, where slavery obtained, which was the subject of discussion at the time, and not the fact that the colored race could not ride in the cars at all. Congress, in the belief that this discrimination was unjust, acted."[77]

The unanimous court characterized the segregation imposed on Kate Brown as a remnant or badge of slavery. One hundred years later, Justice William O. Douglas also characterized segregated railway cars as a badge of slavery.[78] Moreover, scholars have persuasively argued that Davis and the other justices understood that the Fourteenth Amendment, much the same as the charter of the Alexandria and Washington Railroad Company, considered separate but equal facilities as a form of prohibited racial discrimination. For example, Michael W. McConnell demonstrated that the majority of political leaders who supported the Fourteenth Amendment believed that school segregation violated the amendment and that in the years immediately after ratification, between one-half and two-thirds of both houses of Congress voted in favor of school desegregation and against the separate but equal doctrine.[79]

Unfortunately, *Railroad Company v. Brown* played no role in the subsequent debate over the separate but equal doctrine. The Supreme Court's 1896 decision in *Plessy v. Ferguson* barely mentioned the *Brown* case. Instead, it upheld segregation even though the underlying facts in the two cases were virtually identical. Homer Plessy was ordered to move from a whites-only train car to a car designated for Blacks under a Louisiana statute mandating "equal but separate accommodations for the white, and colored races."[80] The Supreme Court, with only Justice John Harlan dissenting, found that the Louisiana statute requiring separate but equal train cars did not violate the Fourteenth Amendment. The majority explained its rationale: "The object of the [Fourteenth] amendment was undoubtedly to enforce the absolute equality of the two races before the law, but, in the nature of things, it could not have been intended to abolish distinctions based upon color, or to enforce social, as distinguished from political, equality, or a commingling of the two races upon terms unsatisfactory to either. Laws permitting, and even requiring, their separation, in places where they are liable to be brought into contact, do not necessarily imply the inferiority of either race to the other."[81]

Davis stated just the opposite in Kate Brown's case. Separate but equal facilities did necessarily imply inferiority, because such a separation of the races was a remnant of slavery. *Plessy* distinguished the holding in *Railroad Company v. Brown* on the basis that in that case the Washington, Alexandria and Georgetown Railroad Company's charter provided that no person could be excluded from the cars on account of color. According to *Plessy*, unlike the Fourteenth Amendment, the charter provision prohibited separate but equal cars for the races. But, as pointed out by Justice Davis in *Brown*, the words found in the charter by themselves could legitimately be interpreted as permitting separate but equal train cars. It was not only the text of the charter but also the temper of Congress at the time of the charter's amendments that made it undeniably certain to Davis that "slavery" obtained by separating the races on trains. The charter amendments of 1863 and 1866 prohibiting segregated rail cars were passed at the time that Congress debated the Thirteenth and Fourteenth Amendments. The attitude of Congress toward racial equality when it considered the constitutional amendments must have been the same as when Congress passed the amendments to the railroad's charter. The same Congress considered the same issue in the same time frame. But thirty years later in deciding *Plessy*, the court ignored the mood of the Reconstruction Congress at the time the Fourteenth Amendment was adopted. Only Justice Harlan in dissent echoed Justice Davis's conclusion that separation of the races in train cars constituted a prohibited badge or remnant of slavery.[82] Thus, *Railroad Company v. Brown* was relegated to a footnote in history. The court did not even mention *Railroad Company v. Brown* in the landmark 1954 decision of *Brown v. Board of Education*, which finally found that the separate but equal doctrine violated the equal protection clause of the Fourteenth Amendment.[83]

Could one of the most shameful decisions in Supreme Court history have been avoided if Davis and his colleagues had sat on the court when *Plessy* was decided? Or is that just wishful thinking? Certainly, Davis and the other members of the court in 1873 viewed the temper and intent of Congress in dealing with racial discrimination differently from the *Plessy* court in 1896. It is difficult to imagine Davis agreeing with the *Plessy* majority that the forced separation of the races was not a badge of inferiority or agreeing with the majority that if Blacks considered separation a badge of inferiority, then it was "not by reason of anything found in the [Louisiana] act, but solely because the colored race chooses to put that construction upon it."[84]

It may be that when Davis wrote the opinion in *Railroad Company v. Kate Brown*, he still held the opinion expressed five years earlier that complete political and social equality between the races was neither wise nor a mark of good statesmanship. After all, five years is a relatively short time, and Davis was admittedly a man of fixed opinions. Assuming the judge's views had not changed, his personal beliefs played no role in his judicial opinion in the railroad company case. To the contrary, his decision mandated social equality in the use of passenger cars in the train ride between Washington, DC, and Alexandria, Virginia. And he made that decision even though the railroad's charter could plausibly be interpreted to permit separate but equal accommodations. Davis may have disagreed with the temper of Congress at the time of Reconstruction, but he accepted his duty to apply the law as intended by the lawmakers. Just as the judge set aside his personal likes and loyalties, he set aside his personal social viewpoints to do what any impartial judge would do: uphold the rule of law.

As a judge, David Davis never wavered from his commitment to impartiality. He stands as a model for other judges in his proven ability to make courtroom decisions free from considerations of friendships, political and social views, and personal feelings toward lawyers and litigants. Equally important, he exhibited a steadfast commitment to the rule of law by independent decision-making unaffected by public clamor, overt threats, unjust criticism, and partisan expectations and demands. Davis has been recognized for his role in the nomination and election of America's greatest president. He deserves equal acclaim for devoting his life on the bench to the most important pillar of any government-sponsored system of dispute resolution: a judiciary resolute in its commitment to fairness and impartiality.

Conclusion

David Davis's most prominent character trait was loyalty. It dictated how he conducted all aspects of his life. Off the bench, loyalty to his friends was foremost, and foremost among his friends was Abraham Lincoln. Judge Davis's unshakable loyalty to the future president developed over the years that they traveled, worked, played, and politicked together. Davis's fidelity, popularity in the Eighth Judicial Circuit, political savvy, and leadership and organizational skills catapulted Lincoln to the presidency.

On the bench, loyalty to his judicial oath dictated Judge Davis's decisions. That oath required impartial rulings based strictly on the evidence. So while pulling every string possible to advance the political career of his friend, Judge Davis honored his sworn duty to impartiality in his rulings in court. That required setting aside his personal loyalty to Lincoln when he appeared in cases before the judge. It also mandated that the judge set aside his personal beliefs and "fixed opinions" on political, social, racial, and partisan issues when deciding cases. And he exhibited a remarkable ability to do so on the trial court bench and the Supreme Court bench.

Davis's vow to loyalty led to his dual legacy, first as Lincoln's close friend and partisan political operative and second as an impartial judge. Today, mixing an active role in politics with a judicial career is strictly outlawed by ethics codes governing the judiciary. Fortunately for the country, in 1860 no ethical rules prohibited a judge's political engagement. If they had, Davis would have had no impact on the executive branch of government. Lincoln simply would not have been nominated or elected, and George Washington would stand alone at the top of the hierarchy of American presidents. And without Lincoln, Davis's impact on the judiciary would have been limited to the trial courts of central Illinois.

Concluding observations are warranted on two important points concerning Davis's legacy. First, the historical record establishes that the close relationship between Davis and Lincoln spawned the judge's unshakable loyalty and dedicated service to his friend. But some scholars deny the existence of an intimate relationship, relying on statements made by Davis during an interview with William Herndon after the president's death. And without doubt, some of the judge's remarks to Herndon concerning the president were unflattering at best. Consequently, no evaluation of the two friends' relationship is complete without an examination of Davis's complaints about Lincoln made during the interview. That examination is conducted in the next section. Second, under the ethical rules existing in Davis's time he was considered a model of judicial impartiality. Under today's rules Davis would be considered just the opposite, a model of judicial partiality and bias. What has changed? A brief explanation is offered for the fundamental shift in what society expects of its judges.

The Lincoln-Davis Relationship in Perspective

The View of Historians

Most historians agree with Ward Lamon and Gustave Koerner that Davis was one of Lincoln's few close and intimate friends. In 1866 newspaper editor and historian Josiah Holland described Davis as a "particular friend" and a "strong personal friend of Mr. Lincoln."[1] Frederick Trevor Hill, a Wall Street lawyer and Lincoln legal scholar, writing in the early twentieth century, characterized Joshua Speed and David Davis as "intimate friends" of Lincoln.[2] Judge Albert A. Woldman, author of *Lawyer Lincoln*, observed that "these two men had been attracted to each other by some inexplicable bonds of affection which continued through to Lincoln's death."[3] Stanley I. Kutler described the friendship as intimate for nearly thirty years.[4] Similarly, Michael Burlingame branded Davis as one of Lincoln's few close friends, and Doris Kearns Goodwin noted that "the evolution of a warm and intimate friendship with Lincoln is evident in the judge's letters home."[5] In the opinion of Professor Leonard M. Niehoff, Davis was "probably the president's best friend."[6] Some scholars, however, deny a personal and confidential relationship between Lincoln and Davis. For example, David Herbert Donald did not include Davis on a list of Lincoln's close or "complete" or "perfect" friends. Rather, continuing with Aristotle's typology of friendship, he classified Davis as a "useful" friend, useful in the sense of a mutual benefit gained from the association. Those like Donald who dispute the closeness of the relationship rely on William Herndon's interview of Davis in 1866.[7]

The Herndon Interview

Over parts of two days in September 1866, William Herndon interviewed Davis about his relationship with Lincoln. During the interview the judge told Herndon that Lincoln would listen to Davis but never asked for or followed his advice except "as to the dollar." Davis added that Lincoln never confided in him or thanked him for anything.[8]

Davis's comments to Herndon in 1866 certainly stand in stark contrast to the sentiments the judge expressed four years earlier when Lincoln appointed him to the Supreme Court. At that time, the new justice expressed his "thankfulness and gratitude" for the president's "distinguished mark of . . . confidence & favor" in placing him on the court.[9] The remarks to Herndon also seem inconsistent with Davis's statement at the time of the president's death that Davis enjoyed a personal friendship with Mr. Lincoln for more than a quarter of a century.[10] Davis's rather harsh comments about Lincoln when interviewed by Herndon may have been colored in part by the pressure Davis felt during the summer and fall of 1866 when he was in the midst of writing the majority opinion in *Ex parte Milligan*. In the opinion, Justice Davis would join the four Democrats on the court in finding that the trials of civilians by Lincoln's specially created military tribunals were unconstitutional.[11] Or it may simply be that the judge was in a bad mood when interviewed by Herndon. Whatever the reason for the sharp words by Davis, they appear to undercut the conclusion that Lincoln had a trusting and confidential relationship with the judge. But Davis's statements to Herndon must be evaluated in context.

On the first day of the interview, Davis's complaint that Lincoln never sought his advice pertained to Davis's association with Lincoln after Davis joined the Supreme Court.[12] The comments came during Davis's description of the president's relationships with cabinet members and Congress, Reconstruction, and Lincoln's request that Davis attend the Republican National Convention in 1864.[13] The truth of the matter is that there was little need to ask the judge for his opinions, because after arriving in Washington, Davis never hesitated to offer the president unsolicited advice. When speaking with Herndon in 1866, Davis could have legitimately felt that Lincoln never followed Davis's advice because on major decisions such as the Emancipation Proclamation, firing cabinet members, and appointing a replacement for Chief Justice Taney, Lincoln patiently listened to Davis but rejected his suggestions.[14] Lincoln did, however, act favorably on many of Davis's requests after the judge arrived in Washington, including the appointment of friends and political supporters to federal jobs.[15]

In his continued statement to Herndon on the following day, Davis broadened his grievance. The judge no longer confined his complaint to the time after he arrived in Washington and appeared to fault Lincoln for not seeking or follow-ing Davis's advice during the time between the presidential election and his appointment to the Supreme Court. If so, the complaint is not supported by the facts and can be chalked up to a fit of pique by Davis. The judge always did have difficulty setting aside what he considered slights, and these real and perceived snubs may have gotten the better of him during the Herndon interview. Besides begrudging Lincoln's failure to ask for Davis's advice on presidential matters, the judge still resented Lincoln's refusal to support him over his shirttail rela-tive Benjamin Edwards when Davis was planning to run for the Eighth Circuit judgeship in 1848. We know the Edwards slight was on Davis's mind because he mentioned it to Herndon during the 1866 interview.[16]

The fact of the matter is that after his election and before placing Davis on the court, the president followed Davis's advice on appointments, including cabinet posts and many, many lesser offices. At the time of the Herndon interview, Da-vis had apparently also forgotten about the privileged treatment afforded the judge between the November election and March inauguration. In December 1860 Davis and Swett were included in Lincoln's confidential discussions with Thurlow Weed. The judge was one of the first two people to review the draft of the first inaugural address. He was invited to join the inaugural train trip, enjoying informal dinners with Lincoln and lavish public events, including din-ners, speeches, the opera, and honored positions in carriage processions. The president exhibited his trust and confidence by including Davis in the discussion on the assassination threat in Baltimore.

Although Lincoln did not often seek out the opinions of friends and col-leagues, it was his nature to listen carefully to others and consider their sugges-tions and points of view. According to Swett, the failure to solicit the opinions of others attached not only to Lincoln's political and presidential decisions but also to Lincoln's decision-making process when representing clients in court. In 1866 Swett told Herndon, "I never knew [Lincoln] in trying a law-suit to ask the advice of any lawyer he was associated with."[17] Davis apparently took Lincoln's failure to seek and follow his advice on matters of state as a personal slight, at least in the mood he was in when talking to Herndon. And that is not surprising. Besides having a high level of confidence (some might say overcon-fidence or unjustified confidence) in the wisdom of his counsel, the judge was accustomed to others obediently following his advice and directions while on Illinois's Eighth Circuit. But Davis knew as well as anyone of Lincoln's confidence in his own judgment and reluctance to solicit or defer to the opinions of others. In the September 1866 interview Davis put it this way: "[Lincoln] had no faith in any mans [*sic*] judgment."[18] Six months earlier, when Davis was in a more charitable mood, he described Lincoln's self-reliance in more positive terms, complimenting his friend's mastery of subjects and the fact that *"he thought* for himself, which is a rare quality nowadays."[19] And it may be that Lincoln seldom if ever said the words "thank you" to Davis.[20] But one wonders if the judge offered thank-yous to Swett any more frequently than Lincoln offered them to Davis.

Lincoln also had complaints about Davis. Chief among those complaints was the judge's constant supplications for jobs and other favors, including the "sharp" message that he sent Attorney General James Speed in 1865 requesting a friend's appointment.[21] But the close bond between the two friends was never broken. Years after Lincoln's relationships with friends such as Norman Judd and Orville Browning faded, Lincoln still treated Davis as his particular friend. In 1864 Lincoln asked then Supreme Court justice Davis to lead Lincoln's re-nomination efforts at the National Convention of the Union Party (a coalition of Republicans and War Democrats) in Baltimore.[22] Not long before his death, Lincoln gave Davis the honor of "attending" to the president in the greeting line at a formal White House reception. After an army lieutenant introduced each guest to Davis, the judge introduced the attendee to Lincoln.[23] And the special relationship was recognized six years later when Justice Davis received the honor of publicly unveiling the statue of the deceased president in the Capitol Rotunda.[24]

Perhaps the best way to evaluate the Lincoln-Davis relationship is to compare it to other friendships cultivated by Lincoln. During the various stages of his life, Lincoln attracted friends with skills fashioned for the events and needs of the time. Davis was the perfect friend and confidant between 1848 and 1860.

Different Friends for Different Times

During the heart of his circuit-riding days, Lincoln was as happy as he could be because he was preoccupied with three things: practicing law, enjoying circuit camaraderie, and attaining elected office. As noted by Swett, Lincoln did not seek the advice of other circuit-riding lawyers about his cases. Neither did he confer with Davis about legal matters. On the circuit, Lincoln simply did not need any-one to talk to about his law practice, the first subject that occupied his thoughts and energies. What Lincoln needed during court days was a boon companion, preferably someone who did not drink, who admired Lincoln, who encouraged his stories, and who placed Lincoln front and center at evening shindigs. He desired a partner with whom he could discuss books, attend events, and take walks, a cohort who would engage in frivolities such as a pillow fight. An accomplice was needed to "sentence" Lincoln at a mock trial for charging low fees and to reprimand him for stealing a tavern's dinner gong.[25] Davis readily filled the role of boon companion. Lincoln's third focus during circuit days—getting elected as senator or president—required a friend of absolute and unforgiving loyalty, integrity, and trustworthiness who knew the political lay of the land, especially in old Whig areas of the state and nation. Davis perfectly fit this role. Few would deny Davis's political savvy, and no one would deny his loyalty to Lincoln. In political matters, Lincoln consulted, coordinated with, and confided in Davis nonstop. Davis was exactly the type of friend that Lincoln needed on the circuit and through his nomination and election as president.

At other times, the concerns controlling Lincoln's life were much different. Thus, the roles played by his closest friends during those periods were in some ways unlike the role filled by Davis. During Lincoln's friendship with Joshua Speed in the late 1830s and early 1840s, Speed and Lincoln lived, ate, socialized, and slept together, just as Davis and Lincoln would do a decade later. Unlike the Davis and Lincoln relationship, however, the Speed-Lincoln friendship began because Speed took pity on Lincoln, who did not have enough money to pay for a bed or food. The topics that dominated the discussions between Speed and Lincoln were earth-shattering to a young Lincoln: romance, lost loves, broken engagements, and reinstituted marriage proposals, all accompanied by bouts of deep depression. Lincoln was lucky to have Speed's intimate friendship, understanding, and help at that critical time.[26] Davis acknowledged the closeness of the Lincoln-Speed relationship.[27] Later, as president, Lincoln needed an outlet for the burdens, stress, and anxiety created by the monumental difficulties facing the nation and the personal tragedy of the loss of his son. Fortunately, the president had Illinois senator Orville Browning with whom to discuss national challenges, to ease Lincoln's apprehension in facing them, and, most importantly, to help with the tragedy of Willie's death.[28] The different periods of Lincoln's life demanded friends with skills fashioned to meet the needs of the time. Davis could never have substituted for Speed or Browning. Neither could Browning have substituted for Speed, nor could he replace Davis. Speed was what Lincoln needed when they both "played the mating game," but he could not have effectively taken the place of Davis on the circuit or the place of Browning in Washington.[29]

Judge Davis and Modern Rules of Judicial Ethics

The political partnership between Judge Davis and Lincoln put Lincoln in the White House. Fortunately for the country, present-day strict judicial ethics rules prohibiting political engagement by judges did not exist in the nineteenth century. Today there could be no political alliance between Judge Davis and lawyer Lincoln and most probably no President Lincoln. There has been a fundamental shift in what society expects of its judges on and off the bench. And that shift has not come without its costs.

In the mid-nineteenth century, lawyers were free to engage in politics by running for office, helping other candidates, speaking for or against office seekers and political parties, holding leadership posts in political organizations, and advocating partisan social, economic, and other policy positions. Judges were free to do the same. In Davis's day, nothing prevented judges from acting as active agents for political, social, and economic change when off the bench. No ethical rules prohibited members of the judiciary from engaging full force in canvassing efforts. Judge Davis certainly took full advantage of this freedom. And he was not the only one. It was accepted practice for off-duty judges to play visible public roles in politics and political campaigns. Brooklyn judge and "prominent Republican" Erastus Dean Culver joined the dignitaries on the dais during Lincoln's famous Cooper Union speech. By "popular demand" Judge Culver addressed the crowd after Lincoln.[30] In the 1860 presidential contest, federal district court judge Ogden Hoffman Jr. endorsed Constitutional Union Party candidate John Bell.[31] During the 1800s Supreme Court justices openly competed for presidential nominations. Besides Justice David Davis's foray into the presidential nomination process, Justice John McLean sought the presidential nod five times between 1836 and 1860. Justice Salmon Chase campaigned for a party nomination four times. Justice Stephen J. Field entered the fray in 1880 and 1884.[32] And the interest of Supreme Court justices in moving into the White House did not end in the nineteenth century. In 1955 Chief Justice Earl Warren led in three out of four Gallup presidential preference polls surveying likely Republican voters and led in all four Gallup polls of independent voters.[33]

Today, the rules of professional responsibility governing lawyers continue to permit attorneys to fully engage in political activities. Like Lincoln, lawyers freely meld political and legal careers into one. To the contrary, modern codes of judicial conduct either flatly prohibit or severely limit a judge's engagement in political activity. To minimize judicial engagement in politics, judges in some states, such as Hawai'i and Rhode Island, are appointed rather than elected.[34] But even in states such as Illinois, where judges are elected, virtually every political action taken by Davis, except campaigning for himself, is now outlawed. The American Bar Association's *Model Code of Judicial Conduct*, which stands as the prototype for state judicial codes, bars judges from (1) publicly endorsing candidates for executive and legislative offices; (2) acting as a leader of a political or campaign organization; (3) speaking on behalf of a political party or candidate; (4) contributing to or soliciting funds for a candidate or party; (5) serving as a delegate to a political convention; and (6) attending political events.[35]

If he had been governed by modern ethics rules, Judge Davis could not have led the Lincoln team in Chicago or even served as a convention delegate. And without Davis's management of the convention, it is almost certain that Lincoln would not have become president. There was simply no one else to successfully lead the floor fight for Lincoln. Our country survived, in part, because the

American Bar Association did not promulgate a model code of judicial conduct until sixty-four years after Lincoln's nomination.

The sea change from a judge's unfettered right to engage in political advocacy in the 1800s to the severe restrictions imposed today is forcefully demonstrated by the reaction to Justice Ruth Bader Ginsburg's criticism of then presidential candidate Donald Trump. In July 2016 Justice Ginsburg publicly stated her dislike of Trump, calling him a "faker" and asserting that "he has no consistency about him. He says whatever comes into his head at the moment. He really has an ego." The justice could not imagine the country with Donald Trump as president and joked that if her husband were alive, he might suggest moving to New Zealand. The *New York Times* and the *Washington Post* immediately condemned the judge's off-the-cuff remarks. The backlash was so severe that Justice Ginsburg apologized for her quips.[36]

So why all the hullabaloo over Justice Ginsburg's critique of the Republican nominee? The justice's opinion of Trump surprised no one who was the least bit familiar with Ginsburg's lifelong political preferences. Nor would it shock anyone that she planned to vote for Hillary Clinton. They shared a political philosophy, and President Bill Clinton put Ginsburg on the bench. Justice Ginsburg's statements were milquetoast when compared to Judge Davis's public political engagement. He actively and publicly opposed and spoke against Democratic candidates and the Democratic Party. Whereas Ginsburg called Trump a faker with a big ego, Davis called Steven Douglas a "demagogue" and Democrats, "Locofocos." Whereas Ginsburg joked about moving to New Zealand, Davis considered moving to czarist Russia after Democratic election victories. Unlike Davis, Justice Ginsburg never hit the stump, recruited volunteers, or solicited funds for a candidate or party. She never led a convention floor fight or contemplated such a move. Davis did all this and more while a member of the judiciary (see chapters 2, 3, and 4).

What has changed? How could the legal profession and the public accept and even welcome Judge Davis's public, persistent, and prolific partisan political engagement and yet severely rebuke Judge Ginsburg for wisecracks that disclosed no political opinions not already widely known? The answer is simple. The manner in which the legal profession and the public evaluate a judge's commitment to independence and impartiality has changed. In Davis's time the standard was straightforward: judges were evaluated by what they did in court. Judges were expected to set aside personal opinions and passions, avoid prejudging cases, ignore "popular or court applause, or distaste," treat the poor and the rich the same, and administer justice "uprightly," "deliberately," and "resolutely."[37] In other words, render fair and impartial decisions based on the law and evidence presented in court. What a judge did off the bench was not considered relevant in assessing judicial impartiality. So there was no need for rules governing extrajudicial activities, even highly partisan undertakings. As a result, judges fully engaged as citizens in the political process. If judges exercised judicial independence and rendered impartial decisions in court, they met the job description regardless of their outside endeavors.

In 1924 the American Bar Association (ABA) became convinced that actual impartiality was insufficient to guarantee public confidence in the judiciary. The ABA believed that judges must also be "above reproach" in their personal lives. That meant that judges could not engage in off-bench activities that might give the appearance of partiality or a lack of integrity. And in the ABA's collective wisdom, the biggest threat to the appearance of judicial impartiality and independence was a judge's political engagement. As the first ABA model judicial code warned, "It is inevitable that suspicion of being warped by political bias will attach to a judge who becomes the active promoter of the interests of one political party as against another."[38] The suspicion of being warped by political influence was enough to render a judge damaged goods. No evidence of actual influence or partiality was required. To avoid the potential perception that a judge was corrupted by partisan entanglements, the political activity routinely undertaken by Davis and other judges of his time was forbidden.

It will come as no surprise that Davis regularly violated modern judicial code mandates other than those restricting political activity. Under current rules, Davis could not have served as the administrator of Lincoln's estate or the estate of anyone other than a family member. He could not have solicited funds for the victims of the Great Chicago Fire or lobby executive and legislative branch officials for governmental appointments, military furloughs, and other favors.[39] Discussing pending and impending cases such as the suppression of the *Chicago Times* with anyone, much less the president, is now taboo.[40] Nor could Davis request that a friend retain Lincoln and send the fee to the judge so that he could forward it to Lincoln.[41] Traveling, eating, sleeping, and socializing with lawyers, witnesses, jurors, and defendants is no longer permitted. Indeed, one court determined that a judge generated an improper appearance by sitting at a table in the courthouse lunchroom with a lawyer on trial before the judge, even though it was the only seat left and the lawyer and judge agreed not to discuss the case.[42] Friendships with lawyers appearing before the judge are now discouraged, resulting in some states automatically disqualifying judges from hearing cases involving lawyers who are Facebook "friends." The disqualification applies regardless of whether the judge ever actually met or conversed with the Facebook friend or recognized the friend's name.[43]

Modern standards would have also affected Justice Davis's ability to hear cases. Regrettably, modern rules would have prevented him from participating in the Supreme Court's decision in *Milligan*. Both federal law and the ABA *Model Code of Judicial Conduct* disqualify judges from hearing appeals from cases in which they participated while serving on a lower court. Since, together with Judge McDonald, Davis heard Milligan's matter in the federal circuit court in Indianapolis, he would have had to sit out the Supreme Court's review of the case. All things being equal, if Davis had been removed from the case, the decision would have been four justices for what is now referred to as the majority opinion and four justices for Chase's concurring opinion.[44] In other words, a tie.

The point is not that we should go back to the good old days before codes of judicial conduct. No one would suggest permitting a judge free rein in the political arena, including coordinating a convention floor fight. Nor should judges engage in ex parte communications about a case pending before the court or share a room with a lawyer who appears before the judge. But maybe we have gone too far in the other direction trying to maintain public confidence in the judiciary by restricting extrajudicial activities that have nothing to do with a judge's impartiality or integrity. Is it fair to conclude, as overprotective judicial ethics committees have, that the public questions a judge's commitment to fairness because the judge attends a spouse's political fundraiser or speaks at a fundraiser for the American Heart Association?[45] Do judge-lawyer Facebook friendships signify such a close relationship so as to require automatic disqualification of a judge? Should Justice Sonia Sotomayor have been forced to resign from a women's business networking group known as the Belizean Grove because of claims that her membership could foreshadow rulings favorable to women or favorable to parties that shared the goals of the networking group? Weren't fears of Justice Sotomayor's partiality allayed by the fact that the justice joined the group only because the men's networking group, the Bohemian Club, barred women from membership?[46] Focusing attention on extrajudicial activities that under strained interpretations might indicate a lack of judicial impartiality only serves to make the public more suspicious of a judge's ability to separate their professional and personal lives. Besides, trying to protect the public from every off-bench activity that could in any way be understood as indicating a bias or prejudice has caused the profession to lose sight of the fundamental value of judicial ethics: actual impartiality in the exercise of judicial duties. The profession should devote its efforts to ensuring actual impartiality on the bench rather than continue its laser focus on secondary cues in assessing a judge's fairness.

The legal profession must reinforce the fact that everyday judges separate their personal beliefs and opinions from their judicial decisions. As former Supreme Court justice John Paul Stevens observed, "Countless judges in countless cases routinely make rulings that are unpopular and surely disliked by at least 50 percent of the litigants who appear before them. It is equally common for them to enforce rules that they think unwise, or that are contrary to their personal predilections."[47]

Lawyers and bar associations are in the best position to teach the public how the job of judges is fundamentally different from the job of legislators and executives. Members of the political branches of government have constituencies to please by promoting the political, social, and economic agendas promised in their campaigns. Judges do not have constituencies, nor can they tailor their decisions to foster outcomes consistent with their personal views. Unlike members of the legislative and executive branches, judges cannot promise anything other than impartiality and neutrality. The Supreme Court has recognized that a political party has the right to designate a "standard bearer who best represents the party's ideologies and preferences."[48] Obviously, that standard bearer will change as Democratic and Republican ideologies and preferences evolve over the years. A standard bearer for the judiciary differs in the respect that the philosophy and values of the judiciary never change. Throughout the centuries, every federal judge has taken the same oath, promising to "administer justice without respect to persons, and do equal right to the poor and to the rich" and to "faithfully and impartially discharge and perform all [judicial] duties" under the Constitution and laws of the country.[49] Unlike the political branches of government and political organizations, the overarching value of the judiciary remains constant: impartial decisions uninfluenced by personal preferences, personal value systems, political interests, public clamor, or fear of criticism.

David Davis certainly enjoyed strong personal and political relationships and held fixed opinions. Some of those opinions were tainted by biases and prejudices based on nationality and race. At the same time, the judge's oath of impartiality and his independence were part of his DNA. He cabined his personal relationships and opinions to the extent humanly possible when deciding cases in the trial court and in the Supreme Court. In that respect, Davis is entitled to serve as the standard bearer of the judiciary in the nineteenth, twentieth, and twenty-first centuries and beyond.

Notes

Abbreviations

ABA   American Bar Association
AL   Abraham Lincoln
DD   David Davis
DDFP   David Davis Family Papers, Abraham Lincoln Presidential Library and
       Museum, Springfield, Illinois
LP   Abraham Lincoln Papers, Library of Congress, https://www.loc.gov/
       collections/abraham-lincoln-papers

Introduction

1. Henry C. Whitney to William H. Herndon, June 23, 1887, in Wilson and Davis, *Herndon's Informants*, 620; Donald, *Lincoln*, 234.

2. *Ex parte* Milligan, 71 U.S. (4 Wall.) 2 (1866).

3. Railroad Company v. Brown, 84 U.S. (17 Wall.) 445 (1873).

4. Plessy v. Ferguson, 163 U.S. 537 (1896) (overruled by Brown v. Board of Education, 347 U.S. 483 [1954]).

Biographical Sketch of David Davis

1. King, *Lincoln's Manager*, 2–7; Creswell, *Oration*, 10; Onofrio, *Maryland Biographical Dictionary*, 167.

2. King, *Lincoln's Manager*, 5, 7; Henkle, "Personal," 30; Bader and Williams, "David Davis," 167.

3. King, *Lincoln's Manager*, 7–12; Chase, *Bishop Chase's Reminiscences*, 2:33; Rutherford B. Hayes to F. A. Hayes, February 5, 1839, in Hayes, *Diary and Letters*, 28.

4. King, *Lincoln's Manager*, 9–12; DD to Ann Mercer Davis Betts, July 1829, DDFP.

5. See, for example, DD to Sarah Davis, October 10, 1847, DDFP.

6. DD to Ann Mercer Davis Betts, July 1829, DDFP.

7. Yale Law School, "Our History," https://law.yale.edu/about-yale-law-school/glance/our-history. New Haven students did not receive degrees from Yale until 1843. See also King, *Lincoln's Manager*, 17n17; certificate certifying that "David Davis of Maryland" attended New Haven Law School from October 1, 1834, until April 22, 1835, in folder 7, box 26, Miscellaneous Papers, 1832–59, David Davis Family Papers, Abraham Lincoln Presidential Library and Museum, Springfield, Illinois.

8. DD to William Perrin Walker, May 1, 1835, DDFP; William Perrin Walker to DD, May 4, 1835, DDFP.

9. King, *Lincoln's Manager*, 20. For a sketch of the life of Levi Davis, see Curran, "Levi Davis."

10. King, *Lincoln's Manager*, 21–24.

11. Morehouse, "Life of Jesse W. Fell," 27.

12. DD to William Perrin Walker, June 20, 1838, DDFP; William Perrin Walker to DD, July 9, 1838, DDFP.

13. Wedding inventory, October 1838, DDFP; King, *Lincoln's Manager*, 31–32.

14. Dent, "David Davis," 559; King, *Lincoln's Manager*, 34; DD and Sarah Davis to William Perrin Walker, January 26, 1839, DDFP.

15. *Evening Critic* (Washington, DC), October 11, 1881, 4; *Iowa County Democrat* (WI), March 24, 1882, 2 (reprinting an article from the *Madison (WI) Democrat*); *Austin (TX) Weekly Statesman*, April 19, 1883, 2; *Weekly Oskaloosa (IA) Herald*, February 1, 1877, 3 (referring to Davis as "that old tub of fat"); *Weekly Caucasian* (MO), March 2, 1872, 2 (describing Davis as "a fat and jolly Illinois millionaire bondholder, who never worked a day in his life").

16. DD to William Perrin Walker, August 16, 1840, DDFP; DD to William Perrin Walker, October 24, 1840, DDFP; Sarah Davis to William Perrin Walker, May 31, 1840, DDFP; DD to William Perrin Walker, November 16, 1840, DDFP; DD to Sarah Davis, March 25, 1841, DDFP; DD to William Perrin Walker, April 25, 1841, DDFP; King, *Lincoln's Manager*, 39. The Davises had seven children. Only two, George and Sallie, survived to adulthood. Bowman, "Sarah Davis."

17. DD to Julius Rockwell, February 10, 1841, DDFP; DD to Julius Rockwell, May 12, 1841, DDFP; *Sangamo Journal*, December 17, 1841, 1.

18. DD to Lucy Adam Walker, June 5, 1842, DDFP; Packard, "The Old Bar," 380; DD to Wells Colton, March 20, 1844, DDFP. Davis consistently complained that his law practice was not profitable enough. DD to Julius Rockwell, May 14, 1844, DDFP; DD to William Perrin Walker, December 31, 1844, DDFP; Burlingame, *Abraham Lincoln*, 1:323 (referring to Davis's reputation as "an outstanding business lawyer"); Bader and Williams, "David Davis," 172.

19. DD to William Perrin Walker, December 31, 1844, DDFP; *Journal of the Convention*, 4.

20. Meites, "1847 Illinois Constitutional Convention," 269, 275, 282–84.

21. Cole, *Constitutional Debates*, 461–62 (statement of David Davis).

22. See *Model Code*, rules 4.1, 4.5.

23. Chapter 5 details the road to Davis's Supreme Court appointment.

24. Goodwin, *Team of Rivals*, 504; see also Donald, *Lincoln*, 483 (stating that Davis remained a "political advisor" to Lincoln while on the Supreme Court); Silver, *Lincoln's Supreme Court*, 81.

25. King, *Lincoln's Manager*, 213–18; DD to AL, June 2, 1864, LP.

26. DD to Sarah Davis, February 23, 1868, DDFP; DD to Sarah Davis, February 8, 1868, DDFP (describing his life as "so uninteresting"); DD to Sarah Davis, March 10, 1868, DDFP ("I feel weary & worn").

27. DD to Sarah Davis, February 21, 1868, DDFP.

28. Morehouse, "Life of Jesse W. Fell," 100–105; Slap, *Doom of Reconstruction*, 146–56.

29. Pratt, "David Davis," 174–75; Emerson, *Giant in the Shadows*, 130–31; Bader and Williams, "David Davis," 206–7.

30. *Chicago Daily Tribune*, January 26, 1877, 5; *Chicago Daily Tribune*, January 12, 1877, 1.

31. Morris, *Fraud of the Century*, 217–20; Pratt, "David Davis," 178. Davis agreed with Justice Bradley, saying that "no good lawyer, not a strict partisan, could decide otherwise" (Hoogenboom, *Rutherford B. Hayes*, 288n38). See also Rehnquist, *Centennial Crisis*, 160, 180 ("a genuine Independent").

32. *Chicago Daily Tribune*, January 26, 1877, 5; King, *Lincoln's Manager*, 291–92.

33. Pratt, "David Davis," 178; *Chicago Daily Tribune*, January 26, 1877, 5; *Richmond (VA) Dispatch*, May 15, 1886, 4; Church, *History of the Republican Party*, 131.

34. King, *Lincoln's Manager*, 301; Atkinson, *Leaving the Bench*, 56; *Chicago Daily Tribune*, October 14, 1881, 1.

35. Cong. Rec., 47th Cong., 1st sess., vol. 13, pt. 1, p. 31 (December 6, 1881) (statement of David Davis).

36. *St. Paul (MN) Daily Globe*, October 14, 1881, 1 (quoting David Davis).

37. "David Davis," *Harper's Weekly*, July 3, 1886, 420; *New York Times*, May 6, 1886, 4; *Huntsville (AL) Gazette*, November 3, 1888, 2.

38. King, *Lincoln's Manager*, 303.

39. Bader and Williams, "David Davis," 203–5.

40. Bowman, "Sarah Davis"; Lucy Forbes Walker Rockwell to Cornelia Livingston Rockwell Bowditch, November 10, 1879, Rockwell Collection, Library, Lenox, Massachusetts.

41. DD to Sarah Davis, March 20, 1864, DDFP. The next year on their twenty-seventh wedding anniversary David gave Sarah an illustrated edition of a book of poetry by Henry Wadsworth Longfellow. Sarah Davis to Frances Mary Walker, October 31, 1865, DDFP. See also DD to Sarah Davis, March 23, 1851, DDFP; DD to Sarah Davis, November 4, 1860, DDFP.

42. Sarah Davis to DD, March 18, 1852, DDFP.

43. Sarah Davis to DD, October 30, 1870, DDFP.

44. King, *Lincoln's Manager*, 298.

45. *Bloomington (IL) Daily Pantagraph*, March 15, 1883, 1; *Bloomington (IL) Weekly Pantagraph*, March 16, 1883, 1; *Cecil Whig* (Elkton, MD), July 3, 1886, 2; *St. Paul (MN) Daily Globe*, March 15, 1883, 4; Sarah Davis to Lucy Adam Walker, December 3, 1838,

DDFP. If her husband had remarried sooner, it would not have surprised Sarah, as she once observed in regard to remarriage, "These widowers don't wait long you know" (Sarah Davis to Frances Mary Walker, September 23, 1865, DDFP).

46. *Proceedings of the Illinois State Bar Association at Its Eighth Annual Meeting*, 39–44.

47. Dent, "David Davis," 557.

48. Laura Swett to DD, December 13, 1862, DDFP; DD to Laura Swett, December 21, 1862, DDFP.

49. *Savannah (GA) Morning News*, June 29, 1886, 3 (reprinting an interview given by Leonard Swett to a Chicago newspaper); Swett, "Memorial Address," 80–81.

50. *Bloomington (IL) Daily Pantagraph*, May 18, 1886, 3 (reprinting an article from the *Chicago Daily News*).

51. Lawrence Weldon to Ward Lamon, June 22, 1886, in Lamon, *Recollections*, xxxii–xxxiii.

52. "Death of Judge David Davis," *Chicago Legal News*, July 3, 1886, 473–74; *Indianapolis Journal*, June 27, 1886, 5; King, *Lincoln's Manager*, 306.

53. David Davis Mansion, "Who Was David Davis," https://daviddavismansion.org/about/2014-10-23-20-28-04 ("at Davis' death, his estate was valued at between four and five million dollars"); Morehouse, "Life of Jesse W. Fell," 102–3n14 ("[Davis] has made two million dollars in fair dealing," quoting Jesse Fell in 1872); *Brenham (TX) Weekly Banner*, November 3, 1881, 1 (reporting Davis's worth at $2 million); *New York Herald*, May 1, 1872, 3 (placing Davis's worth at between $1.5 and $2 million).

54. Ashe, *Biographical History of North Carolina*, 125; "Green, Wharton Jackson," in *Biographical Directory of the United States Congress*, https://bioguideretro.congress.gov/Home/MemberDetails?memIndex=G000419.

Chapter 1. Lincoln's First US Senate Campaign

1. Pratt, "David Davis," 162–63.

2. DD to William P. Walker, May 4, 1844, DDFP ("best stump speaker"); DD to Sarah Davis, October 3, 1847, DDFP; DD to Sarah Davis, October 10, 1847, DDFP; DD to Julius Rockwell, May 14, 1844, DDFP.

3. Pratt, "David Davis," 162. Edward D. Baker was a Springfield lawyer.

4. King, *Lincoln's Manager*, 46; DD, "Memorial Address," 48. Davis handled other types of matters that made up the regular diet of traveling lawyers. For example, in October 1847 he tried two slander cases, one in Piatt County and one in Edgar County. DD to Sarah Davis, October 3, 1847, DDFP; DD to Sarah Davis, October 21, 1847, DDFP.

5. DD to William Perrin Walker, July 1, 1837, DDFP.

6. See, for example, Noe v. Cunningham, File ID L00466, Macon County Circuit Court, May 1838, Law Practice of Abraham Lincoln; Scott v. Davenport, File ID L01165, Tazewell County Circuit Court, September 1843, Law Practice of Abraham Lincoln.

7. Wilson v. Popejoy, File ID L05571, Livingston County Circuit Court, May 1840, Law Practice of Abraham Lincoln.

8. Boggs v. Overton, File ID L01742, Woodford County Circuit Court, April 1844, Law Practice of Abraham Lincoln.

9. See, for example, Robert Patterson and Co. v. Wilbourn, Doolittle and Co., File ID L02189, United States Circuit Court, District of Illinois, Springfield, Illinois, December

1847, Law Practice of Abraham Lincoln; People for the Use of Swallow v. Barnard and Barnard, File ID L01677, McLean County Circuit Court, September 1847, Law Practice of Abraham Lincoln.

10. Lincoln v. Turner and Turner, File ID L00506, DeWitt County Circuit Court, October 1841, Law Practice of Abraham Lincoln; Fraker, *Lincoln's Ladder*, 95–96.

11. DD, "Memorial Address," 52–53. The twenty-two counties were Adams, Calhoun, Cook, Fulton, Greene, Hancock, Henry, Jo Davies, Knox, LaSalle, Macon, McDonough, McLean, Mercer, Morgan, Peoria, Pike, Putnam, Sangamon, Schuyler, Tazewell, and Warren. Moses, *Illinois*, 1:546.

12. Johannsen, *Stephen A. Douglas*, 66, 68.

13. DD, "Memorial Address," 52–53; King, *Lincoln's Manager*, 30–31.

14. King, *Lincoln's Manager*, 34–35; DD to William P. Walker, March 18, 1839, DDFP.

15. King, *Lincoln's Manager*, 23–25; DD to William P. Walker, June 20, 1838, DDFP.

16. King, *Lincoln's Manager*, 37–39.

17. Pratt, "David Davis," 161n19.

18. DD to Julius Rockwell, February 10, 1841, DDFP.

19. Kyle, *Abraham Lincoln*, 42.

20. Sarah Davis to William P. Walker, January 28, 1845, DDFP; Sarah Davis to Lyman Betts, February 23, 1845, DDFP.

21. DD to Sarah Davis, June 7, 1847, DDFP; DD to Sarah Davis, August 2, 1847, DDFP; DD to Sarah Davis, August 8, 1847, DDFP (Davis visits Lincoln's house with twenty invited guests); DD to Sarah Davis, September 5, 1847, DDFP (Davis travels to Tremont with Lincoln); DD to Sarah Davis, June 19, 1847, DDFP (dinner); DD to Sarah Davis, July 1, 1847, DDFP (concert); DD to Sarah Davis, August 29, 1847, DDFP (party).

22. Benjamin Edwards, letter to the editor, *Illinois State Journal*, April 27, 1848, 2; DD to Sarah Davis, June 3, 1848, DDFP; King, *Lincoln's Manager*, 61; *Illinois State Journal*, August 23, 1848, 3.

23. AL to DD, February 12, 1849, in King, *Lincoln's Manager*, 63.

24. DD to AL, June 6, 1849, LP; AL to DD, July 6, 1849, in Basler, *Collected Works, First Supplement*, 15–16; Fraker, *Lincoln's Ladder*, 147.

25. Hill, *Lincoln the Lawyer*, 181.

26. Frank, *Lincoln as a Lawyer*, 23.

27. Burlingame, *Abraham Lincoln*, 1:331.

28. Swett, "Memorial Address," 78.

29. Fenster, *Case of Abraham Lincoln*, 46–48.

30. DD, "Memorial Address," 49–50 ("court days were gala-days with the people, and were looked forward to with ever recurring interest. . . . The weeks of Court were events of the year to the people, who generally attended whether they had business or not"); Pratt, "David Davis," 164 ("To go to court and listen to the witnesses and lawyers was among the chief amusements of the frontier settlements"); Johns, *Personal Recollections*, 62–66.

31. DD to Sarah Davis, October 27, 1851, DDFP.

32. Stevens, *Reporter's Lincoln*, 91 (describing the morning gatherings in McLean County).

33. Whitney, *Life on the Circuit*, 66–67; Swett, "Memorial Address," 77; King, *Lincoln's Manager*, 89; Reynolds, *Abe*, 226–27.

34. DD, "Memorial Address," 49.

35. Lincoln argued 1,257 cases before Judge Davis between 1849 and 1861. See "A Statistical Portrait: Peers and Clients, Lincoln, Douglas, and Davis," Law Practice of Abraham Lincoln.

36. Whitney, *Life on the Circuit*, 62–72; Fraker, *Lincoln's Ladder*, 39–40, 83; DD to Sarah Davis, September 22, 1851, DDFP; DD to Sarah Davis, November 3, 1851, DDFP; DD to Sarah Davis, April 24, 1851, DDFP; DD to Sarah Davis, October 20, 1851, DDFP; DD to Sarah Davis, May 3, 1851, DDFP; DD to Sarah Davis, May 11, 1852, DDFP; DD to Sarah Davis, June 3, 1852, DDFP.

37. DD to Sarah Davis, May 7, 1852, DDFP; Weik, *Real Lincoln*, 77.

38. See, for example, Hunt, "My Personal Recollections," 239 (Davis convinced a reluctant Lincoln to join the lawyers for dinner at the John Albert Jones family house in Tremont in 1850).

39. DD to Sarah Davis, May 3, 1851, DDFP. John Randolph served as a congressman and senator from Virginia. He was the chief prosecutor in the impeachment trial of Supreme Court justice Samuel Chase. See "Randolph, John," in *Biographical Directory*, https://bioguideretro.congress.gov/Home/MemberDetails?memIndex=R000047.

40. King, *Lincoln's Manager*, 69.

41. Dirck, *Lincoln the Lawyer*, 51; Fraker, *Lincoln's Ladder*, 104; "Opinion on Land Titles in Beloit, Wisconsin," March 24, 1856, in Basler, *Collected Works*, 2:336–39, and annotation [1]; "Bill of Exceptions in Case of William R. Coombs," October 14, 1859, and annotation [1], LP.

42. Fraker, *Lincoln's Ladder*, 104. Henry Whitney referred to Lincoln, Davis, and Swett as the "great triumvirate" of the circuit (*Life on the Circuit*, 85).

43. Sarah Davis to DD, September 18, 1853, DDFP; King, *Lincoln's Manager*, 74; DD to Sarah Davis, May 17, 1852, DDFP; DD to Sarah Davis, May 20, 1850, DDFP; DD to Sarah Davis, March 23, 1851, DDFP.

44. DD to Sarah Davis, November 3, 1851, DDFP.

45. King, *Lincoln's Manager*, 69; DD to George Perrin Davis, October 27, 1857, DDFP; DD to George Perrin Davis, April 17, 1854, DDFP; "Inscription in Autograph Album of George P. Davis," December 21, 1858, in Basler, *Collected Works*, 3:347.

46. Fraker, *Lincoln's Ladder*, 172; Whitney, *Life on the Circuit*, 209–10.

47. Donald, *Lincoln*, 167–69; Thomas, *Abraham Lincoln*, 152–54; "Editorial on the Kansas-Nebraska Act," September 11, 1854, in Basler, *Collected Works*, 2:229–30.

48. Donald, *Lincoln*, 179.

49. AL to Charles Hoyt, November 10, 1854, in Basler, *Collected Works*, 2:286, and annotation [1]; AL to Jacob Harding, November 11, 1854, in Basler, *Collected Works*, 2:286; AL to Thomas J. Henderson, November 27, 1854, in Basler, *Collected Works*, 2:288.

50. Elihu B. Washburne to AL, November 14, 1854, LP.

51. Blumenthal, *Wrestling*, 2:432.

52. Donald, *Lincoln's Herndon*, 77. However, Lincoln relinquished much decision-making power to Davis during the 1860 Republican presidential convention. See chapter 3.

53. DD to AL, December 15, 1854, LP; DD to AL, December 8, 1854, LP.

54. AL to Orville Browning, November 12, 1854, in Basler, *Collected Works*, 2:286.

55. Miers, *Lincoln Day by Day*, 2:131–33. Lincoln was involved in legal work on at least December 1, 2, 4, 5, 18, 20, and 21 (2:134–35).

56. "List of Members of the Illinois Legislature in 1855," [January 1, 1855?], in Basler, *Collected Works*, 2:296–98.

57. See, for example, AL to Elihu B. Washburne, December 11, 1854, in Basler, *Collected Works*, 2:292–93; AL to Elihu B. Washburne, December 14, 1854, in Basler, *Collected Works*, 2:293.

58. AL to Elihu B. Washburne, December 14, 1854, in Basler, *Collected Works*, 2:293.

59. Moore and Moore, *Collaborators for Emancipation*, 25; Donald, *Lincoln*, 180–81.

60. Pinsker, "Senator Abraham Lincoln," 7 ("Although the Republicans were suspicious of Lincoln's commitment to fusion and the antislavery cause, their primary objection was regional").

61. Elihu B. Washburne to AL, December 12, 1854, LP.

62. DD, interview with William H. Herndon, September 19, 1866, in Wilson and Davis, *Herndon's Informants*, 347; Burlingame, *Abraham Lincoln*, 1:397 ("Lobbying General Assembly members, Davis persuaded some antislavery militants to support the Springfield attorney").

63. DD to AL, December 15, 1854, LP.

64. Eckley, *Lincoln's Forgotten Friend*, 18–20, 32; King, *Lincoln's Manager*, 104–5.

65. Leonard Swett to AL, December 1, 1854, LP; Leonard Swett to AL, December 19, 1854, LP; Leonard Swett to AL, December 22, 1854, LP; DD to AL, December 8, 1854, LP; DD to AL, December 26, 1854 (stating that Davis would pay Swett's expenses); George, "'Mechem' or 'Mack,'" 28–29.

66. DD to AL, December 26, 1854, LP.

67. DD to AL, December 27, 1854, LP (reproducing letter of Davis's former law partner's sister); DD to AL, December 15, 1854, LP (relating the substance of an article in the *Chicago Daily Democrat* and relating a conversation with the editor of the *Prairie Farmer*); DD to AL, December 26, 1854, LP (relating comments of William Herndon's brother, Elliott Herndon, a Democrat, and quoting from the response to a letter by Davis seeking support for Lincoln).

68. For example, DD to AL, December 26, 1854, LP. In this letter, Davis suggests that Lincoln ask the "leading men" of Vermillion, Coles, and Edgar Counties to contact a newly elected state senator who was a secret Know-Nothing and who had received support from the old Whigs.

69. Elihu N. Powell to AL, November 16, 1854, LP.

70. AL to Noah W. Matheny, November 25, 1854, in Basler, *Collected Works*, 2:287–88.

71. Miller, *Lincoln and His World*, 80; *History of Sangamon County*, 258; DD to AL, December 26, 1854, LP. Broadwell had studied law in the office of Lincoln and Herndon. See Miller, *Lincoln and His World*, 80.

72. AL to Elihu B. Washburne, January 6, 1855, in Basler, *Collected Works*, 2:304.

73. DD to AL, December 26, 1854, LP.

74. DD to AL, December 26, 1854, LP; see also Elihu B. Washburne to AL, December 26, 1854, LP.

75. DD to AL, December 27, 1854, LP, emphasis added; AL to Elihu B. Washburne, January 6, 1855, in Basler, *Collected Works*, 2:304.

76. DD to Julius Rockwell, March 4, 1855, DDFP; Donald, *Lincoln*, 183.

77. DD to William H. Seward, May 23, 1865, in Lamon, *Recollections*, xxxi–xxxii. Davis recommended Lamon for governor of Idaho. Consistent with his brutal honesty, Davis conceded that Lamon "may have faults" (xxxii).

78. King, *Lincoln's Manager*, 63, 100, 113–14; *Journal of the Convention*, 4–5.

79. J. H. Murphy to DD, December 23, 1854, DDFP; King, *Lincoln's Manager,* 107; Murphy, John H., Persons, Papers of Abraham Lincoln Digital Library, https://papersofabrahamlincoln.org/persons/MU06218.

80. Linder, *Reminiscences*, 155, 159; Burlingame, *Abraham Lincoln*, 1:184–85; Logan, Stephen T., Persons, Papers of Abraham Lincoln Digital Library, https://papersofabrahamlincoln.org/persons/LO00310.

81. William Herndon to Jesse W. Weik, February 11, 1887, in Herndon, *Herndon on Lincoln*, 233.

82. DD, interview with William H. Herndon, September 20, 1866, in Wilson and Davis, *Herndon's Informants*, 348.

83. AL to Henry C. Whitney, June 7, 1855, in Basler, *Collected Works*, 2:313. Logan received only 37 percent of the vote in his home county of Sangamon. See Borit, "Lincoln's Opposition," 93n34.

84. DD, interview with William H. Herndon, September 20, 1866, in Wilson and Davis, *Herndon's Informants*, 348.

85. *Journal of the House of Representatives of the Nineteenth General Assembly*, 4–5.

86. DD to AL, December 26, 1854, LP; Moore and Moore, *Collaborators for Emancipation*, 26.

87. Thomas J. Turner to AL, December 10, 1854, LP; "Turner, Thomas Johnston," in *Biographical Directory*, https://bioguideretro.congress.gov/Home/MemberDetails?memIndex=T000429; Harriett Gustason, "Thomas J. Turner Was Freeport's Shining Star," *Freeport (IL) Journal-Standard*, August 9, 2008.

88. *Journal of the House of Representatives of the Nineteenth General Assembly*, 5, 349–60.

89. AL to Elihu B. Washburne, January 6, 1855, in Basler, *Collected Works*, 2:303.

90. *Journal of the House of Representatives of the Nineteenth General Assembly*, 6; AL to Norman B. Judd, December 9, 1859, in Basler, *Collected Works*, 3:506, annotation [2].

91. *Journal of the House of Representatives of the Nineteenth General Assembly*, 6; *Portrait and Biographical Record of Christian County*, 396–97.

92. *Journal of the House of Representatives of the Nineteenth General Assembly*, 6–7; H. S. Thomas to AL, January 29, 1859, LP; Ogg, *Naperville*, 55.

93. *Journal of the House of Representatives of the Nineteenth General Assembly*, 7; Bateman and Selby, *Historical Encyclopedia of Illinois and History of Hancock County*, 2:735.

94. *Journal of the House of Representatives of the Nineteenth General Assembly*, 7; Hanna, Benjamin J. F., Persons, Papers of Abraham Lincoln Digital Library, https://papersofabrahamlincoln.org/persons/HA34087.

95. AL to Elihu B. Washburne, January 6, 1855, in Basler, *Collected Works*, 2:303–4; DD to Julius Rockwell, March 4, 1855, DDFP.

96. *Journal of the House of Representatives of the Nineteenth General Assembly*, 348–49. The five Trumbull devotees were anti-Nebraska Democrats and included state senators Norman Judd, Burton C. Cook, and John M. Palmer and state representatives Henry S. Baker and George T. Allen (349).

97. *Journal of the House of Representatives of the Nineteenth General Assembly*, 350.

98. *Journal of the House of Representatives of the Nineteenth General Assembly*, 351.

99. *Journal of the House of Representatives of the Nineteenth General Assembly*, 352–53; Pinsker, "Senator Abraham Lincoln," 17.

100. *Journal of the House of Representatives of the Nineteenth General Assembly*, 353.

101. *Journal of the House of Representatives of the Nineteenth General Assembly*, 354.

102. *Journal of the House of Representatives of the Nineteenth General Assembly*, 355–56. John Logan received three votes on the sixth ballot (356).

103. *Journal of the House of Representatives of the Nineteenth General Assembly*, 357.

104. *Journal of the House of Representatives of the Nineteenth General Assembly*, 358.

105. *Journal of the House of Representatives of the Nineteenth General Assembly*, 359–60. Archibald Williams received one vote (360). See also Pinsker, "Senator Abraham Lincoln," 18.

106. Leonard Swett to AL, December 22, 1854, LP. Swett also stated in the letter that Joliet Postmaster James McDougall told him that Governor Matteson was not a candidate. See also DD to AL, December 26, 1854, LP; DD to AL, December 27, 1854, LP.

107. AL to Elihu B. Washburne, February 9, 1855, in Basler, *Collected Works*, 2:306.

108. DD to Julius Rockwell, March 4, 1855, DDFP. Davis does not explain why he was "necessarily absent" the day of the vote, but it was more likely a personal matter rather than judicial duties, since the spring session of court had not yet begun.

109. AL to Elihu B. Washburne, February 9, 1855, in Basler, *Collected Works*, 2:306.

110. DD to Julius Rockwell, March 4, 1855, DDFP.

111. DD to Julius Rockwell, March 4, 1855, DDFP. Mary Lincoln's animosity toward Trumbull was more personal. After the election, Mary refused to talk to Trumbull's wife, one of her closest friends, because of her husband's "treachery" (Burlingame, *Abraham Lincoln*, 1:404).

112. AL to Elihu B. Washburne, January 6, 1855, in Basler, *Collected Works*, 2:303.

113. AL to Elihu B. Washburne, February 9, 1855, in Basler, *Collected Works*, 2:305–6; Burlingame, *Abraham Lincoln*, 1:399–402.

114. AL to Elihu B. Washburne, January 6, 1855, in Basler, *Collected Works*, 2:304.

115. DD to AL, December 26, 1854, LP.

116. AL to Elihu B. Washburne, February 9, 1855, in Basler, *Collected Works*, 2:305; Leonard Swett to AL, December 22, 1854, LP.

117. Jesse K. Dubois and DD to AL, May 14, 1860, LP; see also DD to AL, May 18, 1860, LP.

118. Samuel C. Parks, statement for William H. Herndon, [1866], in Wilson and Davis, *Herndon's Informants*, 538.

119. See Lyman Trumbull to AL, January 3, 1858, LP ("I have written you freely & just as I feel, & presume it is unnecessary for me to assure you that I shall continue to labor for the success of the Republican cause in Ill[inoi]s—& the advancement at the next election to the place now occupied by Douglas of that *Friend*, who was instrumental in promoting my own").

120. There is no question that Davis made promises to secure votes at the 1860 convention. It is the precise nature of the promises that remains unclear. See chapter 3.

Chapter 2. Lincoln's Second Senate Defeat

1. DD to Sarah Davis, May 24, 1852, DDFP; DD to William P. Walker, January 6, 1853, DDFP; DD to William P. Walker, March 14, 1853, DDFP; *Laws of the State of Illinois Passed at the First Session* (An Act Fixing the Times of Holding Courts in the Eighth Judicial Circuit), 60; *Laws of the State of Illinois Passed by the Eighteenth General Assembly* (An Act to Reduce the Limits of the Eighth Judicial Circuit), 63.

2. Fraker, *Lincoln's Ladder*, 153, 157; Friends of the Chicago & Alton Depot, "1879 Railroad Depot."

3. DD to George P. Davis, May 21, 1855, DDFP; DD to George P. Davis, May 6, 1855, DDFP; DD to William P. Walker, October 17, 1852, DDFP.

4. "A Statistical Portrait, Peers and Clients, Lincoln and the Railroads," Law Practice of Abraham Lincoln.

5. Illinois Central Railroad v. County of McLean, 17 Ill. 291 (1855); Starr, *Lincoln and the Railroads*, 62–63.

6. Lincoln v. Illinois Central RR, File ID L01660, McLean County Circuit Court, June 1857, Law Practice of Abraham Lincoln; Starr, *Lincoln and the Railroads*, 76–79; King, *Lincoln's Manager*, 91.

7. AL to James F. Joy, September 14, 1855, in Basler, *Collected Works*, 2:325, and annotation [1]; Cundiff v. Illinois Central RR, File ID L00537, Document No. 127881, DeWitt County Circuit Court, November 1854, Law Practice of Abraham Lincoln.

8. DD to Julius Rockwell, December 27, 1855, DDFP; Fraker, *Lincoln's Ladder*, 173–74.

9. Burlingame, *Abraham Lincoln*, 1:417; Whitney, *Life on the Circuit*, 90. Sherman Wakefield lists David Davis as being present at the Bloomington convention (*How Lincoln Became President*, 67).

10. Burlingame, *Abraham Lincoln*, 1:421, 425; Fraker, *Lincoln's Ladder*, 178–85.

11. See Burlingame, *Abraham Lincoln*, 1:433.

12. Burlingame, *Abraham Lincoln*, 1:435, 443; AL to James W. Grimes, August 1857, in Basler, *Collected Works*, 2:413; AL to Jediah F. Alexander, May 15, 1858, in Basler, *Collected Works*, 2:446.

13. Blumenthal, *All the Powers*, 352–53; Donald, *Lincoln*, 202.

14. Goodwin, *Team of Rivals*, 200; Simon, "Union County," 273 (stating that Lincoln wrote off the southernmost Illinois counties); Miers, *Lincoln Day by Day*, 2:211 (entry for February 18, 1858, citing Norman Judd to Lyman Trumbull, April 19, 1858, Lyman Trumbull Papers, Library of Congress).

15. Norman Judd to AL, June 1, 1858, LP; Jesse Fell to AL, January 2, 1861, LP ("I have long since, however, discovered that there is throughout the state, particularly among the whig portion of our party, quite a bitter feeling against [Judd]").

16. AL to Charles L. Wilson, June 1, 1858, LP; Fraker, *Lincoln's Ladder*, 189, 192.

17. Stephen A. Hurlbut to AL, May 29, 1858, LP.

18. AL to Stephen A. Hurlbut, June 1, 1858, in Basler, *Collected Works*, 2:456.

19. AL to Stephen A. Hurlbut, June 1, 1858, in Basler, *Collected Works*, 2:456, annotation [2].

20. *Chicago Daily Tribune*, June 10, 1858, 3; *Chicago Daily Tribune*, June 14, 1858, 2. On June 15, 1858, the *Chicago Daily Tribune* reported that the Republican convention in Lee County unanimously endorsed Lincoln (1).

21. Bateman and Selby, *Historical Encyclopedia of Illinois and History of McLean County*, 2:1029–30.

22. *Proceedings of the Republican State Convention*, 9–12.

23. *Chicago Daily Press and Tribune*, July 12, 1858, 1 (estimating that Lincoln drew 25 percent fewer people than Douglas); Whitney, *Life on the Circuit*, 407.

24. Blumenthal, *All the Powers*, 370; *Chicago Daily Press and Tribune*, July 20, 1858, 2.

25. AL to John Mathers, July 20, 1858, in Basler, *Collected Works*, 2:522; DD to AL, August 25, 1858, LP.

26. AL to Stephen A. Douglas, July 24, 1858, in Basler, *Collected Works*, 2:522.

27. AL to Stephen A. Douglas, July 24, 1858, in Basler, *Collected Works*, 2:522, annotation [1]; Stephen A. Douglas to AL, July 24, 1858, in Basler, *Collected Works*, 2:530, annotation [1].

28. AL to Stephen A. Douglas, July 29, 1858, in Basler, *Collected Works*, 2:528–30; *Chicago Daily Press and Tribune*, July 28, 1858, 1 (reproducing Lincoln's letter and Douglas's response); *Chicago Daily Press and Tribune*, August 3, 1858, 1 (reproducing Lincoln's reply to Douglas).

29. DD to George Perrin Davis, September 22, 1858, DDFP; DD to Julius Rockwell, October 26, 1858, DDFP.

30. DD to AL, August 2, 1858, LP; DD to AL, August 3, 1858, LP; DD to AL, July 30, 1858, LP; DD to AL, September 25, 1858, LP.

31. DD to AL, August 3, 1858, LP; "Fourth Debate with Stephen A. Douglas at Charleston, Illinois," September 18, 1858, in Basler, *Collected Works*, 3:145–46.

32. DD to AL, August 25, 1858, LP.

33. Guelzo, *Lincoln and Douglas*, 144–45; Charles L. Wilson to AL, August 26, 1858, LP; Blumenthal, *All the Powers*, 388–89; Donald, *Lincoln*, 217–19.

34. DD to AL, August 9, 1858, LP; DD to John F. Henry, July 29, 1858, quoted in King, *Lincoln's Manager*, 122. Davis undoubtedly expressed these opinions to Lincoln when he talked with him earlier in Clinton, Illinois. See DD to AL, August 2, 1858, LP.

35. DD to AL, June 14, 1858, LP.

36. Blumenthal, *All the Powers*, 353; King, *Lincoln's Manager*, 115; DD to William P. Walker, December 31, 1844, DDFP ("The abolitionists are hereafter & forever more shut out of the pale of my sympathy").

37. DD to T. Lyle Dickey, July 18, 1856, in Wallace, *Life and Letters*, 74–76; King, *Lincoln's Manager*, 115.

38. James W. Somers to AL, June 22, 1858, LP; Ward Lamon to AL, June 9, 1858, LP.

39. Letter to the editor, "Opposition to Lovejoy," *Chicago Daily Tribune*, June 4, 1858, 2; letter to the editor, "Judge Davis' Position," *Chicago Daily Tribune*, June 11, 1858, 2;

AL to editors, June 8, 1858, in Basler, *Collected Works, First Supplement*, 31–32. See also *Chicago Daily Tribune*, July 25, 1954, 18 ("Credit Lincoln with letter in Tribune in '58").

40. DD to AL, June 14, 1858, LP.

41. Wakefield, *How Lincoln Became President*, 87–91 (quoting the *Bloomington Daily Pantagraph* of September 6, 1858, and December 5, 1935); "Speech at Bloomington, Illinois," September 4, 1858, in Basler, *Collected Works*, 3:85–90; *Illinois State Journal*, September 7, 1858, 2.

42. DD to O. M. Hatch, August 18, 1858, in Schwartz, "Campaign Broadside."

43. Wakefield, *How Lincoln Became President*, 88; DD to Sarah Davis, October 10, 1860, DDFP; *Illinois State Journal*, September 7, 1858, 2.

44. DD to O. M. Hatch, August 18, 1858, in Schwartz, "Campaign Broadside"; DD to AL, August 25, 1858, LP.

45. Blumenthal, *All the Powers*, 388; DD to AL, August 25, 1858, LP; DD to AL, September 25, 1858, LP.

46. DD to AL, November 7, 1858, LP.

47. Fraker, *Lincoln's Ladder*, 193; Johannsen, *Stephen A. Douglas*, 659 (estimating that Douglas spent over $50,000); Guelzo, "Houses Divided," 406–7; Pratt, *Great Debates*, 8 (estimating Lincoln's expenses at $1,000); Pratt, *Personal Finances*, 104–6; AL to Norman Judd, November 16, 1858, in Basler, *Collected Works*, 3:337 (informing Judd that Lincoln spent $250 on the campaign in addition to his ordinary campaign expenses and would contribute $250 toward the $2,500 debt Judd said he incurred from the 1858 Republican campaign).

48. Greeley and Cleveland, *A Political Textbook*, 247.

49. Collins, "The Lincoln-Douglas Contest," 414–15, 408–9.

50. Burlingame, *Abraham Lincoln*, 1:546.

51. Donald, *Lincoln*, 228; Burlingame, *Abraham Lincoln*, 1:546, 549.

52. Fehrenbacher, *Prelude to Greatness*, 116.

53. AL to Norman Judd, October 20, 1858, in Basler, *Collected Works*, 3:229–30.

54. AL to Norman Judd, October 20, 1858, in Basler, *Collected Works*, 3:229–30; *Chicago Daily Press and Tribune*, November 8, 1858, 2.

55. DD to William P. Walker, November 16, 1840, DDFP.

56. DD to Julius Rockwell, October 26, 1858, DDFP; DD to George Perrin Davis, November 7, 1858, DDFP.

57. DD to Edwin Morgan, September 22, 1860, quoted in Burlingame, *Abraham Lincoln*, 1:545–46.

58. *Chicago Daily Press and Tribune*, November 10, 1858, 2.

59. *Illinois State Journal*, November 16, 1858, 2.

60. *Chicago Daily Press and Tribune*, November 25, 1858, 1; *Illinois State Journal*, November 29, 1858, 2 (reprinting an article from the *Chicago Daily Press and Tribune*).

61. Burlingame, *Abraham Lincoln*, 1:547.

62. "The Apportionment," *Illinois State Journal*, November 9, 1858, 2.

63. DD to William Perrin Walker, January 19, 1840, DDFP; DD to Sarah Davis, November 11, 1860, DDFP; see also Illinois State Republican Committee form letter, June 23, 1860, 3, Jesse Fell Papers, Illinois History and Lincoln Collections, University Library, University of Illinois Urbana-Champaign.

64. DD to O. M. Hatch, August 18, 1858, in Schwartz, "Campaign Broadside"; Guelzo, *Lincoln and Douglas*, 143; Donald, *Lincoln*, 231 ("Former Whigs like Judge David Davis resented the prominent role that former Democrats played in the campaign and correctly suspected that Judd was using his position as chairman of the central committee to promote his own gubernatorial prospects"). As the Republican National Convention approached in 1860, Davis wrote Lincoln that he harbored no personal ill-will toward Judd but still believed that his policies as party chair were "unwise" (DD to AL, February 21, 1860, LP).

65. DD to AL, August 3, 1858, LP; DD to AL, August 9, 1858, LP.

66. DD to O. M. Hatch, August 18, 1858, in Schwartz, "Campaign Broadside"; Johannsen, *Stephen A. Douglas*, 655 ("Douglas opened his campaign in Chicago, but it was in central Illinois that the real battle would be fought"); Blumenthal, *All the Powers*, 376 ("[Lincoln] targeted the central counties within eighty miles of Springfield").

67. Jesse Fell to AL, January 2, 1861, LP; Ecelbarger, *Great Comeback*, 20 ("There appear to have been as many Judd detractors within Illinois Republican ranks as there were supporters").

68. Norman Judd to AL, November 15, 1858, LP; Norman Judd to AL, November 20, 1858, LP; AL to Norman Judd, November 16, 1858, in Basler, *Collected Works*, 3:337.

69. Pratt, *Personal Finances*, 78–79, 136–37. The $2,500 loan to Judd was made in September 1857 at 10 percent interest to help Judd purchase property in Iowa. On September 1, 1859, Judd replaced the original note with a new note for $3,000 at 10 percent interest, due in five years.

70. See Donald, *Lincoln*, 231.

71. Davis and Wilson, *Lincoln-Douglas Debates*, xv–xvi; Zarefsky, *Lincoln, Douglas, and Slavery*, 11–15; Donald, *Lincoln*, 203–4.

72. Goodwin, *Team of Rivals*, 197.

73. AL to Lyman Trumbull, December 28, 1857, in Basler, *Collected Works*, 2:430.

74. Lyman Trumbull to AL, January 3, 1858, LP; Stahr, *Seward*, 168–69.

75. Lyman Trumbull to AL, January 3, 1858, LP.

76. *Illinois State Journal*, April 19, 1858, 2 (reproducing an article from the *New York Herald* alleging that a deal had been struck between Douglas and Seward); Burlingame, *Abraham Lincoln*, 1:453. Lincoln did not believe that there was a "secret arrangement" between Douglas and Greeley or Seward. See AL to Charles L. Wilson, June 1, 1858, LP.

77. William Herndon to AL, March 24, 1858, in Herndon and Weik, *Herndon's Lincoln*, 241–42; Lyman Trumbull to AL, January 3, 1858, LP; Donald, *Lincoln's Herndon*, 114–15.

78. Horner, *Lincoln and Greeley*, 140.

79. Horace Greeley to William Herndon, October 6, 1858, in Horner, *Lincoln and Greeley*, 153–54.

80. Ward H. Lamon to AL, June 9, 1858, LP. Lamon's statement that the McLean County Republican Convention "endorsed" Douglas was an exaggeration. See Koos, *Freedom, Land and Community*, 289; Stephen A. Hurlbut to AL, May 29, 1858, LP.

81. AL to editor, *Chicago Daily Journal*, June 1, 1858, in Horner, *Lincoln and Greeley*, 143–44; DD to Julius Rockwell, October 26, 1858, DDFP; DD to AL, November 7, 1858, LP.

82. John J. Crittenden to AL, July 29, 1858, LP.

83. AL to John J. Crittenden, July 7, 1858, in Basler, *Collected Works*, 2:483–84.

84. John J. Crittenden to AL, July 29, 1858, LP.

85. John J. Crittenden to T. Lyle Dickey, August 1, 1858, in Coleman, *Life of John J. Crittenden*, 2:164–66.

86. DD to Julius Rockwell, October 26, 1858, DDFP; Burlingame, *Abraham Lincoln*, 1:542; Guelzo, "Houses Divided," 401.

87. *Illinois State Journal*, October 27, 1858, 2.

88. AL to John J. Crittenden, November 4, 1858, in Basler, *Collected Works*, 3:335–36.

89. DD to AL, November 7, 1858, LP. Davis eventually forgave Dickey so that in 1868 he was able to write to Sarah, "I like him [Dickey] very much" (DD to Sarah Davis, February 21, 1868, DDFP).

90. DD to Julius Rockwell, October 26, 1858, DDFP; DD to AL, November 7, 1858, LP.

91. Browning, *Diary*, 1:245, 246, entries for July 14 and July 18, 1856; see also King, *Lincoln's Manager*, 112.

92. DD to Julius Rockwell, October 26, 1858, DDFP; DD to AL, November 7, 1858, LP.

93. DD to O. M. Hatch, August 18, 1858, in Schwartz, "Campaign Broadside," 7.

94. William Herndon to Theodore Parker, August 31, 1858, in Newton, *Lincoln and Herndon*, 203.

95. Hill, *Lincoln the Lawyer*, 181–82.

96. Donald, *Lincoln*, 211–12; Goodwin, *Team of Rivals*, 208–9.

97. DD to O. M. Hatch, August 16, 1858, LP; DD to AL, August 9, 1858, LP.

98. Guelzo, *Lincoln and Douglas*, 72 (identifying Davis as the principal spokesperson for ex-Whigs in the Third Congressional District).

99. *Proceedings of the Republican State Convention*, 9–12.

100. "Speech at Chicago, Illinois," July 10, 1858, in Basler, *Collected Works*, 2:501.

101. DD to AL, August 3, 1858, LP.

102. "Fourth Debate with Stephen A. Douglas at Charleston, Illinois," September 18, 1858, in Basler, *Collected Works*, 3:145–46.

103. DD to AL, September 25, 1858, LP.

104. See "Opposition to Lovejoy," *Chicago Daily Tribune*, June 4, 1858, 2.

105. Abraham Smith to AL, June 4, 1858, LP.

106. Guelzo, *Lincoln and Douglas*, 73 ("Davis was quietly orchestrating a dump-Lovejoy movement which would nominate Davis instead"); Ward H. Lamon to AL, June 9, 1858, LP (acknowledging that Judge Davis was "beaten"); Burlingame, *Abraham Lincoln*, 1:456 (describing Davis, Swett, and others as spearheading the movement to deny Lovejoy renomination for Congress).

107. See, for example, Guelzo, "Houses Divided," 414.

108. See, for example, "Fourth Debate with Stephen A. Douglas at Charleston, Illinois," September 18, 1858, in Basler, *Collected Works*, 3:145–46.

109. T. Lyle Dickey to AL, November 19, 1854, LP.

110. King, *Lincoln's Manager*, 113.

111. *Chicago Daily Press and Tribune*, November 10, 1858, 2.

112. *Chicago Daily Press and Tribune*, November 10, 1858, 2.

113. DD to AL, September 25, 1858, LP; DD to AL, August 3, 1858, LP.

114. DD to O. M. Hatch, August 18, 1858, in Schwartz, "Campaign Broadside," 7; DD to AL, August 3, 1858, LP. Lincoln also stressed "face to face" personal contact with the voters. See "Lincoln's Plan of Campaign in 1840," January 1840, in Basler, *Collected Works*, 1:180–91.

115. King, *Lincoln's Manager*, 21, 37; DD to O. M. Hatch, August 18, 1858, in Schwartz, "Campaign Broadside"; Benjamin F. James to AL, August 25, 1858, LP.

116. DD to AL, July 30, 1858, LP; DD to Julius Rockwell, December 27, 1855, DDFP.

117. DD to AL, August 2, 1858, LP.

118. DD to AL, August 3, 1858, LP. Owen Lovejoy was an outspoken abolitionist congressman from Illinois.

119. David Kyes to DD, August 7, 1858, LP.

120. DD to David Kyes, August 9, 1858, LP.

121. DD to AL, August 9, 1858, LP.

122. DD to O. M. Hatch, August 16, 1858, LP; DD to AL, August 25, 1858, LP; DD to O. M. Hatch, August 18, 1858, in Schwartz, "Campaign Broadside."

123. DD to O. M. Hatch, August 16, 1858, LP. Republican Thomas J. Pickett was the owner and publisher of the *Tazewell Register* until the spring of 1858, when he sold the paper to John McDonald, who made it a Democratic newspaper. See Scott and James, *Newspapers and Periodicals*, 276–77.

124. DD to O. M. Hatch, August 18, 1858, in Schwartz, "Campaign Broadside."

125. DD to AL, August 25, 1858, LP. Possibly the third precinct was either Delevan or Washington. See Benjamin F. James to AL, August 25, 1858, LP.

126. DD to O. M. Hatch, August 18, 1858, in Schwartz, "Campaign Broadside"; "Speech at Tremont, Illinois," August 30, 1858, in Basler, *Collected Works*, 3:76–77; *Chicago Daily Press and Tribune*, September 2, 1858, 2; "Speech at Pekin, Illinois," October 5, 1858, in Basler, *Collected Works*, 3:206–7.

127. King, *Lincoln's Manager*, 126n44; Guelzo, "Houses Divided," 415.

128. AL to Anson G. Henry, November 19, 1858, in Basler, *Collected Works*, 3:339.

129. King, *Lincoln's Manager*, 126n44; *Illinois State Journal*, November 13, 1858, 2; Guelzo, *Abraham Lincoln*, 57.

130. *Illinois State Journal*, November 13, 1858, 2; Guelzo, "Houses Divided," 415.

131. Fraker, *Lincoln's Ladder*, 207.

132. *Chicago Daily Press and Tribune*, November 8, 1858, 2.

133. DD to AL, September 25, 1858, LP; *Illinois State Journal*, August 21, 1858, 2.

134. Stringer, *History of Logan County*, 1:281–82; Guelzo, "Houses Divided," 415.

135. Fraker, *Lincoln's Ladder*, 132–35.

136. Cochrane, *Centennial History*, 217–18.

137. DD to Sarah Davis, October 27, 1847, DDFP; DD to Judge Walker, June 20, 1838, DDFP; Kyle, *Abraham Lincoln*, 118.

138. James and Loveless, *Bibliography*, 29; Kyle, *Abraham Lincoln*, 64. When William J. Usrey and Charles H. Wingate founded the *Illinois State Chronicle* in 1855, they said that the paper was not linked to any party but would reflect "Republican sentiments" (64).

139. Kyle, *Abraham Lincoln*, 41, 119.

140. *Illinois State Journal*, November 5, 1858, 2; *Illinois State Journal*, November 6, 1858, 2; Kyle, *Abraham Lincoln*, 99.

141. *Illinois State Journal*, November 13, 1858, 2; Kyle, *Abraham Lincoln*, 99.

142. Republicans made gains in Macon County from the 1856 election to the 1858 election. See *Illinois State Journal*, November 22, 1858, 2.

143. DD to AL, November 7, 1858, LP.

144. DD to Julius Rockwell, February 10, 1841, DDFP.

145. DD to O. M. Hatch, August 18, 1858, in Schwartz, "Campaign Broadside."

146. DD to AL, August 9, 1858, LP; DD to AL, August 3, 1858, LP.

147. DD to AL, June 14, 1858, LP.

Chapter 3. *Davis Secures Lincoln's 1860 Presidential Nomination*

1. Blumenthal, *All the Powers*, 233–35, 228–29; Stahr, *Seward*, 160, 163; Bancroft, *Life*, 1:419–20.

2. Stahr, *Seward*, 184 ("Almost everyone expected that Seward would receive the nomination"); Frederick Douglass, "The Chicago Nominations," *Douglass' Monthly* (New York, NY), June 1860, Frederick Douglass Project, University of Rochester, https://rbscp.lib.rochester.edu/4376; DD to Julius Rockwell, December 22, 1862, DDFP.

3. "The Presidential Question," *Morning Courier and New-York Enquirer*, February 11, 1860, reprinted in the *New York Times*, February 22, 1860, 2.

4. Wilson, *Intimate Memories*, 279; *Illinois State Journal*, April 19, 1858, 2, reprinting an article from the *New York Herald*.

5. Bancroft, *Life*, 1:522.

6. Stanton, *Random Recollections*, 212–13; Blumenthal, *All the Powers*, 509–12.

7. Joseph Medill to Frederic Bancroft, February 18, 1896, in Bancroft, *Life*, 1:530–31n.

8. Stahr, *Seward*, 178.

9. Bancroft, *Life*, 1:526–28.

10. *Illinois State Journal*, August 3, 1859, 1; *Chicago Press and Tribune*, November 19, 1859, 2 (reporting the Pennsylvania newspaper's endorsement); *Chicago Press and Tribune*, December 5, 1859, 1; *Chicago Press and Tribune*, January 9, 1860, 2.

11. Warren, *Vice-Presidency*, 4.

12. *Chicago Press and Tribune*, February 10, 1860, 1; DD to Henry E. Dummer, February 20, 1860, in Pratt, *Concerning Mr. Lincoln*, 23. Lincoln replaced Dummer as Stuart's law partner when Dummer moved to Jacksonville, Illinois. Chicago mayor John Wentworth also addressed a Cameron-Lincoln Club, advocating the ticket. *Ford County Journal* (IL), February 2, 1860, 2.

13. Goodwin, *Team of Rivals*, 15; see also Schurz, *Reminiscences*, 2:34 ("Thurlow Weed, the most astute, skillful, and indefatigable political manager ever known"); Stahr, *Seward*, 42.

14. Bancroft, *Life*, 1:523; Bungay, *Traits*, 79–80.

15. Goodwin, *Team of Rivals*, 15; Bancroft, *Life*, 1:522–23.

16. See, for example, Wakefield, *How Lincoln Became President*, 110; Blumenthal, *All the Powers*, 576–77.

17. Swett, "Memorial Address," 79; Norman Judd interview by John Nicolay, February 28, 1876, in Burlingame, *Oral History*, 46.

18. AL to Cyrus M. Allen, May 1, 1860, in Basler, *Collected Works*, 4:46; AL to Richard M. Corwine, May 2, 1860, in Basler, *Collected Works*, 4:47–48.

19. Swett, "Memorial Address," 79.

20. Pratt, *Concerning Mr. Lincoln*, 22.

21. Sarah Davis to William P. Walker, January 28, 1845, DDFP; Ecelbarger, *Great Comeback*, 192.

22. King, *Lincoln's Manager*, 74, 46; DD to Sarah Davis, May 1, 1851, DDFP.

23. Waugh, *One Man Great Enough*, 176; Ecelbarger, *Great Comeback*, 190; King, *Lincoln's Manager*, 307–8; Sarah Davis to DD, July 10, 1848, DDFP; Jesse Fell to AL, January 2, 1861, LP.

24. Henry C. Whitney interview with Jesse W. Weik, [1887–89], in Wilson and Davis, *Herndon's Informants*, 733–34.

25. Whitney, *Life on the Circuit*, 66; Swett, "Memorial Address," 77.

26. DD to William H. Seward, May 23, 1865, in Lamon, *Recollections*, xxxi–xxxii.

27. Leonard Swett to William Herndon, August 29, 1887, in Wilson and Davis, *Herndon's Informants*, 711; White, *Life of Lyman Trumbull*, 144 ("Swett . . . was *Fidus Achates* [faithful friend] of David Davis at all times").

28. Fraker, *Lincoln's Ladder*, 94.

29. DD to George Perrin Davis, April 28, 1857, DDFP; DD to Sarah Davis, October 25, 1860, DDFP; Fraker, *Lincoln's Ladder*, 94–95, 229.

30. William Orme to DD, December 13, 1862, DDFP ("Judge, I would like very much to hear from you. Your advice always has been, and always will be, treasured by me"); DD interview with William Herndon, September 19, 1866, in Wilson and Davis, *Herndon's Informants*, 347.

31. DD to O. M. Hatch, August 18, 1858, in Schwartz, "Campaign Broadside"; DD to AL, August 25, 1858, LP.

32. Wilson, *Intimate Memories*, 194. Rufus Wilson concluded that Davis's "yeoman's services for his friend" at the convention were driven not by shared political beliefs or a hope for future favors but "from a sincere and hearty admiration of Abraham Lincoln's great and noble qualities" and "his honesty, great ability and love of country."

33. Jesse Fell to AL, January 2, 1861, LP.

34. Lamon, *Life*, 312; *Indianapolis Journal*, July 2, 1886, 2 (reprinting a letter from Ward Lamon to the *Denver Tribune*). According to Lincoln, "A man has not time to spend half his life in quarrels." Burlingame and Turner Ettlinger, *Inside Lincoln's White House*, 245, entry for November 8, 1864.

35. Koerner, *Memoirs*, 2:540.

36. Henry C. Whitney, statement to William Herndon, August 27, 1887, in Wilson and Davis, *Herndon's Informants*, 629; Whitney, *Life on the Circuit*, 85. Whitney added that the social status of the three friends was in the order listed.

37. King, *Lincoln's Manager*, 238; see Pratt, *Personal Finances*, 141, quoting a letter from Mary Lincoln to David Davis dated November 18, 1866, in which Mary says, "Please accept my grateful thanks for all your kindness to myself and family." The sincerity of Mary's compliment may be questioned, since at the time she was beseeching Swett and Davis to solicit money from Simon Cameron so that she did not have to live on a "clerk's salary." After the assassination, Davis periodically checked in with Mary Lincoln. See,

for example, Sarah Davis to Frances Mary Walker, September 12, 1865, DDFP (reporting that when Mr. Davis called on Mary Lincoln at the Clifton House in Chicago, she gave him "a good sized photograph of Mr. Lincoln and a small one of Robert & 'Tad'").

38. Robert Todd Lincoln to Thomas Dent, September 12, 1919, quoted in Pratt, *Personal Finances*, 141.

39. AL to James F. Babcock, April 14, 1860, in Basler, *Collected Works*, 4:43; AL to Simon Cameron, August 6, 1860, in Basler, *Collected Works*, 4:91; AL to Whom it may concern, August 2, 1860, in Basler, *Collected Works, First Supplement*, 58.

40. AL to Joseph Holt, November 12, 1861, in Basler, *Collected Works*, 5:21–22.

41. AL to John Wentworth, February 13, 1860, in Basler, *Collected Works, First Supplement*, 48.

42. AL to Elihu B. Washburne, February 9, 1855, LP.

43. DD to AL, November 7, 1858, LP; Donald, *Lincoln*, 234, 242.

44. Weik, *Real Lincoln*, 261.

45. *Cincinnati Daily Press*, May 19, 1860, 2; Ecelbarger, *Great Comeback*, 223.

46. Barton, *Life*, 1:230; Wilson, "*Lincoln's Affair*," 71.

47. AL to William Butler, January 26, 1839, in Basler, *Collected Works*, 1:139–40; Fraker, *Lincoln's Ladder*, 146–47; Burlingame, *Abraham Lincoln*, 1:295.

48. DD to AL, June 6, 1849, LP; Fraker, *Lincoln's Ladder*, 147; William Herndon to Jesse W. Weik, January 15, 1886, in Hertz, *Hidden Lincoln*, 135.

49. William Butler to AL, May 15, 1860, LP. Butler was appointed state treasurer in 1859 and elected to the post in 1860.

50. Browning, *Diary*, 1:382, entry for October 12, 1859; Browning, *Diary*, 1:396, entries for February 20 and 22, 1860; see also Browning, *Diary*, 1:xviii ("There was a suspicion abroad in 1859 that Browning had not been too forward for Lincoln in the campaign of 1858"); Wilson, *Intimate Memories*, 194.

51. Achorn, *Lincoln Miracle*, 118.

52. Plummer, *Lincoln's Rail-Splitter*, 43; Browning, *Diary*, 1:394–95, entry for February 8, 1860; Browning, *Diary*, 1:406–7, entry for May 15, 1860; King, *Lincoln's Manager*, 136.

53. Swett, "Memorial Address," 80; Halstead, *Caucuses of 1860*, 151. Halstead's description of Browning's remarks as "dull" may not be entirely fair. Browning clearly was trying to be humble in victory and conciliatory to New York. See Oldroyd, *Lincoln's Campaign*, 55–57.

54. Browning, *Diary*, 1:407–8, entry for May 17, 1860.

55. Orville Browning to Edgar Cowan, September 6, 1864, quoted in Donald, *"We Are Lincoln Men,"* 138, and see also 109.

56. Browning, *Diary*, 1: 406–7, entries for May 15 and May 16, 1860.

57. Wilson, *Intimate Memories*, 193–94.

58. DD to AL, April 23, 1860, LP; DD to AL, May 5, 1860, LP; Donald, *Lincoln*, 242.

59. Fehrenbacher, *Prelude to Greatness*, 149; Wilson, *Intimate Memories*, 194; Ecelbarger, *Great Comeback*, 37; AL to David L. Phillips, February 17, 1860, in Basler, *Collected Works*, 3:521, annotation [2]; Mary Lincoln to DD, January 17, 1861, in Turner and Turner, *Mary Todd Lincoln*, 71; Samuel C. Parks statement for William H. Herndon, 1866, in Wilson and Davis, *Herndon's Informants*, 538; Donald, *Lincoln*, 231, 242; Blumenthal, *All the Powers*, 522.

60. Jesse W. Fell to AL, January 2, 1861, LP.

61. Jesse W. Fell to AL, January 2, 1861, LP.

62. Donald, *Lincoln*, 231; DD to AL, February 21, 1860, LP. In the letter, Davis claims "no personal feelings of hostility to Mr. Judd" but thought that how he conducted the canvass of 1858 as party chair was "unwise."

63. AL to George W. Dole, Gurdon S. Hubbard, and William H. Brown, December 14, 1859, in Basler, *Collected Works*, 3:507–9.

64. Woldman, *Lawyer Lincoln*, 96.

65. Achorn, *Lincoln Miracle*, 147; AL to Lyman Trumbull, April 29, 1860, in Basler, *Collected Works*, 4:45–46.

66. Villard, *Memoirs*, 1:148. At least in the 1850s Lincoln refused to believe rumors about Yates's drinking problem. AL to Richard Oglesby, September 8, 1854, in Basler, *Collected Works, First Supplement*, 24.

67. Moses, *Biographical Dictionary*, 141–42.

68. Whitney, *Life on the Circuit*, 92.

69. Plummer, *Lincoln's Rail-Splitter*, 156–59; Fraker, *Lincoln's Ladder*, 160.

70. Hearn, *Lincoln*, 5.

71. AL to Norman Judd, December 14, 1859, in Basler, *Collected Works*, 3:509.

72. Koerner, *Memoirs*, 2:80; Goldman, *National Party Chairmen*, 51.

73. Lamon, *Life*, 448; Leonard Swett to Josiah Drummond, May 27, 1860, quoted in Wakefield, *How Lincoln Became President*, 113 ("After the first days we were aided by the arrival of at least 10,000 people from Central Illinois and Indiana").

74. Lamon, *Life*, 448; Wakefield, *How Lincoln Became President*, 180; Morehouse, "Life of Jesse W. Fell," 61n27.

75. Swett, "Memorial Address," 79.

76. Halstead, *Caucuses of 1860*, 145.

77. Goldman, *National Party Chairmen*, 51–52.

78. *Fremont (OH) Journal*, May 18, 1860, 2 (reporting that the Wigwam measured 100 by 180 feet, cost about $6,000, and had a stage accommodating six or seven hundred people, numerous conference rooms, space for a band, and a gallery around three sides of the hall); Norman Judd conversation with John Nicolay, February 28, 1876, in Burlingame, *Oral History*, 46–47.

79. John C. Frémont, May 16, 1860, letter in *Cincinnati Daily Press*, May 17, 1860, 2 (reporting that the Wigwam was overflowing with ten thousand people and that many thousands could not get in).

80. M. Halstead, special to the *Cincinnati Commercial*, May 16, 1860, reprinted in *Cadiz (OH) Democrat Sentinel*, May 23, 1860, 2; Koerner, *Memoirs*, 2:80.

81. DD to Henry E. Dummer, February 20, 1860, in Pratt, *Concerning Mr. Lincoln*, 23.

82. Blumenthal, *All the Powers*, 571–72, 576.

83. And outwork the opposition they did. In a letter to his friend Josiah Drummond, Swett wrote, "No men ever worked as our boys did. I did not, the whole week I was there, sleep two hours a night" (Leonard Swett to J. H. Drummond, May 27, 1860, in Wilson, *Intimate Memories*, 296). Jesse Dubois wrote to Lincoln from the convention, "Judge Davis is furious, never saw him work so hard and so quiet in all my life" (Jesse K. Dubois to AL, May 13, 1860, LP).

84. DD to AL, August 30, 1860, LP (explaining that Davis did not decide the "Davenport case" because he "adjourned the Court for the Chicago Convention").

85. *Chicago Press and Tribune*, May 10, 1860, 1; Blumenthal, *All the Powers*, 576.

86. N. C. McLean to Mrs. N. C. McLean, May 16, 1860, quoted in Elliff, "Views," 6.

87. Swett, "Memorial Address," 79; Pratt, *Personal Finances*, 109 (stating that Davis rented the third floor of the Tremont House for $300); see also the *Sun* (New York, NY), March 15, 1880, 1 (reporting that Davis expended about $700 during the convention and refused Lincoln's offer of reimbursement).

88. Halstead, *Caucuses of 1860*, 122, 132.

89. Leonard Swett to J. H. Drummond, May 27, 1860, in Wilson, *Intimate Memories*, 293–96; Nathan M. Knapp to AL, May 14, 1860, LP; AL to Richard M. Corwine, May 2, 1860, in Basler, *Collected Works*, 4:47; AL to Samuel Galloway, March 24, 1860, in Basler, *Collected Works*, 4:33–34; Goodwin, *Team of Rivals*, 244.

90. Fehrenbacher, *Prelude to Greatness*, 148–49.

91. Leonard Swett to J. H. Drummond, May 27, 1860, in Wilson, *Intimate Memories*, 294; Wakefield, *How Lincoln Became President*, 109; Kyle, *Abraham Lincoln*, 102; Blumenthal, *All the Powers*, 567. For the Ford County Republican Convention resolution naming Lincoln as its first choice for president, see the *Ford County Journal*, March 29, 1860, 2.

92. See DD to Richard Oglesby, April 15, 1860, quoted in Hickey, "Oglesby's Fence Rail Dealings," 6; Blumenthal, *All the Powers*, 568–69.

93. Duis, *Good Old Times*, 280; DD to AL, April 23, 1860, LP; DD to AL, May 5, 1860, LP; DD to Henry E. Dummer, February 20, 1860, in Pratt, *Concerning Mr. Lincoln*, 23; Hickey, "Oglesby's Fence Rail Dealings," 6–7; Kyle, *Abraham Lincoln*, 102.

94. Kyle, *Abraham Lincoln*, 108–9; Lamon, *Life*, 444–45.

95. Kyle, *Abraham Lincoln*, 109–11; Freehling, *Becoming Lincoln*, 244–45; Davis, "Origin," 273; "Remarks to Republican State Convention, Decatur, Illinois," May 9, 1860, in Basler, *Collected Works*, 4:48, annotation [1]; Lamon, *Life*, 445.

96. Kyle, *Abraham Lincoln*, 113–14; Palmer, *Personal Recollections*, 80–81.

97. Fehrenbacher, *Prelude to Greatness*, 154 ("Delegates talked a good deal about their 'second choice'"); Leonard Swett to J. H. Drummond, May 27, 1860, in Wilson, *Intimate Memories*, 294.

98. Leonard Swett to AL, May 25, 1860, LP.

99. Current, *History of Wisconsin*, 282.

100. *Proceedings of the First Three Republican National Conventions*, 149, 152, 153. The proceedings incorrectly recites that Senator Wade received twelve votes from Kentucky on the first ballot. Actually, he received two votes. See Halstead, *Caucuses of 1860*, 146. Kentucky had twelve electoral votes, which translated into twenty-four convention votes. But Kentucky only had twenty-three delegates at the convention and never cast more than twenty-three votes (146–48).

101. John D. Defrees to James Harlan, August 1859, quoted in Herriott, "Republican Presidential Preliminaries," 246–48.

102. *New-York Daily Tribune*, May 15, 1860, 5.

103. Luthin, "Indiana," 386–87.

104. *Indianapolis Daily Journal*, April 19, 1860, quoted in Luthin, "Indiana," 389. The editorial also refuted the claim that it would be better to suffer defeat with Seward or Chase than to win with McLean or Lincoln.

105. Good, *Lincoln for President*, 96.

106. Bailey, "Caleb Blood Smith," 225–26. Indiana went to the Democrats in the four preceding presidential elections (226).

107. Burlingame, *Abraham Lincoln*, 1:608; Swett, "Memorial Address," 76; "David Davis," on stationery of the "Office of George Perrin Davis, Over First National Bank, Cor[ner] Main and Washington Sts Bloomington, Ill. dated 19-," folder F-11, box 26, Miscellaneous Papers, DDFP.

108. Bailey, "Caleb Blood Smith," 220, 222.

109. "Speech at Rockport, Indiana," October 30, 1844, in Basler, *Collected Works*, 1:341–42, annotation [1]; Lighty, "Lincoln's Forgotten Visit"; "Speech at Indianapolis, Indiana," September 19, 1859, in Basler, *Collected Works*, 3:463.

110. Good, *Lincoln for President*, 96.

111. Blumenthal, *All the Powers*, 582; Leonard Swett to Josiah H. Drummond, May 27, 1860, in Wilson, *Intimate Memories*, 294.

112. Luthin, *First Lincoln Campaign*, 139.

113. AL to Lyman Trumbull, April 29, 1860, in Basler, *Collected Works*, 4:46; N. C. McLean to Mrs. N. C. McLean, May 16, 1860, quoted in Elliff, "Views," 7; *Proceedings of the First Three Republican National Conventions*, 149.

114. Blumenthal, *All the Powers*, 579–81; Emery, "Iowa Germans," 425–26; Koerner, *Memoirs*, 2:88–89.

115. Leonard Swett, "To the Editor of the *Tribune*," July 13, 1878, in *Chicago Daily Tribune*, July 14, 1878, 5; *Proceedings of the First Three Republican National Conventions*, 148.

116. Wilson, *Intimate Memories*, 194.

117. Koerner, *Memoirs*, 2:88–89. Allan Nevins correctly concluded that "the precise moment when a majority of Indiana delegates (many of whom had at first leaned toward Bates) decided to vote for Lincoln cannot be determined" (*Emergence of Lincoln*, 2:256). See also *Proceedings of the First Three Republican National Conventions*, 149, 152, 153.

118. Monaghan, *Man Who Elected Lincoln*, 162; Blumenthal, *All the Powers*, 583; see also Woldman, *Lawyer Lincoln*, 279.

119. Charles Ray to AL, May 14, 1860, LP.

120. Caleb B. Smith to DD, January 13, 1861, quoted in Ecelbarger, *Great Comeback*, 197; Donald, *Lincoln*, 249.

121. Hickin, "John C. Underwood," 165–66; Lowe, "Republican Party," 275.

122. Abbott, *For Free Press*, 7; Hickin, "John C. Underwood," 158, 160–61; John C. Underwood to Lyman Trumbull, December 6, 1858, LP.

123. Hickin, "John C. Underwood," 158; Shifflett, "John C. Underwood," 13.

124. John C. Underwood to Lyman Trumbull, December 6, 1858, LP; Lyman Trumbull to AL, December 7, 1858, LP; Lowe, "Republican Party," 275.

125. Lamon, *Recollections*, xxiii; Lamon House, Vermilion County Museum Society, gravesite of Angelina Turner Lamon, Evergreen Memorial Cemetery, Bloomington, IL, http://lamonhouse.org/Lamon_Tree/Ang_Lamon.html; King, *Lincoln's Manager*, 136.

126. *Wheeling (VA) Daily Intelligencer*, May 19, 1860, 2.

127. Miller and Maxwell, *West Virginia*, 13; Lowe, "Republican Party," 276.

128. Horace Greeley to James S. Pike, May 21, 1861, in Pike, *First Blows*, 520 ("We had to rain red-hot bolts on them, however, to keep the majority from going for Seward, who got eight votes here as it was").

129. *Daily Intelligencer*, May 19, 1860, 2.

130. Halstead, *Caucuses of 1860*, 142; Blumenthal, *All the Powers*, 592; Lowe, "Republican Party," 276; *Proceedings of the First Three Republican National Conventions*, 149, 152, 153.

131. *Daily Intelligencer*, May 19, 1860, 2; *Daily Intelligencer*, May 21, 1860, 2.

132. American Presidency Project, Statistics, Election Year 1860, Virginia, https://www.presidency.ucsb.edu/statistics/elections/1860.

133. Reavis, *Life*, 7, 10; *Memorials*, 3–8; Smith, "'Gentlemen,'" 434.

134. "Kentucky Republican State Convention," *Pittsburgh Gazette*, November 21, 1859, 1; Clay, *Life*, 1:249; Harrison, *Lincoln of Kentucky*, 114.

135. Clay, *Life*, 1:241–43, 248; Cassius Clay to William Seward, May 21, 1860, quoted in Burlingame, *Abraham Lincoln*, 1:622.

136. *Proceedings of the First Three Republican National Conventions*, 149. The proceedings incorrectly indicate that Wade received twelve Kentucky votes on the first ballot.

137. Thurlow Weed to William Seward, May 20, 1860, in Van Deusen, "Thurlow Weed's Analysis," 104.

138. *Proceedings of the First Three Republican National Conventions*, 149, 152, 153.

139. Niven, *Gideon Wells*, 296.

140. Swett, "Memorial Address," 79; Wakefield, *How Lincoln Became President*, 16, 112; Eckley, *Lincoln's Forgotten Friend*, 54, 71; Niven, *Gideon Welles*, 296–97; DD and Leonard Swett to AL, November 22, 1860, LP; file for George W. Lawrence, Record Group 59, M650, Applications and Recommendations during the Administrations of Abraham Lincoln and Andrew Johnson 1861–1869, State Department Records, National Archives, Washington, DC.

141. Luthin, *First Lincoln Campaign*, 144.

142. *Proceedings of the First Three Republican National Conventions*, 149.

143. Soodalter, "Stumping"; Corning, *Amos Tuck*, 83.

144. Niven, *Gideon Welles*, 296–97.

145. Miller, *States at War*, 369, 428n49; Corning, *Amos Tuck*, 84.

146. See Burlingame, *Abraham Lincoln*, 1:593, 617–18.

147. *Proceedings of the First Three Republican National Conventions*, 149, 152; Corning, *Amos Tuck*, 84.

148. Thurlow Weed to William Seward, May 20, 1860, in Van Deusen, "Thurlow Weed's Analysis," 103; *Proceedings of the First Three Republican National Conventions*, 152, 153.

149. Wendt, "*Swift Walker*," 13–14, 437.

150. Welles, *Lincoln and Seward*, 22, 36, 27.

151. Goodwin, *Team of Rivals*, 233; Niven, *Gideon Welles*, 291, 296–97; *Proceedings of the First Three Republican National Conventions*, 149, 152, 153.

152. Crockett, *Vermont*, 485–86; Swett, "Memorial Address," 79; Wendt, "*Swift Walker*," 437. Davis may also have assigned Parks to visit the Indiana contingent because Parks

graduated from Indiana University, where his father was a professor. Wylie, *Indiana University*, 104; *Proceedings of the First Three Republican National Conventions*, 149, 152, 153.

153. Huston, "Threat of Radicalism," 90–94, quote at 94.

154. Mark W. Delahay to AL, April 7, 1860, LP; Hawkins Taylor to AL, April 15, 1860, LP; Lyman Trumbull to AL, April 24, 1860, LP.

155. *Chicago Press and Tribune*, April 6, 1860, 1.

156. Huston, "Threat of Radicalism," 90; Thurlow Weed to William Seward, May 20, 1860, in Van Deusen, "Thurlow Weed's Analysis," 103.

157. *Proceedings of the First Three Republican National Conventions*, 149, 152, 153. Rhode Island's first ballot votes were splintered between McLean (five), Bates (one), Chase (one), and John M. Reed [*sic*] of Pennsylvania (one). The second ballot totals were Lincoln (three), Chase (three), and McLean (two). On the third ballot, Lincoln received five votes, and Chase, Seward, and McLean received one vote each.

158. Harrington, *Fighting Politician*, 48. Banks was a Democrat and a Know-Nothing before becoming a Republican. William Schouler to AL, May 21, 1860, annotation [2], LP.

159. Miller, *States at War*, 250–51.

160. "The Inside Facts of Lincoln's Nomination," letter from Thomas H. Dudley to the *Century Illustrated Magazine*, July 1890, 477–78.

161. Nevins, *Emergence of Lincoln*, 2:258n67.

162. Pearson, *Life*, 1:122–23. Andrew was elected governor in November 1860.

163. Browning, *Diary*, 1:406–7, entry for May 15, 1860; Jesse Dubois to AL, May 13, 1860, LP; William Butler to AL, May 16, 1860, LP.

164. DD to Julius Rockwell, February 18, 1858, DDFP; DD to Julius Rockwell, February 18, 1858 (second letter dated February 18, 1858), DDFP; Sarah Davis to Frances Mary Williams, January 17, 1844, DDFP.

165. John Z. Goodrich to AL, March 16, 1865, LP; King, *Lincoln's Manager*, 136; John Z. Goodrich to DD, November 28, 1860, n1, LP.

166. Edward L. Pierce to William Herndon, September 15, 1889, in Wilson and Davis, *Herndon's Informants*, 677. Pierce lived in Chicago from January 1856 to July 1857.

167. *Proceedings of the First Three Republican National Conventions*, 149, 152, 153.

168. Ryan, *Lincoln and Ohio*, 118–21; Edwin A. Parrott to AL, March 5, 1860, LP.

169. Samuel Galloway to AL, March 15, 1860, LP.

170. Jesse K. Dubois to AL, May 13, 1860, LP.

171. *Cleveland Morning Leader*, May 17, 1860, 4; *Maine Union and Journal*, May 18, 1860, 2.

172. William T. Bascom to AL, September 1, 1859, LP; William T. Bascom to AL, September 9, 1859, LP ("There is no man in the Union who under the circumstances can do so much good in Central & Southern Ohio as you can, and more especially to follow Douglas"); Peter Zinn to AL, September 2, 1859, LP.

173. Samuel Galloway to AL, October 13, 1859, LP ("You have secured a host of friends among Republicans"); Edwin A. Parrott to AL, March 5, 1860, LP.

174. Ryan, *Lincoln and Ohio*, 72–74.

175. "Speech at Cincinnati, Ohio," September 17, 1859, in Basler, *Collected Works*, 3:460.

176. Republican Party of Ohio to AL, December 7, 1859, LP; Samuel Galloway to AL, October 13, 1859, LP ("We all think that your visit aided us—and we are grateful for your services"); William T. Bascom to AL, October 13, 1859, LP ("We feel that some of the credit of this result is due to you, and in behalf of our Republican friends I again return you our most grateful thanks").

177. Republican Party of Ohio to AL, December 7, 1859, LP; William Dennison Jr. to Lyman Trumbull, July 21, 1859, LP. The volume was published with the title *Political Debates between Hon. Abraham Lincoln and Hon. Stephen A. Douglas, in the Celebrated Campaign of 1858, in Illinois* (Columbus: Follett, Foster and Company, 1860).

178. *Proceedings of the First Three Republican National Conventions*, 149, 152, 153. For a breakdown of how each Ohio delegate voted on each of the three ballots, see Smith, *History*, 1:116–19.

179. Monaghan, *Man Who Elected Lincoln*, 47; Wendt, *"Swift Walker,"* 419, 437.

180. Jesse K. Dubois to AL, May 13, 1860, LP; William Butler to AL, May 16, 1860, LP.

181. Blumenthal, *All the Powers*, 590.

182. William M. Dickson to AL, May 21, 1860, LP; Robert Hosea to Salmon P. Chase, May 18, 1860, quoted in Luthin, "Indiana," 395.

183. *Chicago Daily Tribune*, April 21, 1895, 47. Medill made the same claim to the *Saturday Evening Post* four years later. *Saturday Evening Post*, August 5, 1899, 85.

184. Ecelbarger, *Great Comeback*, 230n22.

185. William Butler to AL, May 16, 1860, LP.

186. Ecelbarger, *Great Comeback*, 229–30, and n22; *Proceedings of the First Three Republican National Conventions*, 149, 152, 153.

187. Halstead, *Caucuses of 1860*, 149; McClure, *Abraham Lincoln*, 38.

188. Carpenter, "How Lincoln Was Nominated," 858.

189. Davis, *How Abraham Lincoln Became President*, 77–78; Palmer, *Personal Recollections*, 54, 81; Achorn, *Lincoln Miracle*, 264–65.

190. Davis, *How Abraham Lincoln Became President*, 78; Palmer, *Personal Recollections*, 81.

191. Davis, *How Abraham Lincoln Became President*, 78, 81; Palmer, *Personal Recollections*, 81.

192. Maynard, "Dudley," 101–6; Whittlesey, "William Lewis Dayton," 799; Dudley, "Inside Facts," 477–79; *Maine Union and Journal*, May 18, 1860, 2; *Proceedings of the First Three Republican National Conventions*, 149, 153.

193. *Indianapolis Journal*, October 8, 1894, 1–2; Ecelbarger, *Great Comeback*, 200–201.

194. *North American* (Philadelphia), May 11, 1860, quoted in Pflug, "Pennsylvania Politics," 113.

195. *Bradford (PA) Reporter*, March 29, 1860, 2.

196. Goodwin, *Team of Rivals*, 216–17.

197. Thurlow Weed to William Seward, May 20, 1860, in Van Deusen, "Thurlow Weed's Analysis," 103–4. The "confidential letter" would have invested authority in Cummings to withdraw Cameron's name if the circumstances required.

198. "People's State Convention," *Bradford Reporter*, March 1, 1860, 2.

199. "People's State Convention," *Bradford Reporter*, March 1, 1860, 2, emphasis added.

200. "People's State Convention," *Bradford Reporter*, March 1, 1860, 2; "The Election of Delegates to Chicago," *Potter (PA) Journal*, March 22, 1860, 2; *Proceedings of the First Three Republican National Conventions*, 149.

201. Maynard, "Dudley," 103; Blumenthal, *All the Powers*, 589. Maynard and Blumenthal state that Dudley suggested the idea of a Committee of Twelve to Judd.

202. Carpenter, "How Lincoln Was Nominated," 855; Stewart, "Great Winnebago Chieftain," 21.

203. Blumenthal, *All the Powers*, 591.

204. Herman Kreismann to E. B. Washburne, May 16, 1860, cited in Burlingame, *Abraham Lincoln*, unedited manuscript by chapters, vol. 1, chap. 15, p. 1679, n158, https://www.knox.edu/academics/research-and-creative-work/lincoln-studies-center/burlingame-abraham-lincoln-a-life.

205. McClure, *Old Time Notes*, 1:406; *Maine Union and Journal*, May 18, 1860, 2 (reporting as of the evening of May 15).

206. Carpenter, "How Lincoln Was Nominated," 855; McClure, *Old Time Notes*, 1:406. McClure said that Lincoln beat Bates by about six votes. See also Stewart, "Great Winnebago Chieftain," 25–26.

207. Blumenthal, *All the Powers*, 591.

208. Koerner, *Memoirs*, 2:87–89.

209. Carpenter, "How Lincoln Was Nominated," 856–57.

210. Swett, "Memorial Address," 79; Hearn, *Lincoln*, 12; Joseph Casey to Leonard Swett, November 27, 1860, LP.

211. Leonard Swett to AL, November 30, 1860, LP.

212. Carpenter, "How Lincoln Was Nominated," 854–55.

213. Carpenter, "How Lincoln Was Nominated," 857.

214. McClure, *Abraham Lincoln*, 153.

215. Pratt, "David Davis," 167.

216. Jesse W. Fell to AL, January 2, 1861, LP.

217. Whitney, *Life on the Circuit*, 100–101 and n7. According to Whitney, a fourth component of the deal required that the Illinois Republican State Committee endorse Cameron for the cabinet.

218. Achorn, *Lincoln Miracle*, 305.

219. "Endorsement on the Margin of the *Missouri Democrat*," May 17, 1860, in Basler, *Collected Works*, 4:50. In July Lincoln gave a similar written instruction to John Nicolay when he sent his secretary to meet with Indiana Know-Nothing leader Richard Thompson. The instruction was "but commit me to nothing" ("Instructions for John G. Nicolay," July 16, 1860, in Basler, *Collected Works*, 4:83).

220. Herndon and Weik, *Herndon's Life of Lincoln*, 374.

221. See Fehrenbacher and Fehrenbacher, *Recollected Words*, 490 (stating that Whitney tended "to remember past events with mingled accuracy and inaccuracy"); Lehrman, *Lincoln at Peoria*, 62 ("Whitney . . . sometimes exaggerated his own importance and embellished his accounts of events"); "Lincoln's Lost Speech," 5 ("It is difficult to draw any other conclusion than that the Whitney version of Lincoln's 'Lost Speech' is so

largely a product of the imagination that it is entirely unreliable, in substance as well as phraseology").

222. Whitney, *Lincoln the Citizen*, 289.

223. Charles H. Ray to AL, May 14, 1860, LP.

224. Whitney, *Lincoln the Citizen*, 289. Whitney says Lincoln telegraphed back, "I authorize no bargains and will be bound by none" and later sent the handwritten instruction to make no contracts that bound him.

225. King, *Lincoln's Manager*, 140; Donald, *Lincoln*, 249–50; Freehling, *Becoming Lincoln*, 255 ("In fact, Davis bound only himself. He promised only to lobby Lincoln on Cameron's behalf").

226. DD to Thomas Dudley, September 1, 1860, quoted in Burlingame, *Abraham Lincoln*, 1:610; Leonard Swett to J. H. Drummond, May 27, 1860, in Wilson, *Intimate Memories*, 296; Leonard Swett to Thurlow Weed, November 26, 1860, in Weed, *Life*, 2:301.

227. Leonard Swett to AL, November 30, 1860, LP.

228. Herndon and Weik, *Herndon's Lincoln*, 284; Weed, *Life*, 1:612.

229. AL to Simon Cameron, December 31, 1860, in Basler, *Collected Works*, 4:168; Pratt, "Simon Cameron's Fight," 6.

230. "Memorandum on the Charges against Simon Cameron," December 31, 1860, in Basler, *Collected Works*, 4:165; "Memorandum on the Appointment of Simon Cameron," December 31, 1860, in Basler, *Collected Works*, 4:166–67.

231. McClure, *Abraham Lincoln*, 154–55; AL to Simon Cameron, January 3, 1861, in Basler, *Collected Works*, 4:169–70; Pratt, "Simon Cameron's Fight," 6–7.

232. Pratt, "Simon Cameron's Fight," 8, 11.

233. The author of *The Life of Schuyler Colfax* claims that after the nomination, Lincoln complained to some unidentified person that "they have gambled on me all around ... bought and sold me a hundred times. I cannot begin to fill the pledges made in my name" (Hollister, *Life*, 147n1).

234. Joseph Casey to Simon Cameron, May 24, 1860, quoted in Blumenthal, *All the Powers*, 591.

235. Joseph Casey to Leonard Swett, November 27, 1860, LP.

236. *Chicago Tribune*, June 2, 1888, 9. If, as argued, Medill made up the story about obtaining Pennsylvania's vote, it would not have been the first time that he told a Lincoln campaign story that contained "scarcely a word of truth" (Fehrenbacher, *Prelude to Greatness*, 124).

237. Monaghan, *Man Who Elected Lincoln*, 162–63 (providing Medill's description of how Ray obtained Indiana's vote).

238. *Chicago Tribune*, June 2, 1888, 9; *Chicago Tribune*, February 7, 1909, H6.

239. Burlingame, *Abraham Lincoln*, 1:611; McCash, *Jekyll Island*, 63–64; DD to Sarah Davis, February 28, 1868, DDFP; Wilkie, *Sketches and Notices*, 42–44. Dexter handled legal matters with Swett. *Chicago Daily Tribune*, January 15, 1874, 2.

240. Memorandum by Kellogg Fairbank, April 7, 1926, enclosed in Janet Fairbank to Albert J. Beveridge, April 9, 1926, quoted in Burlingame, *Abraham Lincoln*, 1:611. If true, these statements by Davis certainly support Edward Achorn's view that Davis lied to get delegate votes.

241. Nathaniel Fairbank's son, Kellogg Fairbank, was born on February 21, 1869. See *Seventh Report*, 70. David Davis died on June 26, 1886.

242. *Proceedings of the First Three Republican National Conventions*, 149, 152, 153.

243. Edward L. Pierce to William Herndon, September 15, 1889, in Wilson and Davis, *Herndon's Informants*, 677.

244. Ecelbarger, *Great Comeback*, 212.

245. Koerner, *Memoirs*, 2:114.

246. Holtzer, *Lincoln President Elect*, 146; AL to Lyman Trumbull, January 7, 1861, in Basler, *Collected Works*, 4:171 ("[Cameron] is more amply recommended for a place in the cabinet, than any other man").

247. Pratt, *Concerning Mr. Lincoln*, 97n11.

248. Van Deusen, *Thurlow Weed*, 87, 111, 160–62, 166; Weed, *Life*, 1:481–82, 575–78; Watson, "Thurlow Weed," 417.

249. Van Deusen, *Thurlow Weed*, 87.

250. Weed, *Life*, 1:452–53.

251. Donald, *Lincoln's Herndon*, 77 ("There is little reason to believe that at this [1855 senate race] or any other time Lincoln placed the direction of his political career in another man's hands").

252. Tanner, *"The Lobby,"* 408; Weed, *Life*, 2:262.

253. William Seward to Thurlow Weed, March 15, 1860, in Weed, *Life*, 2:261.

254. DD to AL, April 23, 1860, LP; DD to AL, May 5, 1860, LP.

255. Van Deusen, *Thurlow Weed*, 246–47; "Petition Concerning the Gridiron Bills," *New York Herald*, April 11, 1860, 10.

256. Weed, *Life*, 1:476–78.

257. Schurz, *Reminiscences*, 2:177; William Butler to AL, May 15, 1860, LP.

258. Mrs. Henry S. Lane to Alexander Kelly McClure, September 16, 1891, quoted in McClure, *Abraham Lincoln*, 30–31, n.

259. Halstead, *Caucuses of 1860*, 142–43; Taylor, *William Henry Seward*, 6 ("Six months [before the convention, Weed] had contributed funds to the New Hampshire Republicans for use in local elections in the Granite State").

260. Halstead, *Caucuses of 1860*, 140.

261. Schurz, *Reminiscences*, 2:176; Halstead, *Caucuses of 1860*, 140.

262. Gammie, "Pugilists," 267, 269, 271, 294; Rhodes, *History*, 2:462.

263. Jesse Fell to AL, January 2, 1861, LP (noting Davis's "incorruptible integrity"); Freehling, *Becoming Lincoln*, 247 (describing Davis as an "incorruptible judge").

264. William Seward to Francis Seward, January 12, 1831, quoted in Seward and Seward, *William H. Seward*, 1:166; Jesse Fell to AL, January 2, 1861, LP.

265. Watson, "Thurlow Weed," 415 ("Weed would never have introduced innovation in the administration of government as did Seward, but he could make a platform of innovation palatable to the mass of voters").

266. "Mass Meeting at Mackinaw," *Chicago Press and Tribune*, August 1, 1860, 2; King, *Lincoln's Manager*, 5, 207–8; Browning, *Diary*, 1:616, entry for January 19, 1863.

267. Van Deusen, *Thurlow Weed*, 298–300; Thurlow Weed to Preston King, December 10, 1860, in Weed, *Life*, 2:309.

268. Van Deusen, "Thurlow Weed's Analysis," 102.

269. Rhodes, *History*, 2:462.

Chapter 4. Davis and the 1860 General Election

1. *Chicago Daily Tribune*, July 15, 1878, 3; King, *Lincoln's Manager*, 143. During the campaign Seward spoke for Lincoln in fifteen states. Achorn, *Lincoln Miracle*, 417.

2. Thurlow Weed to Lincoln Club of New York, February 12, 1879, quoted in Weed, *Life*, 2:296; *Chicago Daily Tribune*, July 15, 1878, 3.

3. DD to AL, May 23, 1860, LP; Leonard Swett to AL, May 25, 1860, LP; *Chicago Daily Tribune*, July 15, 1878, 3.

4. DD to AL, May 23, 1860, LP.

5. DD to AL, May 24, 1860, LP; AL to DD, May 26, 1860, in Basler, *Collected Works, First Supplement*, 54; King, *Lincoln's Manager*, 144–45.

6. Weed, *Life*, 1:602–3, 2:296.

7. AL to DD, May 26, 1860, in Basler, *Collected Works, First Supplement*, 54.

8. AL to Lyman Trumbull, June 5, 1860, in Basler, *Collected Works*, 4:71; Norman B. Judd to AL, May 25, 1860, LP.

9. American Presidency Project, Statistics, Election Year 1856, https://www.presidency.ucsb.edu/statistics/elections/1856; Gienapp, *Origins*, 414.

10. AL to Simeon Francis, August 4, 1860, in Basler, *Collected Works*, 4:90; see also *Ford County Journal* (IL), July 5, 1860, 2. Minnesota became a state on May 11, 1858.

11. American Presidency Project, Statistics, Election Year 1856, Pennsylvania, https://www.presidency.ucsb.edu/statistics/elections/1856.

12. Wolstoncraft, "Western Pennsylvania," 27.

13. Leonard Swett to Thurlow Weed, July 4, 1860, in Weed, *Life*, 2:298–99; see also Alexander McClure to AL, June 16, 1860, LP (suggesting a visit by Davis and Swett). But see Alexander McClure to AL, July 2, 1860, LP (suggesting that Davis and Swett not come to Pennsylvania).

14. Thurlow Weed to Leonard Swett, July 11, 1860, LP.

15. James E. Harvey to AL, June 5, 1860, LP; AL to Leonard Swett, July 16, 1860, in Basler, *Collected Works*, 4:84; Joseph Medill to AL, July 29, 1860, LP; Leonard Swett to AL, July 1860, LP (enclosing letters Swett received from Joseph Casey and James O. Putnam).

16. Joseph Medill to AL, July 29, 1860, LP.

17. AL to Leonard Swett, July 16, 1860, in Basler, *Collected Works*, 4:84; Leonard Swett to AL, July 18, 1860, LP.

18. Leonard Swett to William H. Herndon, January 17, 1866, in Wilson and Davis, *Herndon's Informants*, 163.

19. DD to AL, July 25, 1860, LP; Leonard Swett to Thurlow Weed, July 4, 1860, in Weed, *Life*, 2:298–99; DD to AL, July 24, 1860, LP.

20. Leonard Swett to AL, July 1860, LP; Leonard Swett to AL, August 17, 1860, LP; Joseph Medill to AL, July 5, 1860, LP (suggesting that "Yates and Swett make a pilgrimage" to the Ninth Congressional District because Republicans there felt neglected, and no speaker from the North would be suitable to send there).

21. DD to AL, July 25, 1860, LP; "Statement of William D. Kelley," in Rice, *Reminiscences*, 262–63; DD to AL, July 24, 1860, LP.

22. DD to AL, August 5, 1860, LP.

23. D. F. Williams to Simon Cameron, June 14, 1858, quoted in Collins, "Democrats' Loss," 521.

24. *Daily Pittsburgh Gazette*, November 21, 1860, 2.

25. Russell Errett to AL, November 21, 1860, LP.

26. Lincoln asked Davis to visit Simon Cameron and Joseph Casey in Harrisburg. See AL to Whom it may concern, August 2, 1860, in Basler, *Collected Works, First Supplement*, 58; DD to AL, August 5, 1860, LP.

27. Pitkin, "Western Republicans," 401, 406–7; *Cleveland Morning Leader*, October 6, 1860, 2; *Buchanan County Guardian* (IA), October 9, 1860, 3.

28. DD to AL, August 5, 1860, LP.

29. Simon Cameron to AL, August 1, 1860, LP.

30. Alexander McClure to AL, June 16, 1860, LP; William M. Reynolds to AL, July 25, 1860, LP.

31. *Daily Pittsburgh Gazette*, February 24, 1860, 2; Pflug, "Pennsylvania Politics," 90.

32. *Lancaster (PA) Intelligencer*, September 25, 1860, 1.

33. AL to G. Yoke Tams, September 22, 1860, in Basler, *Collected Works*, 4:119.

34. "Fragments of a Tariff Discussion," December 1, 1847?, in Basler, *Collected Works*, 1:407–16 and annotations.

35. See, for example, "Speech at Whig Barbecue at Jacksonville, Illinois," October 6, 1843, in Basler, *Collected Works*, 1:329–30; "Speech at Sugar Creek, Illinois," March 1, 1844, in Basler, *Collected Works*, 1:334; "Speech at Rockport, Indiana," October 30, 1844, in Basler, *Collected Works*, 1:341–42; see also "Speech at Lacon, Illinois," July 18, 1846, in Basler, *Collected Works*, 1:381–82; DD to AL, August 5, 1860, LP.

36. Alexander McClure to AL, June 16, 1860, LP.

37. DD to Julius Rockwell, May 14, 1844, DDFP; DD to Julius Rockwell, December 17, 1845, DDFP; DD to Sarah Davis, February 20, 1848, DDFP.

38. Simon Cameron to AL, August 1, 1860, LP; Simon Cameron to DD, October 24, 1860, LP; Cameron offered Davis more money if needed.

39. DD to AL, September 3, 1860, LP.

40. DD to Thurlow Weed, September 3, 1860, Thurlow Weed Papers, River Campus Libraries, University of Rochester, Rochester, NY; Russell Errett to DD, August 27, 1860, LP.

41. John P. Sanderson to DD, August 27, 1860, LP.

42. DD to AL, August 5, 1860, LP; Simon Cameron to AL, August 29, 1860, LP; DD to AL, September 10, 1860, LP.

43. *Daily Pittsburgh Gazette*, September 7, 1860, 2; see also *Raftsman's Journal* (PA), October 31, 1860, 2 (presenting the same defense); *Pennsylvania Daily Telegraph*, September 29, 1860, 1 (reporting Alexander McClure's speech responding to Henry Foster's attack on Lincoln).

44. *Daily Pittsburgh Gazette*, September 7, 1860, 2. The article also defended Hannibal Hamlin's position on the tariff.

45. DD to AL, August 5, 1860, LP.

46. Kahan, *Amiable Scoundrel*, 144.

47. Thurlow Weed to AL, August 13, 1860, LP.

48. DD to AL, August 5, 1860, LP; *Bradford (PA) Reporter*, August 9, 1860, 2; *Carlisle (PA) Herald*, August 10, 1860, 2; DD to AL, October 31, 1860, LP.

49. Alexander McClure to AL, June 16, 1860, LP; Alexander McClure to AL, July 7, 1860, LP.

50. McClure, *Old Time Notes*, 1:409–10; Russell, "A. K. McClure," 340–41.

51. Thurlow Weed to DD, September 25, 1860, LP.

52. Simon Cameron to A. K. McClure, August 1, 1860, https://valley.lib.virginia.edu/papers/F8021; DD to AL, August 5, 1860, LP; John Sanderson to DD, August 27, 1860, LP.

53. *New York Times*, October 13, 1860, 4 (reporting John M. Butler's election to Congress).

54. Kawaguchi, "Diverging Political Affiliations," 14; Paul Jagode to John G. Nicolay, March 31, 1864, LP.

55. *New York Times*, October 12, 1860, 3; "Riche, George Inman," 244.

56. Stillé, *Memorial*, 157.

57. "The People's Convention," *Philadelphia Press*, March 30, 1860, 2; *Philadelphia Press*, January 7, 1861, 1; *North American and United States Gazette* (Philadelphia), February 22, 1861, 1, https://www.loc.gov/exhibits/lincoln/interactives/journey-of-the-president-elect/feb_11/pdf/504i.pdf.

58. John Sanderson to DD, August 27, 1860, LP (listing all committee members).

59. *North Branch (PA) Democrat*, March 14, 1866, 2.

60. See, for example, King, *Digest*.

61. *Alleghanian* (PA), August 9, 1860, 2.

62. *Daily Patriot and Union* (PA), October 19, 1860, 2.

63. Pennsylvania House of Representatives, James Freeborn, Biography.

64. Pennsylvania House of Representatives, William Elliott, Biography. E. G. Waterhouse and Edwin Booth rounded out the nine new Philadelphia committee members. John Sanderson to DD, August 27, 1860, LP.

65. John Sanderson to DD, August 27, 1860, LP.

66. The other interior convention delegates were Andrew Reeder, Joseph Casey, Jacob Haldeman, S. Newton Pettis, Charles Albright, and J. Bowman Bell. *Proceedings of the First Three Republican National Conventions*, 171–72.

67. DD to Sarah Davis, March 7, 1848, DDFP; William Walker to DD, May 7, 1857, DDFP; Lucy Adam Walker to William Perrin Walker, June 2 and June 4, 1840, DDFP.

68. John Sanderson to DD, August 27, 1860, LP.

69. AL to Whom it may concern, August 2, 1860, in Basler, *Collected Works, First Supplement*, 58.

70. Alexander McClure to AL, August 11, 1860, LP.

71. McClure, *Abraham Lincoln*, 46.

72. AL to Whom it may concern, August 2, 1860, in Basler, *Collected Works, First Supplement*, 58.

73. McClure, *Abraham Lincoln*, 46; Alexander McClure to AL, August 27, 1860, LP.

74. Alexander McClure to AL, August 21, 1860, LP; Alexander McClure to AL, August 27, 1860, LP. It may be that recalling events thirty years later, McClure incorrectly related that all the precincts were covered at the time of Davis's visit.

75. McClure, *Old Time Notes*, 1:411.

76. See Alexander McClure to AL, August 11, 1860, LP; Alexander McClure to AL, September 24, 1860, LP; Alexander McClure to AL, October 3, 1860, LP; see also Myers, "Influence," 247.

77. Alexander McClure to AL, September 27, 1860, LP.

78. Alexander McClure to AL, June 16, 1860, LP.

79. McClure, *Old Time Notes*, 1:411.

80. Myers, "Influence," 247 (Clay, Curtin, Cameron, Corwin, and Wade); McClure, *Old Time Notes*, 1:418 (Schurz); Baker, *Works*, 4:111 (Seward); *Alleghanian* (PA), September 20, 1860, 2 (Seward); *Daily Pittsburgh Gazette*, September 28, 1860, 2 (Corwin, Wade, Campbell, Caldwell, and Armour); *Bedford (PA) Gazette*, September 28, 1860, 1 (announcing Carl Schurz's Harrisburg speech in less than flattering terms); Alexander McClure to AL, October 3, 1860 (Burlingame and Blair); Alexander McClure to AL, August 11, 1860, LP (Hazelhurst and Ullman); *Jeffersonian* (PA), August 30, 1860, 2 (Giddings).

81. *Bedford (PA) Inquirer*, September 28, 1860, 2; *Daily Pittsburgh Gazette*, October 4, 1860, 2; *Jeffersonian* (PA), August 2, 1860, 2.

82. Alexander McClure to Simon Cameron, April 12, 1860, Cameron Papers, https://valley.lib.virginia.edu/papers/F8582.

83. See 1860 Presidential General Election Results—Pennsylvania, in *Dave Leip's Atlas*; Alexander McClure to AL, October 10, 1860, LP (advising that Curtin won by thirty thousand votes and predicting that Lincoln would carry the state by fifty thousand votes).

84. McClure, *Old Time Notes*, 1:410–11, 414, 417.

85. Russell Errett to Joseph Medill, July 24, 1860, LP; Simon Cameron to DD, October 24, 1860, LP.

86. McClure, *Abraham Lincoln*, 41–43; McClure, *Old Time Notes*, 1:419–20.

87. *New York Herald*, October 16, 1860, 6; *New York Herald*, October 2, 1860, 4.

88. *Daily Pittsburgh Gazette*, September 22, 1860, 2.

89. John Z. Goodrich to Henry Dawes, June 8, 1860, quoted in Luthin, "Pennsylvania," 77.

90. Joseph Casey to DD, July 31, 1860, quoted in Sarah Davis to DD, August 5, 1860, DDFP.

91. Alexander K. McClure to AL, August 1, 1860, LP; Alexander K. McClure to AL, August 21, 1860, LP.

92. DD to AL, August 12, 1860, LP.

93. Alexander K. McClure to AL, September 12, 1860, LP.

94. Alexander K. McClure to AL, August 11, 1860, LP.

95. Alexander K. McClure to AL, August 11, 21, 27, 1860, LP; Alexander K. McClure to AL, September 12, 24, 27, 1860, LP; Alexander K. McClure to AL, October 3, 10, 12, 19, 1860, LP; see also John P. Sanderson to DD, August 27, 1860, LP; Simon Cameron to DD, October 24, 1860, LP; Thomas Dudley to DD, September 17, 1860, LP; DD to AL,

August 24, 1860, LP; Russell Errett to DD, August 27, 1860, LP; Russell Errett to DD, September 11, 1860, LP; Edwin D. Morgan to DD, September 10, 1860, with a note from DD to AL, September 15, 1860, LP.

96. King, *Lincoln's Manager*, 5–8, 13; Steiner, *Life*, 40.

97. Holden, "Training," 420; Boynton, *History*, 250–51.

98. Sherman, *John Sherman's Recollections*, 1:177–79; Jenkins and Stewart, *Fighting*, 222–23; *Proceedings of the First Three Republican National Conventions*, 118, 160.

99. Winter Davis to DD, July 27, 1860, partially copied in Sarah Davis to DD, August 5, 1860, DDFP.

100. "Speech before the Electors of the Fourth Congressional District of Maryland, September 27, 1860," in Davis, *Speeches*, 186, 148.

101. Winter Davis to DD, June 28, 1860, LP; DD to AL, July 5, 1860, LP.

102. John T. Graham to AL, November 10, 1860, LP; Worthington G. Snethen to AL, October 31, 1860, LP; DD to AL, August 14, 1860, LP; Winter Davis to DD, July 27, 1860, quoted in Sarah Davis to DD, August 5, 1860, DDFP; "Speech before the Electors," 178–81.

103. Henry Winter Davis to DD, August 22, 1860, LP.

104. Henry Winter Davis to DD, August 22, 1860, LP. Sherman was appointed to fill Salmon P. Chase's seat in the Senate in March 1861.

105. Henry Winter Davis to DD, September 1860, LP; see also Sherman, *John Sherman's Recollections*, 1:201.

106. DD to AL, August 14, 1860, LP.

107. Henry Winter Davis to DD, September 1860, LP; Sherman, *John Sherman's Recollections*, 1:225.

108. Henry Winter Davis to DD, September 1860, LP; "Speech before the Electors," 147–86.

109. Henry Winter Davis to DD, October 1, 1860, LP.

110. "Speech before the Electors," 158, 163, 166–67, 171, 178–82.

111. Henry Winter Davis to DD, October 1, 1860, LP.

112. *New York Times*, September 28, 1860, 1; *New York Times*, September 29, 1860, 1 (publishing speech); *Lewistown (PA) Gazette*, October 4, 1860, 1; *Cleveland Morning Leader*, October 3, 1860, 3; *Muscatine (IA) Weekly Journal*, October 5, 1860, 2; *Daily Exchange* (Baltimore, MD), September 28, 1860, 1.

113. *Lewistown (PA) Gazette*, October 4, 1860, 1.

114. *Cleveland Morning Leader*, October 3, 1860, 3; *Philadelphia Press*, September 28, 1860, 2.

115. See, for example, *Jeffersonian* (PA), October 11, 1860, 1.

116. DD to AL, August 14, 1860, LP.

117. *New-York Daily Tribune*, May 30, 1860, 4 (listing subscriber and circulation figures for April 1860). The figures included the *Daily Tribune*, the *Semi-Weekly Tribune*, and the *Weekly Tribune*.

118. *New-York Daily Tribune*, July 4, 1860, 4; *New-York Daily Tribune*, July 27, 1860, 4; *New-York Daily Tribune*, May 19, 1860, 7 ("Mr. Lincoln's romantic personal history, his eloquence as an orator, and his firm personal integrity, give augury of a successful campaign—one of the 1840 stamp"); *New-York Daily Tribune*, July 16, 1860, 4; *New York Times*, July 17, 1860, 1.

119. DD to AL, August 18, 1860, LP.

120. "Know-Nothing Convention in Syracuse," *New York Times*, May 10, 1855, 4. In January 1859 Governor Edwin D. Morgan appointed Benjamin Welch Jr. commissary general of the New York State Militia. *New York Times*, January 13, 1859, 1.

121. Benjamin Welch Jr. to AL, August 17, 1860, LP; Benjamin Welch Jr. to AL, November 3, 1860, LP. It was important to visit Fogg because he did not always see eye to eye with Seward and Weed. See George G. Fogg to AL, February 5, 1861, LP.

122. DD to AL, August 14, 1860, LP.

123. Burlingame, *Abraham Lincoln*, 1:641.

124. DD to AL, August 18, 1860, LP; DD to Thurlow Weed, August 24, 1860, in Weed, *Life*, 2:300; American Presidency Project, Statistics, Election Year 1860, Rhode Island, https://www.presidency.ucsb.edu/statistics/elections/1860.

125. Starr Clark to Thurlow Weed, August 1, 1860, LP.

126. Leonard Swett to Thurlow Weed, July 4, 1860, in Weed, *Life*, 2:298–99.

127. Thomas Dudley to DD, August 24, 1860, LP.

128. Illinois State Republican Central Committee form letter, June 23, 1860, Jesse Fell Papers, Illinois History and Lincoln Collections, University of Illinois.

129. Illinois State Republican Central Committee form letter, June 23, 1860; Baringer, "Campaign Techniques," 248.

130. Leonard Swett to Thurlow Weed, July 4, 1860, in Weed, *Life*, 2:299.

131. Illinois State Republican Central Committee form letter, June 9, 1859, Fell Papers; Baringer, "Campaign Techniques," 204–5.

132. Pratt, *Personal Finances*, 105, quoting Ozias M. Hatch.

133. Norman B. Judd to AL, August 1, 1860, LP; DD to AL, June 5, 1860, LP.

134. Ezekiel Boyden to DD, September 10, 1860, LP.

135. *Chicago Press and Tribune*, September 28, 1860, 2.

136. Fraker, *Lincoln's Ladder*, 235; Neely, *Boundaries*, 63 ("To examine the papers of a nineteenth-century presidential candidate is to be left wondering where the money came from").

137. King, *Lincoln's Manager*, 149; DD to AL, June 5, 1860, LP; Pratt, *Personal Finances*, 110–11; *Sun* (New York, NY), March 15, 1880, 1; Swett, "Memorial Address," 79; Egerton, *Year of Meteors*, 182.

138. Weik, *Real Lincoln*, 283–85.

139. Browne, *Abraham Lincoln*, 2:468–69.

140. DD to AL, May 24, 1860, LP. After the June 1, 1860, state central committee meeting the members of the committee proceeded to the Lincolns' home for supper. Mary Lincoln to Amos Tuck, June 4, 1860, in Hickey and Lincoln, "Lincolniana," 208; DD to AL, July 5, 1860, LP; DD to AL, October 31, 1860, LP; DD to AL, October 5, 1860, LP.

141. Reid, *Ohio*, 1:727.

142. Norman B. Judd to Hon. R. Schenck, August 13, 1860, LP. Schenck came to Illinois. David L. Phillips to Jesse K. Dubois, October 29, 1860, LP.

143. *Chicago Press and Tribune*, August 15, 1860, 1; Robert Wilson to AL, October 16, 1860, LP.

144. Wabash County Illinois Republicans to AL, August 5, 1858, LP; J. H. McKee to AL, July 9, 1860, LP.

145. Leonard Swett to AL, July 1860, LP.

146. *Chicago Press and Tribune*, August 1, 1860, 4 (Fairfield, Centralia, Vandalia); *Illinois State Journal*, August 11, 1860, 2 (Fairfield); *Illinois State Journal*, August 4, 1860, 2 (Burnt Prairie); *Chicago Press and Tribune*, August 18, 1860, 4 (debate at Carmi); Page, *History*, 73.

147. *Chicago Press and Tribune*, August 8, 1860, 4 (Grayville, Mount Carmel, Albion, Olney); *Chicago Press and Tribune*, August 14, 1860, 2 (Mattoon); *Chicago Press and Tribune*, August 25, 1860, 2 (reporting that Swett's three-and-one-half-hour speech in Albion moved some listeners to tears).

148. Leonard Swett to AL, August 17, 1860, LP. Swett was a regular on the Illinois campaign trail. The *Illinois State Journal* listed his speaking "appointments" from October 15 through October 22 to include Galva (Henry County), Oquawka (Henderson County), Aledo (Mercer County), Monmouth (Warren County), Knoxville (Knox County), and Springfield (Sangamon County). *Illinois State Journal*, October 15, 1860, 3.

149. Burlingame, *Lincoln's Journalist*, 7.

150. DD to AL, August 3, 1858, LP.

151. Brush, "Political Career," 31–32; *Chicago Press and Tribune*, July 13, 1860, 2 (reporting that the state central committee was expending force in central and southern Illinois because "the people are beginning to think that Republicans are not all insurrectionists and cut-throats"); *Chicago Press and Tribune*, October 6, 1860, 2 (reprinting an article from the *Schuyler Citizen* [Rushville, IL]).

152. *Chicago Press and Tribune*, October 6, 1860, 2 (reprinting an article from the *Schuyler Citizen*).

153. Heinzel, "'To Protect,'" 382; *Illinois State Journal*, October 15, 1860, 3 (Lawrence, Marion, Christian, Woodford); *Illinois State Journal*, July 24, 1860, 2 (Jersey, Greene, Macoupin); *Illinois State Journal*, September 10, 1860, 2 (Morgan); *Illinois State Journal*, October 31, 1860, 3 (Sangamon); *Chicago Press and Tribune*, July 28, 1860, 4 (DeWitt, Ford, Iroquois, Champaign, Vermillion).

154. *New York Times*, September 19, 1860, 8; Heinzel, "'To Protect,'" 381–82; *Cong. Globe*, 36th Cong., 1st sess., 202–7 (speech of Hon. Owen Lovejoy, April 5, 1860).

155. Owen Lovejoy to Jesse Fell, July 21, 1860, quoted in Brush, "Political Career," 32 ("No one will doubt the wisdom of your councils hereafter in regard to my going to Egypt. I was as glad for you as for me").

156. *Ottawa (IL) Free Trader*, September 29, 1860, 2.

157. Cleveland, *Tribune Almanac*, 56.

158. Cleveland, *Tribune Almanac*, 56. Marion County gave Lincoln 858 votes, Douglas 1,715 votes, and 93 votes went to Bell and Breckinridge combined. In 1856 the vote totals for Marion County were 150 votes for Republican Frémont, 1,150 votes for Democrat Buchanan, and 413 votes for American (Know-Nothing) Fillmore. In 1860 Christian County gave Lincoln 968, Douglas 1,408, and Bell and Breckinridge combined 29 votes. In 1856 Christian County totals were 239 for Frémont, 884 for Buchanan, and 299 for Fillmore. In 1860 Greene County voted 979 for Lincoln, 2,173 for Douglas, and 71 for Bell and Breckinridge combined. In 1856 in Greene County Frémont received 245 votes, Buchanan 1,565, and 719 for Fillmore.

159. Cleveland, *Tribune Almanac*, 56. In 1856 White County gave the Democrats 55 percent of the vote to Fillmore's 44 percent. In 1860 Democrats received 66 percent of the vote.

160. *Illinois State Journal*, July 10, 1860, 3.

161. *Chicago Press and Tribune*, August 1, 1860, 2.

162. *Chicago Press and Tribune*, August 1, 1860, 2.

163. *Chicago Press and Tribune*, August 3, 1860, 2.

164. *Chicago Press and Tribune*, September 10, 1860, 2.

165. *Illinois State Journal*, August 9, 1860, 2; Angle, *Here I Have Lived*, 246–48.

166. DD to AL, July 24, 1860, LP.

167. *Illinois State Journal*, August 27, 1860, 2; *Chicago Press and Tribune*, August 7, 1860, 1; Fehrenbacher, *Chicago Giant*, 180–83.

168. DD to AL, October 5, 1860, LP.

169. AL to DD, July 27, 1860, in Basler, *Collected Works, First Supplement*, 57.

170. Fehrenbacher, *Chicago Giant*, 183; *Watertown (WI) Republican*, June 29, 1860, 2.

171. DD to AL, June 12, 1860, LP; AL to Robert W. Thompson, July 10, 1860, in Basler, *Collected Works*, 4:82–83.

172. DD to AL, July 24, 1860, LP; *Illinois State Journal*, August 9, 1860, 2.

173. *Illinois State Journal*, August 9, 1860, 2; *Illinois State Journal*, August 13, 1860, 2 (quoting the *State Democrat*).

174. *Illinois State Journal*, August 9, 1860, 2; DD to AL, September 3, 1860, LP. Henry S. Baker was one of the five anti-Nebraska Democrats who along with John Palmer and Norman Judd stood by Trumbull in his senatorial contest against Lincoln in 1859. Bateman and Selby, *Historical Encyclopedia of Illinois and History of Christian County*, 1:32.

175. *Illinois State Journal*, August 9, 1860, 2; Angle, *Here I Have Lived*, 246–47.

176. DD to AL, September 10, 1860, LP; *Illinois State Journal*, September 13, 1860, 2.

177. Illinois State Agricultural Society to AL, August 30, 1858, LP; H. P. Sloan, Winnebago County Agricultural Society to AL, July 12, 1858, LP; Grundy County Illinois Agricultural Society to AL, July 28, 1859, LP.

178. David Atwood to AL, May 23, 1860, LP; "Address before the Wisconsin State Agricultural Society, Milwaukee, Wisconsin, September 30, 1859," in Basler, *Collected Works*, 3:471–82.

179. DD to Julius Rockwell, October 1, 1864, DDFP; DD to William P. Walker, October 7, 1847, DDFP; "Possible Presidential Candidates: Hon. David Davis, of Illinois," *Frank Leslie's Illustrated Newspaper* (New York, NY), April 24, 1880, 118. See admission tickets in David Davis's name to various state and county agricultural fairs from 1858 until 1884 in folder F-14, box 26, Miscellaneous Papers, n.d., DDFP.

180. *Illinois State Journal*, September 15, 1860, 3; *Illinois State Journal*, September 14, 1860, 3.

181. DD to AL, September 10, 1860, LP.

182. DD to AL, April 23, 1860, LP. Davis used the term "[D]utch" to include Germans. So did Lincoln. Koerner, *Memoirs*, 2:32–33. A "smart politician" would use the word "Germans" instead, at least when speaking to Germans (2:33).

183. DD to AL, June 7, 1860, LP.

184. Koerner, *Memoirs*, 2:89, 98–100; *Chicago Press and Tribune*, October 12, 1860, 1; *Chicago Press and Tribune*, September 4, 1860, 1.

185. Koerner, *Memoirs*, 2:92.

186. DD to Thurlow Weed, September 11, 1860, in Luthin, "Indiana," 398; *Daily Pittsburgh Gazette*, September 7, 1860, 2.

187. Carl Schurz to AL, May 22, 1860, LP.

188. *Evansville (IN) Daily Journal*, October 29, 1860, 1.

189. McClure, *Old Time Notes*, 1:418; *Evansville Daily Journal*, August 21, 1860, 1.

190. *Richmond (IN) Palladium*, August 23, 1860, 2; *Randolph County Journal* (IN), September 20, 1860, 2; *Evansville Daily Journal*, August 21, 1860, 1; *Evansville Daily Journal*, October 29, 1860, 1; *Evansville Daily Journal*, August 9, 1860, 1 (listing Schurz's speaking appointments).

191. *Chicago Press and Tribune*, July 13, 1860, 1.

192. *Chicago Press and Tribune*, August 9, 1860, 2; *Watertown (WI) Republican*, August 10, 1860, 2.

193. *Chicago Press and Tribune*, September 26, 1860, 1; *Chicago Press and Tribune*, September 20, 1860, 1, 2; *Watertown (WI) Republican*, August 31, 1860, 2; *Bedford (PA) Gazette*, September 28, 1860, 1; *Jeffersonian* (PA), September 13, 1860, 2.

194. *Ashtabula (OH) Weekly Telegraph*, October 6, 1860, 2.

195. Carl Schurz to AL, October 10, 1860, LP; *Chicago Press and Tribune*, October 23, 1860, 1; *Chicago Press and Tribune*, October 25, 1860, 4; *Watertown (WI) Republican*, October 26, 1860, 2.

196. *Chicago Press and Tribune*, July 21, 1860, 4. Faust, *German Element*, 131n2. Hassaurek also spoke in northern Illinois. *Chicago Press and Tribune*, July 30, 1860, 1.

197. Rose, "Upland Southerners," 244–47; Adams, "Illinois South," 43–45; Lynch, "Flow of Colonists," 3–6.

198. Julian, *Political Recollections*, 115.

199. In the 1856 presidential election the Democratic ticket in Indiana received 50.41 percent of the vote, the Republicans 40.09 percent, and the American Party 9.51 percent. In Illinois the vote percentages were Democrats 44.09 percent, Republicans 40.23 percent, and Americans 15.68 percent. See 1856 Presidential General Election Data— National by State, in *Dave Leip's Atlas*, https://uselectionatlas.org/RESULTS/national .php?f=o&year=1856. The need to draw votes from the Fillmore block was obvious.

200. DD to AL, August 5, 1860, LP.

201. DD to Thurlow Weed, August 24, 1860, in Weed, *Life*, 2:299–300.

202. DD to Thurlow Weed, August 24, 1860, in Weed, *Life*, 2:299.

203. DD to Thurlow Weed, August 24, 1860, in Weed, *Life*, 2:300; AL to Edwin Morgan, September 20, 1860, in Basler, *Collected Works*, 4:116–17.

204. DD to Thurlow Weed, August 24, 1860, in Weed, *Life*, 2:300; John Defrees to Thurlow Weed, August 25, 1860, quoted in Luthin, "Indiana," 400.

205. Caleb Smith to DD, August 30, 1860, LP; see also Jesse Williams to DD, August 31, 1860, LP; *Wabash (IN) Express*, October 3, 1860, 3.

206. DD to Edwin Morgan, September 22, 1860, quoted in Burlingame, *Abraham Lincoln*, 1:545–46.

207. AL to Norman Judd, October 20, 1858, in Basler, *Collected Works*, 3:330.

208. DD to Thurlow Weed, September 3, 1860, Weed Papers. Davis may have made the second request for New York money not because of the letters describing pipe-laying efforts but because of Caleb Smith's complaint that New York had not responded to Indiana's initial request for funds. Caleb Smith to DD, August 30, 1860, LP.

209. Thurlow Weed to DD, September 7, 1860, LP. In the same letter Weed told Davis that he was assigning George G. Fogg and John Z. Goodrich to deal with Pennsylvania so as "not to awaken jealousies" lingering from the Chicago convention. See also Edwin Morgan to DD, September 10, 1860, LP.

210. DD to Thurlow Weed, September 11, 1860, Weed Papers; see Luthin, "Indiana," 398.

211. John Z. Goodrich to AL, March 16, 1865, LP; King, *Lincoln's Manager*, 154; Egerton, *Year of Meteors*, 182; DD to Sarah Davis, October 10, 1860, a.m., DDFP ("John Z. Goodrich [if Indiana has gone right] will plume himself very much on the result").

212. Leonard Swett to DD, October 1, 1860, LP; Zimmerman, "Origin and Rise," 396–97; DD to George P. Davis, November 7, 1858, DDFP.

213. DD to AL, October 5, 1860, LP.

214. *Evansville (IN) Daily Journal*, September 29, 1860, 3; *Evansville Daily Journal*, October 8, 1860, 1. Swett's appointment to speak in Evansville on October 6 was rescheduled. *Evansville Daily Journal*, October 5, 1860, 1; DD to AL, October 1860, LP; *Wabash (IN) Express*, October 3, 1860, 2.

215. Zachary, "Henry S. Lane," 108.

216. See Zimmerman, "Origin and Rise," 385 (repeating a claim made by the *New Albany [IN] Daily Ledger*).

217. Schuyler Colfax to AL, May 30, 1860, LP.

218. Roll, "Richard W. Thompson," 183–84, 188–89, 196–97, 199; Zimmerman, "Origin and Rise," 396.

219. AL to Richard Thompson, June 18, 1860, in Basler, *Collected Works*, 4:79, annotation [1]; AL to Richard Thompson, July 10, 1860, in Basler, *Collected Works*, 4:82–83; AL to Richard Thompson, July 16, 1860, in Basler, *Collected Works*, 4:84.

220. See *Wabash (IN) Express*, August 22, 1860, 1; Roll, "Richard W. Thompson," 201–3.

221. DD to AL, September 3, 1860, LP; Henry Lane to Richard Thompson, September 3, 1860, quoted in Roll, "Richard W. Thompson," 202.

222. *Wabash (IN) Express*, October 3, 1860, 1; *Evansville (IN) Daily Journal*, October 4, 1860, 1.

223. Roll, "Richard W. Thompson," 203–4.

224. *Cincinnati Daily Press*, September 29, 1860, 1; *Wabash (IN) Express*, October 3, 1860, 3 (claiming that less than half of the delegation from Kentucky attending the rally returned home and instead wandered the streets looking for temporary work in Indianapolis); Jesse Williams to DD, August 31, 1860, LP.

225. *Richmond (IN) Palladium*, October 4, 1860, 2; *Evansville (IN) Daily Journal*, October 3, 1860, 1; *Democratic Press* (OH), October 4, 1860, 2.

226. *Richmond (IN) Palladium*, October 4, 1860, 2. The Democratic newspapers refuted the claim reporting that the crowd was made up mostly of voters. *Democratic Press* (OH), October 4, 1860, 2.

227. DD to George Perrin Davis, September 30, 1860, DDFP.

228. DD to George Perrin Davis, September 30, 1860, DDFP.

229. DD to Sarah Davis, October 15, 1860, DDFP; DD to George Perrin Davis, October 18, 1860, DDFP.

230. See, for example, Leonard Swett to DD, October 1, 1860, LP; DD to AL, October 5, 1860, LP; DD to AL, October 1860, LP.

231. DD to Sarah Davis, October 10, 1860, p.m., DDFP.

232. DD to George Perrin Davis, October 5, 1860, DDFP; DD to Sarah Davis, October 15, 1860, DDFP.

233. DD to George Perrin Davis, November 1, 1860, DDFP; DD to AL, October 5, 1860, LP; DD to Sarah Davis, November 4, 1860, DDFP; DD to Sarah Davis, October 15, 1860, DDFP; DD to Sarah Davis, November 2, 1860, DDFP.

234. DD to Sarah Davis, October 18, 1860, DDFP; DD to Sarah Davis, October 22, 1860, DDFP.

235. DD to Sarah Davis, October 30, 1860, DDFP.

236. DD to George Perrin Davis, November 4, 1860, DDFP; DD to Sarah Davis, November 4, 1860, DDFP.

237. American Presidency Project, Statistics, Election Year 1860, https://www.presidency.ucsb.edu/statistics/elections/1860.

238. DD to George Perrin Davis, November 4, 1860, DDFP; DD to Sarah Davis, November 4, 1860, DDFP; DD to Sarah Davis, November 11, 1860, DDFP; DD to Sarah Davis, November 9, 1860, DDFP; DD to George Perrin Davis, November 14, 1860, DDFP.

239. Stanton, *Random Recollections*, 221.

240. See, for example, Joseph Casey to DD, November 19, 1860, LP; John Z. Goodrich to DD, November 23 and 28, 1860, LP; B. Rush Petrikin to DD, November 26, 1860, LP; Charles T. Jones to DD, December 3, 1860, LP; A. H. Connor to DD, December 6, 1860, LP; William P. Small to DD, December 6, 1860, LP; Thomas Dudley to DD, December 7, 1860, LP; Eric Locke to DD, December 26, 1860, LP; John Defrees to DD, January 16, 1861, LP; Edgar Cowan to DD, January 30, 1861, LP.

241. Mary Lincoln to DD, January 17, 1861, quoted in King, *Lincoln's Manager*, 172.

242. For example, Russell Errett to AL, November 21, 1860, LP.

243. DD to AL, November 19, 1860, LP; DD to AL, November 20, 1860, LP; James R. Partridge to DD, November 21, 1860, LP; DD to AL, December 10 and 12, 1860, LP; DD to AL, January 28, 1861, LP.

244. King, *Lincoln's Manager*, 167; Weed, *Life*, 1:605–12 (Weed provides a detailed recollection of the discussion concerning the candidates for cabinet posts); AL to Lyman Trumbull, December 21, 1860, in Basler, *Collected Works*, 4:158–59; Leonard Swett, letter to the editor, *Chicago Daily Tribune*, July 14, 1878, 5.

245. Henry Whitney, statement to William Herndon, 1887, in Wilson and Davis, *Herndon's Informants*, 649; Burlingame, *Abraham Lincoln*, 2:83–84; Jones, John A., Persons, Papers of Abraham Lincoln Digital Library, https://papersofabrahamlincoln.org/persons/JO08859.

246. Holzer, *Lincoln President Elect*, 292.

247. Donald, *Lincoln*, 273–75; *New York Herald*, February 21, 1861, 1.

248. DD to Sarah Davis, February 17, 1861, DDFP. Lincoln had a similar experience getting supper on the evening the train arrived in Indianapolis. He had to "wait nearly half an hour for his slender share of the repast" (Villard, *Lincoln*, 78–79).

249. Lamon, *Recollections*, 34; Thurlow Weed to Willard, February 19, 1861, in Lamon, *Recollections*, 34.

250. For a reference to an informal dinner, see DD to Sarah Davis, February 17, 1861, DDFP.

251. *New York Herald*, March 1, 1861, 1.

252. DD to Sarah Davis, February 17, 1861, DDFP.

253. *Sun* (New York, NY), February 20, 1861, 2; King, *Lincoln's Manager*, 177; *New York Herald*, February 21, 1861, 1.

254. Norman Judd to Allan Pinkerton, November 3, 1867, in Pinkerton, *History and Evidence*, 17–23; Lamon, *Life*, 522–23; Donald, *Lincoln*, 277–78.

255. Lamon, *Life*, 522.

256. Norman Judd to Allan Pinkerton, November 3, 1867, in Pinkerton, *History and Evidence*, 21–22.

257. "Allan Pinkerton Agency (Report Furnished to William H. Herndon) 1861," in Wilson and Davis, *Herndon's Informants*, 298. In his biography of Lincoln, Lamon says that at the time he felt the Baltimore threat was real, but that upon years of reflection he concluded that the plot never existed. Lamon, *Life*, 512–13.

258. Norman Judd to Allan Pinkerton, November 3, 1867, in Pinkerton, *History and Evidence*, 21–22; Lamon, *Life*, 522.

259. Lamon, *Life*, 522; Norman Judd to Allan Pinkerton, November 3, 1867, in Pinkerton, *History and Evidence*, 22.

260. *New York Herald*, February 24, 1861, 1. Sarah Davis also feared for her husband's safety (Sarah Davis to DD, March 1, 1861, DDFP). See also Norman Judd to Allan Pinkerton, November 3, 1867, in Pinkerton, *History and Evidence*, 22.

261. Norman Judd to Allan Pinkerton, November 3, 1867, in Pinkerton, *History and Evidence*, 22.

262. Wilson, *Intimate Memories*, 116.

263. Holzer, *Lincoln President-Elect*, 392–95.

264. Stanton, *Random Recollections*, 221.

Chapter 5. Lincoln Puts Davis on the Supreme Court

1. McGinty, *Lincoln and the Court*, 92, 94–95.

2. Henry Winter Davis to AL, March 6, 1861, LP; William Seward to AL, March 9, 1861, LP; John S. Carlile to AL, March 10, 1861, LP.

3. McGinty, *Lincoln and the Court*, 98.

4. Orville H. Browning to AL, April 9, 1861, LP; Eliza H. Browning to AL, June 8, 1861, LP.

5. *Cincinnati Daily Press*, January 29, 1862, 2 (reprinting an article from the *New York Evening Post*); McGinty, *Lincoln and the Court*, 107.

6. Kutler, *Judicial Power*, 14–20; McGinty, *Lincoln and the Court*, 108–9.

7. Fairman, *Mr. Justice Miller*, 50, 26, 28, 17, 29–32.

8. AL to DD, August 27, 1862, in McGinty, *Lincoln and the Court*, 115.

9. Wilson, *Intimate Memories*, 194.

10. Leonard Swett to AL, January 25, 1862, LP.

11. Browning, *Diary*, 1:xix–xx; Donald, *"We Are Lincoln Men,"* 114 ("Lincoln was obviously delighted to have the Brownings in Washington, old friends whom he could absolutely trust. He knew that the Illinois senator would never betray a confidence, never leak information to his colleagues or to the press, never even hint that he had inside information").

12. Browning, *Diary*, 1:475–76, entry for July 3, 1861.

13. Browning, *Diary*, 1:477, entry for July 6, 1861.

14. Browning, *Diary*, 1:477–78, entry for July 8, 1861.

15. Browning, *Diary*, 1:478, entry for July 9, 1861.

16. Browning, *Diary*, 1:479–81, entries for July 11, 13, 1861.

17. Browning, *Diary*, 1:481–82, entry for July 15, 1861.

18. Browning, *Diary*, 1:482–83, entries for July 16, 17, 19, 1861.

19. Browning, *Diary*, 1:530–31, entries for February 20, 21, 22, 23, 24, 1862. The Brownings also spent the night of February 25 with the president. Browning, *Diary*, 1:531, entry for February 25, 1862; Donald, *"We Are Lincoln Men,"* 120.

20. Leonard Swett to William Herndon, August 29, 1887, in Wilson and Davis, *Herndon's Informants*, 710–11; Leonard Swett to AL, August 15, 1861, LP.

21. Leonard Swett to AL, January 28, 1862, LP (transmitting a petition from members of the state constitutional convention); Illinois State Convention to AL, January 21, 1862, LP; Robert Campbell and Wayman Crow to Leonard Swett, February 10, 1862, LP (cover letter for a petition in support of Davis); Leonard Swett to AL, February 13, 1862, LP (enclosing a petition from Missouri lawyers); Bader and Williams, "David Davis," 188 ("the support for Davis was immense").

22. John T. Stuart to AL, January 24, 1862, LP; Leonard Swett to AL, January 25, 1862, LP.

23. Leonard Swett to AL, January 25, 1862, LP.

24. DD to Julius Rockwell, March 4, 1855, DDFP; AL to Elihu B. Washburne, February 9, 1855, in Basler, *Collected Works*, 2:306; DD to Julius Rockwell, October 26, 1858, DDFP; DD to AL, November 7, 1858, LP.

25. Browning, *Diary*, 1:407, entry for May 16, 1860.

26. Baxter, "Orville H. Browning," 437 ("As Lincoln rose to political prominence, Browning's attitude toward him, though amicable on the surface, was marked by a strange indifference that may have concealed some jealousy").

27. Magdol, *Owen Lovejoy*, 278.

28. Leonard Swett to Mrs. Laura Swett, August 10, 1862, quoted in McGinty, *Lincoln and the Court*, 115.

29. Browning, *Diary*, 1:xvii.

30. Donald, *"We Are Lincoln Men,"* 128.

31. Donald, *"We Are Lincoln Men,"* 128.

32. John P. Usher to DD, May 1, 1862, quoted in King, *Lincoln's Manager*, 194; DD to John P. Usher, May 15, 1862, quoted in McGinty, *Lincoln and the Court*, 114–15. Accord-

ing to King, *Lincoln's Manager*, 195, Davis recommended another judge for the court of claims position.

33. See, for example, Samuel C. Pomeroy et al. to AL, January 7, 1861, LP; Bradley F. Granger to AL, August 13, 1862, LP; Missouri Delegates in Congress to AL, March 18, 1862, LP.

34. Bader and Williams, "David Davis," 208.

35. Silver, *Lincoln's Supreme Court*, 78.

36. AL to DD, August 27, 1862, in McGinty, *Lincoln and the Court*, 115.

37. Silver, *Lincoln's Supreme Court*, 71.

38. DD to AL, September 1, 1862, in McGinty, *Lincoln and the Court*, 116.

39. DD to Sarah Davis, March 2, 1862, DDFP; Palmer, *Bench and Bar*, 1:545.

40. DD to Leonard Swett, November 26, 1862, in Pratt, *Concerning Mr. Lincoln*, 99; DD to William Orme, December 9, 1862, quoted in Pratt, "David Davis," 171; King, *Lincoln's Manager*, 191.

41. King, *Lincoln's Manager*, 201–3; DD to Julius Rockwell, June 25, 1878, DDFP.

42. DD to Julius Rockwell, November 30, 1870, quoted in King, *Lincoln's Manager*, 277.

43. For example, Bell v. Railroad Company, 71 U.S. (4 Wall.) 598 (1866); The Des Moines, 154 U.S. 584 (1872); Haldeman v. United States, 91 U.S. 584 (1875).

44. See DD to Julius Rockwell, February 19, 1865, DDFP ("I dread the effect of this universal & widespread corruption").

45. Randall v. Brigham, 74 U.S. (7 Wall.) 523, 535–36 (1868).

46. Bradley v. Fisher, 80 U.S. (13 Wall.) 335, 350–57 (1871).

47. Bradley v. Fisher, 80 U.S. 357 (Davis, J., dissenting).

48. Stephenson, "The Waite Court," 477; United States v. Union Pacific Railroad, 91 U.S. (1 Otto) 72 (1875).

49. Swett, "Memorial Address," 77; Gaines v. New Orleans, 73 U.S. (6 Wall.) 642 (1867).

50. Browning, *Diary*, 1:616, entries for January 17 and 19, 1863; AL to DD, April 13, 1865, in Basler, *Collected Works, First Supplement*, 286–87.

51. DD to AL, July 27, 1862, LP; DD to AL, June 2, 1864, LP; DD to AL, October 4, 1864, LP; DD to AL, November 29, 1864, LP; DD to AL, October 22, 1864, LP.

52. See Fraker, *Lincoln's Ladder*, 79, 82, 177, 229; DD to Sarah Davis, December 21, 1862, DDFP; DD to Sarah Davis, January 22, 1862, DDFP; William Orme to DD, December 13, 1862, DDFP; King, *Lincoln's Manager*, 193.

53. Burlingame, *Inner World*, 167, quoting DD to Leonard Swett, January 23, 1863, DDFP.

54. King, *Lincoln's Manager*, 205. In the end, Davis's wishes were granted, and Orme received a promotion and leave to go home to settle his father's estate (205–6). See also DD to Sarah Davis, January 28, 1863, DDFP ("I got Orme's leave & it was very hard to do it"). At the time Davis was assisting Orme he was negotiating a leave for another Illinois soldier. DD to Sarah Davis, January 28, 1863, DDFP. And Davis's favor seeking for friends did not end upon Lincoln's death. See, for example, DD to William H. Seward, July 1, 1865, William H. Seward Papers, River Campus Libraries, University of Rochester.

55. Boutwell, *Reminiscences*, 2:29 (reporting that Lincoln said, "We cannot ask a [Supreme Court nominee] what he will do, and if we should, and he should answer us, we should despise him for it. Therefore we must take a man whose opinions are known"); see Kutler, "David Davis," 526.

56. DD to Julius Rockwell, September 16, 1863, DDFP; Ex parte Milligan, 71 U.S. (4 Wall.) 2 (1866).

57. DD statement to William H. Herndon, September 20, 1866, in Wilson and Davis, *Herndon's Informants*, 348–49.

Chapter 6. Justice Davis and Wartime Presidential Edicts

1. White, "Strangely Insignificant Role," 215; DD to Julius Rockwell, September 16, 1863, DDFP.

2. *Prize Cases*, 67 U.S. (2 Black) 635 (1862); McGinty, *Lincoln and the Court*, 142.

3. *Prize Cases*, 67 U.S. 660–62, 665–71.

4. *Prize Cases*, 67 U.S. 682–99 (Nelson, J., dissenting).

5. *Prize Cases*, 67 U.S. 669.

6. Ex parte Vallandigham, 68 U.S. (1 Wall.) 243 (1863).

7. Nicolay and Hay, "Abraham Lincoln," 127n2, 128; Klement, *Limits of Dissent*, 103, 152–54, 76, 142; *Ex parte Vallandigham*, 68 U.S. 244–45; McGinty, *Lincoln and the Court*, 184–86.

8. Karamanski, *Rally 'round the Flag*, 191.

9. *Ex parte Vallandigham*, 68 U.S. 244.

10. Nicolay and Hay, "Abraham Lincoln," 128–30; *Ex parte Vallandigham*, 68 U.S. 244–47.

11. AL to Erastus Corning and others, June 12, 1863, in Basler, *Collected Works*, 6:266. Lincoln tried to put the matter to rest by transporting Vallandigham to Confederate authorities. Once in Virginia, however, Vallandigham took a circuitous route from Richmond to Canada, where he managed his successful campaign for the Ohio Democrat gubernatorial nomination, losing badly in the general election. Nicolay and Hay, "Abraham Lincoln," 135–36.

12. Ex parte Vallandigham, 28 F. Cas. 874, 922–24 (S.D. Ohio 1863); AL to Erastus Corning and others, June 12, 1863, in Basler, *Collected Works*, 6:268. On the factual and legal aspects of the Vallandigham matter, see Curtis, "Lincoln, Vallandingham," 117–31; and Klement, *Limits of Dissent*.

13. *Ex parte Vallandigham*, 68 U.S. 251–53; see also Hyde v. Shine, 199 U.S. 62, 85 (1905) ("Petitions for habeas corpus are frequently accompanied by applications for certiorari as ancillary thereto, and both are awarded or denied together").

14. *Ex parte Vallandigham*, 68 U.S. 254.

15. Silver, *Lincoln's Supreme Court*, 153.

16. Ex parte Merryman, 17 F. Cas. 144 (1861).

17. A. E. Keir Nash, "John Catron," in Urofsky, *Biographical Encyclopedia*, 123.

18. *Ex parte Vallandigham*, 28 F. Cas. 874, 920; William Bosch, "Noah Haynes Swayne," in Urofsky, *Biographical Encyclopedia*, 522 (stating that when the *Vallandigham* case reached the Supreme Court, Justice Swayne "voted that the civilian courts could not review a trial by [a] military court").

19. In re Winder, 30 F. Cas. 291–94 (D. Mass. 1862).

20. DD interview with William Herndon, September 20, 1866, in Wilson and Davis, *Herndon's Informants*, 349.

21. Sarah Davis to DD, December 11, 1863, DDFP; Sarah Davis to DD, December 28, 1863, DDFP; Sarah Davis to George Perrin Davis, February 1, 1864, DDFP. Davis authored multiple opinions for the court's December 1863 term. See, for example, Woods v. Freeman, 68 U.S. (1 Wall.) 398 (1863); Eames v. Godfrey, 68 U.S. (1 Wall.) 78 (1863); Ryan v. Bindley, 68 U.S. (1 Wall.) 66 (1863).

22. Karamanski, *Rally 'round the Flag*, 190–92; General Orders, No. 84, June 1, 1863, in *War of the Rebellion*, ser. 1, vol. 23, pt. 2, p. 381.

23. *Chicago Daily Tribune*, June 4, 1863, 4; Curtis, "Lincoln, Vallandingham," 132–33.

24. *New York Times*, June 4, 1863, 8 (quoting Judge Drummond).

25. Browning, *Diary*, 1:632, entry for June 3, 1863.

26. Browning, *Diary*, 1:632, entry for June 3, 1863; *New York Times*, June 4, 1863, 8 (stating that Davis was expected to act with Judge Drummond in the *Chicago Times'* request for an injunction); Sallie Davis to George Perrin Davis, June 4, 1863, DDFP; King, *Lincoln's Manager*, 211.

27. DD and William Herndon to AL, June 2, 1863, quoted in Tenney, "To Suppress," 255; DD statement to William Herndon, September 20, 1866, in Wilson and Davis, *Herndon's Informants*, 349. Davis described the telegram as informing Lincoln that the suppression of the *Times* was an "error."

28. DD to E. M. Stanton, May 27, 1863, in *War of the Rebellion*, ser. 1, vol. 23, pt. 2, p. 369. Davis's title, "Judge of Supreme Court," appeared below his name on the telegram. The governor of Indiana, O. P. Morton, simultaneously sent a telegram to Stanton requesting Hascall's removal. O. P. Morton to E. M. Stanton, May 27, 1863, in *War of the Rebellion*, ser. 1, vol. 23, pt. 2, p. 369.

29. Lyman Trumbull and Isaac N. Arnold to AL, June 3, 1863, in *War of the Rebellion*, ser. 1, vol. 23, pt. 2, p. 385.

30. "The Chicago Times Establishment Taken Possession of by the Military Authorities-Meeting of Its Friends in the Evening," *Chicago Daily Tribune*, June 4, 1863, 4; *New York Times*, June 4, 1863, 8; Paul, "Suppression," 111–13.

31. AL to Edwin M. Stanton, June 4, 1863, in Basler, *Collected Works*, 6:248; General Orders, No. 91, June 4, 1863, in *War of the Rebellion*, ser. 1, vol. 23, pt. 2, p. 386.

32. DD interview with William Herndon, September 20, 1866, in Wilson and Davis, *Herndon's Informants*, 349; see also AL to Isaac N. Arnold, May 25, 1864, in Basler, *Collected Works*, 7:361 ("I am far from certain to-day that the revocation was not right").

33. Karamanski, *Rally 'round the Flag*, 195–96. After delivering the message lifting the suspension of the publication to the editor of the *Times*, Burnside received a second telegram from Lincoln telling him to postpone rescinding the suppression order. Burnside ignored the second telegram.

34. Towne, "'Such Conduct,'" 46–49; McKirdy, *Lincoln Apostate*, 89; *Journal of the Convention*, 4–5; DD to Sarah Davis, October 27, 1851, DDFP; AL to John M. Clayton, May 13, 1849, in Basler, *Collected Works*, 2:48; DD to Julius Rockwell, May 28, 1850, DDFP; AL to James A. Pearce, January 13, 1851, in Basler, *Collected Works*, 2:97, annotation [1].

35. McKirdy, *Lincoln Apostate*, 108–9; Towne, "'Such Conduct,'" 59–60; *Chicago Daily Tribune*, April 8, 1863, 1.

36. *Chicago Daily Tribune*, April 9, 1863, 2.

37. See, for example, Samuel Treat to DD, November 20, 1862, LP; Samuel Treat to DD, November 21, 1862, LP.

38. DD to George Perrin Davis, April 7, 1863, DDFP; DD to Julius Rockwell, April 8, 1863, DDFP (both letters sent from Bloomington).

39. *Illinois State Journal*, April 8, 1863, 3.

40. Sampson, "'Pretty Damned Warm Times,'" 99–102, 110–13; Coleman and Spence, "Charleston Riot," 15, 18–27, 27–29 (listing casualties).

41. Barry, "'I'll Keep Them,'" 20–22; DD to AL, July 4, 1864, in Barry, "'I'll Keep Them,'" 27, exhibit 2; Coleman and Spence, "Charleston Riot," 37–39.

42. DD to AL, July 1, 1864, in Barry, "'I'll Keep Them,'" 27, exhibit 1.

43. AL to DD, July 2, 1864, in Basler, *Collected Works*, 7:421; AL to S. H. Treat, July 2, 1864, in Basler, *Collected Works*, 7:422; S. H. Treat to AL, July 4, 1863, quoted in Basler, *Collected Works*, 7:422–23, annotation [1]; telegram, AL to DD, July 2, 1864, in Basler, *Collected Works*, 7:422, annotation [1].

44. DD to AL, July 4, 1864, in Barry, "'I'll Keep Them,'" 27, exhibit 2, 29, exhibit 3. Davis added in his letter to Lincoln that the abstract prepared by the defense lawyers was accurate.

45. Coleman and Spence, "Charleston Riot," 45–47.

46. *Ex parte Milligan*, 71 U.S. 2, 6–7.

47. Towne, "Persistent Nullifier," 303–4, 328, 331–32.

48. Howell, "Wartime Judgments," 1796.

49. Burton, "Two Significant Decisions," 122.

50. Dewey, "Hoosier Justice," 184, entry for May 7, 1864.

51. DD to AL, October 4, 1864, LP; DD to AL, November 29, 1864, LP.

52. Dewey, "Hoosier Justice," 190, entry for September 24, 1864, 195, entry for December 17, 1864.

53. DD to Sarah Davis, January 6, 1868, DDFP; DD to Sarah Davis, February 8, 1868, DDFP.

54. *Ex parte Milligan*, 71 U.S. 8.

55. Dewey, "Hoosier Justice," 203, entry for May 9, 1865.

56. Whitney, *Life on the Circuit*, 76–77.

57. Dewey, "Hoosier Justice," 207, 207n45, entries for June 5–11, 1865; United States v. Scott, 70 U.S. (3 Wall.) 642 (1865).

58. Dewey, "Hoosier Justice," 203–4, entries for May 9 and 11, 1865.

59. Brief of Amicus Curiae Civil War Historians in Support of Petitioner, 29, Al-Marri v. Spagone, 555 U.S. 1545 (2009) (No. 08–368) (stating that McDonald and Davis "feigned disagreement and certified their supposed split decision to the Supreme Court").

60. *Ex parte Milligan*, 71 U.S. 8.

61. Dewey, "Hoosier Justice," 203–4, entry for May 11, 1865; DD and David McDonald to President Johnson, May 11, 1865, quoted in Johnson, *Papers*, 8:60.

62. Foulke, *Life*, 1:428; Oliver P. Morton to Andrew Johnson, May 11, 1865, in Johnson, *Papers*, 8:60–61.

63. Klement, *Dark Lanterns*, 226; Andrew Johnson to Alvin P. Hovey, May 16, 1865, in *War of the Rebellion*, ser. 2, vol. 8, p. 587.

64. Edwin M. Stanton to Alvin P. Hovey, May 30, 1865, in *War of the Rebellion*, ser. 2, vol. 8, pp. 583–84.

65. McGinty, *Lincoln and the Court*, 254–56; *Daily Ohio Statesman*, April 4, 1866, 3.

66. White, "Internal Powers," 1490–91.

67. See, for example, McGinty, *Lincoln and the Court*, 256.

68. See, for example, White, "Internal Powers," 1490–91.

69. King, *Lincoln's Manager*, 254.

70. In re Egan, 8 F. Cas. 367 (C.C. N.D. N.Y. 1866) (No. 4,303).

71. *Ex parte Milligan*, 71 U.S. 109, 118–20.

72. *Ex parte Milligan*, 71 U.S. 121.

73. *Ex parte Milligan*, 71 U.S. 121.

74. *Ex parte Milligan*, 71 U.S. 122.

75. *Ex parte Milligan*, 71 U.S. 126–27.

76. *Ex parte Milligan*, 71 U.S. 120–21.

77. *Ex parte Milligan*, 71 U.S. 135–36 (Chase, C. J., concurring).

78. *Ex parte Milligan*, 71 U.S. 139–41 (Chase, C. J., concurring).

79. *Review of the Decision*, 256.

80. *Review of the Decision*, 5, 9, 11, 12.

81. *Review of the Decision*, 19.

82. *Chicago Tribune*, January 18, 1867, 2; *Chicago Tribune*, January 30, 1867, 2; see also "Political Questions in the Supreme Court," *The Nation*, January 10, 1867, reproduced in Lurie, *Supreme Court*, 76–78.

83. *New York Herald*, January 2, 1867, 4.

84. *New York Herald*, December 23, 1866, 4; see also *Carson (NV) Daily Appeal*, January 26, 1867, 2; *Wheeling (WV) Daily Intelligencer*, January 4, 1867, 1 (reprinting an article from the *New York Herald*).

85. *Delaware (OH) Gazette*, January 18, 1867, 2; *New York Times*, January 3, 1867, 4.

86. *Marshall County Republican* (IN), December 27, 1866, 2.

87. For example, *Evansville (IN) Daily Journal*, February 5, 1867, 2.

88. Warren, *Supreme Court*, 2:433, 433n1.

89. *Staunton (VA) Spectator*, January 8, 1867, 2.

90. Warren, *Supreme Court*, 2:437–39.

91. *National Intelligencer*, December 31, 1866, 2, in Lurie, *Supreme Court*, 72.

92. *Louisiana Democrat*, January 16, 1867, 2.

93. Clinton, "Mandatory View," 1594n288 ("*Ex parte Milligan* was the major case creating Congress' fear of the Court's reaction to the Reconstruction program"); see also Fairman, *Reconstruction*, 221.

94. Cong. Globe, 39th Cong., 2nd sess. 251 (1867) (statement of Thaddeus Stevens); Cong. Globe, 39th Cong., 2nd sess. 1484–85 (1867) (statement of James Wilson); *Daily Gate City* (IA), March 7, 1867, 2 (reproducing Wilson's speech).

95. *Chicago Tribune*, December 28, 1866, 2; *Raftsman's Journal* (PA), February 20, 1867, 2.

96. "Summary of Events."

97. "Summary of Events," 573–74; see also "The New Dred Scott," *Harper's Weekly*, January 19, 1867, in Lurie, *Supreme Court*, 79 ("Like the Dred Scott decision, it is not a

judicial opinion-it is a political act"); "Political Questions in the Supreme Court," *The Nation*, January 10, 1867, in Lurie, *Supreme Court*, 76–78.

98. Dewey, "Hoosier Justice," 203–4, entries for May 11 and May 14, 1865.

99. Klingaman, "Abraham Lincoln," 236.

100. *Bloomington (IL) Daily Pantagraph*, January 8, 1867, quoted in Fairman, *Reconstruction*, 218–19; Sarah Davis to DD, January 14, 1867, DDFP; Sarah Davis to DD, January 20, 1867, DDFP.

101. DD to Julius Rockwell, February 24, 1867, in Fairman, *Reconstruction*, 232. Davis was surprised that the Republicans authorized military trials for civilians after the end of the war: "I did not suppose the Republican party would endorse such trials after the war is over. Yet they do it" (232).

102. Yoo, "Lincoln and Habeas," 529; Neely, *Fate of Liberty*, 176–77; Mississippi v. Johnson, 71 U.S. (4 Wall.) 475 (1866); Georgia v. Stanton, 73 U.S. (6 Wall.) 50 (1867).

103. DD interview with William Herndon, September 20, 1866, in Wilson and Davis, *Herndon's Informants*, 348.

104. DD to Julius Rockwell, February 24, 1867, in Fairman, *Reconstruction*, 232–34.

105. DD to Julius Rockwell, February 24, 1867, in Fairman, *Reconstruction*, 234. Folder F-12, box 26 of the David Davis Family Papers contains an undated list of more than 140 persons to whom Justice Davis planned to send a copy of the *Milligan* opinion.

106. DD to Julius Rockwell, April 22, 1868, DDFP.

107. Warren, *Supreme Court*, 2:427; Bader and Williams, "David Davis," 213; Rostow, "Japanese American Cases," 524; Barry, "*Ex parte Milligan*," 355; Hensel, "Jeremiah Sullivan Black," 195.

108. Hamdi v. Rumsfeld, 542 U.S. 507, 567n1 (2004) (Scalia, J., dissenting) (quoting Reid v. Covert, 354 U.S. 1, 30 [1957]); see also Barry, "'I'll Keep Them,'" 21n4.

109. Neely, *Fate of Liberty*, 184; Rana, "Freedom Struggles," 1039, 1045.

110. Herndon and Weik, *Herndon's Lincoln*, 300.

111. As part of his charge to the Indianapolis grand jury in May 1863, Davis instructed the jurors:

> It is charged that there are secret organizations in some of the States of this Union, with "grips, signs and passwords," having for their objects—resistance to law, and the overthrow of the Government.
>
> It is hard to conceive of so great a depravity and wickedness, but if such organizations do exist, they should be speedily overthrown if we would avoid further trouble and calamity. If anywhere in this State, bad men have combined together for such wicked purposes, I pray you, bring them to light, and let them receive the punishment due to their crimes. ("U.S. Circuit Court at Indianapolis," 49)

112. Pratt, "David Davis," 174–75.

113. McKoski, "Reestablishing," 275–76.

Chapter 7. Impartiality on the Trial Court Bench

1. See, for example, Blaustein and Mersky, *First One Hundred Justices*, 38–39 (ranking Davis as an average Supreme Court justice).

2. *Bloomington (IL) Weekly Pantagraph*, July 2, 1886, 4 (quoting an article in the *Chicago Inter-Ocean*).

3. *Bloomington (IL) Weekly Pantagraph*, July 2, 1886, 4 (quoting an article in the *Chicago Inter-Ocean*).

4. *Bloomington (IL) Weekly Pantagraph*, July 2, 1886, 4.

5. *Illinois State Journal*, March 30, 1849, 2; King, *Lincoln's Manager*, 63; *Illinois State Journal*, April 27, 1857, 2.

6. *Biographical and Genealogical Record*, 2:441–42; Kirby Benedict to DD, February 19, 1849, DDFP; Hunt, *Kirby Benedict*, 33–34, 40–42; John D. Caton to AL, February 4, 1862, LP; King, *Lincoln's Manager*, 63.

7. *Illinois Citizen* (Danville), May 29, 1850, quoted in King, *Lincoln's Manager*, 78.

8. Cullom, *Fifty Years*, 36 ("Judge Davis was a remarkedly popular man on his circuit"); *Sun* (New York, NY), March 15, 1880, 1; Edward Finegan to David Davis, June 5, 1860, DDFP.

9. *Chicago Daily Tribune*, June 14, 1858, 2 (reproducing part of the Will County Bar Association's resolution); Stevens, *Past and Present*, 2:497, 458, 461–62.

10. *Urbana (IL) Union*, April 15, 1858, 3, quoted in Fraker, *Lincoln's Ladder*, 39.

11. Thomas M. Moffett et al. to DD, March 30, 1855, in Basler, *Collected Works*, 2:310; *Illinois State Journal*, April 13, 1855, 3. Along with other Democrats, George W. Shutt signed the letter. Shutt supported Douglas in 1860 and spoke at a rally for Douglas in Pleasant Plains in August 1860. *Illinois State Journal*, August 22, 1860, 3; DD to Thomas Moffett and other members of the Springfield Bar Association, April 10, 1855, reprinted in *Illinois State Journal*, April 13, 1855, 3.

12. See, for example, Champaign County, Illinois, Bar Association to AL, January 30, 1862, LP; Whiteside, Illinois, Bar Members to AL, 1862, LP; Macon County, Illinois, Members of the Bar to AL, 1862, LP; La Salle County, Illinois, Members of the Bar to AL, 1862, LP; *Illinois State Journal*, November 12, 1862, 2 (reproducing a resolution of the Logan County Bar Association).

13. Dent, "David Davis," 544.

14. Whitney, *Life on the Circuit*, 80; *Sun* (New York, NY), March 15, 1880, 1. During Davis's time as a trial judge, a litigant was statutorily entitled to a change of judge upon the filing of a perfunctory affidavit claiming judicial bias. See, for example, McGoon v. Little, 7 Ill. (2 Gilm.) 42 (1845).

15. See, for example, Allen v. Illinois Central Railroad, File ID L00767, DeWitt County Circuit Court, October 1855, Law Practice of Abraham Lincoln.

16. Hill, *Lincoln the Lawyer*, 182.

17. *Chicago Tribune*, March 23, 1872, 4.

18. "An Act Concerning Practice," in *Revised Laws*, 496; "Who May Be Witnesses in Criminal Cases," in *Revised Statutes*, 153–54; and "Evidence and Depositions," in *Revised Statutes*, sec. 23, pp. 232–37; Fishback, "Illinois Legislation," 422–28.

19. Voegeli, *Free but Not Equal*, 170–71; Avins, "Right to Be a Witness," 488.

20. United States v. Rhodes, 27 F. Cas. 785, 787 (C.C.D. Ky. 1866).

21. *Chicago Press and Tribune*, June 14, 1859, 1.

22. Koos, *Freedom, Land, and Community*, 382 (quoting from the *Bloomington [IL] Daily Pantagraph*, September 18, 1862); Dred Scott v. Sandford, 60 U.S. (19 How.) 393, 407 (1857). Koos views Judge Davis's ruling as "prefiguring the Fourteenth Amendment" (382).

23. People v. Hill, File ID L04244, Sangamon County Circuit Court, June 1854, Law Practice of Abraham Lincoln; People v. Tomlinson, File ID L04319, Sangamon County Circuit Court, March 1854, Law Practice of Abraham Lincoln; Florville v. Stockdale et al., File ID L03260, Sangamon County Circuit Court, August 1849, Law Practice of Abraham Lincoln. William Florville was Haitian. He was born in Cap-Haïtien, Haiti, in 1807. See also Moreland, "Law for Rulers," 29; Dirck, *Lincoln the Lawyer*, 149 ("Race was a negligible presence in [Lincoln's] practice").

24. Linder, *Reminiscences*, 21, 35–36, 182; "President's Annual Address," in *Proceedings of the Illinois State Bar Association, at Its First Annual Meeting*, 25; Palmer, *Bench and Bar*, 2:656; Coleman, *Abraham Lincoln*, 124.

25. Linder, *Reminiscences*, 182–83. Linder did not claim that Davis's rulings were influenced by the political affiliation of lawyers, public or political pressure, or the judge's personal relationship with the parties.

26. Whitney, *Life on the Circuit*, 81.

27. Hill, *Lincoln the Lawyer*, 215.

28. Whitney, *Life on the Circuit*, 65–66.

29. Linder, *Reminiscences*, 184.

30. For a description of the lecture, see DD to Sarah Davis, May 19, 1848, DDFP.

31. King, *Lincoln's Manager*, 83; DD to Sarah Davis, October 20, 1851, DDFP; Browning, *Diary*, 2:381, entry for April 23, 1874.

32. Coleman, *Abraham Lincoln*, 124; Swett, "Memorial Address," 76–77.

33. DD to Sarah Davis, May 11, 1852, DDFP.

34. Linder, *Reminiscences*, 183–84; DD to Sarah Davis, May 17, 1852, DDFP.

35. Burlingame, *Abraham Lincoln*, 1:323; Angle, "Abraham Lincoln," 38.

36. Letter to the editor, "Opposition to Lovejoy," *Chicago Daily Tribune*, June 4, 1858, 2.

37. *New York Herald*, May 1, 1872, 3.

38. See, for example, *Illinois State Register*, November 23, 1850, 2; *Illinois State Register*, November 22, 1851, 2.

39. "An Act to Establish the Eighteenth Judicial Circuit," in *Laws of the State of Illinois Passed by the Twentieth General Assembly*, 14; *Illinois State Register*, April 20, 1857, 2; Abrams and Fisher, *Lincoln's Last Trial*, 57.

40. *Illinois State Register*, April 22, 1857, 2 (two articles).

41. *Illinois State Journal*, April 23, 1857, 2.

42. *Illinois State Register*, April 25, 1857, 2.

43. *Illinois State Journal*, April 27, 1857, 2.

44. *Illinois State Register*, October 18, 1862, 2; *Illinois State Register*, October 25, 1862, 2.

45. Chittenden, *Recollections*, 173.

46. "The Final Report Made by the Commission on War Claims at St. Louis," March 10, 1862, 37th Cong., 2nd sess., H.R. Executive Document No. 94, https://reader.library.cornell.edu/docviewer/digital?id=may920305#mode/1up. Davis hired Leonard Swett to help investigate some of the claims because Davis knew that Swett was perpetually in debt. Eckley, *Lincoln's Forgotten Friend*, 93, 101–2, 118.

47. Samuel T. Glover to AL, February 14, 1862, LP; John R. Shepley to AL, February 25, 1862, LP.

Chapter 8. Impartiality on the Supreme Court Bench

1. See Warren, *Supreme Court*, 2:427–34; Fairman, *Reconstruction*, 221; Moreland, "Law for Rulers," 116–17.

2. Cong. Globe, 39th Cong., 2nd sess., 286 (January 4, 1867).

3. Cong. Globe, 39th Cong., 2nd sess., 210 (December 20, 1866).

4. Ewing, *History and Law*, 41–42; Barkow, "More Supreme Than Court?," 287–90; Rehnquist, *Centennial Crisis*, 157–60; Rhodes, *History*, 7:250–52, 262–63; *New York Times*, November 9, 1916, 6.

5. *Chicago Daily Tribune*, February 11, 1877, 5 (reporting the statement made by F. E. Richards at the Democratic City Executive Committee meeting on February 10, 1877).

6. Hoogenboom, *Rutherford B. Hayes*, 288n38 (quoting William Henry Smith to Rutherford B. Hayes, February 17, 1877). But later, Davis told his brother-in-law that he "had no doubt that Tilden was cheated" (DD to Julius Rockwell, June 25, 1878, Judge Julius Rockwell Collection, Lenox, Massachusetts, Library, https://lenoxlib.org/wp-content/uploads/2020/10/DD-to-JR-June-25-1878-transcription.pdf).

7. *Quincy (IL) Weekly Whig*, February 8, 1877, 4; *Daily Quincy (IL) Herald*, December 6, 1877, 2.

8. *Washington Bee* (Washington, DC), April 7, 1883, 3 (quoting the *Globe Democrat*); *Washington Bee*, April 30, 1887, 2.

9. *Chicago Daily Tribune*, January 26, 1877, 4 (two articles).

10. DD to Julius Rockwell, March 18, 1882, DDFP. Others did not see such a high-minded motive in Davis's refusal to caucus with either party. See Samuel Miller to William P. Ballinger, December 5, 1875, in Fairman, *Mr. Justice Miller*, 373–74. Justice Miller claimed that "every act" of Davis's life was governed "by his hope of the Presidency." Justice Miller added, however, that Davis was "as honest a man as [he] ever knew."

11. *Weekly Louisianian* (New Orleans), May 3, 1879, 1; *Weekly Louisianian*, January 8, 1881, 2.

12. Kutler, "David Davis," 527.

13. Dent, "David Davis," 557; *St. Paul (MN) Daily Globe*, October 14, 1881, 1.

14. Atkinson, *Leaving the Bench*, 56; Swett, "Memorial Address," 80.

15. *St. Paul (MN) Daily Globe*, October 14, 1881, 1 (quoting David Davis); see also *Huntsville (AL) Gazette*, October 22, 1881, 1; *Huntsville Gazette*, March 10, 1883, 1.

16. King, *Lincoln's Manager*, 303.

17. "Mass Meeting at Mackinaw," *Chicago Press and Tribune*, August 1, 1860, 2.

18. DD to Leonard Swett, November 26, 1862, in Pratt, *Concerning Mr. Lincoln*, 99.

19. "Mass Meeting at Mackinaw," *Chicago Press and Tribune*, August 1, 1860, 2; DD to Julius Rockwell, July 15, 1854, DDFP; DD to Julius Rockwell, February 18, 1858, DDFP.

20. Meites, "1847 Illinois Constitutional Convention," 282.

21. *Cecil (MD) Whig*, June 24, 1882, 3.

22. Perry Vezey to DD, January 6, 1876, DDFP; DD to John Mercer Walker, January 23, 1876, DDFP; Perry Vezey to DD, December 24, 1879, DDFP; Perry Vezey to DD, April 14, 1875, DDFP; Perry Vezey to DD, April 30, 1880, DDFP; *Cecil Whig*, June 24, 1882, 3.

23. DD to Julius Rockwell, August 5, 1882, DDFP; *Cecil Whig*, June 24, 1882, 3; *Chillicothe (IL) Independent*, June 10, 1882, 2; *Indianapolis Leader*, June 24, 1882, 2.

24. *Daily Republican* (DE), June 7, 1882, 1.

25. Koerner, *Memoirs*, 2:539.

26. Schley, "Voices from History," 1; Sarah Davis to Fanny Walker, January 10, 1842, DDFP; Tangorra, "Back of the House," 4, 20. Catharine, the housekeeper, milked the cows, tended the fire, ran errands, and did a great many "odds and ends." She was sixteen years old and originally from Lenox, Massachusetts. She came to the Davises under a contract of indenture in 1841. DD to William Perrin Walker, March 2, 1844, and annotations 6 and 7, DDFP; DD to Sarah Davis, August 6, 1848, DDFP.

27. Sarah Davis to Harriette Worthington et al., February 7, 1839, DDFP.

28. *Indianapolis Leader*, October 22, 1881, 1.

29. DD to AL, October 14, 1862, LP.

30. Browning, *Diary*, 1:616, entries for January 17 and 19, 1863; DD to AL, October 14, 1862, LP; Allardice, "'Illinois Is Rotten!,'" 105–11.

31. "The 1860 Presidential General Election Results—Illinois" and "The 1860 Presidential General Election Results—Indiana," both in *Dave Leip's Atlas*.

32. DD to W. W. Orme, October 20, 1862, quoted in Burlingame, *Abraham Lincoln*, 2:419; see Charles Sumner to AL, November 8, 1862, in *Proceedings of the Massachusetts Historical Society*, 44:602–3 ("I deplore the result in New York. It is worse for our country than the bloodiest disaster on any field of battle").

33. Silbey, *Respectable Minority*, 143–44; Burlingame, *Abraham Lincoln*, 2:419; Browning, *Diary*, 1:582, entry and editor's note for November 4, 1862; *Manitowoc (WI) Pilot*, November 14, 1862, 2.

34. David D. Field to AL, November 8, 1862, LP; Browning, *Diary*, 1:582, entry and editor's note for November 4, 1862.

35. Browning, *Diary*, 1:592, entry for December 5, 1862.

36. Browning, *Diary*, 1:585, entry for November 12, 1862.

37. DD to William Orme, October 15, 1862, William Ward Orme Papers, Illinois History and Lincoln Collection, University of Illinois Urbana-Champaign Library, Urbana, IL; Isaac N. Arnold to AL, November 5, 1862, n1, LP; Browning, *Diary*, 1:625, entry for March 28, 1863; DD to Julius Rockwell, July 1, 1863, DDFP ("In the Western Country until the Emancipation proclamation, the people were united in the support of the War"); DD to George Perrin Davis, February 9, 1863, DDFP.

38. Tap, "Race, Rhetoric, and Emancipation," 102, 116, 122; DD to AL, October 14, 1862, LP; see Stahr, *Stanton*, 248; Robert Smith to Richard Yates, October 13, 1862, LP.

39. Allardice, "'Illinois Is Rotten!,'" 105.

40. Cole, *Era of the Civil War*, 260, 267; *Journal of the Illinois House of Representatives*, January 8, 1863, 78, 80–83. A Republican resolution supporting rigid enforcement of the Emancipation Proclamation was killed by a vote of forty-nine to thirty-one (83).

41. Browning, *Diary*, 1:616, entry for January 19, 1863; Burlingame, *Abraham Lincoln*, 2:422.

42. DD to Julius Rockwell, April 22, 1868, DDFP; AL to Michael Hahn, March 13, 1864, in Basler, *Collected Works*, 7:243; King and Nevins, "Constitution," 30 ("Up to the time of his death [Lincoln] was opposed to giving Negroes the vote, except possibly to the small minority who could read and write and who had served in the army during the war").

43. Cong. Globe, 39th Cong., 1st sess., 685 (February 6, 1866).

44. DD to Julius Rockwell, April 22, 1868, DDFP; Dyer, "One Hundred Years," 6; Burlingame, *With Lincoln*, 171.

45. DD to Julius Rockwell, April 22, 1868, DDFP.

46. Woodburn, "George W. Julian's Journal," 327, entry for February 1, 1865; *Burlington (IA) Weekly Hawk-Eye*, February 11, 1865, 4; McGinty, *Lincoln and the Court*, 243–45.

47. Charles Sumner to Salmon Chase, December 21, 1864; Salmon Chase to Charles Sumner, December 21, 1864; Charles Sumner to Salmon Chase, January 15, 1865; Salmon Chase to Charles Sumner, January 15, 1865; Salmon Chase to Charles Sumner, January 23, 1865, all in Sumner, *Charles Sumner*, 97–98.

48. *New-York Daily Tribune*, February 7, 1865, 8; see also *Loyal Georgian* (Augusta), February 3, 1866, 2; see generally Brown, "Genesis," 171–72.

49. DD to Julius Rockwell, February 19, 1865, Manuscript Division, Library of Congress. A transcription of the letter is available at David & Sarah Davis Family Correspondence, Illinois Wesleyan University, Bloomington, IL, https://collections.carli.illinois.edu/digital/collection/iwu_davis/id/1419/rec/1; Sarah Davis to Frances Mary Walker, February 8, 1865, DDFP; Sarah Davis to Frances Mary Walker, March 19, 1865, DDFP. Davis missed Lincoln's inauguration in March 1865 because doctors would not let him travel to Washington. King, *Lincoln's Manager*, 225.

50. DD to Julius Rockwell, February 19, 1865, quoted in Fairman, *Reconstruction*, 60.

51. In 1890 Everett J. Waring became the first African American lawyer to argue before the Supreme Court. Smith v. United States, 137 U.S. 224 (1890); Smith, "Exact Justice," 11.

52. John S. Rock to F. W. Bird, "Mr. Rock's Experience in Washington," *National Anti-Slavery Standard*, March 4, 1865; *Alleghanian* (PA), February 9, 1865, 2; Contee, "Teacher, Healer, Lawyer," 85.

53. DD to Julius Rockwell, February 25, 1864, LP; DD to Julius Rockwell, April 22, 1868, DDFP.

54. *Liberator*, March 16, 1860, 2 (publishing the speech of Dr. John S. Rock).

55. DD to Sarah Davis, February 23, 1868, DDFP.

56. DD to Julius Rockwell, February 19, 1865, DDFP; Railroad Company v. Brown, 84 U.S. 445 (1873).

57. About seven weeks after John Rock's admission to the Supreme Court bar, Davis wrote to his brother-in-law that if he had been well enough to be in Washington during the preceding months, he "would have tried to have prevented the doing of certain things which were done." There is no mention of Rock in the letter and no indication that Davis was referring to Rock's admission. Indeed, the letter complains about Lincoln's appointment of John Lowell to replace Peleg Sprague as the district court judge in Massachusetts. Davis was "chagrined & mortified" about the selection and would have telegraphed Lincoln if he had had forewarning of the appointment. A year before, Davis told the president that "Judge Sprague was old & infirm and that [Davis] did not expect that he would live out his administration & that [Davis] wanted [Julius Rockwell] appointed" (DD to Julius Rockwell, March 20, 1865, DDFP).

58. Senate Report No. 131, 40th Cong., 2nd sess., 1868, 1–2, 12–14 (testimony of Kate Brown), https://www.senate.gov/artandhistory/history/resources/pdf/KateBrownReport.pdf.

59. Senate Report No. 131, 7–9 (testimony of B. H. Hinds). Another witness testified that Mrs. Brown was removed bodily from the train after a severe struggle but received no "rough treatment" (15 [testimony of Thomas Norfleet]).

60. Senate Report No. 131, 1, 3.

61. Cong. Globe, 40th Cong., 2nd sess., 1122, 1125 (February 12, 1868).

62. Senate Report No. 131, 12–14 (testimony of Kate Brown), 23–25 (testimony of Dr. Alexander T. Augusta); Masur, "Patronage and Protest," 1062.

63. Senate Report No. 131, 17–22 (testimony of Oscar A. Stevens).

64. Senate Report No. 131, 18–19 (testimony of Oscar A. Stevens).

65. Senate Report No. 131, 2.

66. Senate Report No. 131, 2–3.

67. See, for example, *National Republican* (Washington, DC), March 2, 1868, 3; *Alexandria (VA) Gazette*, March 9, 1868, 3; *New York Herald*, June 18, 1868, 3; *Richmond (VA) Dispatch*, June 19, 1868, 3; *Evening Star* (Washington, DC), June 17, 1868, 1.

68. *Evening Star* (Washington, DC), March 21, 1870, 4.

69. Masur, "Patronage and Protest," 1063–64; *Alexandria Gazette*, March 23, 1870, 3.

70. *Railroad Company*, 84 U.S. 448–49; *Evening Star* (Washington, DC), March 25, 1870, 4; *Evening Star*, March 24, 1870, 4; *Evening Star*, March 21, 1870, 4.

71. *Railroad Company*, 84 U.S. 451.

72. *Railroad Company*, 84 U.S. 446; An Act Authorizing the Extension of the Alexandria and Washington Railroad into the District of Columbia, and Conferring Certain Privileges on the Baltimore and Ohio Railroad Company, published in the *Daily Union* (Washington, DC), August 6, 1854, 2.

73. *Railroad Company*, 84 U.S. 446, 451–52; An Act to Extend the Charter of the Alexandria and Washington Railroad Company, and for Other Purposes, approved March 3, 1863, published in the *Daily Pittsburgh Gazette*, July 15, 1863, 1.

74. *Railroad Company*, 84 U.S. 452.

75. *Railroad Company*, 84 U.S. 449; Senate Report No. 131, 18–19 (testimony of Oscar A. Stevens).

76. *Railroad Company*, 84 U.S. 452–53. The unanimous court decision bears witness to the fact that each justice, regardless of philosophical, social, or political ideology, viewed the antidiscriminatory mood of Congress between 1863 and 1868 as unmistakable.

77. *Railroad Company*, 84 U.S. 452–53.

78. *Railroad Company*, 84 U.S. 452–53; Jones v. Mayer, 392 U.S. 409, 445 (1968) (Douglas, J., concurring); see also Goldstein, "The Second Amendment," 391–92.

79. McConnell, "Originalism," 953, 1117–19; see also Calabresi and Perl, "Originalism," 547–48.

80. Plessy v. Ferguson, 163 U.S. 537, 540–41 (1896) (overruled by Brown v. Board of Education, 347 U.S. 483 [1954]).

81. *Plessy*, 163 U.S. 544.

82. *Plessy*, 163 U.S. 555, 563 (Harlan, J., dissenting).

83. *Brown*, 347 U.S. 483.

84. *Plessy*, 163 U.S. 551.

Conclusion

1. Holland, *Life*, 97, 132.

2. Hill, *Lincoln the Lawyer*, 175.

3. Woldman, *Lawyer Lincoln*, 263.

4. Kutler, "David Davis," 520. Kutler also stated that "upon Davis' death, he was referred to as 'Lincoln's closest friend.'"

5. Burlingame, *Abraham Lincoln*, 1:331; Goodwin, *Team of Rivals*, 150. Other historians have arrived at similar conclusions. See, for example, Hearn, *Lincoln*, 7 ("great friends"); Bader and Williams, "David Davis," 214 ("close friends and colleagues"); Barnes, *Supreme Court*, 93 ("intimate personal and political friend"); Fraker, *Lincoln's Ladder*, 105 (close friends); Beveridge, *Abraham Lincoln*, 1:511 ("Judge David Davis . . . was as intimate with Lincoln as any other man except Herndon"); Wilson, *Intimate Memories*, 67 ("one of Lincoln's closest friends"); Gray, *Illinois*, 177 (intimate friends).

6. Niehoff, "David Davis," 184; *Chicago Tribune*, June 27, 1886, 4.

7. Dirck, *Lincoln the Lawyer*, 52–53; Donald, *"We Are Lincoln Men,"* xvi, 66–67. Often added to the evidence of a lack of a close friendship is Davis's comment to Orville Browning shortly after the president's death that Lincoln had "neither strong friendships nor enmities" and had not asked Davis's opinion on any topic since becoming president. Browning, *Diary*, 2:24–25, entry for April 22, 1865.

8. DD interview with William Herndon, September 19, 1866, in Wilson and Davis, *Herndon's Informants*, 346–47; DD interview with William Herndon, September 20, 1866, in Wilson and Davis, *Herndon's Informants*, 348.

9. DD to AL, September 1, 1862, LP; DD to AL, October 30, 1862, LP.

10. *Daily State Sentinel* (Indianapolis, IN), May 20, 1865, 3 (reporting the eulogy delivered by David Davis during the "Proceedings of the United States District Court [Indianapolis] in Relation to the Death of President Lincoln").

11. King, *Lincoln's Manager*, 254.

12. This conclusion finds support in Davis's similar complaint to Orville Browning eight days after the assassination that Lincoln "had never written him a line, nor asked his opinion upon any subject since he was elected President." Davis added that during the election campaign Lincoln wrote him very often but had never done so since. Browning, *Diary*, 2:24–25, entry for April 22, 1865.

13. DD interview with William Herndon, September 19, 1866, in Wilson and Davis, *Herndon's Informants*, 346–47. Davis told Herndon that Lincoln never mentioned a word on Reconstruction to him. DD interview with William Herndon, September 19, 1866, in Wilson and Davis, *Herndon's Informants*, 347.

14. Browning, *Diary*, 1:616, entries for January 17 and 19, 1863; DD to AL, November 29, 1864, LP; DD to AL, October 22, 1864, LP; AL to DD, April 13, 1865, in Basler, *Collected Works, First Supplement*, 286–87; King, *Lincoln's Manager*, 208, 228–29; DD to Leonard Swett, December 16, 1862, DDFP.

15. DD to AL, July 27, 1862, and n1, LP ("My Dear Sir—I am very solicitous for the appointment of my nephew, Jos. A. Scranton, of Scranton, Luzerne Co. Pa. Collector for the Congressional district in which he resides"); DD to AL, June 2, 1864, LP; DD to AL, October 4, 1864, LP.

16. DD interview with William H. Herndon, September 20, 1866, in Wilson and Davis, *Herndon's Informants*, 349.

17. Leonard Swett to William Herndon, January 17, 1866, in Wilson and Davis, *Herndon's Informants*, 167.

18. DD statement to William Herndon, 1866, in Wilson and Davis, *Herndon's Informants*, 529.

19. DD statement to William Herndon, February 22, 1866, in Wilson and Davis, *Herndon's Informants*, 218.

20. Davis was in good company in not receiving words of appreciation from Lincoln. When Matilda Edwards was asked if Lincoln "ever [m]entioned the subject of his love to her," Matilda responded that Lincoln never mentioned the subject and "never even Stooped to pay [her] a Compliment" (Elizabeth Todd Edwards interview with William Herndon, 1865–66, in Wilson and Davis, *Herndon's Informants*, 444).

21. King, *Lincoln's Manager*, 228–30.

22. DD interview with William H. Herndon, September 19, 1866, in Wilson and Davis, *Herndon's Informants*, 346; DD to AL, June 2, 1864, LP.

23. Stevens, *Reporter's Lincoln*, 96–97, reporting the recollections of Albert Blair. Blair placed the White House reception in February 1865. The date is likely incorrect, since Davis spent the month of February in Bloomington recuperating from an illness.

24. *New National Era* (Washington, DC), February 2, 1871, 2; Sarah Davis to Lucy Forbes Walker Rockwell, January 8, 1871 (misdated January 8, 1870), DDFP. The sculptor, Vinnie Ream, invited Davis and a few other Lincoln friends to preview the statue on January 7, 1871. According to Sarah, her husband thought it "very good."

25. DD to Sarah Davis, May 3, 1851, DDFP; Leonard Swett interview with Jesse W. Weik, ca. 1887–89, in Wilson and Davis, *Herndon's Informants*, 731–32; Henry C. Whitney interview with Jesse W. Weik, ca. 1887–89, in Wilson and Davis, *Herndon's Informants*, 733–34; King, *Lincoln's Manager*, 89; Reynolds, *Abe*, 226–27.

26. See Donald, *"We Are Lincoln Men,"* 29–36, 39–55.

27. DD to Gideon Welles, July 27, 1872 (referring to Joshua Speed as one of Lincoln's "cherished friends"), folder 1860 (Misc.), box 9, 1860 National Convention—January—1861, David Davis Family Papers, Chicago History Museum (apparently misfiled).

28. See Donald, *"We Are Lincoln Men,"* 114–22.

29. Donald, *"We Are Lincoln Men,"* 41. Donald characterized Browning as Lincoln's "closest wartime friend" (xvii).

30. *New-York Daily Tribune*, February 28, 1860, 6.

31. Fritz, *Federal Justice*, 24.

32. McKoski, "Reestablishing," 282.

33. Murphy, *Congress and the Court*, 264. The polling questions assumed that President Dwight Eisenhower would not run for reelection in 1956.

34. National Center for State Courts, Judicial Selection, https://www.ncsc.org/consulting-and-research/areas-of-expertise/court-leadership/judicial-selection.

35. *Model Code of Judicial Conduct 2007*, rules 4.1, 4.2; see New York Advisory Committee on Judicial Ethics, Opinion 96–07 (1996); Nevada Standing Committee on Judicial

Ethics and Election Practices, Opinion JE12–004 (2012). Judicial conduct codes in states that elect judges vary as to the type of political activity permitted for judges and judicial candidates. Illinois rules permit more political activity than most other jurisdictions, but even in Illinois, Judge Davis could not today endorse, speak on behalf of, or solicit funds for an executive branch candidate; serve as a convention delegate; or lead a convention floor fight. *Illinois Code of Judicial Conduct of 2023*, rule 4.1.

36. Joan Biskupic, "Justice Ruth Bader Ginsburg Calls Trump a 'Faker,' He Says She Should Resign," *CNN Politics*, July 13, 2016, https://www.cnn.com/2016/07/12/politics/justice-ruth-bader-ginsburg-donald-trump-faker/index.html; Adam Liptak, "Ginsburg Has a Few Words about Trump," *New York Times*, July 11, 2016, 1; Editorial Board, "Justice Ginsburg's Inappropriate Comments on Donald Trump," *Washington Post*, July 12, 2016, https://www.washingtonpost.com/opinions/justice-ginsburgs-inappropriate-comments -on-donald-trump/2016/07/12/981df404–4862–11e6-bdb9–701687974517_story.html; Editorial Board, "Mr. Trump Is Right about Justice Ginsburg," *New York Times*, July 13, 2016, 18; David G. Savage, "Justice Ginsburg Apologizes for 'Ill-Advised' Trump Remarks," *Chicago Tribune*, July 15, 2016, 14.

37. McKoski, "Reestablishing," 280–81 (quoting Matthew Hale, *Lord Hale's Rules for His Judicial Guidance: Things Necessary to Be Continually Had in Remembrance*, reproduced in *In re* Code of Judicial Conduct, 643 So. 2d 1037, 1038n2 [Florida 1994]).

38. "Canons of Judicial Ethics 1924," canon 28.

39. For Davis's participation in raising funds for the victims of the Great Chicago Fire, see Pratt, "David Davis," 160.

40. See *Model Code of Judicial Conduct 2007*, rule 3. ("Appointment to Fiduciary Positions"), rule 3.7(A)(2) ("Participation in Educational, Religious, Charitable, Fraternal, or Civic Organizations and Activities"), rule 1.3 ("Avoiding Abuse of the Prestige of Judicial Office"), rule 2.9 ("Ex Parte Communications").

41. Dillingham v. Fisher, File No. L02512, Document Nos. 4171, 4168, Rock County Circuit Court (Wisconsin), February 1856, Law Practice of Abraham Lincoln.

42. Wells v. Del Norte School District C-7, 753 P.2d 770, 772 (Colorado Ct. App. 1987).

43. See, for example, Massachusetts Committee on Judicial Ethics, Opinion 2016–01 (2016); Connecticut Committee on Judicial Ethics, Opinion 2013-06 (2013); Oklahoma Judicial Ethics Advisory Panel, Opinion 2011–3 (2011). Some states take the more realistic view that the designation of Facebook "friendship" is virtually meaningless and does not in itself require a judge to recuse from cases in which a lawyer is a Facebook friend. For example, Law Offices of Herssein and Herssein v. United Services Automobile Association, 271 So.3d 889, 898–99 (Florida 2018).

44. 28 U.S.C. § 47; *Model Code of Judicial Conduct 2007*, rule 2.11(A)(6)(d). Under modern rules, Justice Field could not have sat on the case either because his brother, David Dudley Field, was one of the attorneys representing Milligan. McGinty, *Lincoln and the Court*, 252; *Model Code of Judicial Conduct 2007*, rule 2.11(A)(2)(b).

45. *Model Code of Judicial Conduct 2007*, rule 3.7(A)(4). Rule 3.7(A)(4) permits judges to speak only at fundraising events of law-related organizations.

46. McKoski, "Reestablishing," 292–93.

47. Republican Party of Minnesota v. White, 536 U.S. 765, 798 (2002) (Stevens, J., dissenting).

48. Eu v. San Francisco County Democratic Central Committee, 489 U.S. 214, 224 (1989) (quoting Ripon Society v. National Republican Party, 525 F.2d 567, 601 [D.C. Cir. 1975]).

49. Judiciary Act of 1789, chap. 20, § 8, 1 Stat. 73, 76 (now 28 U.S.C. § 453).

Bibliography

Books, Articles, and Documents

Abbott, Richard H. *For Free Press and Equal Rights: Republican Newspapers in the Reconstruction South.* Edited by John W. Quist. Athens: University of Georgia Press, 2004.

Abrams, Dan, and David Fisher. *Lincoln's Last Trial: The Murder Case That Propelled Him to the Presidency.* Toronto: Hanover Square, 2018.

Achorn, Edward. *The Lincoln Miracle: Inside the Republican Convention That Changed History.* New York: Atlantic Monthly Press, 2023.

Adams, Joseph. "The Illinois South: Culture and Identity in Southern Illinois." *Western Illinois Historical Review* 8 (Spring 2017): 43–78.

Allardice, Bruce S. "'Illinois Is Rotten with Traitors!': The Republican Defeat in the 1862 State Election." *Journal of the Illinois State Historical Society* 104, no. 1–2 (Spring–Summer 2011): 97–114.

Andreasen, Byron C. *Looking for Lincoln in Illinois: Lincoln and Mormon Country.* Carbondale: Southern Illinois University Press, 2015.

Angle, Paul M., ed. *Abraham Lincoln, by Some Men Who Knew Him: Being Personal Recollections of Judge Owen T. Reeves, Hon. James S. Ewing, Col. Richard P. Morgan, Judge Franklin Blades, John W. Bunn.* Chicago: Americana House, 1950.

Angle, Paul M. "Abraham Lincoln: Circuit Lawyer." Lincoln Centennial Association Papers. Springfield, IL: Lincoln Centennial Association, 1928.

Angle, Paul M. *Here I Have Lived: A History of Lincoln's Springfield, 1821–1865.* New Brunswick, NJ: Rutgers University Press, 1950.

Angle, Paul M., ed. "The Recollections of William Pitt Kellogg." *Abraham Lincoln Quarterly* 3, no. 7 (September 1945): 319–39.

Ankrom, Reg. *Stephen A. Douglas: The Political Apprenticeship, 1833–1843.* Jefferson, NC: McFarland, 2015.

Ashe, Samuel A., ed. *Biographical History of North Carolina from Colonial Times to the Present.* Vol. 2. Greensboro, NC: Charles L. Van Noppen, 1905.

Atkinson, David N. *Leaving the Bench: Supreme Court Justices at the End*. Lawrence: University Press of Kansas, 1999.

Avins, Alfred. "The Right to Be a Witness and the Fourteenth Amendment." *Missouri Law Review* 31, no. 4 (Fall 1966): 471–504.

Bader, William D., and Frank J. Williams. "David Davis: Lawyer, Judge, and Politician in the Age of Lincoln." *Roger Williams University Law Review* 14, no. 2 (Spring 2009): 163–214.

Bader, William D., and Frank J. Williams. *Unknown Justices of the United States Supreme Court*. Buffalo, NY: William S. Hein, 2011.

Bailey, Louis J. "Caleb Blood Smith." *Indiana Magazine of History* 29, no. 3 (September 1933): 213–39.

Baker, George E., ed. *The Works of William H. Seward*. 5 vols. Boston: Houghton Mifflin, 1884.

Bancroft, Frederic. *The Life of William H. Seward*. 2 vols. New York: Harper and Brothers, 1900.

Baringer, William Eldon. "Campaign Techniques in Illinois, 1860." In *Illinois State Historical Society Transactions for the Year 1932*, 203–81. Publication 39. Springfield: Illinois State Historical Library, 1932.

Barkow, Rachel E. "More Supreme Than Court? The Fall of the Political Question Doctrine and the Rise of Judicial Supremacy." *Columbia Law Review* 102, no. 2 (March 2002): 237–336.

Barnes, William Horatio. *The Supreme Court of the United States: A Series of Biographies*. Washington, DC: W. H. Barnes, 1877.

Barry, Peter J. "*Ex parte Milligan*: History and Historians." *Indiana Magazine of History* 109, no. 4 (December 2013): 355–79.

Barry, Peter J. "'I'll Keep Them in Prison Awhile . . . ': Abraham Lincoln and David Davis on Civil Liberties in Wartime." *Journal of the Abraham Lincoln Association* 28, no. 1 (Winter 2007): 20–29.

Barton, William E. *The Life of Abraham Lincoln*. 2 vols. Indianapolis, IN: Bobbs-Merrill, 1925.

Basler, Roy P., ed. *The Collected Works of Abraham Lincoln*. 9 vols. New Brunswick, NJ: Rutgers University Press, 1953–55.

Basler, Roy P., ed. *The Collected Works of Abraham Lincoln, First Supplement 1832–1865*. Westport, CT: Greenwood, 1974.

Basler, Roy P., and Christian O. Basler, eds. *The Collected Works of Abraham Lincoln, Second Supplement 1848–1865*. New Brunswick, NJ: Rutgers University Press, 1990.

Bateman, Newton, and Paul Selby, eds. *Historical Encyclopedia of Illinois and History of Christian County*. 2 vols. Chicago: Munsell, 1918.

Bateman, Newton, and Paul Selby, eds. *Historical Encyclopedia of Illinois and History of Hancock County*. 2 vols. Chicago: Munsell, 1921.

Bateman, Newton, and Paul Selby, eds. *Historical Encyclopedia of Illinois and History of McLean County*. 2 vols. Chicago: Munsell, 1908.

Baxter, Maurice G. "Orville H. Browning: Lincoln's Colleague and Critic." *Journal of the Illinois State Historical Society* 48, no. 4 (Winter 1955): 431–55.

Beveridge, Albert J. *Abraham Lincoln 1809–1858*. 2 vols. New York: Houghton Mifflin, 1928.

Billings, Roger, and Frank J. Williams, eds. *Abraham Lincoln, Esq.: The Legal Career of America's Greatest President.* Lexington: University Press of Kentucky, 2010.

Biographical and Genealogical Record of La Salle and Grundy Counties, Illinois. 2 vols. Chicago: Lewis Publishing, 1900.

Bishop, John Leander. *A History of American Manufactures from 1608 to 1860.* Vol. 1. Philadelphia: Edward Young, 1864.

Blaustein, Albert P., and Roy M. Mersky. *The First One Hundred Justices: Statistical Studies on the Supreme Court of the United States.* Hamden, CT: Archon Books, 1978.

Blumenthal, Sidney. *All the Powers of Earth: The Political Life of Abraham Lincoln, 1856–1860.* New York: Simon and Schuster, 2019.

Blumenthal, Sidney. *Wrestling with His Angel: The Political Life of Abraham Lincoln, 1849–1856.* New York: Simon and Schuster, 2017.

Borit, G. S. "Lincoln's Opposition to the Mexican War." *Journal of the Illinois State Historical Society* 67, no. 1 (February 1974): 79–100.

Boutwell, George S. *Reminiscences of Sixty Years in Public Affairs.* 2 vols. New York: McClure Phillips, 1902.

Bowman, Anthony. "Sarah Davis (1814–1879)." McLean County Museum of History, Biographies, Davis, Sarah (2009). https://mchistory.org/research/biographies/davis-sarah.

Boynton, Edward C. *History of West Point, and Its Military Importance during the American Revolution.* 2nd ed. New York: D. Van Nostrand, 1871.

Brown, Charles Summer. "The Genesis of the Negro Lawyer in New England." Part 2. *Negro History Bulletin* 22, no. 8 (May 1959): 171–77.

Browne, Robert Henry. *Abraham Lincoln and the Men of His Time: His Cause, His Character, and True Place in History, and the Men, Statesmen, Heroes, Patriots, Who Formed the Illustrious League about Him.* 2 vols. Rev. 2nd ed. Chicago: Blakely-Oswald, 1907.

Browning, Orville Hickman. *The Diary of Orville Hickman Browning.* 2 vols. Edited with an introduction and notes by Theodore Calvin Pease and James G. Randall. Springfield: Trustees of the Illinois State Historical Library, 1925.

Bungay, George W. *Traits of Representative Men.* New York: Fowler and Wells, 1882.

Burlingame, Michael. *Abraham Lincoln: A Life.* 2 vols. Baltimore, MD: Johns Hopkins University Press, 2008.

Burlingame, Michael. *The Inner World of Abraham Lincoln.* Urbana: University of Illinois Press, 1994.

Burlingame, Michael, ed. *Lincoln's Journalist: John Hay's Anonymous Writings for the Press, 1860–1864.* Carbondale: Southern Illinois University Press, 1998.

Burlingame, Michael, ed. *An Oral History of Abraham Lincoln: John G. Nicolay's Interviews and Essays.* Carbondale: Southern Illinois University Press, 1996.

Burlingame, Michael, ed. *With Lincoln in the White House: Letters, Memoranda, and Other Writing of John G. Nicolay 1860–1865.* Carbondale: Southern Illinois University Press, 2000.

Burlingame, Michael, and John R. Turner Ettlinger, eds. *Inside Lincoln's White House: The Complete Civil War Diary of John Hay.* Carbondale: Southern Illinois University Press, 1997.

Burton, Harold H. "Two Significant Decisions: *Ex parte Milligan* and *Ex parte McCardle.*" *American Bar Association Journal* 41, no. 2 (February 1955): 121–24, 176–77.

Calabresi, Steven G., and Michael W. Perl. "Originalism and *Brown v. Board of Education.*" *Michigan State Law Review* 2014, no. 3 (2014): 429–574.

"Canons of Judicial Ethics 1924." In *The Development of the ABA Judicial Code,* by Lisa L. Milord, 131–43. Chicago: American Bar Association, 1992.

Carpenter, Frank B. "How Lincoln Was Nominated." *Century Magazine* 24, no. 6 (October 1882): 853–59.

Chadwick, Bruce. *Lincoln for President.* Naperville, IL: Sourcebooks, 2009.

Chase, Philander. *Bishop Chase's Reminiscences: An Autobiography.* 2 vols. 2nd ed. Boston: James B. Dow, 1848.

Chittenden, Lucius Eugene. *Recollections of President Lincoln and His Administration.* New York: Harper and Brothers, 1891.

Church, Charles A. *History of the Republican Party in Illinois 1854–1912.* Rockford, IL: Wilson Brothers, 1912.

Clay, Cassius Marcellus. *The Life of Cassius Marcellus Clay: Memoirs, Writings, and Speeches.* Cincinnati: J. Fletcher Brennan, 1886.

Cleveland, John F., ed. *The Tribune Almanac and Political Register for 1861.* New York: Tribune Association, 1860.

Clinton, Robert N. "A Mandatory View of Federal Court Jurisdiction: Early Implementation of and Departures from the Constitutional Plan." *Columbia Law Review* 86, no. 8 (December 1986): 1515–1621.

Cochrane, Joseph. *Centennial History of Mason County, Including a Sketch of the Early History of Illinois.* Springfield, IL: Rokker, 1876.

Cole, Arthur Charles, ed. *The Constitutional Debates of 1847.* Springfield: Trustees of the Illinois State Historical Library, 1919.

Cole, Arthur Charles. *The Era of the Civil War, 1848–1870.* Springfield: Illinois Centennial Commission, 1919.

Coleman, Ann Mary, ed. *The Life of John J. Crittenden: With Selections from His Correspondence and Speeches.* 2 vols. Philadelphia: J. B. Lippincott, 1871.

Coleman, Charles H. *Abraham Lincoln and Coles County, Illinois.* New Brunswick, NJ: Scarecrow, 1955.

Coleman, Charles H., and Paul H. Spence. "The Charleston Riot, March 28, 1864." *Journal of the Illinois State Historical Society* 33, no. 1 (March 1940): 7–56.

Collins, Bruce. "The Democrats' Loss of Pennsylvania in 1858." *Pennsylvania Magazine of History and Biography* 109, no. 4 (October 1985): 499–536.

Collins, Bruce. "The Lincoln-Douglas Contest of 1858 and Illinois' Electorate." *Journal of American Studies* 20, no. 3 (December 1986): 391–420.

Contee, Clarence G. "Teacher, Healer, Lawyer: The Supreme Court Bar's First Black Member." In *Yearbook 1976: Supreme Court Historical Society,* 82–85. Washington, DC: Supreme Court Historical Society, 1975.

Corning, Charles R. *Amos Tuck.* Exeter, NH: News-Letter Press, 1902.

Creswell, John A. J. *Oration on the Life and Character of Henry Winter Davis.* Washington, DC: Government Printing Office, 1866.

Crockett, Walter Hill. *Vermont, the Green Mountain State.* Vol. 3. New York: Century History, 1921.

Cullom, Shelby Moore. *Fifty Years of Public Service: Personal Recollections of Shelby M. Cullom, Senior United States Senator from Illinois.* 2nd ed. Chicago: A. C. McClurg, 1911.

Curran, Nathaniel B. "Levi Davis, Illinois' Third Auditor." *Journal of the Illinois State Historical Society* 71, no. 1 (February 1978): 2–12.

Current, Richard N. *The History of Wisconsin.* Vol. 2, *The Civil War Era, 1848–1873.* Madison: State Historical Society of Wisconsin, 1976.

Curtis, Michael Kent. "Lincoln, Vallandigham, and Anti-war Speech in the Civil War." *William and Mary Bill of Rights Journal* 7, no. 1 (December 1998): 105–91.

Davis, David. "Memorial Address: The Life and Services of John Todd Stuart." In *Proceedings of the Illinois State Bar Association, at Its Ninth Annual Meeting, Held at the City of Springfield, January 12 and 13, 1886,* 47–55. Springfield, IL: H. W. Rokker, 1886.

Davis, Henry Winter. *Speeches and Addresses Delivered in the Congress of the United States, and on Several Public Occasions, by Henry Winter Davis, of Maryland.* New York: Harper and Brothers, 1867.

Davis, J. McCan. *How Abraham Lincoln Became President.* Centennial ed. Springfield: Illinois Company, 1909.

Davis, J. McCan. "Origin of the Lincoln Rail: As Related by Governor Oglesby." *Century Illustrated Monthly Magazine* 60, no. 33 (June 1900): 271–75.

Davis, Rodney O., and Douglas L. Wilson, eds. *The Lincoln-Douglas Debates.* Urbana: Knox College Lincoln Studies Center and University of Illinois Press, 2008.

Dent, Thomas. "David Davis of Illinois—a Sketch." *American Law Review* 53, no. 4 (July/August 1919): 535–60.

Denton, Lawrence M. *William Henry Seward and the Secession Crisis: The Effort to Prevent Civil War.* Jefferson, NC: McFarland, 2009.

Dewey, Donald O. "Hoosier Justice: The Journal of David McDonald, 1864–1868." *Indiana Magazine of History* 62, no. 3 (September 1966): 175–232.

Dirck, Brian. *Lincoln the Lawyer.* Urbana: University of Illinois Press, 2007.

Dittenhoefer, Abram J. *How We Elected Lincoln.* New York: Harper and Brothers, 1916.

Donald, David Herbert. *Charles Sumner and the Rights of Man.* New York: Knopf, 1970.

Donald, David Herbert. *Lincoln.* New York: Simon and Schuster, 1995.

Donald, David Herbert. *Lincoln's Herndon.* New York: Knopf, 1948.

Donald, David Herbert. *"We Are Lincoln Men": Abraham Lincoln and His Friends.* New York: Simon and Schuster, 2003.

Dudley, Thomas H. "The Inside Facts of Lincoln's Nomination." *Century Illustrated Monthly Magazine* 40, no. 3 (July 1890): 477–79.

Duis, E. *The Good Old Times in McLean County, Illinois.* Bloomington, IL: Leader, 1874.

Dyer, Brainerd. "One Hundred Years of Negro Suffrage." *Pacific Historical Review* 37, no. 1 (February 1968): 1–20.

Ecelbarger, Gary. "Before Cooper Union: Abraham Lincoln's 1859 Cincinnati Speech and Its Impact on His Nomination." *Journal of the Abraham Lincoln Association* 30, no. 1 (Winter 2009): 1–17.

Ecelbarger, Gary. *The Great Comeback: How Abraham Lincoln Beat the Odds to Win the 1860 Republican Nomination.* New York: St. Martin's Press, 2008.

Eckley, Robert S. *Lincoln's Forgotten Friend, Leonard Swett.* Carbondale: Southern Illinois University Press, 2012.

Eckley, Robert S. Review of *"We Are Lincoln Men": Abraham Lincoln and His Friends,* by D. H. Donald. *Journal of the Abraham Lincoln Association* 25, no. 2 (Summer 2004): 71–81.

Edmonds, Franklin Spencer. *History of the Central High School of Philadelphia.* Philadelphia: J. B. Lippincott, 1902.

Egerton, Douglas R. *Year of Meteors: Stephen Douglas, Abraham Lincoln, and the Election That Brought on the Civil War.* New York: Bloomsbury, 2010.

Egle, William Henry. *Life and Times of Andrew Gregg Curtin.* Philadelphia: Thompson, 1896.

Elliff, John T. "Views of the Wigwam Convention: Letters from the Son of Lincoln's 1856 Candidate." *Journal of the Abraham Lincoln Association* 31, no. 2 (Summer 2010): 1–11.

Ellis, Richard J. *The Development of the American Presidency.* New York: Routledge, 2012.

Emerson, Jason. *Giant in the Shadows: The Life of Robert T. Lincoln.* Carbondale: Southern Illinois University Press, 2012.

Emery, Charles Wilson. "The Iowa Germans in the Election of 1860." *Annals of Iowa* 22, no. 6 (October 1940): 421–54.

Ewing, Elbert William Robinson. *History and Law of the Hayes-Tilden Contest before the Electoral Commission: The Florida Case, 1876–1877.* Washington, DC: Cobden Publishing, 1910.

Fairman, Charles. *Mr. Justice Miller and the Supreme Court, 1862–1890.* Cambridge, MA: Harvard University Press, 1939.

Fairman, Charles. *Reconstruction and Reunion 1864–1868, Part One.* Vol. 6 of *Oliver Wendell Holmes Devise History of the Supreme Court of the United States.* New York: Macmillan, 1971.

Faust, Albert Bernhardt. *The German Element in the United States.* Vol. 2. Boston: Houghton Mifflin, 1909.

Fehrenbacher, Don E. *Chicago Giant: A Biography of "Long John" Wentworth.* Madison, WI: American History Research Center, 1957.

Fehrenbacher, Don E. *Prelude to Greatness: Lincoln in the 1850's.* Stanford, CA: Stanford University Press, 1962.

Fehrenbacher, Don E., and Virginia Fehrenbacher, eds. *Recollected Words of Abraham Lincoln.* Stanford, CA: Stanford University Press, 1996.

Fenster, Julie M. *The Case of Abraham Lincoln: A Story of Adultery, Murder, and the Making of a Great President.* New York: Palgrave Macmillan, 2007.

Field, Henry M. *The Life of David Dudley Field.* New York: Charles Scribner's Sons, 1898.

Finkelman, Paul. "Prelude to the Fourteenth Amendment: Black Legal Rights in the Antebellum North." *Rutgers Law Journal* 17, no. 3–4 (Spring and Summer 1986): 415–82.

Fishback, Mason M. "Illinois Legislation on Slavery and Free Negroes 1818–1865." In *Transactions of the Illinois State Historical Society for the Year 1904,* 414–32. Publication 9. Springfield: Illinois State Historical Library, 1904.

Foner, Eric. *Free Soil, Free Labor, Free Men: The Ideology of the Republican Party before the Civil War.* New York: Oxford University Press, 1970.

Foulke, William Dudley. *Life of Oliver P. Morton: Including His Important Speeches.* 2 vols. Indianapolis, IN: Bowen-Merrill, 1899.

Foy, Charles R., and Michael I. Bradley. "The African American Community in Brushy Fork, Illinois, 1818–1861." *Journal of the Illinois State Historical Society* 112, no. 2 (Summer 2019): 129–62.

Fraker, Guy C. *Lincoln's Ladder to the Presidency: The Eighth Judicial Circuit.* Carbondale: Southern Illinois University Press, 2012.

Frank, John P. *Lincoln as a Lawyer.* Urbana: University of Illinois Press, 1961.

Freehling, William W. *Becoming Lincoln.* Charlottesville: University of Virginia Press, 2018.

Fridlington, Robert. *The Reconstruction Court 1864–1888.* Millwood, NY: Associated Faculty Press, 1987.

Friends of the Chicago & Alton Depot. "1879 Railroad Depot, History of the Depot, 1847–1947." https://www.chicagoalton1879depot.org/history.

Fritz, Christian G. *Federal Justice in California: The Court of Ogden Hoffman, 1851–1891.* Lincoln: University of Nebraska Press, 1991.

Gammie, Peter. "Pugilists and Politicians in Antebellum New York: The Life and Times of Tom Hyer." *New York History* 75, no. 3 (July 1994): 265–96.

Garrett, Romeo B. "The Negro in Peoria, 1773–1905." *Negro History Bulletin* 17, no. 7 (April 1954): 147–50.

George, Tom M. "'Mechem' or 'Mack': How a One-Word Correction in the *Collected Works of Abraham Lincoln* Reveals the Truth about an 1856 Political Event." *Journal of the Abraham Lincoln Association* 33, no. 2 (Summer 2012): 20–33.

Gerhardt, Michael J. *Lincoln's Mentors: The Education of a Leader.* New York: Harper-Collins, 2021.

Gienapp, William E. *The Origins of the Republican Party, 1852–1856.* New York: Oxford University Press, 1987.

Goldman, Ralph M. *The National Party Chairmen and Committees: Factionalism at the Top.* Armonk, NY: M. E. Sharpe, 1990.

Goldstein, Leslie Friedman. "The Second Amendment, the *Slaughter-House Cases* (1873), and *United States v. Cruikshank* (1876)." *Albany Government Law Review* 1, no. 2 (2008): 365–418.

Good, Timothy S. *Lincoln for President: An Underdog's Path to the 1860 Republican Nomination.* Jefferson, NC: McFarland, 2009.

Goodwin, Doris Kearns. *Team of Rivals: The Political Genius of Abraham Lincoln.* New York: Simon and Schuster, 2005.

Gray, James. *The Illinois.* New York: Farrar and Rinehart, 1940.

Greeley, Horace, and John F. Cleveland, eds. *A Political Textbook for 1860: Comprising a Brief View of Presidential Nominations and Elections.* New York: Tribune Association, 1860.

Gresham, Matilda. *Life of Walter Quintin Gresham, 1832–1895.* 2 vols. Chicago: Rand McNally, 1919.

Grimsley, Elizabeth Todd. "Six Months in the White House." *Journal of the Illinois State Historical Society* 19, no. 3/4 (October 1926–January 1927): 43–73.

Guelzo, Allen C. *Abraham Lincoln as a Man of Ideas*. Carbondale: Southern Illinois University Press, 2009.

Guelzo, Allen C. "Houses Divided: Lincoln, Douglas, and the Political Landscape of 1858." *Journal of American History* 94, no. 2 (September 2007): 391–417.

Guelzo, Allen C. *Lincoln and Douglas: The Debates That Defined America*. New York: Simon and Schuster, 2008.

Halstead, Murat. *Caucuses of 1860: A History of the National Political Conventions of the Current Political Campaign*. Columbus, OH: Follett, Foster, 1860.

Harrington, Fred Harvey. *Fighting Politician: Major General N. P. Banks*. Philadelphia: University of Pennsylvania Press, 1948.

Harrison, Lowell. *Lincoln of Kentucky*. Lexington: University Press of Kentucky, 2000.

Harrison, Victoria L. "We Are Here Assembled: Illinois Colored Conventions, 1853–1873." *Journal of the Illinois State Historical Society* 108, no. 3–4 (Fall/Winter 2015): 322–46.

Hayes, Rutherford B. *Diary and Letters of Rutherford Birchard Hayes: Nineteenth President of the United States*. Edited by Charles Richard Williams. Vol. 1. Columbus: Ohio State Archaeological and Historical Society, 1922.

Hearn, Chester G. *Lincoln, the Cabinet, and the Generals*. Baton Rouge: Louisiana State University Press, 2010.

Heinzel, Sally. "'To Protect the Rights of the White Race': Illinois Republican Racial Politics in the 1860 Campaign and the Twenty-Second General Assembly." *Journal of the Illinois State Historical Society* 108, no. 3–4 (Fall/Winter 2015): 374–406.

Henkle, W. D., ed. "Personal." *Ohio Educational Monthly and National Teacher* 28, no. 1 (January 1879): 29–30.

Hensel, W. U. "Jeremiah Sullivan Black, Chief-Justice of Pennsylvania and Attorney-General of the United States." *Green Bag* 2, no. 5 (May 1890): 189–97.

Herndon, William H. *Herndon on Lincoln: Letters*. Edited by Douglas L. Wilson and Rodney O. Davis. Urbana: University of Illinois Press, 2016.

Herndon, William H., and Jesse W. Weik. *Herndon's Life of Lincoln: The History and Personal Recollections of Abraham Lincoln as Originally Written by William H. Herndon and Jesse W. Weik with Introduction and Notes by Paul M. Angle*. New York: Albert and Charles Boni, 1930.

Herndon, William H., and Jesse W. Weik. *Herndon's Lincoln*. Edited by Douglas L. Wilson and Rodney O. Davis. Urbana: University of Illinois Press, 2006.

Herriott, F. I. "Republican Presidential Preliminaries in Iowa—1859–1860." *Annals of Iowa* 9, no. 4 (January 1910): 241–83.

Hertz, Emanuel, ed. *Abraham Lincoln, the Tribute of the Synagogue*. New York: Bloch, 1927.

Hertz, Emanuel. *The Hidden Lincoln: From the Letters and Papers of William H. Herndon*. New York: Viking, 1938.

Hickey, James T. "Oglesby's Fence Rail Dealings and the 1860 Decatur Convention." *Journal of the Illinois State Historical Society* 54, no. 1 (Spring 1961): 5–24.

Hickey, James T., and Mary Lincoln. "Lincolniana." *Journal of the Illinois State Historical Society* 65, no. 2 (Summer 1972): 206–9.

Hickin, Patricia. "John C. Underwood and the Antislavery Movement in Virginia, 1847–1860." *Virginia Magazine of History and Biography* 73, no. 2 (April 1965): 156–68.

Hill, Frederick Trevor. *Lincoln the Lawyer.* New York: Century, 1906.

History of Sangamon County, Illinois; Together with Sketches of Its Cities, Villages and Townships . . . Portraits of Prominent Persons, and Biographies of Representative Citizens. Chicago: Inter-State Publishing, 1881.

Holden, Edward S. "Training of Cadets for the U.S. Army." *Journal of the Military Service Institution of the United States* 34 (1904): 420–30.

Holland, Josiah Gilbert. *The Life of Abraham Lincoln.* Springfield, MA: Gurdon Bill, 1866.

Hollister, Ovando J. *Life of Schuyler Colfax.* New York: Funk and Wagnalls, 1886.

Holzer, Harold. *Lincoln President-Elect: Abraham Lincoln and the Great Secession Winter, 1860–1861.* New York: Simon and Schuster, 2008.

Hoogenboom, Ari. *Rutherford B. Hayes: Warrior and President.* Lawrence: University Press of Kansas, 1995.

Horner, Harlan Hoyt. *Lincoln and Greeley.* Urbana: University of Illinois Press, 1953.

Howell, William G. "Wartime Judgments of Presidential Power: Striking Down but Not Back." *Minnesota Law Review* 93, no. 5 (May 2009): 1778–1819.

Hunt, Aurora. *Kirby Benedict: Frontier Federal Judge.* Glendale, CA: Arthur H. Clark, 1961.

Hunt, Eugenia Jones. "My Personal Recollections of Abraham and Mary Todd Lincoln." *Abraham Lincoln Quarterly* 3, no. 5 (March 1945): 235–52.

Huston, James L. "The Threat of Radicalism: Seward's Candidacy and the Rhode Island Gubernatorial Election of 1860." *Rhode Island History* 41, no. 3 (August 1982): 87–99.

James, Edmund J., and Milo J. Loveless. *A Bibliography of Newspapers Published in Illinois prior to 1860.* Springfield, IL: Phillips Brothers, 1899.

Jenkins, Jeffery A., and Charles Stewart. *Fighting for the Speakership: The House and the Rise of Party Government.* Princeton, NJ: Princeton University Press, 2012.

Johannsen, Robert W. *Stephen A. Douglas.* Urbana: University of Illinois Press, 1997.

Johns, Jane Martin. *Personal Recollections of Early Decatur, Abraham Lincoln, Richard J. Oglesby, and the Civil War.* Decatur, IL: Decatur Chapter Daughters of the American Revolution, 1912.

Johnson, Andrew. *The Papers of Andrew Johnson.* Vol. 8. Edited by Paul Bergeron. Knoxville: University of Tennessee Press, 1989.

Johnson, John W., ed. *Historic U.S. Court Cases: An Encyclopedia.* 2 vols. New York: Routledge, 2001.

Journal of the Convention, Assembled at Springfield, June 7, 1847, in Pursuance of an Act of the General Assembly of the State of Illinois . . . Approved, February 20, 1847, for the Purpose of Altering, Amending, or Revising the Constitution of the State of Illinois. Springfield, IL: Lanphier and Walker, 1847.

Journal of the House of Representatives of the Fourteenth General Assembly of the State of Illinois. Springfield, IL: Walters and Weber, 1844.

Journal of the House of Representatives of the Nineteenth General Assembly of the State of Illinois. Springfield, IL: Lanphier and Walker, 1855.

Julian, George W. *Political Recollections, 1840 to 1872*. Chicago: Jansen, McClurg, 1884.

Kahan, Paul. *Amiable Scoundrel: Simon Cameron, Lincoln's Scandalous Secretary of War*. Lincoln: University of Nebraska Press, 2016.

Karamanski, Theodore J. *Rally 'round the Flag: Chicago and the Civil War*. Lanham, MD: Rowman and Littlefield, 2006.

Kawaguchi, Lesley Ann. "Diverging Political Affiliations and Ethnic Perspectives: Philadelphia Germans and Antebellum Politics." *Journal of American Ethnic History* 13, no. 2 (Winter 1994): 3–29.

King, Robert P. *A Digest of Laws Relating to the City of Philadelphia from Its Territorial Extension, by Act of Assembly, Approved February 2d, 1854, until the Close of the Session of the Legislature in 1865*. Philadelphia: King and Baird, 1865.

King, Willard L. *Lincoln's Manager, David Davis*. Cambridge, MA: Harvard University Press, 1960.

King, Willard L., and Allan Nevins. "The Constitution and Declaration of Independence as Issues in the Lincoln-Douglas Debates." *Journal of the Illinois State Historical Society* 52, no. 1 (Spring 1959): 7–32.

Klement, Frank L. *Dark Lanterns: Secret Political Societies, Conspiracies, and Treason Trials in the Civil War*. Baton Rouge: Louisiana State University Press, 1984.

Klement, Frank L. *The Limits of Dissent: Clement L. Vallandigham and the Civil War*. New York: Fordham University Press, 1998.

Klingaman, William K. *Abraham Lincoln and the Road to Emancipation, 1861–1865*. New York: Penguin Publishing Group, 2001.

Knapp, Charles Merriam. *New Jersey Politics during the Period of the Civil War and Reconstruction*. Geneva, NY: W. F. Humphrey, 1924.

Koerner, Gustave. *Memoirs of Gustave Koerner, 1809–1896: Life-Sketches Written at the Suggestion of His Children*. 2 vols. Edited by Thomas J. McCormack. Cedar Rapids, IA: Torch, 1909.

Koos, Greg. *Freedom, Land and Community: A History of McLean County, Illinois 1730–1900*. Bloomington, IL: McLean County Museum of History, 2021.

Kutler, Stanley I. "David Davis." In *The Justices of the United States Supreme Court, 1789–1969: Their Lives and Major Opinions*, rev. ed., edited by Leon Friedman and Fred L. Israel, 2:520–28. New York: Chelsea House, 1997.

Kutler, Stanley I. *Judicial Power and Reconstruction Politics*. Chicago: University of Chicago Press, 1968.

Kyle, Otto R. *Abraham Lincoln in Decatur*. New York: Vantage, 1957.

Lamon, Ward Hill. *The Life of Abraham Lincoln from His Birth to His Inauguration as President*. Boston: James R. Osgood, 1872.

Lamon, Ward Hill. *Recollections of Abraham Lincoln, 1847–1865*. 2nd ed. Edited by Dorothy Lamon Teillard. Washington, DC: Published by the editor, 1911.

Laws of the State of Illinois Passed at the First Session of the Sixteenth General Assembly. Springfield, IL: Charles H. Lanphier, 1849.

Laws of the State of Illinois Passed by the Eighteenth General Assembly Convened January 3, 1853. Springfield, IL: Lanphier and Walker, 1853.

Laws of the State of Illinois, Passed by the Fifteenth General Assembly, at Their Session Begun and Held in the City of Springfield, December 7, 1846. Springfield, IL: Charles H. Lanphier, 1847.

Laws of the State of Illinois Passed by the Twentieth General Assembly Convened January 5, 1857. Springfield, IL: Lanphier and Walker, 1857.

Lehrman, Lewis E. *Lincoln at Peoria: The Turning Point.* Mechanicsburg, PA: Stackpole Books, 2008.

Leonard, Elizabeth D. *Lincoln's Forgotten Ally: Judge Advocate General Joseph Holt of Kentucky.* Chapel Hill: University of North Carolina Press, 2011.

Lighty, S. Chandler. "Lincoln's Forgotten Visit to Indianapolis." *Indiana History Blog,* Indiana Historical Bureau of the Indiana State Library, September 15, 2016. blog.history .in.gov/abraham-lincolns-indy-speech-retitle-obviously.

"Lincoln's Lost Speech." *Bulletin of the Abraham Lincoln Association* 21, no. 1 (December 1930): 3–5.

Linder, Usher F. *Reminiscences of the Early Bench and Bar of Illinois.* Chicago: Chicago Legal News, 1879.

Lovejoy, Owen. *His Brother's Blood: Speeches and Writings, 1838–1864.* Edited by William F. Moore and Jane Ann Moore. Urbana: University of Illinois Press, 2004.

Lowe, Richard G. "The Republican Party in Antebellum Virginia, 1856–1860." *Virginia Magazine of History and Biography* 81, no. 3 (July 1973): 259–79.

Lurie, Jonathan. *The Supreme Court and Military Justice.* Thousand Oaks, CA: CQ Press, 2013.

Luthin, Reinhard H. *The First Lincoln Campaign.* Cambridge, MA: Harvard University Press, 1944.

Luthin, Reinhard H. "Indiana and Lincoln's Rise to the Presidency." *Indiana Magazine of History* 38, no. 4 (December 1942): 385–405.

Luthin, Reinhard H. "Pennsylvania and Lincoln's Rise to the Presidency." *Pennsylvania Magazine of History and Biography* 67, no. 1 (January 1943): 61–82.

Lynch, William O. "The Flow of Colonists to and from Indiana before the Civil War." *Indiana Magazine of History* 11, no. 1 (March 1915): 1–7.

Magdol, Edward. *Owen Lovejoy, Abolitionist in Congress.* New Brunswick, NJ: Rutgers University Press, 1967.

Masur, Kate. "Patronage and Protest in Kate Brown's Washington." *Journal of American History* 99, no. 4 (March 2013): 1047–71.

Maynard, Douglas H. "Dudley of New Jersey and the Nomination of Lincoln." *Pennsylvania Magazine of History and Biography* 82, no. 1 (January 1958): 100–108.

McCash, June Hall. *The Jekyll Island Cottage Colony.* Athens: University of Georgia Press, 1998.

McClure, Alexander K. *Abraham Lincoln and Men of War-Times: Some Personal Recollections of War and Politics during the Lincoln Administration.* 4th ed. Philadelphia: Times Publishing, 1892.

McClure, Alexander K. *Old Time Notes of Pennsylvania.* 2 vols. Philadelphia: John C. Winston, 1905.

McConnell, Michael W. "Originalism and the Desegregation Decisions." *Virginia Law Review* 81, no. 4 (May 1995): 947–1140.

McGinty, Brian. *The Body of John Merryman: Abraham Lincoln and the Suspension of Habeas Corpus.* Cambridge, MA: Harvard University Press, 2011.

McGinty, Brian. *Lincoln and the Court.* Cambridge, MA: Harvard University Press, 2008.

McKirdy, Charles R. *Lincoln Apostate: The Matson Slave Case.* Jackson: University Press of Mississippi, 2011.

McKoski, Raymond J. "The Political Activities of Judges: Historical, Constitutional, and Self-Preservation Perspectives." *University of Pittsburgh Law Review* 80, no. 2 (Winter 2018): 245–314.

McKoski, Raymond J. "Reestablishing Actual Impartiality as the Fundamental Value of Judicial Ethics: Lessons from 'Big Judge Davis.'" *Kentucky Law Journal* 99, no. 2 (2011): 259–325.

Meites, Jerome B. "The 1847 Illinois Constitutional Convention and Persons of Color." *Journal of the Illinois State Historical Society* 108, no. 3–4 (Fall/Winter 2015): 266–95.

Memorials of the Life and Character of Stephen T. Logan. Springfield, IL: H. W. Rokker, 1882.

Miers, Earl Schenck, ed. *Lincoln Day by Day: A Chronology, 1809–1865.* 3 vols. Washington, DC: Lincoln Sesquicentennial Commission, 1960.

Miller, Richard F., ed. *States at War.* Vol. 1, *A Reference Guide for Connecticut, Maine, Massachusetts, New Hampshire, Rhode Island, and Vermont in the Civil War.* Hanover, NH: University Press of New England, 2013.

Miller, Richard Lawrence. *Lincoln and His World.* Vol. 4, *The Path to the Presidency, 1854–1860.* Jefferson, NC: McFarland, 2012.

Miller, Thomas Condit, and Hu Maxwell. *West Virginia and Its People.* Vol. 2. New York: Lewis Historical, 1913.

Model Code of Judicial Conduct 2007. American Bar Association. April 14, 2020. https://www.americanbar.org/groups/professional_responsibility/publications/model_code_of_judicial_conduct_2007/.

Monaghan, Jay. *The Man Who Elected Lincoln.* Indianapolis, IN: Bobbs-Merrill, 1956.

Moore, William F., and Jane Ann Moore. *Collaborators for Emancipation: Abraham Lincoln and Owen Lovejoy.* Urbana: University of Illinois Press, 2014.

Morehouse, Frances Milton Irene. "The Life of Jesse W. Fell." *University of Illinois Studies in the Social Sciences* 5, no. 2 (June 1916): 9–123.

Morris, Roy, Jr. *Fraud of the Century: Rutherford B. Hayes, Samuel Tilden, and the Stolen Election of 1876.* New York: Simon and Schuster, 2004.

Moses, John, ed. *Biographical Dictionary and Portrait Gallery of the Representative Men of the United States: Illinois Volume.* Chicago: Lewis Publishing, 1896.

Moses, John. *Illinois, Historical and Statistical, Comprising the Essential Facts of Its Planting and Growth as a Province, County, Territory, and State.* 2 vols. Chicago: Fergus, 1889.

Murphy, Walter F. *Congress and the Court: A Case Study in the American Political Process.* Chicago: University of Chicago Press, 1962.

Myers, C. Maxwell. "The Influence of Western Pennsylvania in the Campaign of 1860." *Western Pennsylvania Historical Magazine* 24, no. 4 (December 1941): 229–50.

Nagle, John Copeland. "How Not to Count Votes." *Columbia Law Review* 104, no. 6 (October 2004): 1732–64.

National Center for State Courts. Judicial Selection. https://www.ncsc.org/consulting-and-research/areas-of-expertise/court-leadership/judicial-selection.

Neely, Mark E., Jr. *The Boundaries of American Political Culture in the Civil War Era.* Chapel Hill: University of North Carolina Press, 2005.

Neely, Mark E., Jr. *The Fate of Liberty: Abraham Lincoln and Civil Liberties.* New York: Oxford University Press, 1991.

Nester, William. *The Age of Lincoln and the Art of American Power, 1848–1876.* Lincoln: University of Nebraska Press, 2013.

Nevins, Allan. *The Emergence of Lincoln.* 2 vols. New York: Charles Scribner's Sons, 1950.

Newton, Joseph Fort. *Lincoln and Herndon.* Cedar Rapids, IA: Torch Press, 1910.

Nicolay, John G., and John Hay. "Abraham Lincoln: A History. The President and the Draft—Vallandigham—the Peace Party at the Polls." *Century Illustrated Monthly Magazine* 38, no. 1 (May 1889): 123–49.

Niehoff, Leonard M. "David Davis." In *The Supreme Court Justices: Illustrated Biographies 1789–1995,* 2nd ed., edited by Clare Cushman, 181–85. Washington, DC: CQ Press, 1995.

Niven, John. *Gideon Welles: Lincoln's Secretary of the Navy.* New York: Oxford University Press, 1973.

Oaks, Dallin H., and Marvin S. Hill. *Carthage Conspiracy: The Trial of the Accused Assassins of Joseph Smith.* Urbana: University of Illinois Press, 1975.

Ogg, Bryan J. *Naperville: A Brief History.* Charleston, SC: History Press, 2018.

Oldroyd, Osborn H. *Lincoln's Campaign or the Political Revolution of 1860.* Chicago: Laird and Lee, 1896.

Onofrio, Jan. *Maryland Biographical Dictionary.* Saint Clair Shores, MI: Somerset Publishers, 1999.

Packard, W. "The Old Bar of McLean County." In *Transactions of the McLean County Historical Society,* 1:379–90. Bloomington, IL: Pantagraph Printing, 1899.

Page, O. J. *History of Massac County, Illinois; with Life Sketches and Portraits.* Metropolis, IL: O. J. Page, 1900.

Palmer, John M. *The Bench and the Bar of Illinois: Historical and Reminiscent.* 2 vols. Chicago: Lewis, 1899.

Palmer, John M. *Personal Recollections of John M. Palmer: The Story of an Earnest Life.* Cincinnati: Robert Clarke, 1901.

Paull, Bonnie E., and Richard E. Hart. *Lincoln's Springfield Neighborhood.* Charleston, SC: History Press, 2015.

Pearson, Henry Greenleaf. *The Life of John A. Andrew: Governor of Massachusetts, 1861–1865.* 2 vols. Boston: Houghton Mifflin, 1904.

Pennsylvania House of Representatives Archives. Members of the House of Representatives, Member Biographies. https://archives.house.state.pa.us/people/house-historical-biographies.

Pierce, Bessie Louise. *A History of Chicago.* Vol. 2, *From Town to City 1848–1871.* Chicago: University of Chicago Press, 1940.

Pike, James S. *First Blows of the Civil War: The Ten Years of Preliminary Conflict in the United States from 1850 to 1860.* New York: American News, 1879.

Pinkerton, Allan. *History and Evidence of the Passage of Abraham Lincoln: From Harrisburg, Pa., to Washington, D.C., on the 22d and 23d of February, 1861.* New York: Rode and Brand, 1906.

Pinsker, Matthew. "Senator Abraham Lincoln." *Journal of the Abraham Lincoln Association* 14, no. 2 (Summer 1993): 1–21.

Pitkin, Thomas M. "Western Republicans and the Tariff in 1860." *Mississippi Valley Historical Review* 27, no. 3 (December 1940): 401–20.

Plummer, Mark A. *Lincoln's Rail-Splitter: Governor Richard J. Oglesby.* Urbana: University of Illinois Press, 2001.

Portrait and Biographical Record of Christian County, Illinois. Chicago: Lake City, 1893.

Portrait and Biographical Record of Macon County, Illinois. Chicago: Lake City, 1893.

Pratt, Harry E., ed. *Concerning Mr. Lincoln: In Which Abraham Lincoln Is Pictured as He Appeared to Letter Writers of His Time.* Springfield, IL: Abraham Lincoln Association, 1944.

Pratt, Harry E. "David Davis, 1815–1886." In *Transactions of the Illinois State Historical Society for the Year 1930,* 157–83. Publication 37. Springfield: Illinois State Historical Library, 1930.

Pratt, Harry E. *The Great Debates.* Springfield: Illinois State Historical Library, 1955.

Pratt, Harry E. "'Judge' Abraham Lincoln." *Journal of the Illinois State Historical Society* 48, no. 1 (Spring 1955): 28–39.

Pratt, Harry E. *The Personal Finances of Abraham Lincoln.* Springfield, IL: Abraham Lincoln Association, 1943.

Pratt, Harry E. "Simon Cameron's Fight for a Place in Lincoln's Cabinet." *Bulletin of the Abraham Lincoln Association* 49, no. 1 (September 1937): 3–11.

Proceedings of the First Three Republican National Conventions of 1856, 1860 and 1864. Minneapolis: Charles W. Johnson, 1893.

Proceedings of the Illinois State Bar Association at Its Eighth Annual Meeting, Held at the City of Springfield, January 13 and 14, 1884. Springfield, IL: H. W. Rokker, 1885.

Proceedings of the Illinois State Bar Association, at Its First Annual Meeting, Begun and Held at the City of Springfield, January 3d, 1878. Springfield: Illinois State Bar Association, 1878.

Proceedings of the Massachusetts Historical Society October, 1910–June, 1911. Boston: Massachusetts Historical Society, 1911.

Proceedings of the Republican State Convention Held at Springfield, Illinois, June 16, 1858. Springfield, IL: Bailhache and Baker, 1858.

Rana, Aziz. "Freedom Struggles and the Limits of Constitutional Continuity." *Maryland Law Review* 71, no. 4 (2012): 1015–51.

Rawley, James A. *A Lincoln Dialogue.* Lincoln: University of Nebraska Press, 2014.

Reavis, L. U. *The Life and Public Services of Richard Yates, the War Governor of Illinois.* St. Louis: J. H. Chambers, 1881.

Rehnquist, William H. *Centennial Crisis: The Disputed Election of 1876.* New York: Knopf, 2004.

Reid, Whitelaw. *Ohio in the War: Her Statesmen, Generals, and Soldiers.* 2 vols. Columbus, OH: Eclectic Publishing, 1893.

Review of the Decision of the U.S. Supreme Court, in the Cases of Lambdin P. Milligan and Others, the Indiana Conspirators. Published by the Union Congressional Executive Committee. Washington, DC: Chronicle, 1867.

Revised Laws of Illinois: Containing All Laws . . . Passed by the Eighth General Assembly . . . Commencing on the Third Day of December, 1832, and Ending the Second Day of March, 1833, Together with All Laws Required to Be Re-published by the Said General Assembly. Vandalia, IL: Greiner and Sherman, 1833.

Revised Statutes of the State of Illinois: Adopted by the General Assembly . . . at Its Regular Session, Held in the Years, A.D., 1844–'5, Together with an Appendix. Springfield, IL: Walters and Weber, 1845.

Reynolds, David S. *Abe: Abraham Lincoln in His Times.* New York: Penguin Press, 2020.

Rhodes, James Ford. *History of the United States from the Compromise of 1850 to the Final Restoration of Home Rule at the South in 1877.* 7 vols. New York: Macmillan, 1910.

Rice, Allen Thorndike, ed. *Reminiscences of Abraham Lincoln by Distinguished Men of His Time.* New York: North American, 1886.

"Riche, George Inman." In *Appleton's Cyclopaedia of American Biography,* rev. ed., edited by James G. Wilson and John Fiske, 5:244. New York: D. Appleton, 1900.

Roll, Charles. "Richard W. Thompson: A Political Conservative in the Fifties." *Indiana Magazine of History* 27, no. 3 (September 1931): 183–206.

Rose, Gregory S. "Upland Southerners: The County Origins of Southern Migrants to Indiana by 1850." *Indiana Magazine of History* 82, no. 3 (September 1986): 242–63.

Rostow, Eugene V. "The Japanese American Cases—a Disaster." *Yale Law Journal* 54, no. 3 (June 1945): 489–533.

Russell, William H. "A. K. McClure and the People's Party in the Campaign of 1860." *Pennsylvania History* 28, no. 4 (October 1961): 335–45.

Ryan, Daniel Joseph. *Lincoln and Ohio.* Columbus: Ohio State Archeological and Historical Society, 1923.

Sampson, Robert D. "'Pretty Damned Warm Times': The 1864 Charleston Riot and 'The Inalienable Right of Revolution.'" *Illinois Historical Journal* 89, no. 2 (Summer 1996): 99–116.

Sandburg, Carl. *Abraham Lincoln: The Prairie Years.* 2 vols. New York: Harcourt Brace, 1926.

Schley, Pat. "Voices from History: Getting Ready for Winter." David Davis Mansion, November 23, 2018. https://daviddavismansion.org/about/archived-research/75-voices -from-history-getting-ready-for-winter.

Schurz, Carl. *The Reminiscences of Carl Schurz.* 3 vols. New York: McClure, 1907–8.

Schwartz, Bernard. *A History of the Supreme Court.* New York: Oxford University Press, 1993.

Schwartz, Thomas F. "A Campaign Broadside." *For the People: A Newsletter of the Abraham Lincoln Association* 4, no. 3 (Autumn 2002): 6–7.

Scott, Frank William, and Edmund Janes James. *Newspapers and Periodicals of Illinois, 1814–1879.* Springfield: Trustees of the Illinois State Historical Library, 1910.

Seventh Report of the Class of 1890 of Harvard College 1920, Thirtieth Anniversary. Concord, NH: Rumford Press, 1921.

Seward, William Henry, and Frederick William Seward. *William H. Seward: An Autobiography from 1801 to 1834. With a Memoir of His Life, and Selections from His Letters, 1831–1836.* New York: Derby and Miller, 1891.

Sherman, John. *John Sherman's Recollections of Forty Years in the House, Senate and Cabinet.* 2 vols. Chicago: Werner, 1895.

Silbey, Joel H. *A Respectable Minority: The Democratic Party in the Civil War Era, 1860–1868.* New York: Norton, 1977.

Silver, David M. *Lincoln's Supreme Court.* Urbana: University of Illinois Press, 1956.

Silverman, Jason H. *Lincoln and the Immigrant.* Carbondale: Southern Illinois University Press, 2015.

Simon, John Y. "Union County in 1858 and the Lincoln-Douglas Debate." *Journal of the Illinois State Historical Society* 62, no. 3 (August 1969): 267–92.

Slap, Andrew L. *The Doom of Reconstruction: The Liberal Republicans in the Civil War Era.* New York: Fordham University Press, 2010.

Smith, J. Clay, Jr. "Exact Justice and the Spirit of Protest: The Case of *Plessy v. Ferguson* and the Black Lawyer." *Howard Scroll: The Social Justice Law Review* 4, no. 1 (Fall 1999): 1–15.

Smith, John David. "'Gentlemen, I Too, Am a Kentuckian': Abraham Lincoln, the Lincoln Bicentennial, and Lincoln's Kentucky in Recent Scholarship." *Register of the Kentucky Historical Society* 106, no. 3–4 (Summer/Autumn 2008): 433–70.

Smith, Joseph P., ed. *History of the Republican Party in Ohio.* 2 vols. Chicago: Lewis Publishing, 1898.

Somers, W. H. "A New Light on Lincoln as an Advocate." Edited by Allen Henry Wright. *Green Bag* 20, no. 2 (February 1908): 78–80.

Soodalter, Ron. "Stumping in New Hampshire." *America's Civil War* 23, no. 5 (November 2010): 23–24.

Stahr, Walter. *Seward: Lincoln's Indispensable Man.* New York: Simon and Schuster, 2012.

Stahr, Walter. *Stanton: Lincoln's War Secretary.* New York: Simon and Schuster, 2017.

Stanton, Henry B. *Random Recollections.* New York: Harper and Brothers, 1887.

Starr, John W., Jr. *Lincoln and the Railroads: A Biographical Study.* New York: Dodd, Mead, 1927.

Steiner, Bernard C. *Life of Henry Winter Davis.* Baltimore, MD: John Murphy Company, 1916.

Stephenson, Donald Grier, Jr. "The Waite Court at the Bar of History." *Denver University Law Review* 81, no. 2 (2003): 449–95.

Stephenson, Donald Grier, Jr. *The Waite Court: Justices, Rulings, and Legacy.* Santa Barbara, CA: ABC-CLIO, 2003.

Stevens, W. W. *Past and Present of Will County, Illinois.* 2 vols. Chicago: S. J. Clarke, 1907.

Stevens, Walter B. *A Reporter's Lincoln.* Edited by Michael Burlingame. Lincoln: University of Nebraska Press, 1998.

Stewart, A. J. D., ed. *The History of the Bench and Bar of Missouri: With Reminiscences of the Prominent Lawyers of the Past, and a Record of the Law's Leaders of the Present.* St. Louis: Legal Publishing, 1898.

Stewart, John D. "The Great Winnebago Chieftain: Simon Cameron's Rise to Power, 1860–1867." *Pennsylvania History* 39, no. 1 (January 1972): 20–39.

Stillé, Charles J. *Memorial of the Great Central Fair for the U.S. Sanitary Commission, Held at Philadelphia, June 1864*. Philadelphia: U.S. Sanitary Commission, 1864.

Stone, Geoffrey R. *Perilous Times: Free Speech in Wartime from the Sedition Act of 1798 to the War on Terrorism*. New York: W. W. Norton, 2004.

Strevey, Tracy. "Joseph Medill and the *Chicago Tribune* in the Nomination and Election of Abraham Lincoln." In *Papers in Illinois History and Transactions for the Year 1938*, edited by Paul M. Angle, 39–63. Springfield: Illinois State Historical Society, 1939.

Stringer, Lawrence B. *History of Logan County, Illinois: A Record of Its Settlement, Organization, Progress and Achievement*. Chicago: Pioneer, 1911.

Sullivan, Frank, Jr. "Indianapolis Judges and Lawyers Dramatize *Ex parte Milligan*, a Historical Trial of Contemporary Significance." *Indiana Law Review* 37, no. 3 (2004): 661–66.

"Summary of Events: Milligan's Case." *American Law Review* 1, no. 3 (April 1867): 572–75.

Sumner, Charles. *Charles Sumner: His Complete Works*. Vol. 12. Boston: Lee and Shepard, 1900.

Swett, Leonard. "Memorial Address: The Life and Services of David Davis." In *Proceedings of the Illinois State Bar Association at Its Tenth Annual Meeting, Held at the City of Springfield, January 11 and 12, 1887*, 75–81. Springfield, IL: H. W. Rokker, 1887.

Tanner, Hudson C. *"The Lobby," and Public Men from Thurlow Weed's Time*. Albany, NY: George MacDonald, 1888.

Tap, Bruce. "Race, Rhetoric, and Emancipation: The Election of 1862 in Illinois." *Civil War History* 39, no. 2 (June 1993): 101–25.

Taylor, A. A. "The Negro in South Carolina during the Reconstruction: The Convention of 1868." *Journal of Negro History* 9, no. 4 (October 1924): 381–408.

Taylor, John M. *William Henry Seward: Lincoln's Right Hand*. New York: HarperCollins, 1991.

Tenney, Craig D. "To Suppress or Not to Suppress: Abraham Lincoln and the *Chicago Times*." *Civil War History* 27, no. 3 (September 1981): 248–59.

Thomas, Benjamin P. *Abraham Lincoln: A Biography*. New York: Knopf, 1952.

Thomas, Dale. *Lincoln's Old Friends of Menard County, Illinois*. Charleston, SC: History Press, 2012.

Tocklin, Adrian M. "*Pennoyer v. Neff*: The Hidden Agenda of Stephen J. Field." *Seton Hall Law Review* 28, no. 1 (1997): 75–141.

Towne, Stephen E. "The Persistent Nullifier: The Life of Civil War Conspirator Lambdin P. Milligan." *Indiana Magazine of History* 109, no. 4 (December 2013): 303–54.

Towne, Stephen E. "'Such Conduct Must Be Put Down': The Military Arrest of Judge Charles H. Constable during the Civil War." *Journal of Illinois History* 9 (Spring 2006): 43–62.

Turner, Justin G., and Linda Levitt Turner, eds. *Mary Todd Lincoln: Her Life and Letters*. New York: Knopf, 1972.

Urofsky, Melvin I., ed. *Biographical Encyclopedia of the Supreme Court: The Lives and Legal Philosophies of the Justices*. Washington, DC: CQ Press, 2006.

"U.S. Circuit Court at Indianapolis. Charge of Judge Davis to the Grand Jury." *Western Law Monthly* 5 (June 1863): 48–50.

Van Deusen, Glyndon G., ed. "Thurlow Weed's Analysis of William H. Seward's Defeat in the Republican Convention of 1860." *Mississippi Valley Historical Review* 34, no. 1 (June 1947): 101–4.

Van Deusen, Glyndon G. *Thurlow Weed: Wizard of the Lobby.* Boston: Little, Brown, 1947.

Villard, Henry. *Lincoln on the Eve of '61: A Journalist's Story.* Edited by Harold G. Villard and Oswald Garrison Villard. New York: Knopf, 1941.

Villard, Henry. *Memoirs of Henry Villard, Journalist and Financier, 1835–1900.* 2 vols. Boston: Houghton Mifflin, 1904.

Voegeli, V. Jacque. *Free but Not Equal: The Midwest and the Negro during the Civil War.* Chicago: University of Chicago Press, 1967.

Wakefield, Sherman Day. *How Lincoln Became President.* New York: Wilson-Erickson, 1936.

Wallace, Isabel. *Life and Letters of General W. H. L. Wallace.* Chicago: R. R. Donnelley, 1909.

War Claims at St. Louis: Letter from the Secretary of War, Transmitting the Final Report Made by the Commission on War Claims at St. Louis. March 10, 1862. 37th Cong., 2nd sess., H.R. Exec. Doc. No. 94. https://reader.library.cornell.edu/docviewer/digital?id=may920305#mode/1up.

The War of the Rebellion: A Compilation of the Official Records of the Union and Confederate Armies. 70 vols. Washington, DC: Government Printing Office, 1880–1901.

Warren, Charles. *The Supreme Court in United States History.* Rev. ed. 2 vols. Boston: Little, Brown, 1926.

Warren, Louis A. "The Vice-Presidency Twice Beckons Lincoln." *Lincoln Lore: Bulletin of the Lincoln National Life Foundation,* no. 1646 (April 1975): 1–4.

Watson, Richard L., Jr. "Thurlow Weed, Political Boss." *New York History* 22, no. 4 (October 1941): 411–25.

Waugh, John C. *One Man Great Enough: Abraham Lincoln's Road to Civil War.* Orlando, FL: Harcourt, 2007.

Weed, Thurlow. *Life of Thurlow Weed Including His Autobiography and a Memoir.* Edited by Harriet A. Weed. 2 vols. Boston: Houghton Mifflin, 1884.

Weik, Jesse W. *The Real Lincoln: A Portrait.* Boston: Houghton Mifflin, 1922.

Welles, Gideon. *Lincoln and Seward: Remarks upon the Memorial Address of Chas. Francis Adams, on the Late Wm. H. Seward.* New York: Sheldon, 1874.

Wendt, Lloyd. *"Swift Walker": An Informal Biography of Gurdon Saltonstall Hubbard.* Chicago: Regnery Books, 1986.

White, G. Edward. "The Internal Powers of the Chief Justice: The Nineteenth-Century Legacy." *University of Pennsylvania Law Review* 154, no. 6 (June 2006): 1463–1510.

White, Horace. *The Life of Lyman Trumbull.* Boston: Houghton Mifflin, 1913.

White, Jonathan W. "The Strangely Insignificant Role of the U.S. Supreme Court in the Civil War." *Journal of the Civil War Era* 3, no. 2 (June 2013): 211–38.

White, Ronald C., Jr. *A. Lincoln: A Biography.* New York: Random House, 2009.

Whitney, Henry Clay. *Life on the Circuit with Lincoln.* Edited by Paul M. Angle. Caldwell, ID: Caxton, 1940.

Whitney, Henry Clay. *Lincoln the Citizen (February 12, 1809, to March 4, 1861).* New York: Current Literature, 1907.

Whittlesey, Walter Lincoln. "William Lewis Dayton, 1825: Senator—Presidential Candidate—Civil War Minister to France—a Forgotten Princetonian Who Served His Country Well." *Princeton Alumni Weekly,* May 9, 1930, 797–802.

Widmer, Ted. *Lincoln on the Verge: Thirteen Days to Washington.* New York: Simon and Schuster, 2020.

Wilkie, Franc B. *Sketches and Notices of the Chicago Bar; Including the More Prominent Lawyers and Judges of the City and Suburban Towns.* Chicago: Henry A. Sumner, 1871.

Wilson, Douglas L. *Honor's Voice: The Transformation of Abraham Lincoln.* New York: Knopf, 1998.

Wilson, Douglas L. "Lincoln's Affair of Honor." *Atlantic Monthly,* February 1998, 64–71.

Wilson, Douglas L., and Rodney O. Davis, eds. *Herndon's Informants: Letters, Interviews, and Statements about Abraham Lincoln.* Urbana: University of Illinois Press, 1998.

Wilson, Rufus Rockwell, ed. *Intimate Memories of Lincoln.* Elmira, NY: Primavera, 1945.

Wilson, Rufus Rockwell, ed. *Lincoln among His Friends: A Sheaf of Intimate Memories.* Caldwell, ID: Caxton Printers, 1942.

Woldman, Albert A. *Lawyer Lincoln.* Boston: Houghton Mifflin, 1936.

Wolstoncraft, Joseph B. "Western Pennsylvania and the Election of 1860." *Western Pennsylvania Historical Magazine* 6, no. 1 (January 1923): 25–38.

Woodburn, James A., ed. "George W. Julian's Journal: The Assassination of Lincoln." *Indiana Magazine of History* 11, no. 4 (December 1915): 324–37.

Woollen, William Wesley. *Biographical and Historical Sketches of Early Indiana.* Indianapolis, IN: Hammond, 1883.

Wylie, Theophilus A. *Indiana University: Its History from 1820, When Founded, to 1890: With Biographical Sketches of Its Presidents, Professors and Graduates, and a List of Its Students from 1820 to 1887.* Indianapolis, IN: Wm. B. Burford, 1890.

Yale Law School. "Our History." https://law.yale.edu/about-yale-law-school/glance/our-history.

Yoo, John. "Lincoln and Habeas: Of Merryman and Milligan and McCardle." *Chapman Law Review* 12, no. 3 (Spring 2009): 505–33.

Zarefsky, David. *Lincoln, Douglas, and Slavery: In the Crucible of Public Debate.* 2nd ed. Chicago: University of Chicago Press, 1993.

Zimmerman, Charles. "The Origin and Rise of the Republican Party in Indiana from 1854 to 1860." *Indiana Magazine of History* 13, no. 3 (September 1917): 211–69.

Newspapers and Periodicals

Alexandria (VA) Gazette
Alleghanian (PA)
Ashtabula (OH) Weekly Telegraph
Austin (TX) Weekly Statesman
Bedford (PA) Gazette
Bedford (PA) Inquirer
Bloomington (IL) Daily Pantagraph
Bloomington (IL) Weekly Pantagraph

Bradford (PA) Reporter
Brenham (TX) Weekly Banner
Brooklyn (NY) Daily Eagle
Buchanan County Guardian (IA)
Burlington (IA) Weekly Hawk-Eye
Cadiz (OH) Democrat Sentinel
Carlisle (PA) Herald
Carson (NV) Daily Appeal
Cecil Whig (Elkton, MD)
Chicago Daily Journal
Chicago Daily Tribune
Chicago Inter-Ocean
Chicago Legal News
Chicago Press and Tribune
Chicago Tribune
Chillicothe (IL) Independent
Cincinnati Commercial
Cincinnati Daily Press
Cleveland Morning Leader
Daily Exchange (Baltimore, MD)
Daily Gate City (IA)
Daily Intelligencer (VA)
Daily Patriot and Union (PA)
Daily Pittsburgh Gazette
Daily Quincy (IL) Herald
Daily Republican (DE)
Daily State Sentinel (Indianapolis, IN)
Daily Union (Washington, DC)
Delaware (OH) Gazette
Democratic Press (OH)
Democratic Watchman (PA)
Douglass' Monthly (New York, NY)
Evansville (IN) Daily Journal
Evening Critic (Washington, DC)
Evening Star (Washington, DC)
Ford County Journal (IL)
Frank Leslie's Illustrated Newspaper (New York, NY)
Freeport (IL) Journal-Standard
Fremont (OH) Journal
Globe (PA)
Harper's Weekly (New York, NY)
Harrisburg (PA) Telegraph
Huntsville (AL) Gazette
Illinois State Journal

Illinois State Register
Indianapolis Daily Journal
Indianapolis Journal
Indianapolis Leader
Iowa County Democrat (WI)
Jasper (IN) Weekly Courier
Jeffersonian (PA)
Lancaster (PA) Intelligencer
Lewistown (PA) Gazette
Liberator (MA)
Louisiana Democrat
Louisville (KY) Courier-Journal
Loyal Georgian (Augusta)
Maine Union and Journal
Manitowoc (WI) Pilot
Marshall County Republican (IN)
Maryland Free Press
Milwaukee Daily Free Democrat
Morning Courier and New-York Enquirer
Muscatine (IA) Weekly Journal
Nation (New York, NY)
National Anti-Slavery Standard (New York, NY)
National Intelligencer (Washington, DC)
National Republican (Washington, DC)
New Albany (IN) Daily Ledger
New National Era (Washington, DC)
New-York Daily Tribune
New York Herald
New York Times
New-York Tribune
North American and United States Gazette (Philadelphia)
North Branch (PA) Democrat
Ottawa (IL) Free Trader
Pennsylvania Daily Telegraph
Philadelphia Press
Potter (PA) Journal
Quincy (IL) Weekly Whig
Raftsman's Journal (PA)
Randolph County Journal (IN)
Richmond (VA) Dispatch
Richmond (VA) Enquirer
Richmond (IN) Palladium
Sangamo Journal (Springfield, IL)
Saturday Evening Post

Savannah (GA) Morning News
Springfield (IL) Republican
Staunton (VA) Spectator
St. Paul (MN) Daily Globe
Sun (New York, NY)
Wabash (IN) Express
Washington Bee (Washington, DC)
Watertown (WI) Republican
Weekly Caucasian (MO)
Weekly Louisianian (New Orleans)
Weekly Oskaloosa (IA) Herald
Western Citizen (Chicago, IL)
Wheeling (VA) Daily Intelligencer

Court Cases

Brown v. Board of Education of Topeka, Shawnee County, Kansas, 347 U.S. 483 (1954).
Eames v. Godfrey, 68 U.S. (1 Wall.) 78 (1863).
Ex parte Milligan, 71 U.S. (4 Wall.) 2 (1866).
Ex parte Vallandigham, 28 F. Cas. 874 (C.C. S.D. Ohio 1863).
Ex parte Vallandigham, 68 U.S. (1 Wall.) 243 (1863).
Georgia v. Stanton, 73 U.S. (6 Wall.) 50 (1867).
Hamdi v. Rumsfeld, 542 U.S. 507 (2004).
Hyde v. Shine, 199 U.S. 62 (1905).
In re Egan, 8 F. Cas. 367 (C.C. N.D. N.Y. 1866).
In re Winder, 30 F. Cas. 288 (C.C. D. Mass. 1862).
Marks v. Butler, 24 Ill. 567 (1860).
Maybin v. Coulon, 4 U.S. (4 Dal.) 298 (1804).
Mississippi v. Johnson 71 U.S. (4 Wall.) 475 (1866).
Plessy v. Ferguson, 163 U.S. 537 (1896).
Prize Cases, 67 U.S. (2 Black) 635 (1862).
Railroad Company v. Brown, 84 U.S. (17 Wall.) 445 (1873).
Ryan v. Bindley, 68 U.S. (1 Wall.) 66 (1863).
United States v. Rhodes, 27 F. Cas. 785 (C.C. D. Ky. 1866).
United States v. Scott, 70 U.S. (3 Wall.) 642 (1865).
United States v. Union Pacific Railroad, 91 U.S. (1 Otto) 72 (1875).
Woods v. Freeman, 68 U.S. (1 Wall.) 398 (1863).

Theses and Honors Projects

Brush, Elizabeth Parnham. "The Political Career of Owen Lovejoy." Master's thesis, University of Illinois, 1912. https://www.ideals.illinois.edu/items/53444.
Huddleston, D. Mark. "A Developing Frontier: Logan County, Illinois to 1872." Master's thesis, Eastern Illinois University, 1976. https://thekeep.eiu.edu/cgi/viewcontent.cgi?article=4447&context=theses.
Moreland, John L. "A Law for Rulers and People: David Davis, Ex Parte Milligan, and Constitutional Liberalism during the Civil War Era." Master's thesis, Illinois

State University, 2016. https://ir.library.illinoisstate.edu/cgi/viewcontent.cgi?article =1587&context=etd.

Paul, Norma Ann. "Suppression of the *Chicago Times:* June 1863." Master's thesis, Loyola University of Chicago, 1932. https://ecommons.luc.edu/luc_theses/315.

Pflug, Oliver L. "Pennsylvania Politics 1854–1860." Master's thesis, University of Montana, 2002. https://scholarworks.umt.edu/etd/5226.

Shifflett, Crandall A. "John C. Underwood: A Carpetbagger Reconsidered, 1860–1873." Master's thesis, University of Virginia, 1971. https://libraetd.lib.virginia.edu/public _view/3x816m736.

Tangorra, Gina C. "The Back of the House as Viewed from the Front of the House: Sarah Davis and the Irish Domestic Servants of Clover Lawn from 1872 to 1879." Honors Projects, Illinois Wesleyan University, 2010. https://digitalcommons.iwu.edu/ history_honproj/44.

Zachary, Lauren E. "Henry S. Lane and the Birth of the Indiana Republican Party, 1854–1861." Master's thesis, Indiana University, 2013. https://scholarworks.iupui.edu/ bitstream/handle/1805/4668/Zachary,%20Lauren%20E.%20Thesis.pdf?sequence=1.

Select Online Resources

Abraham Lincoln Papers. Library of Congress. https://www.loc.gov/collections/abraham -lincoln-papers.

American Presidency Project. Statistics, Data Archive, Elections. University of California, Santa Barbara. https://www.presidency.ucsb.edu/statistics/elections.

Biographical Directory of the United States Congress 1774-Present. https://bioguideretro .congress.gov/home.

Burlingame, Michael. *Abraham Lincoln: A Life.* Unedited manuscript by chapters. https://www.knox.edu/academics/research-and-creative-work/lincoln-studies-center/ burlingame-abraham-lincoln-a-life.

Chronicling America: Historic American Newspapers. https://chroniclingamerica.loc.gov.

Collected Works of Abraham Lincoln. https://quod.lib.umich.edu/l/lincoln/.

Dave Leip's Atlas of U.S. Presidential Elections. http://uselectionatlas.org.

David & Sarah Davis Family Correspondence. Illinois Wesleyan University, Blooming-ton, IL. https://collections.carli.illinois.edu/digital/collection/iwu_davis.

David Davis Mansion. https://daviddavismansion.org.

Frederick Douglass Project. University of Rochester. https://rbscp.lib.rochester.edu/ frederick-douglass-project.

Hoosier State Chronicles: Indiana's Digital Historic Newspaper Program. https://newspapers .library.in.gov/.

Illinois Code of Judicial Conduct of 2023. Illinois Supreme Court Rules, Article XI. https:// www.illinoiscourts.gov/rules/supreme-court-rules?a=xi.

Illinois Digital Archives. http://www.idaillinois.org.

Illinois Digital Newspaper Collections. https://idnc.library.illinois.edu.

The Law Practice of Abraham Lincoln: Complete Documentary Edition. 2nd ed. Edited by Martha L. Benner, Cullom Davis, et al. http://www.lawpracticeofabrahamlincoln.org.

Papers of Abraham Lincoln Digital Library, Abraham Lincoln Presidential Library and Museum. https://papersofabrahamlincoln.org.

Pennsylvania Newspaper Archive. https://panewsarchive.psu.edu.

Archives

David Davis Family Papers. Abraham Lincoln Presidential Library and Museum, Springfield, Illinois.

Fell, Jesse W. Papers. Illinois History and Lincoln Collections, University of Illinois Urbana-Champaign Library, Urbana, IL.

Orme, William Ward. Papers. Illinois History and Lincoln Collections, University of Illinois Urbana-Champaign Library, Urbana, IL.

Seward, William H. Papers. River Campus Libraries, University of Rochester.

State Department Records. National Archives, Washington, DC.

Weed, Thurlow. Papers. River Campus Libraries, University of Rochester, Rochester, NY.

Index

Raymond J. McKoski is a retired Illinois Circuit Judge and adjunct professor at the University of Illinois Chicago School of Law. He is the author of *Judges in Street Clothes: Acting Ethically Off-the-Bench.*

The University of Illinois Press
is a founding member of the
Association of University Presses.

———————————————

Composed in 10.5/13 Minion Pro
by Lisa Connery
at the University of Illinois Press
Manufactured by Sheridan Books, Inc.

University of Illinois Press
1325 South Oak Street
Champaign, IL 61820–6903
www.press.uillinois.edu